UNDERSTANDING THE SELF-HELP ORGANIZATION

UNDERSTANDING THE SELF-HELP ORGANIZATION

FRAMEWORKS AND FINDINGS

THOMAS J. POWELL

SAGE Publications
International Educational and Professional Publisher
Thousand Oaks   London   New Delhi

For information address:

SAGE Publications, Inc.
2455 Teller Road
Thousand Oaks, California 91320

SAGE Publications Ltd.
6 Bonhill Street
London EC2A 4PU
United Kingdom

SAGE Publications India Pvt. Ltd.
M-32 Market
Greater Kailash I
New Delhi 110 048 India

Printed in the United States of America

Library of Congress Cataloging-in-Publication Data

Understanding the self-help organization: frameworks and findings/
   edited by Thomas J. Powell.
        p. cm.
   Includes bibliographical references and index.
   ISBN 0-8039-5487-5 (cl).—ISBN 0-8039-5488-3 (pk)
   1. Self-help groups. I. Powell, Thomas J.
HV547.U53 1994
361.4—dc20   94-3376

94 95 96 97 98   10 9 8 7 6 5 4 3 2 1

Sage Production Editor: Diana E. Axelsen

Contents

Preface:
Some Comments on Knowledge Development in the Self-Help Field

THOMAS J. POWELL

A s a field such as self-help matures, increasing interest is attached to identifying the areas in which knowledge needs to be developed. This interest is necessarily an emerging one because in the early period, it may not even be clear what areas need to be explored. Premature identification (or, worse, foreclosing) of areas would almost certainly retard development in important areas. Yet to go on without taking stock of whether important areas are being addressed may mean important areas continue to be overlooked. This volume organizes the chapters into sections so as to invite consideration of whether attention is being given to important areas and what the state of knowledge is in each of these areas. It focuses attention on four important areas: public policy and self-help; participation—especially by minorities—in self-help; explanatory frameworks; and, finally, a loose category containing an accumulation of important findings about self-help. The reader might wish to ponder what other areas should be on this list and what is known about each of them. But even in anticipation of that, it may be observed that public policy is underdeveloped. For example, what policies should govern the referrals and facilitation of participation in self-help programs by professional services providers? Such questions need to be addressed, as no field can realize its potential without a well-developed public policy that is both critical and supportive. It would also seem evident that progress is being made in identifying, developing, and applying new explanatory frameworks to self-help phenomena. Although much remains to be done, it is encouraging to note the inclusion of minority themes related to sexual orientation and race in many of the chapters. In the Findings section, it is refreshing to see the Nike approach to qualitative studies emerge. Hopefully, this will prompt more of us to do it, instead of only encouraging others to do it.

Of course, the primary justification for the selection of these chapters is that they, independently, offer original insights about self-help. Some essays meeting this criterion first appeared in the *Journal of Applied Behavioral Science*: Lieberman and Snowden; Humphreys and Woods; Luke, Roberts, and Rappaport; Rappaport; Maton; Kaufmann; Meissen and Warren; Nash and Kramer. These works are referred to in my chapter, "Self-Help Research and Policy Issues," which also appeared in that journal. Other essays were prepared specially for this volume.

Several of the contributors (Kennedy et al.; Schubert & Borkman; Saulnier; and Kurtz) preparing special chapters for this volume have gone beyond simply calling for more qualitative research and have done it. It is especially refreshing to have studies that include richly detailed and vivid accounts of self-help activities. These studies also limit the tendency to idealize self-help processes by describing their complicated realities and the adjustments they make to their participants, for example, the acceptance of dating among the participants of Lesbian Al-Anon (Saulnier).

Snowden and Lieberman, and Powell, in their specially prepared chapters, contribute to the ongoing campaign to include minority concerns in self-help research. Meissen and Warren elucidate the advantages of viewing self-help from the vantage point of the clearinghouses. Kingree and Ruback provide an exemplar for the use of social psychological theory in self-help research. Noordsy, Schwab, Fox, and Drake provide another kind of exemplar for the inclusion of self-help oriented practice and research in psychiatric rehabilitation programs.

With this guide to the structure and content of this volume, the reader is encouraged to read deeply and critically, keeping in mind the possibility of contributing to the next stage of maturity in the self-help field. Lest this seem to be going too far, consider that those involved in a field inevitably have an impact it. Among the ways they do this is to develop new practices or solidify existing ones. In so doing they make one kind—a very important kind—of policy about self-help. Whether their impact is beneficial or their policy progressive may depend on the extent to which they have a critical understanding of the state of knowledge in the self-help field.

1. Self-Help Research and Policy Issues

THOMAS J. POWELL

The question often asked by those just turning their attention to self-help groups is, are they helpful? This is like asking are mental health services helpful. What is the referent? Does it refer, for example, to medication, psychotherapy, or supported employment services? And to whom is the service to be administered? Does it refer to people facing a current stressor, to people with an ongoing anxiety disorder, or to people with a severe mental illness?

Similarly, asking about whether self-help works is also a complex question. Although self-help research has produced numerous positive findings, their interpretation is complicated by a number of factors. These factors are associated with loosely defined samples (e.g., people who have identified themselves as emotionally disturbed or mentally ill; Galanter, 1988; Raiff, 1982; see also Rappaport, this volume); people who are in a mental hospital aftercare program (Gordon, Edmunson, & Bedell, 1982); parents who have lost a child (Videka-Sherman & Lieberman, 1985); people with alcohol abuse problems (Emrick, Tonigan, Montgomery, & Little, 1993); and people with scoliosis (Hinrichsen, Revenson, & Shinn, 1985). Another factor com-

AUTHOR'S NOTE: The author wishes to thank Keith Humphreys, Kenneth I. Maton, Gregg Meissen, and Douglas Noordsy for their comments on an earlier draft of this chapter, which was first presented in a workshop on self-help research. The workshop, funded by MH-46399 from the National Institute of Mental Health, was held February 17-18, 1993, in Ann Arbor, Michigan.

1

plicating the interpretation of these positive findings is that much remains unknown about the "black box" self-help program that produced them. Even Alcoholics Anonymous (AA), with the standardization built into its Twelve Steps and Twelve Traditions and its comprehensive and often cited General Service Conference-approved literature, varies greatly from one meeting to another. Inevitably, then, this leaves doubts about what varieties of AA the positive findings might generalize to cover (Emrick et al., 1993; Kurtz, 1993). The external validity of research on other less well-standardized self-help programs is even more uncertain.

Still another factor raising doubts about the interpretability of positive findings is evident when they are produced by weak or flawed designs. The typical weakness of randomized controlled trials is that they assign people, such as aftercare patients (Gordon et al., 1982) and widows (Vachon, Lyall, Rogers, Freedman-Letofsky, & Freeman, 1980), to a self-help group of questionable authenticity, one that is created, and in some measure maintained, by professionals. The comment about experimental designs in the landmark 1976 special issue of the *Journal of Applied Behavioral Science* on self-help groups (still a valuable conceptual resource) continues to hold: "The common 'pre-post' measurement of outcomes in treatment groups, in comparison with control groups, is an awkward model to apply to self-help groups" (Lieberman & Borman, 1976, p. 459). Moreover, such designs leave doubt about the equivalence of the comparison groups. The studies of Compassionate Friends (Videka-Sherman & Lieberman, 1985), a support group for parents and siblings grieving the death of a child, and the Scoliosis Groups (Hinrichsen et al., 1985) were quasi-experiments, leaving many unanswered questions about what "treatment" the experimental group was exposed to and about whether the experimental group and the nonequivalent comparison group were similar enough in the beginning to justify comparing outcomes. Furthermore, some benefit and some do not, and those who do benefit do so in some ways but not in others.

Last, there are the interpretability questions associated with "single group" or correlation design studies, such as those with Recovery, Inc. (Galanter, 1988; Raiff, 1982) and with the 20-odd AA studies reviewed by Emrick et al. (1993). These studies can only assess associations between outcome and involvement in self-help activities. Accordingly, they invite speculation about numerous factors other than self-help, ones that might account for the improvement. This brief critique of a purposive sample of outcome studies raises the question of what conclusions can be drawn. Certainly, more studies need to be done with more tightly defined samples and with more carefully described interventions. And wherever possible, stronger experimental designs should be used, short of distorting the nature of the self-help experience or intervention. Most important, and this further qualifies the above conclusion about stronger designs, more appropriate studies along the lines recommended by the authors of this volume need to be undertaken. Some examples of their recommendations are that future studies must be guided by more complex ecological frameworks (see Maton, this volume), must use more culturally diverse samples (see Humphreys & Woods, this volume), and must employ more sensitive measures of the outcomes actually sought by self-help groups themselves (see Rappaport, 1994).

Shifting attention to the many other kinds of studies, such as those related to participation and process, the question is, should they be placed on hold until more outcome studies are done? Not reasonably so. Although much remains to be discovered about who benefits from what kinds of self-help and how they benefit, the available evidence is consistent with an assumption that participants do benefit. However, this limited assumption does not imply meeting some ideal standard of effectiveness. Instead, it rests on meeting a real-world standard of probable and selective effectiveness—selective with respect to both who the person is and how the improvement manifests itself. This resembles standards operative in the professional services sphere. To insist on a uniquely strict standard for self-help would be to discount a set of experiences and services that seem likely to be beneficial and, in so doing, to minimize the numbers who have access or can participate in them.

HOW MANY PARTICIPATE?
HOW CULTURALLY DIVERSE ARE THEY?
HOW DO THEY DISTRIBUTE THEMSELVES
AMONG THE VARIOUS GROUPS?

Happily the era of "guesstimating" the number of self-help group members has given way to data-based estimates, albeit still in an early stage of development. These estimates will become increasingly trustworthy as more is learned about what kind of data is necessary to make them accurate. Jacobs and Goodman (1989) began the new era by extrapolating from actual community survey data. However, as their data were limited (to the state of Illinois) and indirect (the growth rate for individuals was estimated from changes in the number of groups in New Jersey), their national estimate was perforce very approximate. The next advance came with the availability of national probability samples, first in Canada (Gottlieb & Peters, 1991) and then in the United States (Narrow, Regier, Rae, Manderscheid, & Locke, 1993; Regier et al., 1993). Lieberman and Snowden (this volume) have analyzed the U.S. Epidemiological Catchment Area (ECA) database and reported the associations between self-help and diagnosis and the use of professional services. They also examine the ethnicity of self-help members. Still, these studies are difficult to interpret and compare with one another. A simple difference is that the ECA study reports 6-month and lifetime prevalence, whereas the Canadian study reports 12-month prevalence.

But a more important difference concerns the questions asked: The U.S. question was "Have you ever gone to a self-help group, like Alcoholics Anonymous, etc.?," whereas the Canadian question was "Since last November [i.e., in the past 12 months], did you participate in a self-help mutual aid group such as a single-parents group, bereaved parents or AA?" Although it is tempting to speculate on the effect of the extra elements in the Canadian question—the reference to "mutual aid" and to the examples of "single parents" and "bereaved parents" along with AA, which was mentioned in the ECA study—it would focus attention on a secondary point.

The primary point is that no single question is adequate to obtain the desired information. When asking about the use of professional services, the ECA study used upward of 20 items (National Institute of Mental Health [NIMH], 1988a). This reflects the privileged position held by professional services relative to other ways in which people find help. Ignoring other ways, such as participation in self-help programs, has caused an imbalance in our research agenda. Some national organization (e.g., NIMH or the National Center for Health Statistics in the United States or Statistics Canada in that country) could begin to right the balance and advance their agenda by either asking, or funding others to ask, a set of questions about the use of self-help with a national probability sample. A number of separate questions (the actual number required is likely to be about the same as used for professional services) will be needed to elicit information that people variously categorize under the headings of support groups, advocacy groups, community groups, self-help, and mutual-aid groups. Moreover, it will be necessary to distinguish between groups that are professionally facilitated and those that rely on the experiential wisdom of the self-help members. In terms of the nature of the activity, it will be necessary to separate the solitary from those that are social and imbued with the spirit of mutual aid and fellowship.

A next step would be to ask respondents about self-help groups in the various self-help areas, such as the addictions, mental health, physical health, family life, and so on. After that, they need to be asked about their connection to the problem. Caregivers typically have different concerns from the persons with the condition or actually in the situation. To parallel the ECA structure, additional questions would be required about frequency of use (e.g., in the past 6 months or over a lifetime). But this is more complex than asking about professional services, as knowledge about the use of self-help must include information about contacts and activities outside the formal sessions. Although these inquiries have no parallel in the ECA structure, they would be essential, as self-help groups encourage outside activities and often consider them necessary to benefit from the program.

Self-Help Clearinghouses

The foregoing could be a useful approach to answer questions related to who goes to self-help groups, with what kinds of conditions, or in what kinds of situations. It is not as well-suited, however, to answer questions about the population ecology of these organizations (Maton, Leventhal, Madara, & Julien, 1989). What is the distribution of these organizations in particular geographic areas? What are the correlates of birth, survival, and disbandment for these organizations? For these questions, the self-help clearinghouses can be an invaluable aid to investigators searching for a suitable sampling frame and again when they need to obtain access to the members of these organizations who end up in the sample (Meissen & Warren, this volume). A clearinghouse database would also enhance the opportunity to study interactions between individual, group, and community characteristics. By systematically sampling participants from different groups and different communities, much can be learned about the important but mostly neglected interactions across these levels of analysis (see Maton, 1994).

Unfortunately, the capacity of clearinghouses to perform these research functions—not to mention their already underfunded referral and group development functions—is severely hampered by inadequate and unstable funding. Only a handful of state mental health agencies or other state agencies recognize the contribution that clearinghouses make, or could make, to a comprehensive system of care by providing significant funding. Federal agencies might also find it to their advantage to recognize the actual and potential contribution of clearinghouses to their missions by referring to clearinghouses in their announcements and requests for proposals for demonstration and research programs. Clearinghouses have an important role to play in serving people with long-term mental illness and, more broadly, people who need or obtain support from a variety of community support systems. They should be routinely considered when initiatives are undertaken to improve access, develop resources, and coordinate services.

Through its Canadian Council on Social Development, Canada has been more supportive of self-help and the clearinghouse concept. In 1992 Ottawa energized the field by sponsoring the International Conference on Self-Help and Mutual Aid. Earlier (1987), the U.S. Surgeon General sponsored a landmark meeting in Los Angeles. The Surgeon General's Workshop on Self-Help and Public Health (Department of Health and Human Services, 1988) developed an impressive agenda for the field of self-help. Unfortunately, this has been allowed to languish. A new national initiative is needed to recapture the enthusiasm generated by this workshop and to invigorate its far-reaching recommendations.

The Role of Professional Privilege

The number of people knowing about or using self-help is limited by the prevailing and not often commented on culture of professional privilege. This concept of cultural privilege echoes similar ones formulated by other disenfranchised minorities, such as those in the feminist, independent living, and gay movements. Yet some think the discrimination is more deliberate. They attribute the lack of recognition for self-help groups to deliberate efforts to marginalize them. For them, it goes beyond simply being socialized in a culture of professional privilege (Chamberlin, Rogers, & Sneed, 1989; Emerick, 1990).

Whether happenstance or not, the consequence is a policy imbalance. In the mental health area, for example, state mental health and human service agencies and their federal counterparts allocate the lion's share of their resources to the study and improvement of professional services, apparently little cognizant of the diverse ways by which people get help. The literature mirrors the near monopoly privilege of professionals. In what was heralded as a comprehensive position statement on the diagnosis and treatment of major depression, the American Psychiatric Association estimates that 20% to 35% of the population will experience persistent and severe residual symptoms (Karasu et al., 1993). Yet in this 1,600-line article, only 4 lines are related to "consumer oriented support groups," with nary an indication that people might want to investigate affiliates of the National Depressive and Manic-Depressive Association, a self-help organization with over 35,000 members. Until professionals, most probably through their preprofessional and continuing education experiences, become more aware of how their privileged position results in ignorance about self-help programs, their clients and patients will be denied access to them. Unless professionals convey this information, clients are unlikely to be sufficiently informed to make a decision about their potential usefulness. Professionals, after all, are well-positioned in their roles as acute care specialists or as crisis regulators to open the gates to participation in these services. The role of the researchers is to develop valid information about self-help programs that will enable professionals to become better informed about the structural characteristics, change processes, and probable outcomes for people who use these services. In this way, professionals can be transformed from often unwitting gate-blockers to knowledgeable facilitators of self-help services.

One aspect of this research should be to address some of the professional biases head-on, as Chesler (1990) did in his study of the dangers professionals associated with the use of self-help groups. Ninety percent of his health care professionals thought their colleagues believed there were serious risks, whereas only 24% of them had observed any evidence of dangerous behavior. Isn't this discrepancy another evidence of the bias associated with professional privilege?

Diversity in Membership

In this volume, new ground has been broken in terms of both the methodology used to study affiliation and the findings produced by these studies. This is so even considering the disappointing ECA findings about the low rates of participation by African Americans (see Lieberman & Snowden, 1994). Humphreys and Woods (1994) direct attention to a neglected aspect of minority participation. They highlight the importance of contextual variables while challenging conventional wisdom about who joins and who continues in self-help organizations. They go beyond the important statewide study in Missouri, which suggested that both Blacks and Whites affiliated with (and benefited from) AA and Narcotics Anonymous (NA). Despite these encouraging findings, the Missouri study found that Blacks were referred less often (DenHartog, Homer, & Wilson, 1986). Humphreys and Woods go on to identify the conditions under which African Americans affiliate with AA and NA at rates equal to or exceeding that of Whites. African Americans affiliate at higher rates in urban areas where they are in the majority. Conversely, Whites affiliate at a higher rate in the suburban and small-city areas where they are in the majority. This suggests that referrals are more apt to succeed when they are made to culturally compatible groups. This invites inquiry as to whether the cultural compatibility threshold varies in communities with varying levels of minority population. It might be that the cultural compatibility threshold is lower or more relaxed in communities that already have a definite, or perhaps even a predominant, African-American character. In research terms, how is the percentage in the population of specific minority groups related to the success rate of referrals from that population? If it were found that the standard for cultural compatibility is more relaxed in minority communities, there would be important implications for national self-help organizations seeking to improve their cultural diversity. It would suggest that first consideration should be given to concentrating their recruitment efforts in predominantly minority communities instead of following what seems like the more common pattern of attempting to recruit prospective minority members to groups in majority communities.

Whereas Humphreys and Woods' (1994) data relate to the community context of participation, Luke, Roberts, and Rappaport (this volume) deal with group context. Although group context can reflect community context, there is no necessary connection. It is perhaps not uncommon to have a predominantly White group in a predominantly Black community or vice versa. Therefore, it is important to examine, as Luke et al. (1994) do, the relationship between participation and group characteristics directly. Unfortunately, there was not enough ethnic minority variation in this sample to study the ethnic context of the group. Fortunately, Luke et al. were able to examine gender context. They found that when women predominate in the group, there is a higher rate of dropout for men and, even less expected, a higher dropout rate for women. The generalizability of this startling finding about the relationship between ongoing participation and the proportion of women in groups invites further study.

Conventional wisdom about who participates has been challenged in another study examining participation in an organization for people with manic depressive and major depressive illness. Experience at the Center for Self-Help Research indicates that younger males are as open to participation as older females. Given the various ways in which gender can be related to participation and the enormous practical significance of these relationships, it would be wise to encourage such studies. Similarly, studies need to be encouraged of the color status of the host community, of the self-help group, and of the prospective members. Important relationships across these different levels of analysis and participation seem likely to exist and remain to be discovered. Such studies might be suggested as potentially high-payoff, organization-building, action research projects for major national self-help organizations, such as the National Alliance for the Mentally Ill (NAMI) or Recovery, Inc. (Israel, Schurman, & Hugentobler, 1992). The project might begin with a survey of the members of these national self-help organizations to further clarify the relationship between these variables and participation. Next, longitudinal data might be collected on participation from existing groups with contrasting patterns of participation. This could be followed by quasi-experiments that follow those who are encouraged to participate, comparing the experimental group with another group that does not have access to the particular self-help group. As knowledge increases and the questions become increasingly sharp and compelling, it might be appropriate to conduct true experiments in which prospective members would be randomly encouraged (assigned) to two or more groups. Based on previous research and theory, one group would be presumed to be maximally attractive and a best fit while the other groups would be presumed to vary in degree of attraction and fit. Studies proceeding in this ascending order, and undertaken in the context of a collaborative action research project with the self-help groups, could provide important information about effective recruitment and retention strategies and about the likely effects of participation.

With appropriate congressional and agency policy development, there are a number of models that could be used to fund these projects. Using a model developed by the Office of Rural Health Policy in the Health Research Services Administration, consumer and self-help groups could be given contracts to conduct the surveys. Such projects might also be supported by the Center for Mental Health Services within the Substance Abuse and Mental Health Administration. This could be done via a specific announcement that would have demonstration and evaluation components. It might follow the pattern of the service improvement grants, which are often focused on consumer and family self-help and advocacy projects. However, instead of restricting applicant eligibility to state departments of mental health, self-help organizations might also be made eligible applicants. In some instances, the current indirect route through the departments of mental health could cloud the self-help focus and complicate project management.

Other initiatives of the Center for Mental Health Services, such as Project Share (Philadelphia, PA) and the National Empowerment Center (Lawrence,

MA), might be expanded to include a services research component. The marvelously productive conference on Research on Alcoholics Anonymous (Miller & McCrady, 1993), supported by a grant from the National Institute for Alcohol Abuse and Alcoholism (NIAAA), needs to be followed up with research funding if it is to have the impact it deserves. As far as direct federal agency involvements in self-help demonstrations and research, they have been too little and too few.

A current grant program of the National Institutes of Health could be used as a model for enabling self-help organizations to become applicants. The Small Business Technology Transfer Program requires the business to be the applicant but also requires the business applicant to collaborate with a research institution. The legislative intent is to "stimulate and foster scientific . . . and technological innovation through cooperative R&D carried out between small business and research institutions" (National Institutes of Health, 1993, p. 2). In this quote, substitute the words *services* for "technological" and *self-help* for "business" and—alas—an instrument has been created for empowering self-help organizations to conduct services research.

Another model could be created from the Public Academic Liaison (PAL) program sponsored by the NIMH (1988b). It would use the mechanism designed to contribute to the development of publicly supported professional services programs to focus more attention on mission-relevant self-help services. Continuing the parallel with professional services, it might be called the Self-Help (Consumer) Academic Liaison (SHAL) program. Such a program would have a number of benefits. It would contribute to increased professional awareness of self-help groups, to a better balance in the country's service development agenda, and to a better use of cost-free self-help services.

An unusual opportunity now exists to fund self-help services research. The ADAMHA Reorganization Act of 1992, transferring NIMH, NIAAA, and the National Institute on Drug Abuse (NIDA) to the National Institutes of Health, provides that "of the amounts appropriated . . . the Director[s] shall obligate not less than 15% to carry out health services research" (sec. 201). This represents a substantial increase in services research funding for all the institutes, and it could be used to achieve a better balance between self-help and professional services research. These funding and programmatic policy developments might well be considered potential advocacy goals for self-help organizations and services researchers.

THE NEED FOR MORE
COLLABORATIVE, CULTURALLY
COMPATIBLE MODELS OF SELF-HELP RESEARCH

Alternatives to the Professional Services Model

Traditional models used in professional services research have a number of limitations for understanding the processes and outcome of self-help programs. The services model assumes a sharp dichotomy between those who are formally enrolled in a services program and those who are not. Self-help groups typically do not use such dichotomies. They neither screen in nor screen out potential members provided, of course, they present themselves as having the qualifying condition. (But even the term *qualifying condition* needs comment, as relatives and friends are often welcome, observers are welcome in open meetings, and, in some groups, such as Adult Children of Alcoholics, it is difficult to define who has the condition and there might be little interest in determining whether members meet the definition.)

Formal enrollment procedures are rare (although activities to recognize months or years of membership are not), and new people are accepted as members if they so regard themselves. Attendance at meetings is likely on an irregular, as needed basis, with the definition of need controlled by the user rather than the provider. The services model, unlike a model that would be more appropriate to self-help, focuses almost exclusively on presence or absence at formal sessions. Even within this model, however, it is possible to devise acceptable research procedures. Yeaton (in press), for example, has devised an innovative method based on the use of partial Social Security numbers to measure attendance in self-help groups while still preserving the anonymity of members.

Still, the services model is not well-suited to deal with those extrasession contacts that combine friendship with coping—an especially serious omission, as it is precisely these kinds of activities that have been found to be related to benefiting from self-help group participation (Galanter, 1988; Videka-Sherman & Lieberman, 1985). Another problem with the services model is that outcomes are assessed using traditional scales that are more attuned to the worldview and therapeutic techniques of psychotherapy than to self-help.

Rappaport (1994) describes a different model that can be used to understand self-help processes and outcomes. Participants begin to identify with the community narrative. The narrative is gradually used to organize the person's story. The structure of the community narrative is gradually adopted as the structure for the member's personal narrative. The personal narrative is closely linked to the member's personal identity, and both, in turn, are hypothesized to be closely related to the person's functioning. This raises a question whether research review groups will be receptive to such models. To be specific, will the Initial Review Groups of the NIMH (or NIAAA or NIDA) or will the Centers for Mental Health Services, Substance Abuse Prevention and Treatment of the Substance Abuse and Mental Health Services Administration be receptive to self-help and also to new conceptual models for dealing with the topic? The alternative view is that the culture of professional privilege as it is played out in the application scoring process will be less receptive to these newer, more qualitative and naturalistic models. Yet these newer models are needed because they are more compatible with models that self-help members use to monitor their own progress. These models can be inferred from the way that members in Twelve Step groups tell stories about working a particular step, from the way that members in groups affiliated with the National Depressive and Manic Depressive Association relate their ongoing battle to resist the temptation to deny their illness, or from the way that members, in a final illustration from Recovery, Inc., tell stories, which in their language means "give examples," attributing good outcomes to the conscientious practice of the Recovery method.

Collaboration

Kaufmann's chapter (this volume) challenges us to think about how to conduct more collaborative research, a goal, incidentally, that would be furthered by greater respect for the community narrative model. Consumers or self-help leaders (using these terms synonymously for present purposes) are beginning to be recognized as stakeholders not only in self-help research but in all research that purports to benefit them. Simultaneously, large organizations, such as the National Depressive and Manic Depressive Association and NAMI, have formulated ambitious and sophisticated neuroscience research agendas. Less attention, however, has been paid to the development of a psychosocial research agenda. Such an agenda would address the day-to-day issues their members face in terms of stigma, jobs, education, housing, and their satisfaction with mental health services. Even less attention has been paid to the kind of information that would empower their own organizations and the movement as a whole. An exception is the work of Sommer (1992) and his associates and the California Alliance for the Mentally Ill. Additional progress could be made if self-help leaders drew up a series of questions about their own organizations and their members. These questions might include who their members are, how their organization functions, who benefits, and how. The NAMI made progress along these lines when it used MacArthur Foundation funding to sponsor a survey of its membership (Skinner, Steinwachs, & Kasper, 1992). NAMI provided useful information about the membership, their representativeness in terms of the eligible population, and their satisfaction with professional services. Hopefully, later reports of this survey will include more information about the experiences, satisfactions, and desires of members of NAMI, which describes itself as a "grassroots, self-help support and advocacy organization of families and friends of people with serious mental illnesses and consumers themselves." Insofar as leaders seek information about the usefulness of their own organization to the members, they will demonstrate that they understand the importance of their own organization as well as the importance of professional services and neuroscience research.

With more collaborative research under way and in the offing, a number of strategic and ethical issues are emerging. These issues will be all the more salient the longer studies remain in the field and the more they use longitudinal designs to pursue answers to complex and consequential questions. Before most of these studies collect their data and issue their reports, their principal investigators are likely to be involved in discussions about whether one cohort of self-help leaders can commit the next cohort of self-help leaders and members to cooperation with outside researchers. These discussions could become more tense if they are associated with frequent, unplanned turnover among the self-help leaders. The implicit or explicit veto power that this decision about continuance gives to self-help leaders is a kind of absolute power that can be very intimidating. The mere threat might deter some investigators from even considering projects, especially with self-help groups that are more activist and critical of professional services. Others, perhaps more naive or committed than reckless, can expect to find themselves in potential conflict situations, some of which might simply be expressions of the legitimate tensions between research and the more direct organizational and movement-building activities of self-help organizations. The tedious research procedures and the long delays inherent in research, especially when it is longitudinal, can be reason enough to want to abandon them for some other quicker payoff organizational development activities. However, it could also be the expression of a less generous impulse. The threat to revoke permission to complete a study can also be a power play. The irony is that it might signify that the time has come when it is not only professionals who have the potential to misuse the research process.

What is needed is a new vision of mutually beneficial organizational relationships between research and self-help organizations (Powell, 1990). Casual input from occasional focus groups is no longer enough. Research sponsors or funders must also assume some responsibility, perhaps through developing some guidelines for these collaborative relationships. In any event, they might reasonably expect to see letters of agreement that spell out the mechanisms that will be used to resolve the expectable difficulties. On the whole, they should expect more contractual relationships between the self-help and the research organizations, and along with this they should be prepared for the added costs of the negotiating and coordinating activities necessary to maintain understanding and support for these arrangements. Therefore, it might also be expected that services research will cost more in the self-help sector than in the professional sector because of the greater complexity of the self-help sector.

Referral Processes

Studies of referral have become an important research focus and, as noted above, the chapters in this volume by Luke et al., Maton, and Humphreys and Woods take us beyond the domain of individual-level variables. They cross domains as they present data and theory about the importance of individual-group match and community context variables. The knowledge obtained by this approach will be useful to develop referral procedures and to construct a model of how the process works. A number of authors have discussed elements of effective referral processes (Farquharson, 1990; Levy & Derby, 1992; McCrady & Irvine, 1989; Medvene, Lin, Mendoza, Harris, & Miller, 1993; Nowinski & Baker, 1992; Powell, 1987). All agree that simply mentioning a group is insufficient. Referrals must be made by informed persons who are positive but realistic about the focal self-help group. Moreover, these authors contribute to an emerging norm that several partial or full sessions are desirable to impart information about the self-help group and deal with any difficulties experienced by the prospective member in his or her early contacts with the self-help group.

Our own research with the Manic Depressive and Depressive Association of Metropolitan Detroit has produced promising findings about the effectiveness of a facilitation process that capitalizes on the referent power of veteran members to provide information about the group (French & Raven, 1959). In this study, veteran members, or sponsors as they were called, introduced prospective members to the self-help organization. They discussed how the organization helped them and then, after the prospective members gave their permission, accompanied them to a "rap group" meeting. This procedure resulted in more than half of the experimental group attending at least one meeting on their own in contrast to a very small proportion of the control group (Powell et al., 1992).

Noordsy, Schwab, Fox, and Drake (this volume) found that aggressive promotion of Alcoholics Anonymous and Narcotics Anonymous by professional case managers (not self-helpers) among people with dual diagnoses also led to a similar high rate of attendance for at least one self-help meeting. However, ongoing affiliation occurred less often. An ethnographic analysis revealed that these techniques led to resentment among many consumers, and the approach has since been modified to be less confrontive.

Another of our research studies, this time with dual recovery AA groups suggests that the organizational context of the referral makes a difference (Kurtz, Puscas, Harrison, Powell, & Garvin, 1992). People with dual diagnoses who appeared similar, except with respect to whether they received treatment in a substance abuse facility, differed in their response to referral. Those who had been treated in a substance abuse agency participated more often in the dual recovery AA groups designed for people with co-occurring problems. Noordsy et al. (1994) also found an association between inpatient addictions treatment and affiliation with community AA groups among people with dual diagnoses. Similar findings are reported by Humphreys and Woods (1994) for those with primary alcohol or drug diagnoses. People who had been treated in inpatient settings affiliated in higher proportion than those in outpatient settings. But, of course, future studies will need to rule out other unmeasured variables. Length of time a person has the problem could make a difference. And then there are a host of potentially important variables related to who makes the referral and how.

Some might argue that in light of the low rate of participation in professional services (Regier et al., 1993), people should not be expected to affiliate with self-help groups at any higher rates. There is likely to be a ceiling on self-help participation just as there seems to be on the use of professional services. Moreover, it would be inappropriate for self-help to substitute for professional care. Self-help should not be thought of as a "poor person's psychotherapy" or, perhaps more aptly, as "uninsured person's psychotherapy." Nonetheless, it is quite appropriate to discourage costly, excessive professional care by providing access to more appropriate self-help programs. The budgetary advantage arises from the self-help system, in which consumers become "prosumers," producers of what they consume (Gartner & Riessman, 1984). Note, however, this is a substitution policy only insofar as it discourages the substitution of less appropriate, less effective, albeit more expensive, professional care for self-help services. Moreover, it is a policy that might be especially appropriate for people in particular circumstances—for example, people who are recovering or are coping with long-term conditions or need to implement or maintain lifestyle changes to manage their conditions effectively.

Moreover, contrary to conventional wisdom, it would be wise to consider, based on evidence presented in this volume and elsewhere, that those assumed to be unresponsive to self-help (e.g., African Americans) simply have not been given the opportunity (DenHartog et al., 1986). Nash and Kramer (this volume) describe a very substantial network of self-help groups established and maintained solely by African Americans. Surely, much remains to be done to investigate how these and other organizations attract those previously assumed to be difficult to attract. But such an undertaking will take more resources and stronger connections to the world of academic research than has characterized this field to date. Hopefully, efforts to make these connections will build on the important, informally developed, self-help/academic liaisons at the Universities of Illinois, Michigan, California (Berkeley), and Wichita State. Notwithstanding the many challenges still before us, when this volume, together with the special issue of the *American Journal of Community Psychology* (Borkman, 1991), is compared with the 1976 issue of the *Journal of Applied Behavioral Science,* one is forced to conclude that the field has come a long way. These publications highlight many opportunities for researchers and self-help organizations and for the funding agencies who can do so much to foster creative partnerships between them.

REFERENCES

ADAMHA Reorganization Act of 1992. sec. 124, 42 U.S.C., sec. 201.

Borkman, T. J. (Ed.). (1991). Self-help groups [special issue]. *American Journal of Community Psychology, 19*(5).

Chamberlin, J., Rogers, J. A., & Sneed, C. S. (1989). Consumers, families, and community support systems. *Psychosocial Rehabilitation Journal, 12*(3), 93-106.

Chesler, M. A. (1990). Action research in the voluntary sector: A case study of scholar-activist roles in self-help groups. In S. Wheelan & E. Pepitone (Eds.), *Advances in field theory* (pp. 265-280). Newbury Park, CA: Sage.

DenHartog, G. L., Homer, A. L., & Wilson, R. B. (1986). *Cooperation: A tradition in action. Self-help involvement of clients in Missouri alcohol and drug abuse treatment programs.* Missouri Department of Mental Health.

Department of Health and Human Services, Public Health Service. (1988). *Surgeon general's workshop on self-help and public health* (HRSA, Bureau of Maternal and Child Health and Resource Development Publication No. 224-250). Washington, DC: U.S. Government Printing Office.

Emerick, R. (1990). Self-help groups for former patients: Relations with mental health professionals. *Hospital and Community Psychiatry, 41*(4), 401-407.

Emrick, C. D., Tonigan, J. S., Montgomery, H., & Little, L. (1993). Alcoholics Anonymous: What is currently known. In B. S. McCrady & W. R. Miller (Eds.), *Research on Alcoholics Anonymous: Opportunities and alternatives* (pp. 41-78). New Brunswick, NJ: Rutgers Center of Alcohol Studies.

Farquharson, A. (1990). *A guide to competency profile of human service professionals working with self-help groups.* Victoria, Canada: University of Victoria Press.

French, J.R.P., & Raven, B. (1959). The bases of social power. In D. Cartwright (Ed.), *Studies in social power* (pp. 150-167). Ann Arbor: University of Michigan, Institute for Social Research.

Galanter, M. (1988). Zealous self-help groups as adjuncts to psychiatric treatment: A study of Recovery, Inc. *American Journal of Psychiatry, 145*(10), 1248-1253.

Gartner, A., & Riessman, F. (1984). *The self-help revolution.* New York: Human Sciences Press.

Gordon, R. E., Edmunson, E., & Bedell, J. (1982). Reducing rehospitalization of state mental patients: Peer management and support. In A. Yaeger & R. Slotkin (Eds.), *Community mental health.* New York: Plenum.

Gottlieb, B. H., & Peters, L. (1991). A national demographic portrait of mutual aid group participants in Canada. *American Journal of Community Psychology, 19*(5), 651-666.

Hinrichsen, G. A., Revenson, T. A., & Shinn, M. (1985). Does self-help help? An empirical investigation of scoliosis peer support groups. *Journal of Social Issues, 41*(1), 65-87.

Humphreys, K., & Woods, M. D. (1994). Researching mutual-help group participation in a segregated society. In T. J. Powell (Ed.), *Understanding the self-help organization: Frameworks and findings.* Thousand Oaks, CA: Sage.

Israel, B. A., Schurman, S. J., & Hugentobler, M. K. (1992). Conducting action research: Relationships between organization members and researchers. *Journal of Applied Behavioral Science, 28*(1), 74-101.

Jacobs, M. K., & Goodman, G. (1989). Psychology and self-help groups: Predictions on a partnership. *American Psychologist, 44*(3), 536-545.

Karasu, T. B., Docherty, J. P., Gelenberg, A., Kupfer, D. J., Merriam, A. E., & Shadoan, R.A.P.A. (1993). Practice guidelines for major depressive disorder in adults: Work group on major depressive disorder. *American Journal of Psychiatry Supplement, 150*(4), 1-26.

Kaufmann, C. L. (1994). Consumer roles in self-help group research. In T. J. Powell (Ed.), *Understanding the self-help organization: Frameworks and findings.* Thousand Oaks, CA: Sage.

Kurtz, E. (1993). Research on Alcoholics Anonymous: The historical context. In B. S. McCrady & W. R. Miller (Eds.), *Research on Alcoholics Anonymous: Opportunities and alternatives* (pp. 13-26). New Brunswick, NJ: Rutgers Center of Alcohol Studies.

Kurtz, L. F., Puscas, N., Harrison, S., Powell, T. J., & Garvin, C. D. (1992, August). *AA attendance by seriously mentally ill substance abusers.* Paper presented at the International Congress on Alcohol and Drug Dependence, Glasgow, Scotland.

Levy, L. H., & Derby, J. F. (1992). Bereavement support groups: Who joins, who does not, and why. *American Journal of Community Psychology, 20,* 649-662.

Lieberman, M. A., & Borman, L. D. (Eds.). (1976). Special Issue: Self-help groups. *Journal of Applied Behavioral Science, 12*(3), 261-463.

Lieberman, M. A., & Snowden, L. R. (1994). Problems in assessing prevalence and membership characteristics of self-help group participants. In T. J. Powell (Ed.), *Understanding the self-help organization: Frameworks and findings.* Thousand Oaks, CA: Sage.

Maton, K. I. (1994). Moving beyond the individual level of analysis in mutual-help group research: An ecological paradigm. In T. J. Powell (Ed.), *Understanding the self-help organization: Frameworks and findings.* Thousand Oaks, CA: Sage.

Maton, K. I., Leventhal, G. S., Madara, E. J., & Julien, M. (1989). Factors affecting the birth and death of mutual-help groups: The role of national affiliation, professional involvement, and member focal problem. *American Journal of Community Psychology, 17*(5), 643-671.

McCrady, B. S., & Irvine, S. (1989). Self-help groups. In R. K. Hester & W. R. Miller (Eds.), *Handbook of alcoholism treatment approaches: Effective alternatives* (pp. 153-169). New York: Pergamon.

Medvene, L. J., Lin, K., Mendoza, R., Harris, N., & Miller, M. (1993). *Mexican-American participation in family support groups: Psychological, cultural and organizational factors.* Manuscript under review.

Meissen, G., & Warren, M. L. (1994). The self-help clearinghouse: A new development in action research for community psychology. In T. J. Powell (Ed.), *Understanding the self-help organization: Frameworks and findings.* Thousand Oaks, CA: Sage.

Miller, W. R., & McCrady, B. S. (1993). The importance of research on Alcoholics Anonymous. In B. S. McCrady & W. R. Miller (Eds.), *Research on Alcoholics Anonymous: Opportunities and alternatives* (pp. 3-12). New Brunswick, NJ: Rutgers Center of Alcohol Studies.

Narrow, W. E., Regier, D. A., Rae, D. S., Manderscheid, R. W., & Locke, B. Z. (1993). Use of services by persons with mental and addictive disorders: Findings from the National Institute of Mental Health Epidemiologic Catchment Area program. *Archives of General Psychiatry, 50*(2), 95-107.

Nash, K. B., & Kramer, K. D. (1994). Self-help for sickle cell disease in African-American communities. In T. J. Powell (Ed.), *Understanding the self-help organization: Frameworks and findings.* Thousand Oaks, CA: Sage.

National Institute of Mental Health. (1988a). *ECA public use wave 1 codebook.* Rockville, MD: Author.

National Institute of Mental Health. (1988b). Public-academic liaison (PAL) for research on serious mental disorders. *Catalog of Federal Domestic Assistance, 13.242,* 1-8.

National Institutes of Health. (1993). Small business technology transfer program. *NIH Guide for Grants and Contracts, 22*(32), 2.

Noordsy, D., Schwab, B., Fox, L., & Drake, R. E. (1994). The role of self-help programs in the rehabilitation of persons with mental illness and substance abuse disorders. In T. J. Powell (Ed.), Understanding the self-help organization: Frameworks and findings. Thousand Oaks, CA: Sage.

Nowinski, J., & Baker, S. (1992). *The twelve-step facilitation handbook: A systematic approach to early recovery from alcoholism and addictionism.* New York: Lexington Books.

Powell, T. J. (1987). *Self-help organizations and professional practice.* Silver Spring, MD: National Association of Social Workers.

Powell, T. J. (1990). Professional help and informal help: Competing or complementary systems. In T. J. Powell (Ed.), *Working with self-help* (pp. 31-49). Silver Spring, MD: National Association of Social Workers.

Powell, T. J., Hill, E. M., Warner, L., Yeaton, W., Silk, K., Callahan, J., & Janssen, J. (1992). *Encouraging attendance at a self-help group for people with mood disorders: A preliminary report.* Ann Arbor: University of Michigan, Center for Self-Help Research & Knowledge Dissemination.

Raiff, N. R. (1982). Self-help participation and quality of life: A study of the staff of Recovery, Inc., helping people help themselves. *Prevention in Human Services, 1*(3), 79-89.

Rappaport, J. (1994). Narrative studies, personal stories, and identity transformation in the mutual-help context. In T. J. Powell (Ed.), *Understanding the self-help organization: Frameworks and findings.* Thousand Oaks, CA: Sage.

Regier, D. A., Narrow, W. E., Rae, D. S., Manderscheid, R. W., Locke, B. Z., & Goodwin, F. K. (1993). The de facto U.S. mental and addictive disorders service system: Epidemiologic catchment area prospective 1-year prevalence rates of disorders and services. *Archives of General Psychiatry, 50*(2), 85-94.

Skinner, E. A., Steinwachs, D. M., & Kasper, J. A. (1992). Family perspectives on the service needs of people with serious and persistent mental illness: Part 1: Characteristics of families and consumers. *Innovations & Research, 1*(3), 23-30.

Sommer, R. (1992). Collaborative research with a family support organization. *Psychiatry, 55,* 111-118.

Vachon, M.L.S., Lyall, W.A.L., Rogers, J., Freedman-Letofsky, K., & Freeman, S.J.J. (1980). A controlled study of self-help intervention for widows. *American Journal of Psychiatry, 137*(11), 1380-1384.

Videka-Sherman, L., & Lieberman, M. (1985). The effects of self-help and psychotherapy intervention on child loss: The limits of recovery. *American Journal of Orthopsychiatry, 55*(1), 70-81.

Yeaton, W. H. (in press). The development and assessment of valid measures of service delivery to enhance inference in outcome-based research: Measuring attendance at self-help group meetings. *Journal of Consulting and Clinical Psychology.*

2. Agency Involvement With Self-Help Programs and Quality of Mental Health Services for Older Adults

THOMAS J. POWELL

The question of whether self-help involvement is an additional resource complementing professional care or substitutes for it concerns self-help leaders and sympathetic professionals alike (Department of Health and Human Services, 1988). Professionals understandably fear that budget-oriented policymakers will promote self-help as a substitute for professional care. Self-help leaders recoil from the suggestion that their services might be used to justify a retreat from public responsibility for services. Of course, neither professionals nor self-helpers oppose the reduction of excessive professional care which may be a consequence of the lack of access to more appropriate self-help experiences. But aside from reducing inappropriate use, participation in self-help programs may stimulate appropriate service demand, as it leads some people to become aware of services, or more assertive in asking for them, or more inclined to see them in a positive light (Nicholaichuk & Wollert, 1989; Powell, 1979; Riessman, Moody, & Worthy, 1984).

AUTHOR'S NOTE: This research was supported by a grant from the Ittelson Foundation.

At the agency level, parallel questions exist. Does agency involvement with self-help programs simply (and happily) complement professional services, or is it linked to an increase or decrease of professional services? If involvement, assuming its desirability, were linked to an increase, it could be incorporated into a broader strategy to expand services to underserved populations, such as older adults (Colenda & van Dooren, 1993; Flemming & Rickards, 1986). Although there are no data directly relevant to the relationship between agency involvement with self-help and changes in service output, there are data indicating that when general service agencies become involved with specialized external agencies, their services to these populations increase. For example, health planning agencies which became involved with aging network agencies gave more attention to long-term care (Benjamin, Lindeman, Budetti, & Newacheck, 1984). Increased mental health services were available to seniors in those mental health centers that coordinated their services with aging network agencies (Lebowitz, Light, & Bailey, 1987). This knowledge may be further refined by the tentative findings that certain types of relationships, or particular types of cooperative interactions, between mental health and aging network agencies were found to be stronger predictors of increased services to senior adults than others (Chapleski, Moles, Gibson, & Powell, 1991; Moles, Chapleski, & Powell, 1992). And although no formal study exists of the link between self-help and increased professional services, covariation has been observed between the growth of AA and alcoholism treatment centers (National Institute for Alcohol Abuse and Alcoholism, 1983).

These considerations give rise to a number of research questions: The first asks how involved are community mental health agencies serving older adults with self-help programs relevant to this population? The second asks whether there is a relationship between agency involvement in self-help and increases or decreases in the agency's services to older adults. The third asks whether Area Agencies on Aging (AAA), which are presumed to be strongly committed to older adult services, are also heavily involved with self-help programs. The fourth asks whether the relationship between community mental health agencies (CMH) and self-help programs is different for older ethnic minorities than it is for older adults in general (Baker, Weiner, Levine, & Gordon, 1984). These questions were addressed with data on changes in mental health services for older adults in Michigan from 1983 to 1986. This was a period in which the state department of mental health offered agencies special initiatives to improve their services for older adults (Grady & Maynard, 1987; Powell & Fellin, 1987).

METHODS

Sample

The CMH sample was made up of the 55 CMH boards in Michigan and 10 major contract agencies in the Detroit area. The AAA sample was made up of the 14 Area Agencies on Aging. Questionnaires were returned by 72 of the 79 CMH and AAA agencies, for a 91% response rate. The rates for the three subsamples were: 80% (8/10) for the contract agencies, 91% (50/55) for the community mental health boards, and 100% (14/14) for the AAAs. The agency-designated respondents usually functioned as aging specialists in the agency. In descending order, the professional affiliations of the respondents were: social work (54%), psychology (19%), and nursing (9.5%). A majority of them held master's degrees.

Questionnaire

The instrument was a mailed, self-administered questionnaire. Data were elicited about their perceptions of the extent to which their agencies were involved with self-help programs. Among the programs offered as examples were: the Older Women's League, the Gray Panthers, Parkinson groups, Alzheimer groups, Widow to Widow programs, Make Today Count groups, Survivors of Suicide, Dignity, Self-Help for the Hard of Hearing (SHH), and the many groups for people with ostomies, stroke, and the other conditions disproportionately affecting older adults (Borkman, 1982). Eleven items were used to assess the nature of CMH and AAA agency involvement with self-help groups. One item was used to assess perceived changes in services for older adults during the last 3 years (1983-1986). Two items were used to assess minority access to services. The respondents were asked to indicate to what extent each item was true on a scale of 1 to 5 (1 = *no extent,* 2 = *little extent,* 3 = *some extent,* 4 = *considerable extent,* and 5 = *great extent*).

Analyses

The percentage of CMH agencies engaged in various types of involvement with self-help programs was calculated. For each type of involvement (11 items), a chi square test was used to examine whether the proportions of involved and noninvolved CMHs differed in terms of the expected proportions improving or not improving their services for older adults. The percentages of CMHs and AAAs engaged in each type of involvement were compared to assess whether the AAAs, as predicted, were more involved. Lastly, a chi square test was used to examine whether the involved and noninvolved CMHs differed in terms of improving services to minorities as measured by two variables (reduction in barriers and increase in services).

FINDINGS

Involvement With Self-Help

Table 2.1 indicates the percentages of respondents who rated the items as true, combining the categories *to some extent, to a considerable extent, or a great extent.* The items indicating sustained involvement (Items 4-7) are rated as true nearly half the time or more. The statements indicating that the CMHs learn or benefit from self-help organizations (Items 9-11) are rated as true less often, about a third of the time. At the opposite pole, the items which could be rated true in the absence of a behavioral commitment (Items 1-2) are endorsed most frequently.

Relationship Between Self-Help and
Increased Services for Older Adults

Five of the 11 types of CMH involvement with self-help were related to increases in mental health services for older adults from 1983-1986. Four of the chi square relationships were significant at the .05 level as indicated by a double asterisk in Table 2.1. The fifth showed a trend toward significance— $p = < .10$, as indicated by a single asterisk.

To check the validity of the involvement with self-help measure as an indicator of commitment to older adults, the amount of involvement by AAAs was compared with the CMHs. The reasoning is as follows: AAAs have only one priority, whereas service to older adults is one of several CMH priorities. Thus AAAs might be expected to have higher levels of involvement with self-help than the CMHs. Table 2.2, which displays these data, shows that AAA involvement with self-help was greater than that of CMH in 10 of 11 comparisons. Although only three of these relationships are

TABLE 2.1   The Percentage of Community Mental Health Agencies Indicating Various Types of Involvement With Self-Help Programs

Item	Percent	N
1. Could make effective use of self-help organizations if they were available	95	58
2. Self-help organizations are likely to become an important factor in plans to provide services	69	58
3. Independent (external) self-help groups or organizations play an important role	63	57
4. Have tried to stimulate the development of self-help or mutual-aid resources	62**	56
5. Make effective use of agency-sponsored (internal) support groups	55	56
6. Have effective relationships with independent self-help groups or organizations	48**	58
7. Have linkages or consultation arrangements with self-help organizations	45	58
8. Staff has been assigned to liaison with specific self-help organizations	38**	58
9. Professionals attend the (open) meetings of self-help organizations to learn more about them	36**	58
10. Self-help organizations assist in attaining agency objectives	34*	56
11. Self-help organizations offer consultation or technical assistance to agency	24	58

NOTE: $*p \leq .10$; $**p \leq .05$.

significant, 10 of the 11 comparisons were in the predicted direction. The small size of the AAA sample (14) meant there was limited power to establish significance.

Another way to check the validity of these findings is to ask whether self-help involvement is possibly confounded with the agencies' broader outreach orientation. This would render the relationship between self-help and services spurious, as it would be a function of the broader and prior outreach orientation. This possibility was checked by examining three variables: involvement with voluntary organizations, religious organizations, and governmental organizations. When the relationships between these variables and increased services for older adults were examined, none of the relationships were significant. The relationships between these three outreach variables and involvement with self-help were also examined. Again, these relationships were not significant. In a final check of the independence of the self-help variable, the AAAs, which did show more self-help involve-

TABLE 2.2 The Percentage of Community Mental Health Agencies (CMHs) and Area Agencies on Aging (AAAs) Indicating Various Types of Involvement With Self-Help Programs

Item	CMHs Percent	AAAs Percent
1. Could make effective use of self-help organizations if they were available	95	86
2. Self-help organizations are likely to become an important factor in plans to provide services	69	77
3. Independent (external) self-help groups or organizations play an important role	63	91
4. Have tried to stimulate the development of self-help or mutual-aid resources	55	82
5. Make effective use of agency-sponsored (internal) support groups	62	79
6. Have effective relationships with independent self-help groups or organizations	48	79
7. Have linkages or consultation arrangements with self-help organizations	45	64
8. Staff has been assigned to liaison with specific self-help organizations	38	64**
9. Professionals attend the (open) meetings of self-help organizations to learn more about them	34	64**
10. Self-help organizations assist in attaining agency objectives	36	50
11. Self-help organizations offer consultation or technical assistance to agency	24	57**

NOTE: **$p \leq .05$.

ment, did not show more outreach involvement than the CMHs. Thus involvement with self-help does not appear to be simply part of a broader orientation to become involved in community outreach activities.

Minorities

To what extent did involvement with self-help improve services to minorities? Two items were used as measures. In one item, respondents were asked to what extent the percentage of services to minority elderly had increased during the past 3 years. In the other, they were asked to what extent they perceived a reduction in the barriers to service for minority elderly during the past 3 years. The responses indicated some improvement on both outcome variables but not as much as for older adults in general. Of the 22 tests

(11 self-help involvement items by the two service outcome items—increase in services and reduction in barriers), 6 were significant. Two of the eleven self-help items were related to an increase in the percentage of minority elderly served whereas four of them were related to a reduction in the barriers to service for minority elderly. This ratio of 6/22 compares unfavorably with the ratio of 5/11 when the question was about self-help involvement with older adults in general. This finding is consistent with the earlier findings of a related study, in which minorities did not benefit as much from special funding and technical assistance programs as older adults in general (Fellin & Powell, 1988).

DISCUSSION

Findings from cross-sectional designs and small, geographically restricted samples are usually considered tentative. In this instance, they might be considered even more tentative, given the nature of the data. This was not a study of the actual behavior of the CMH agencies. Instead, it was a study of the perceptions of the representatives of these agencies. Nonetheless, there are some reasons for confidence in the data. The variation among the self-help involvement variables suggests the data were not overwhelmingly affected by a social desirability response set. The variation in the (dependent) service variables is likewise confidence enhancing. Still, it cannot be considered a definitive study. However, it might well be used to support future research budgets sufficient to collect objective, longitudinal observations about self-help involvement and services to older adults. Another improvement would be to include comparison groups. It would be advantageous even if it were not possible to randomly assign agencies to an experimenter-manipulated self-help involvement condition and some other non-self-help condition. Such a quasi-experimental design would lower the threat to validity and increase the plausibility that it was self-help and not some other confounding variable which accounted for the findings (Cook & Campbell, 1979). Quasi, or better yet, true experiments would also lower the plausibility that the causal direction could be reversed, with increased services leading to more involvement with self-help programs rather than the reverse, as proposed here.

Notwithstanding the caution that must be observed, the study supports the following interpretations. There was a substantial level of professional involvement in self-help. Moreover, the nature of the involvement went beyond the simple sending and receiving of referrals. Many CMHs provided and received consultation and technical assistance. CMH staff often went to the open meetings of self-help organizations and took on liaison assignments with specific organizations. This range of involvement is consistent with the idea that a comprehensive conception of the service delivery system should include self-help as an integral component (Lenrow & Burch, 1981). The system envisions that self-help entities would provide technical assistance to professional agencies, as well as the other way around. If this is to happen, supportive public policies need to be developed and implemented, including ones that alter the culture of professional privilege which has resulted in a definition of the system as made up of only its own inputs (Powell, this volume).

Some reason for hope may be found in a comparison of the findings of the present study with those of an earlier study. More than 10 years ago, Levy (1978) surveyed mental health professionals about their use of self-help groups. In making this comparison, it must be kept in mind that Levy used a national sample and was concerned with self-help groups in general and not the more specific subset of those serving older adults. Still, unless one assumes these are the only important differences, the data suggest the level of professional recognition and involvement with self-help may be on the rise. Forty-six percent of Levy's respondents said that "self-help groups may have an important or very important role to play in a comprehensive mental health delivery system," whereas 95% of the present respondents indicated they "could make effective use of self-help organizations if they are available." In Levy's sample 48% were "making either frequent or occasional referrals to self-help groups," whereas 63% of the present sample indicate that "independent (external) self-help groups or organizations play an important role." Lastly, 31% of the national sample said that "their agencies would-be interested in trying to integrate their services with the activities of self-help groups," whereas 69% of the later Michigan sample indicated that self-help organizations "are likely to become an important factor . . . in plans to provide services."

This apparent growth in involvement could also be attributable to differences in the wording of questions or to the more organizational emphasis of the present study, as well as to the differences mentioned above. But unless one is inclined to assess these methodological differences as the determining ones, it seems more plausible to conclude that there have been some changes in the behavior of mental health professionals and their agencies over the 10-year period.

Involvement by itself serves no purpose unless it is related to some favorable outcome. The most important finding of this study is that involvement with older adult-oriented self-help programs was related to developing more adequate services for older adults. CMHs involved with self-help significantly increased their services to this underserved group over a 3-year period. Thus it can be cautiously concluded that involvement is not a substitute, but a stimulus, for the development of more services.

Yet the benefits of involvement were not equally distributed to minorities. Although CMH involvement with self-help programs had some benefit for minorities, the relationship between self-help and increased services was not as strong for minorities as it was for older adults in general. Thus, special initiatives need to be considered with minority-friendly self-help organizations or with those that have the potential to become accessible and sensitive to minorities. To qualify for this status, self-help organizations need to step up to the challenge to form chapters in minority communities. Too often the onus is on the potential recruit, who is expected to make contact with strange groups in nonminority communities (Humphreys & Woods, this volume). Self-help organizations must also do a better job of linking with other helping systems in minority communities (Nash & Kramer, this volume). Most importantly perhaps, professionals need to challenge the unwarranted but, unfortunately, no less self-fulfilling prophecy about the futility of making referrals of minorities to self-help groups. These negative prophecies are consistent only with the present low levels of participation where the onus is on the help-seeking minority person (Snowden & Lieberman, this volume). They are not consistent with, and need to be challenged by, the systematic studies indicating that given appropriate circumstances, African Americans affiliate with self-help groups as often as nonminorities (DenHartog, Homer, & Wilson, 1986; Humphreys & Woods, 1994).

The findings of this study, together with those concerned with the effects of specific cooperative interactions (Chapleski et al., 1991; Moles et al., 1992) suggest that agencies might improve their services by attending open meetings and assigning staff to liaison with specific self-help groups and organizations. Agencies are also likely to find it advantageous to ask self-help organizations to assist them in carrying out their missions. Frequently this should take the form of asking them to provide consultation and technical assistance to the professional staff. Note that these kinds of involvement imply a reciprocal relationship. They suggest professionals must be ready to invite self-help organizations to assist the agency, not just to be assisted by it, as is the current discriminatory pattern (Kurtz, 1985; Toseland & Hacker,

1982). In working this out, ways must also be found to minimize the risks of competition and cooptation to self-help groups (Hasenfeld & Gidron, 1993). However, it should also be clear that agencies have much to lose if they avoid these relationships. They need self-help groups to understand and connect with the culture and needs of their clients. By engaging in this process, professionals will gain an appreciation for the distinctive helping mechanisms of the self-help group and for how these might be used to complement professional help. In developing egalitarian relationships with self-help organizations, professionals will come to appreciate a marvelous irony: As professional organizations risk opening themselves up to be helped by self-help organizations, they will become more effective as professional organizations.

However, if this vision is to be realized, policy developments are needed in a number of areas. Self-help needs to become a more central focus of services research (Powell, 1994). Curriculum policies governing the education of health and human service professionals need to refer explicitly to the potentially complementary role of self-helpers and professionals. State service agency initiatives and federal demonstration (and research) projects need to define self-help programs as part of the relevant domain (Salzer, McFadden, & Rappaport, in press). The program announcements of funding agencies need to explicitly refer to self-help groups as they invite proposals to encourage various kinds of collaboration and service coordination. Based on the findings of this study, it might be said that if public policy is to carry out its guiding role, it must be informed by activity at the grassroots level, and if grassroots activity is to flourish it must obtain the nutrients that can only be supplied by a supportive public policy.

REFERENCES

Baker, F. M., Weiner, O., Levine, M., & Gordon, J. B. (1984). Utilization of mental health services by the aging. *Journal of the National Medical Association, 76,* 455-460.

Benjamin, A. E., Lindeman, D. A., Budetti, P. P., & Newacheck, P. W. (1984). Shifting commitments to long-term care: The role of coordination. *The Gerontologist, 24,* 598-603.

Borkman, T. (1982). Where are older persons in mutual self-help groups? In A. Kalhen & P. Ahmed (Eds.)., *Aging* (pp. 257-284). New York: Elsenier Biomedical.

Chapleski, E. E., Moles, E. L., Gibson, R. C., & Powell, T. J. (1991). *The effect of cooperative efforts between mental health and aging network agencies on improved mental health services to older adults and older minorities.* Paper presented at the Annual Scientific Meeting of the Gerontological Society of America, San Francisco, CA.

Colenda, C. C., & van Dooren, H. (1993). Opportunities for improving community mental health services for elderly persons. *Hospital & Community Psychiatry, 44,* 531-533.

Cook, T. D., & Campbell, D. T. (1979). *Quasi-experimentation.* Chicago: Rand McNally.

Den Hartog, G. L., Homer, A. L., & Wilson, R. B. (1986). *Cooperation: A tradition in action: Self-help involvement of clients in Missouri alcohol and drug abuse treatment programs.* Missouri: Missouri Department of Mental Health.

Department of Health and Human Services, Public Health Service. (1988). *Surgeon general's workshop on self-help and public health* (HRSA, Bureau of Maternal and Child Health and Resource Development Publication No. 224-250). Washington, DC: U.S. Government Printing Office.

Fellin, P. A., & Powell, T. J. (1988). Mental health services and older adult minorities: An assessment. *The Gerontologist, 28*(4), 442-447.

Flemming, A. S., & Rickards, L. D. (1986). *Findings and recommendations: Mental health recommendations of the 1981 White House Conference on Aging.* Washington, DC: White House Conference on Aging.

Grady, S. C., & Maynard, C. L. (1987). Building ties: A mental health and aging project. *The Gerontologist, 27,* 428-429.

Hasenfeld, Y., & Gidron, B. (1993). Self-help groups and human service organizations: An interorganizational perspective. *Social Service Review, 67,* 217-236.

Humphreys, K., & Woods, M. D. (1994). Researching mutual-help group participation in a segregated society. In T. J. Powell (Ed.), *Understanding the self-help organization: Frameworks and findings.* Thousand Oaks, CA: Sage.

Kurtz, L. F. (1985, Spring). Cooperation and rivalry between helping professionals and members of AA. *Health & Social Work, 10,* 104-112.

Lebowitz, B. D., Light, E., & Bailey, F. (1987). Mental health center services for the elderly: The impact of coordination with area agencies on aging. *The Gerontologist, 27,* 699-702.

Lenrow, P. B., & Burch, R. W. (1981). Mutual aid and professional service: Opposing or complementary? In B. J. Gottlieb (Ed.), *Social networks and social support.* Beverly Hills, CA: Sage.

Levy, L. H. (1978). Self-help groups viewed by mental health professionals: A survey and comments. *American Journal of Community Psychology, 6,* 305-313.

Moles, E. L., Chapleski, E. E., & Powell, T. J. (1992). *Interagency cooperation and awareness and acceptance of mental health services.* Paper presented at annual meeting of the Gerontological Society of America, Initiatives to Reduce Barriers to Mental Health Service Use: Addressing Cultural Factors, Washington, DC.

Nash, K. B., & Kramer, K. D. (1994). Self-help for sickle cell disease in African-American communities. In T. J. Powell (Ed.), *Understanding the self-help organization: Frameworks and findings.* Thousand Oaks, CA: Sage.

National Institute on Alcohol Abuse and Alcoholism. (1983, February). Growth of AA, treatment cited over past 15 years. *NIAAA Information and Feature Service, 104,* 2.

Nicholaichuk, T., & Wollert, R. (1989, Spring). The effects of self-help on health status and health-services utilization. *Canadian Journal of Community Mental Health, 8,* 17-30.

Powell, T. J. (1979). Comparisons between self-help groups and professional services. *Social Casework, 60,* 561-565.

Powell, T. J. (1994). Self-help research and policy issues. In T. J. Powell (Ed.), *Understanding the self-help organization: Frameworks and findings.* Thousand Oaks, CA: Sage.

Powell, T. J., & Fellin, P. A. (1987). *Mental health services for older adults in Michigan: Progress, problems, and prospects, executive summary.* Lansing, MI: The University of Michigan and Michigan Department of Mental Health.

Riessman, F., Moody, M. R., & Worthy, E. H. (1984). Self-help and the elderly. *Social Policy, 14,* 19-26.

Salzer, M. S., McFadden, L., & Rappaport, J. (in press). Professional views of self help groups: A comparative and contextual analysis. *Administration and Policy in Mental Health.*

Snowden, L. R., & Lieberman, M. A. (1994). African-American participation in self-help groups. In T. J. Powell (Ed.), *Understanding the self-help organization: Frameworks and findings.* Thousand Oaks, CA: Sage.

Toseland, R. W., & Hacker, L. (1982). Self-help groups and professional involvement. *Social Work, 27,* 341-348.

3. Problems in Assessing Prevalence and Membership Characteristics of Self-Help Group Participants

MORTON A. LIEBERMAN
LONNIE R. SNOWDEN

The development of contemporary forms of self-help or mutual-aid groups is generally ascribed to Alcoholics Anonymous, which was initiated in 1935. In the short span of a half century, such groups have evolved from an oddity and suspect human service to a vigorous, diverse endeavor known to all who watch daytime talk shows. Newspaper stories during the past several years have reported on a wide range of such groups. African Americans have organized to combat poverty, and others banding together for support include young cancer patients, "psychics," breast cancer patients, survivors of English boarding schools, grandparents who are parents once again, the hearing impaired, bereaved gays, young wives, stressed-out entrepreneurs, executives of takeover companies, family members of politicians, former public officials testifying before Congress, and people who have problems with the IRS. Issues that form the focus of groups range from litigation, unemployment, and fake illness to abortion and impotence. Such diversity and specificity of common problems testify to the vigor and scope of self-help groups.

Social scientists and health professionals were slow to recognize both the existence and import of self-help groups; systematic inquiry is of even more recent origin. Today, we can easily locate studies covering a wide variety of self-help groups addressing innumerable illnesses and dilemmas that plague us. Despite the vigorous growth of empirical research in the past 2 decades, simple demographic information on "how many and who" participate in U.S. support groups remains virtually unknown. Information about self-help groups is of particular importance in the current debate over expected changes in human service delivery. The role such groups can and will play requires such basic descriptive information.

The absence of good epidemiological data has not prevented constant references, both in professional journals and in the media, stating that "many millions" seek out self-help groups. Unfortunately, these estimates are rarely based on adequate empirical studies. The first scholarly appraisal, using an analysis of group growth trends of self-help group membership, was reported by Tracy and Gussow (1976). Their tabulation of functioning chapters in six self-help organizations over a 30-year period, 1942 to 1972, indicated an increase of 67 chapters formed each year since the 1950s. These growth rates were based on information from the International Laryngectomee Association, International Parents Organization, United Ostomy Club, Gam-Anon, and Parents Anonymous. Alcoholics Anonymous (AA), a much larger organization, exhibited a similar growth rate. By 1972, the number of functioning chapters of AA had reached 18,612; by 1978, there were over 30,000 chapters, revealing a growth rate of 50% in 6 years.

Lieberman and Borman (1979) reported on the growth rates of six self-help organizations: Mended Hearts, Compassionate Friends, Widows' Groups, Mothers of Twins, Mothers' Groups, and Women's Consciousness-Raising Groups. Estimates based on the number of chapters listed by the national organizations and their reported membership were found to be biased. Field visits to chapters identified by the national organization revealed that a number of such chapters existed in name only; they had neither a membership beyond the one isolated contact person nor evidence of ever having held a meeting. Clearly, reliance on data from the organization itself can lead to erroneous estimates of participants and their characteristics. Moreover, although most of what we commonly think of as self-help groups are formally linked to national organizations, there are large numbers of identifiable self-help groups that are not. Unfortunately, this number is unknown.

Several recently published studies provide some important corrections to inaccurate epidemiological information. In one of the few estimates to appear in the literature based on a probability sample, Gottlieb and Peters (1991) reported the extent of participation in self-help groups in Canada.

About 2% of the Canadian population reported having been in a self-help or mutual-aid group during the preceding 12 months. Participants tended to be female, 25-44 years old, and to live in either the western provinces or Ontario. Unfortunately, no information was provided on the participants' problems nor on other sources of help to address them. Without such data, the niche for self-help groups in a human service system is impossible to evaluate.

A recent study by Room and Greenfield (1991) using a 1990 nationwide study of drinking practices ($N = 2,058$) provided excellent information on AA membership. The survey reported that 3.1% of respondents—1.5% in the last year— had attended an AA meeting at some point in their life for help with alcohol problems. Interestingly, the overall lifetime rate of attendance at an AA meeting was 9.0%, 3.4% in the past year. Unfortunately, the survey does not reflect what motivations, other than drinking problems, prompted such attendance. Room (1993) concluded, based on the analysis of the survey, that 13.3% of the population had attended a Twelve Step group at some point in their life, and 5.3% had done so during the past year.

The National Institute of Mental Health (NIMH) has considered use of self-help groups as part of its attempt to understand the de facto mental health service system. Capitalizing on longitudinal design of the Epidemiological Catchment Area (ECA) survey, Narrow, Regier, Rae, Manderscheid, and Locke (1993) calculated prevalence rates for use of self-help groups for the year interval between two face-to-face interviews included in the study. About .7% of the sample reported self-help group use. Among participants, approximately 7.9% had substance abuse disorders, 9.7% comorbidity marked by substance abuse and mental problems, and 5.1% nonsubstance abuse disorders. Use of self-help groups represented 12.6% of the total service use among those with a nonsubstance abuse diagnosis and about 20.6% among substance abuse disorders; self-help group users attended more sessions than did users of every other type of help.

The present chapter, using secondary analysis of three surveys, examines the prevalence of self-help group use. Two of the surveys rely on large household probability samples and the third on the population of self-help groups in California. Highlighted in this chapter are the problems of accurately assessing self-help group participation based on current survey information.

STUDY 1: THE ECA SURVEY

The Epidemiological Catchment Area study (Robins & Regier, 1991) is a large community survey ($N = 20,000$) designed to determine the incidence and prevalence of specific psychiatric disorders and to better understand the use of medical and mental health services. The ECA data are unique in that detailed data were collected on health services use, sociodemographics, and diagnosis of mental health problems, using a core of identical questions and instruments across five ECA sites. The secondary analysis presented here used 18,000 subjects, excluding all those residing in institutional settings at the time of the survey. The survey asked a series of questions about helping resources used for emotional disorders, nerves, drugs, alcohol, or other mental health problems. Among these questions was a probe that asked "Have you ever gone to a self-help group, like Alcoholics Anonymous, etc.?" Both lifetime use and past 6 months' use were requested.

Findings

Demographics

Lifetime use of self-help groups was 3.6% for men and 2.2% for women. The Caucasian rate was 3.6%, Hispanic, 2.2%, and African American, 1.1%. The mean age of self-help group participants was 43.1 years, and mean level of education was 12 years (compared to 11 years for the general population). Analyses of social class indicated that self-help group use (as for most other services) increased with higher socioeconomic status (SES).

Table 3.1 displays the demographic information associated with self-help group participation. Table 3.1 also provides similar information on professional mental health (MH) services use (defined by a positive response to seeking out a mental health specialist, health plan or clinic, private practice, mental health center, psychiatric outpatient clinic at a general hospital, outpatient clinic in a psychiatric hospital, an outpatient clinic in a VA hospital, or a drug or an alcohol clinic). Both prevalence (past year use) and lifetime use are shown. Columns 1 and 2 show the ratio of professional mental health services to the proportion of the population using self-help groups, columns 3 and 4 the percentage of lifetime self-help group and MH service use, and columns 5 and 6 the figures for past-year use. Note that these figures do not reflect exclusive use; the same individual could be using both self-help groups and professional mental health services. In fact, the overlap is 31%; that is, 31% of those who during the past year participated in a self-help group also sought out the help of a professional mental health provider. The lifetime use overlap is much higher—71%.

Men are more likely than women to use self-help services rather then professional mental health services. The divorced/separated use self-help

TABLE 3.1 Frequency of Mental Health Services (MHS) Use Compared to Self-Help Group (SHG) Use: ECA Sample (in percentages)

Respondent Characteristics	Ratio SHG /MHS Lifetime	Ratio SHG /MHS 1-Year	Lifetime SHG	Past Year SHG	Lifetime MHS	Past Year MHS
Men	.25	.19	3.6	.6	14.4	3.1
Women	.14	.16	2.2	.6	15.7	3.8
Married	.19	.20	2.3	.5	11.9	2.5
Widowed	.17	.13	1.4	.2	8.1	1.5
Separated	.22	.14	4.7	.8	21.0	5.6
Divorced	.18	.17	5.7	1.5	30.9	8.6
Single	.17	.13	2.9	.6	17.4	4.8
Black	.10	.03	1.1	.1	10.8	3.0
Latino	.27	.21	3.2	.6	11.8	2.9
Caucasian	.20	.18	3.6	.7	18.0	3.8
SES lowest quarter	.17	.11	1.8	.3	10.4	2.7
SES second quarter	.21	.20	2.7	.6	13.0	3.0
SES third quarter	.20	.18	3.6	.7	18.3	3.8
SES highest quarter	.14	.15	3.1	.8	22.8	5.4
Age 18-29	.15	.14	2.3	.5	15.4	3.6
30-45	.17	.14	3.9	.9	23.1	6.4
46-59	.23	.16	3.6	.7	16.0	4.3
Over 60	.14	.31	1.8	.4	7.4	1.3

groups more frequently than do the never married and the married. However, the ratio of self-help group to professional help is highest for the currently married. Ethnic groups are highly skewed, with Caucasians showing the highest use, closely followed by Hispanics, with the African-American group the lowest. Self-help group participation is linearly related to social class, with the lowest quartile showing the smallest usage. This parallels the use of professional mental health services. The highest use of self-help groups is among those 30 to 45 years old, next highest is the 46-59 age group, and the lowest is for those over 60 years of age. This also parallels the use of professional services. Overall, for every member in our society who within a 1-year period participated in a self-help group to address mental health and substance abuse problems, 5.8 turned to a professional.

TABLE 3.2   Use of Self-Help Group (SHG) or Professional Mental Health
Services (MHS), Associated With Presence of DSM-III Diagnosis
(in percentages)

	No DSM-III Diagnosis	Lifetime DSM-III Diagnosis	No Past Year DSM-III Diagnosis	Past Year DSM-III Diagnosis
Lifetime SHG use	0.5	2.3	1.2	1.6
No SHG use	59.6	37.6	71.3	26.0
Past year SHG use	0.1	0.5	0.3	0.3
No SHG use past year	63.7	35.7	74.4	25.0
Lifetime MHS use	5.0	10.2	8.0	7.1
No MHS use	55.1	29.7	64.5	20.4
Past year MHS use	1.0	2.5	1.6	2.0
No MHS use past year	62.8	33.7	73.2	23.3

NOTE: Lifetime SHG use = 2.8%; Past year SHG use = .6%; Lifetime MHS use = 15.2%; past year MHS use = 3.5%.

Self-Help Group Participation
and Psychopathology

Beyond demographic differences, what other characteristics were associated with self-help group participation? Were self-help group members more likely to manifest signs of psychopathology? The ECA survey provides a number of ways of examining the level of emotional distress. Table 3.2 shows the prevalence rate both for the past year and over one's lifetime. Two different classifications of diagnosis are used: lifetime occurrence (column 2) and past year occurrence (column 4). Columns 1 and 3 show the percentage of service use for respondents who did not reach iagnostic criteria set by the Diagnostic and Statistical Manual of Mental Disorders (DSM-III).

As shown in Table 3.2, self-help group participants are five times more likely than nonparticipants over their lifetime to manifest symptoms of sufficient magnitude and frequency to be classified as mentally ill using DSM-III criteria. These differences disappear, however, when current use and current DSM-III diagnosis are examined. Rather than a 5:1 ratio, self-help group participation is equally divided between respondents manifesting illness and those who were not. Perhaps many who are currently participating in self-help groups are in remission. As a large number of the participants are substance abusers, this could explain the difference between past and current DSM-III diagnosis. For example, many current members of AA would not meet current DSM-III diagnostic criteria. Comparisons between the frequency of self-help group participation with use of professional mental health services reveal that the ratio of lifetime use of mental health professionals and lifetime DSM-III diagnosis is much smaller for professional services than it is for self-help group use; only about twice as many people who indicate they have ever used a mental health professional had a lifetime DSM-III diagnosis compared to the 5:1 ratio in self-help groups.

Types of Mental Illness and Service Use

Table 3.3 shows usage rates for professional services compared to self-help groups for the major clusters of mental disorders: schizophrenias, the affective disorders, substance abuse, and anxiety disorders.

The most illuminating contrasts shown in Table 3.3 are those between the percentages of psychiatrically ill currently using professional services and self-help group participation. Approximately 30% currently manifesting schizophrenic disorders sought out professional service, compared to 3% for self-help groups, a 10:1 ratio. For the affective disorders, about 17% used professional mental health services, with approximately 2.5% using self-help groups, a ratio of 6.5:1. For substance abuse, 10% use professional services and 2.5% self-help groups, a ratio of 4.5:1. For the anxiety disorders, approximately 20% use professional services and 2% self-help groups, a ratio of almost 10:1. Thus, although a higher percentage of people suffering from schizophrenic disorders use self-help groups, the ratio comparisons indicate that self-help groups represent a larger share of total use for substance abuse, with the affective disorders next and both the schizophrenic disorders and anxiety disorders much lower. These ratio comparisons are, of course, not an indicator of the prevalence of the disorders nor an indicator of how many people are served.

The composition of self-help groups based on the diagnostic categories of membership is portrayed in Figure 3.1. As might have been anticipated from the previous discussion, substance abuse and affective disorders represent nearly half of the self-help group membership, with an additional 8% drawn from the anxiety disorders and 5% from the schizophrenias. Self-help groups addressing the emotional problems of their participants are primarily directed toward substance abuse and affective disorders.

TABLE 3.3 Use of Self-Help Groups (SHG) and Professional Mental Health Services (MHS), Associated With Specific Diagnoses (in percentages)

Diagnosis	Schizophrenia	Affective Disorders	Substance Abuse	Anxiety Disorders	Any DSM-III Diagnosis
Current SHG use	3.1	2.6	2.4	2.0	1.3
Current MHS use	29.4	16.7	11.1	19.6	4.5
Lifetime SHG use	4.3	10.1	14.2	10.4	6.7
Lifetime MHS professional use	63.4	51.4	38.0	51.2	30.5

NOTE: Schizophrenia also includes schizophreniform. Affective disorders include mania, major depression, grief, or dysthymia. Substance abuse may involve alcohol or drugs. Anxiety disorders may be somatic or panic or obsessive-compulsive or anorexia.

STUDY 2: MELLINGER-BALTER SURVEY

The Institute for Research in Social Behavior's national survey of 3,161 households focused on psychotropic drug use (Mellinger & Balter, 1983). Respondents were asked, "During the past twelve months, have you received treatment, advice or help from a psychiatrist, psychologist, a social worker or counselor?" In addition, they were asked, "During the past twelve months, did you take part in any personal growth or self-help group or training activity such as EST, meditation, Alcoholics Anonymous, Weight Watchers, or assertiveness training? What group was that?" Measures indexing psychiatric disturbance were available for each respondent: psychiatric distress (the number and intensity of psychiatric symptoms); the amount of life stress; and role impairment (a measure of how well subjects were functioning in their major roles: parent, husband or wife, student, worker).

This survey provided another source for estimating the incidence of self-help group participation compared to professional helping resources. More important, it provided information on type of groups used by the respondents, permitting categorization of self-help groups into those providing behavioral "correction," those providing support, and groups used for growth.

Findings

The prevalence rates during 1980 indicate that 5.6% of adults used a mental health professional, 2.9% participated in a self-help group, and 2.2%

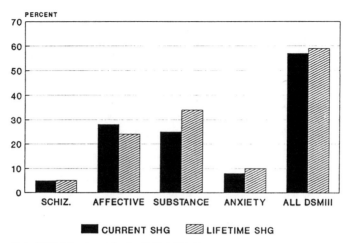

Figure 3.1. SHG Membership, by DSM-III Diagnosis

participated in some type of experiential education ("growth group") (Lieberman, 1989). Table 3.4 shows selected demographic characteristics of self-help group participants contrasted to those who use professional mental health services and growth groups. The characteristics of self-help group participants are roughly parallel to those found in the ECA survey: Highest users of self-help groups were the divorced/separated (note that the pattern is different for growth groups), and age is associated with less use (excepting the youngest cohort). Education level was used as a marker of SES; the results are parallel to the ECA study, with low SES associated with low self-help group participation. The college educated, however, are relatively low in use (again, note the distinct pattern shown by growth group participants).

Stress and Psychopathology

Figures 3.2 and 3.3 depict the relationships between stress (Figure 3.2) and psychiatric symptoms (Figure 3.3) with helping sources. As stress increases, the proportion of survey respondents seeking out mental health services increases dramatically, as does participation in growth groups. There is a substantial linkage between self-help group and the highest stress level. Turning to psychiatric symptoms, increases in symptoms are associated with increased use of mental health services. No appreciable relationship, however, was found between psychiatric symptoms and self-help group participation. This observation differs from the reported positive association

TABLE 3.4 Selected Demographic Characteristics of Help Users:
Mellinger-Balter Survey (in percentages)

	Use of Mental Health Services	Use of Self-Help Group	Use of Growth Group
Married	4.1	3.8	1.9
Separated/divorced	11.8	3.5	3.7
Widowed	4.9	1.7	.5
Single	7.8	2.0	4.9
Age			
18-24	14.6	.9	4.3
25-34	13.3	4.5	3.3
35-49	11.2	5.3	2.1
50-64	11.0	3.7	2.0
Over 65	7.7	.9	.7
Education			
< High school	4.9	2.3	1.2
High school	5.0	6.0	1.6
Some college	6.3	7.3	3.5
≥ College	6.8	4.5	5.7
Caucasian	5.0	3.5	2.8
Noncaucasian	9.3	2.3	.5

found in the ECA study. Most likely the methods used in each of the surveys to inquire about self-help group participation explains the differences in findings. This is addressed more fully in the Discussion section.

STUDY 3: SURVEY OF CALIFORNIA SELF-HELP GROUPS—THE UCLA SURVEY

The California Self-Help Center (UCLA) developed a file of over 3,000 self-help groups (1991 resurvey indicated the number of groups is currently close to 4,000). This file represents the most complete listing of active self-help groups currently available anywhere in the United States. Included in the available information are a description of each group, its goals, frequency of meeting, requirements for attendance, characteristics of participants, focus of the group, history of formation, fee requirements, types of group activities stressed, number of members, service features, characteristics of the leader (member chosen by the group; trained professional,

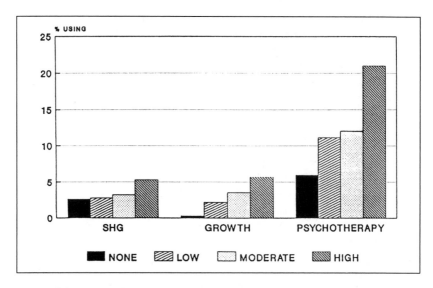

Figure 3.2. Level of Stress and Helping Sources

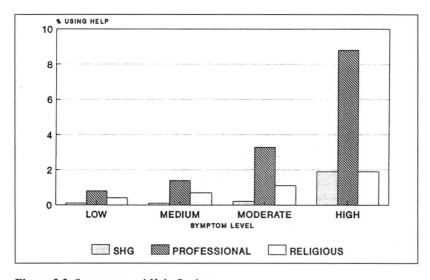

Figure 3.3. Symptoms and Help Settings

volunteer or paid; trained nonprofessional), processes and procedural characteristics, external source of funding, and national affiliation.

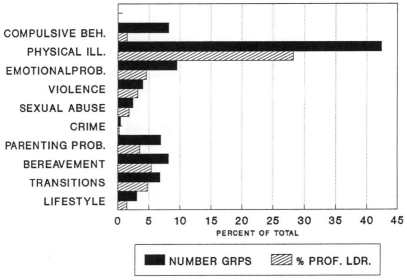

N=2925 Groups excluding substance abuse

Figure 3.4. Problem Areas Served by California SHGs

Problems Addressed by Groups

Figure 3.4 shows the number of groups for each common problem area (excluding substance abuse groups) served by California self-help groups. Also displayed is the number of groups led by professionals. Close to half of the groups address the management of physical illness. Unlike the data portrayed in the ECA survey, only 10% of the self-help groups directly address specific mental illnesses. (Although 227 self-help groups directly serve the mentally ill and their families, this number, of course, underestimates services to the mentally ill. No accurate information was available on the number of substance abuse groups. Included are 9 phobia, 5 depression, 8 manic/depression, 5 schizophrenic, and 5 suicide self-help groups; 113 address a range of serious mental disorders, and 91 address families of the seriously mentally ill).

Number of Participants

Estimates of participation were based on measures used to assess group size: number of members participating in a typical session and the total number of members associated with the group. One quarter of the groups reported less than 10 participants at a typical meeting; one quarter, 10-14; one quarter, 15-24; and one quarter, 25-100. Based on group reports (minus substance abuse groups, such as AA), the mean number of attendees per meeting is 20.9, SD = 18.7, and the mean membership per group chapter is 94.2, SD = 157.7. Based on the 1991 survey of 4,000 groups, we would estimate that during a 1-week period 83,000 Californians participate in self-help groups, representing a total membership of 373,000 (excluding substance abuse). A more accurate estimate, extrapolating from the ECA survey, suggests that approximately 15.2% of the adult population has during their lifetime met the criteria for a DSM-III diagnosis of substance abuse. Of that number, 24.3% had at some time in their lives used a self-help group and 5.5% had done so in the past year. Adding this to the prior estimate, approximately 500,000 Californians were active self-help group members during the past year.

Selected Characteristics of Self-Help Groups

Leadership

There are wide differences in both orientation and style of self-help group leaders. Clients lead 13.5% of all groups, 62% are led by paid professionals, 18% by voluntary professionals (unpaid), and 7% by trained nonprofessionals (often former clients). Nearly one third (32%) of the groups were started by professionals. Groups were designated as being led by a professional leader if, on the survey questionnaire, the informant named a specific professional by name or by category (physician, psychologist, nurse, social worker, etc.). In other parts of the survey, the informant might have indicated that his or her self-help group was jointly led or that there was a shared leadership arrangement. The group was classified as professionally led in those instances. Further compromising the survey information was our inability to determine if the professional leader shared the group's common problem, circumstances that might modify the professionalism of leadership in the direction of peer-led.

New Members

Groups differ markedly in the procedures for admission of new participants, ranging from no entrance requirements to formal screening procedures. The majority (65%) do not require a prospective participant to call or make any other arrangements before attending a meeting. Only a handful of the groups set up specific requirements (must have a diagnosis, prescreening, and the like). As might be anticipated, looking at the range of self-help groups listed in the UCLA data, requirements such as prescreening are most often associated with professionally run groups. Groups also differ on the level of openness to new members. Some groups are close-ended and during a specific time will not admit new members; others weekly add new members weekly.

Services

Services provided by self-help groups vary widely: from those that only offer support to groups that provide multiple services as well as programs directed toward social or political change. For example, in the self-help groups providing services to the seriously mentally disabled, 80% provide phone help, 46% incorporate a buddy system, 21% have a home visiting program, 36% provide peer counseling, and 27% train peer counselors. Most (81%) state that they have access for the handicapped, 11% provide transportation, only slightly more than 1% provide babysitting, and only 2% provide economic assistance. Sixty percent produce a newsletter, 35% state that they are involved in ongoing public education, about the same percentage provide a speakers bureau, and 25% aid in prevention programs for the community at large.

DISCUSSION

A review of the survey data does not build confidence in estimating past or current use of self-help groups. Nevertheless, if forced to estimate, we believe that the best information available is from the Mellinger-Balter 1980 survey; the range of problems that respondents could attach to help-seeking was wider. Furthermore, the survey responses included group names, enabling us to independently classify the help setting with greater precision. Based on that survey, we estimated that in 1980 approximately 5.3 million people participated in a self-help group. Using the 3% growth figure of self-help groups (based, unfortunately, on out-of-date information) a rough estimate of 1992 participants is 7.5 million.

As has been widely suspected, self-help group use for mental health problems appears to be a predominately White, middle-class phenomenon.

An important and unexpected finding, based on the ECA survey, was the high incidence of self-help group use among Latinos, which was only slightly lower than that of the White population. All ethnic groups used professional services much more frequently than self-help groups to address emotional and substance abuse problems. Problems with substance abuse and affective disorders predominate in those who seek out self-help groups; for these disorders, the mutual-aid community plays an especially significant role in the overall service system. Perhaps most telling was the finding that usage of services is overlapping; those who seek out help do so in multiple service delivery modalities.

The analysis presented in this chapter is only a small beginning in answering the basic epidemiological questions raised at the outset. Accurate epidemiological information requires the unambiguous identification of the phenomena under study. The findings of an apparent increase in professionalization—the large number of self-help groups led by professionals, most of whom are paid—if representative of other regions than California, poses a major hurdle for self-help group survey studies. How do we distinguish traditional professional services from those provided in a self-help group? In short, what constitutes a self-help group? Is the report of a respondent who states that he or she had participated in a self-help group sufficient? We think not.

Since the inception of self-help groups, their image has been shaped by a few simple yet powerful ideas: Ordinary people with a common problem come together in settings they own and control, share their problems, and learn from one another without need of professionals. As attractive as this populist view might be, the UCLA study's findings that 60% (omitting substance abuse groups) were led by professionally trained leaders, many of whom were paid, creates dissonance (Lieberman, 1992). The apparent blurring of the traditional boundaries between professional services and mutual-aid groups magnifies the problem of correctly reporting rates of self-help group participation.

The ideal portrait of self-help groups presented in texts does not match empirical reality (Lieberman, 1992; Lieberman & Borman, 1979). The classical picture of such groups, often based on the AA model, appears not to match current self-help group activity; diversity and change over time is the rule. Some groups begin as small face-to-face support systems but soon develop into complex multifaceted client-run social agencies; others start as social protest or social action movements that evolve into quasi-therapeutic settings; still others whose origins were based on face-to-face help and support move in the opposite direction, becoming social action settings more intent on changing society than on changing themselves.

How, then, given both the apparent increasing professionalization of self-help groups and the enormous diversity of their clients and goals, do we define the realm for discourse? The traditional definition of self-help groups as those led by the clients themselves is an appealing one, as it provides a conceptual basis for a boundary. Professional leaders operate from a specific set of perspectives and use behaviors that are different from those of nonprofessionals. Professional leaders manifest greater psychological distance between themselves and their participants. They have an organized and, at times, distinctive view of the cause of illness. They generally believe, despite variations in theory, that the curative powers of therapeutic groups are derived from their social microcosm characteristics; examination of the interaction among members is the central therapeutic task. Self-help groups do not commonly emphasize such examinations. From this perspective, professionalization of self-help groups could have profound impact on how such self-help groups provide help to their members and the types of outcomes (e.g., participants' feelings of mastery, control, and empowerment). A definition of self-help groups based on nonprofessional leaders sharing the common problem of the group, although appealing conceptually, does not match current practice.

On the other hand, equating self-help groups with peer leadership poses an equally serious definitional problem. Intervention studies using peer therapists have been well-represented in the literature since the early 1960s (Cowen, Gardner, & Zax, 1967). However, the community mental health movement of the 1960s, with its emphasis on client-provided services, is not equivalent to self-help. The community mental health movement's treatment ideology, the source of control, and ownership of the treatment setting were professional.

Are we simply to conclude that self-help groups are a poorly defined and unbounded area, where arbitrary judgments rather than conceptual structure are the rule? We think not. Despite the difficulty in precisely defining them, self-help groups are distinct and differ in important ways from professionally delivered help. Self-help groups are complex entities. They create experiences such as the inculcation of hope, the development of understanding, and the experience of being loved that are thought to be therapeutic. They are also cognitive restructuring systems possessing elaborate ideologies about the cause and source of difficulty and about the way individuals need to think about their dilemmas in order to be helped (Antze, 1976). Additionally, they are social linkage systems where people form relationships, and in that sense, self-help groups provide social support (Lieberman & Videka-Sherman, 1986).

The available empirical evidence also suggests that self-help groups differ not only from traditional group therapy but among themselves. There is also increasing evidence (Levy, 1984; Lieberman & Borman, 1979; Lieberman & Videka-Sherman, 1986) that even within any one type of self-help organization, which may involve hundreds of groups, variation is the rule. The ability to specify a class of activities that covers hundreds of organizations with thousands of groups is obviously limited (Levy, 1976). Clearly, then, surveys that rely on a few simple questions about self-help group participation are prima facie inadequate. Accurate survey research to identify the prevalence of self-help group use and the client characteristics will require increases in the details about the groups and their processes; without such information the potential for error is very high.

REFERENCES

Antze, P. (1976). The role of ideologies in peer psychotherapy organizations: Some theoretical considerations and three case studies. *Journal of Applied Behavioral Science, 12,* 323-346.

Cowen, C. L., Gardner, F. A., & Zax, M. (Eds.). (1967). *Emergent approaches to mental health problems.* New York: Appleton-Century-Crofts.

Gottlieb, B., & Peters, L. (1991). A national portrait of mutual aid group participants in Canada. *American Journal of Community Psychology, 19,* 651-666.

Levy, L. H. (1976). Self-help groups, types and psychological processes. *Journal of Applied Behavioral Science, 12,* 310-322.

Levy, L. H. (1984). Issues in research and evaluation. In R. Gartner & F. Riessman (Eds.), *The self help revolution* (pp. 155-172). New York: Human Science Press.

Lieberman, M. A. (1989). Mutual aid groups: An underutilized resource among the elderly. In *Annual review of gerontology and geriatrics* (Vol. 9, pp. 285-320). New York: Springer.

Lieberman, M. A. (1992). Bereavement self-help groups: A review of conceptual and methodological issues. In M. S. Strobe & R. O. Hanson (Eds.), *Bereavement: A sourcebook of research and intervention.* Cambridge: Cambridge University Press.

Lieberman, M. A., & Borman, L. (1979). *Self-help groups for coping with crises: Origins, members, processes and impact.* San Francisco: Jossey-Bass.

Lieberman, M. A., & Videka-Sherman, L. (1986). The impact of self-help groups on the mental health of widows and widowers. *Journal of Orthopsychiatry, 56,* 435-449.

Mellinger, G., & Balter, M. (1983). *Collaborative project: GMIRSB report.* Washington, DC: National Institute of Mental Health.

Narrow, W. E., Regier, D. A., Rae, P. S., Manderscheid, R. W., & Locke, B. Z. (1993). Use of services by persons with mental and addictive disorders. *Archives of General Psychiatry, 50,* 95-107.

Robins, L. N., & Regier, D. A. (1991). *Psychiatric disorders in America.* New York: Free Press.

Room, R. (1993). Alcoholics Anonymous as a social movement. In B. S. McCrady & W. R. Miller (Eds.), *Research on Alcoholics Anonymous.* New Brunswick, NJ: Rutgers Center of Alcohol Studies.

Room, R., & Greenfield, T. (1991). *Alcoholics Anonymous, other 12 step movements and psychotherapy in the U.S. population, 1990* (Working Paper No. F281). Berkeley, CA: Alcohol Research Group, Medical Research Institute of San Francisco.

Tracy, G., & Gussow, Z. (1976). Self-help groups: A grass-root response to a need for services. *Journal of Applied Behavioral Sciences, 12,* 381-396.

4. African-American Participation in Self-Help Groups

LONNIE R. SNOWDEN
MORTON A. LIEBERMAN

Increasing scholarly attention is focused on the help-seeking patterns of African Americans suffering from health, mental health, and substance abuse problems (Cheung & Snowden, 1990). "Black underutilization" has become a concern: Critics of service systems have argued that owing to organizational, financial, and attitudinal barriers, African-American people have been deterred from seeking needed treatment. When services have been sought, there has been too great a reliance on psychiatric hospitalization (Snowden & Cheung, 1990). Critics also have raised the possibility of African-American preference for culturally based alternatives to formal mental health treatment.

The system of help for dealing with problems in living has increasingly come to include not only the health, mental health, substance abuse, and social service sectors, but also self-help groups. Despite the difficulty in precisely defining them, self-help groups are distinct and differ in important ways from professionally delivered help. Self-help groups are complex entities. They create experiences such as the inculcation of hope, the development of understanding, and the experience of being loved which are thought to be therapeutic. They are also cognitive restructuring systems possessing elaborate ideologies about the cause and source of difficulty and about the way individuals need to think about their dilemmas in order to be helped (Antze, 1976). Additionally, they are social linkage systems where people form relationships, and in that sense, self-help groups provide social support. The available empirical evidence also suggests that self-help groups differ not only from traditional group therapy, but also among themselves. Even within any one type of self-help organization, which may involve hundreds of groups, variation is the rule (Levy, 1984; Lieberman & Borman, 1979). The ability to generalize a class of activities to hundreds of organizations with thousands of groups is obviously limited (Levy, 1976).

However defined, self-help groups include a large number of Americans. Based on the best epidemiological sources of data available, one estimate placed the number of Americans who had been involved in self-help groups at some time during their lifetime at 7.5 million (Lieberman & Snowden, this volume).

Little has been written about minority involvement in self-help. In one of the few contributions to appear in the literature, Neighbors, Elliot, and Gant (1990) emphasized a long tradition of civil and fraternal organizations maintained by African Americans and devoted to the betterment of African-American communities. These economic, social, and political structures embody a broad concept of self-help; they are not a reflection of African-American participation in face-to-face mutual assistance directed toward physical and mental illness.

Maton (1984) focused on the inner city poor, many of whom are African American, and speculated on reasons for their lack of participation in the spectrum of self-help. He suggested lack of awareness of existing self-help groups and lack of access to a full array of types of groups, along with the possibility that both cultural norms and a realistic fear of strangers limit the willingness to engage in self-disclosure. Jason et al. (1988) described a project aimed at increasing minority participation in self-help in a predominantly African-American (86%) inner city neighborhood. After confirming that few groups were in fact available, the project initiated various educational and public relations activities designed to increase awareness of self-help and promote the development of groups. Six self-help groups had been established within 1 year of the initiation of the project.

Humphreys and Woods (this volume) examined the use of Twelve Step groups by African Americans and Whites 1 year after treatment for substance abuse. Although limited by consideration of only one type of self-help, the study represents one of only a handful of empirical contributions. The data indicated comparable rates of self-help group participation for the races but differences in the variables that predicted use. Whites who were relatively unlikely to attend suffered from substance abuse problems of greater severity, had come into treatment under legal pressure, were treated outside of a residential setting, and were treated for a briefer period. Blacks who were relatively unlikely to attend also spent less time in treatment but suffered from more severe psychological problems. Living in an area whose residents were of predominantly the same race as that of the client also was associated with self-help group involvement: Blacks living in Black areas and Whites in White areas were more likely to attend.

Despite widespread acceptance of the view that African Americans and other ethnic minority group members are underrepresented in mutual assistance/self-help (Hamilton, 1990), little evidence has been presented to document this claim. A significant limitation in attempting to assess levels of African-American participation is an absence of good epidemiological data on use of self-help groups not only for African Americans but among the population at large (Lieberman & Snowden, 1994). In one of the few studies to appear in the literature, Gottlieb and Peters (1991) used data from the Volunteer Activity Survey, in which a representative sample of Canadians was asked about their participation in "self help mutual aid groups" (Gottlieb & Peters, 1991). In their report, the authors did not describe participation by persons of African descent.

As one source of data, the present study relied on the Epidemiology Catchment Area (ECA) Program. The ECA is a large multisite study sponsored by the National Institute of Mental Health (NIMH) in an effort to determine the incidence and prevalence of specific psychiatric disorders and to better understand the use of medical and mental health services. Among surveys inquiring about self-help group use, only the ECA obtained a significant number of African Americans as subjects, owing both to the size of the ECA sample and oversampling of Blacks at one of the ECA sites (St. Louis).

Earlier reports have made use of the ECA data to estimate the extent of self-help group participation (Lieberman & Snowden, 1994; Narrow, Regier, Rae, Manderscheid, & Locke, 1993), but none has emphasized racial differences. The present study has made use of data from the ECA to consider the question of African-American participation in self-help. The intention was to document the extent of African-American participation, to compare it with the extent of White and Latino/Latina participation, and to evaluate socioeconomic status (SES) and any general tendency not to seek help from formal helping resources for problems in mental health as explanations for Black-White differences. The study presents for the first time, national, comparative data on African Americans in self-help.

As will be seen, the ECA data provide estimates of participation rates for self-help groups addressing only mental health and substance abuse problems. The multitude of other human concerns served by self-help groups are beyond the scope of the ECA data. There are no known sources of data on individuals that address African-American participation in such groups.

In a complementary effort, data were examined involving a shifting of orientation from the individual person/potential user of self-help groups to the group itself. One source of data gathered from this perspective is maintained by the California Self-Help Center, a statewide program providing consultation, technical assistance, information, and referral. The center houses a roster of active self-help groups that includes information on racial composition. By comparing African-American representation in groups for problems other than those involving mental health and substance abuse with African-American representation in the state, the extent of Black utilization was assessed.

METHOD

The Epidemiological Catchment Area Study

The ECA data were collected at five sites: New Haven (Connecticut), Baltimore, St. Louis, North Carolina, and Los Angeles. The investigators at all sites collected a common core of information on sociodemographic factors and service utilization. Information was also collected permitting diagnosis under criteria of the Diagnostic and Statistical Manual of Mental Disorders (DSM-III), the Diagnostic Interview Schedule.

The Baltimore ECA covered the eastern third of the city of Baltimore, where about 38% of the population was Black. The St. Louis ECA consisted of three noncontinuous mental health catchment areas: the central business district of St. Louis, the northern part of St. Louis County, and three neighboring suburban and agricultural counties. About 20% of the St. Louis ECA was Black. The North Carolina ECA sampled a five-county area in the north central piedmont of North Carolina. About 38% of the North Carolina sample was Black. The New Haven and Los Angeles sites contributed relatively few African Americans to the sample. In all, there were 4,300 African Americans surveyed across the five sites: 420 in New Haven, 148 in Los Angeles, 1,082 in Baltimore, 1,058 in St. Louis, and 1,392 in North Carolina. Across the five sites, the sample also included 12,152 Whites.

Respondents were asked a series of questions regarding helping resources they had used for problems with "emotions, nerves, drugs, alcohol or other mental health problems." Among the potential sources of help for such problems they might have used was the following probe: "Have you ever gone to a self-help group like Alcoholics Anonymous, etc.?" The question was asked covering both the course of a lifetime and the past 6 months. All respondents, Black and White, were asked the same question. Answers to this question furnish estimates of the proportions of African-American and White self-help group users but not of the frequencies of their use. The question of racial differences in the numbers of meetings attended by self-help group participants is an important one but lies beyond our present capacity to answer.

Included within the ECA was a survey of the institutionalized population at the five sites. African Americans were overrepresented in certain institutions, especially prisons and mental hospitals. Owing to the special opportunities and obstacles to using self-help groups facing institutional residents, the present analysis concerns itself solely with community respondents. Thus, estimates reported as findings are based on percentages of self-help group participation among community respondents.

The California Study

The California Self-Help Center (UCLA) has developed an active file of almost 4,000 self-help groups. This file represents the most complete listing of active self-help groups currently available anywhere in the United States. Various kinds of information are included: a description of each group, its goals, frequency of meeting, requirements for attendance, characteristics of participants, focus of the group, history of formation, fee requirements, types of group activities stressed, number of members, service features, characteristics of the leader (member chosen by the group, trained professional [volunteer or paid], trained nonprofessional), some process or procedures characteristics, external source of funding, and national affiliation. The file is brought up to date at regular intervals, most recently in 1991.

FINDINGS

ECA: African Americans and
Mental Health Substance Abuse Problems

Over the course of a lifetime about 3.6% of Whites and about 1.1% of Blacks reported having used self-help groups. During the past year about .7% of Whites and .1% of Blacks reported self-help group use. Differences according to socioeconomic standing are reported in Table 4.1. African-American lifetime use rose from 1.1% at the lowest socioeconomic level to 1.8% at the highest. White lifetime use rose from 2.3% to 4.5% at Level 3 and declined to 3.5% at Level 4. African-American participation was substantially lower than that of Whites at every social class quartile. By contrast, levels of self-help group use were greater than those of African Americans and comparable to those of Whites.

A more exact estimation of the contribution of ethnicity and social class was accomplished through the use of logistic regression equations, one for lifetime use of self-help groups, the other for lifetime use of professional mental health services. The order of entry was: (a) socioeconomic standing, (b) race, and (c) race by social class interaction. Statistical improvement in the predictive model for professional mental health services was found for SES, chi-square improvement = 137.1; $p < .01$, as well as race, chi-square improvement = 95.6; $p < .01$. The interaction, Ethnicity X SES, yielded a chi square of 1.6, NS. The findings for lifetime use of self-help groups were: SES, chi-square improvement = 11.3, $p < .01$; race, chi-square improvement = 11.3, $p < .01$; interaction, chi-square improvement = .2, NS. Thus ethnicity and social class were independent factors linked to use of both professional mental health and self-help group services; the association between ethnicity and use was comparable throughout the socioeconomic hierarchy.

Ratios comparing professional services to self-help group use were computed. These ratios express self-help group use as a proportion of professional service use and control for general racial difference in seeking help. Self-help group use was 18% of professional service use among Caucasians and 21% among Latinos/Latinas, but only 3% among African Americans. Black use of self-help groups was disproportionately low, even taking account of their low use of professional services.

TABLE 4.1 Epidemiological Catchment Area Survey: Percent Reporting
Having Ever Used a Self-Help Group

SES/Diagnosis	African American (N = 4,287)		Hispanic (N = 1,433)		White (N = 12,152)	
	Used Self-Help Group	Total	Used Self-Help Group	Total	Used Self-Help Group	Total
Level 1 (Low)	1.1	36.5	2.3	35.0	2.3	18.9
Level 2	1.0	36.3	3.7	38.2	3.4	32.1
Level 3	1.2	20.1	3.4	21.1	4.5	31.8
Level 4	1.8	7.1	3.9	5.7	3.5	17.2
Any DSM III Diagnosis	2.3	38.4	8.7	33.2	8.3	29.6

Considering persons with a lifetime DSM-III diagnosis, the difference between African Americans and Whites in lifetime self-help use was also pronounced (see Table 4.1). Among the 29.6% of Whites reporting any diagnosis, about 8.3% had used a self-help group. Only about 2.3% of the 38.4% of African Americans with a lifetime DSM-III diagnosis reported self-help group use.

Among persons who have mental health needs—the heaviest self-help group users (Lieberman & Snowden, 1994)—the racial discrepancy was widest. Were African Americans turning instead to religious figures or natural healers? Data on lifetime use of religious figures and natural healers for problems in mental health are presented in Table 4.2. Again, logistic regression permitted a controlled test of racial differences. Statistical improvement in the predictive model for use of a religious figure was significant for SES, chi-square improvement = 32.9, $p < .01$; race, chi-square improvement = 4.7, $p < .01$; but not for the SES X race interaction, chi-square improvement = .03, $p > .86$). The racial difference found was such that Whites, not African Americans, were more likely to use a religious figure. In predicting use of a natural healer, no effect proved statistically significant: SES, chi-square improvement = .3, $p > .59$; race, chi-square improvement = .00, $p > .97$; interaction, chi-square improvement = 2.3, $p > .12$).

There was no evidence of greater use of religious figures or nontraditional healers to offset the relative lack of use by African Americans of self-help groups.

TABLE 4.2 Percentage of Users of Selected Formal and Informal Sources of Help

Socioeconomic Status	Religious Figure			Natural Healer		
	Black	Hispanic	White	Black	Hispanic	White
Level 1	4.2	3.4	4.4	0.9	1.0	0.4
Level 2	4.5	6.4	5.7	0.3	1.7	0.6
Level 3	5.9	6.6	7.1	0.7	2.1	0.8
Level 4	5.7	7.4	7.1	0.4	0	0.9

California Self-Help Center: African Americans and Transitions, Lifestyles, Health, and Other Problems

Self-help groups for common concerns other than mental health or substance abuse were described in the following categories (percentage of total number of groups is presented in parentheses): physical illness (51.5%), violence (4.8%), sexual abuse (2.9%), crime (.5%), parenting (8.4%), bereavement (10.0%), transitions (8.2%), and lifestyle (3.7%). These groups reported having 1,400 African-American members. Based on an estimated total membership of 373,000 (Lieberman & Snowden, 1994), the African-American membership was .4%. In 1990, the African-American population of California was 7.4% (Statistical Abstract of the United States, 1991).

DISCUSSION

The ECA data provide strong evidence of African-American underrepresentation in self-help groups. Overall, African Americans were about one third as likely as Whites to indicate involvement in a self-help group over the course of their lifetime, and only about one seventh as likely to report involvement in the past year. Among persons with a diagnosis of mental illness and who were relatively heavy users of self-help groups, the difference in levels of use shrank somewhat but, for lifetime use, remained pronounced. Only among persons reporting mental illness during the past year was the difference between races less than statistically significant.

The results from the ECA cannot be attributed to socioeconomic standing. In multivariate analysis, SES emerged as a significant correlate of self-help group use, as did race controlling for SES.

Nor do the results reflect a more general tendency often attributed to African Americans to avoid professional sources of help for problems in mental health. Taking self-help group use as a proportion of use of specialty mental health services, African Americans were found to make relatively little use of self-help groups, far less again than Whites. Even by the standard of general African-American use of mental health services, use of self-help groups remains especially slight.

African Americans were also underrepresented also when findings were considered for concerns other than those related to mental health and substance abuse. African Americans made up less than 1% of the membership of groups devoted to transition, lifestyle, health, and other problems. Black underrepresentation cannot be attributed to lesser need; African Americans tend to have more illness and greater cause for death-related bereavement than Whites and to experience more parenting-related and transition-related sources of stress (cf. Jaynes & Williams, 1989). Race-related socioeconomic differences may play a role but scarcely seem sufficient to explain the extremely low rate of Black membership.

In interpreting the present findings, several methodological limitations must be borne in mind. The ECA study ascertained self-help group use on the basis of a single question. The question asked about problems with drugs and alcohol, as well as in mental health. The self-help probe used AA as its only example. This approach may have led to an underreporting of use of groups other than Twelve Step groups. On the other hand, racial disparities may be least for use of Twelve Step groups (Humphreys & Woods, 1994); the ECA data may understate racial disparities in self-help group involvement.

The data from the California Self-Help Center include many but not all self-help groups. It is possible that groups not listed have as members more African Americans than groups that were listed. The existence of unaffiliated self-help groups in African-American communities cannot be ruled out. To compensate for underrepresentation in affiliated groups, nevertheless, any such system of unrecognized groups must be vast.

In the end, shortcomings of the present data can only be overcome by conducting large-scale surveys in which African Americans are oversampled. Questions must be written listing specific types of problems (e.g., depression, alcohol abuse, cancer, etc.) and asking about possible self-help group use for help with each. Respondents should be asked to name the group, indicate when and how frequently they attended, where the group met, how they learned about it, and what its membership was. Only from a comprehensive approach will we learn precisely the scope and nature of racial differences.

Granting their validity, there are several possible explanations to account for the present findings. Self-help groups tend to define the problems they are designed to address in terms that may be alien to African Americans suffering from these problems. For national and ethnic groups, African Americans have evolved cultural traditions that include in certain instances indigenous ways to define problems in living. Anthropologists, for example, have documented folk disorders that are widely recognized in certain African-American communities (e.g., Camino, 1989). Beliefs in such syndromes may have originated in the rural South, to which the great majority of African Americans can trace their origins. These traditions may have survived Black migration to the North, owing to the facts that the bulk of migration is relatively recent, visits to relatives in the rural South appear to be common, and residential patterns in the North tend to be segregated by race.

Also related to cultural differences is the possibility of a differential preference for the style of helping practiced in self-help groups. Disclosure of intimate details about one's life in the company of persons who are neither family members nor close friends may hold less appeal for African Americans than Whites. Cultural sanction for self-help group participation need not be equal.

Yet another possible explanation for the relatively low rate of participation by African Americans in self-help groups is the existence of cultural analogues or culturally preferred alternatives. The Black church in particular has been suggested as a substitute. Religious belief and prayer—demonstrated to be a preferred coping style for African Americans—may serve to meet existential needs and provide personal comfort available to others through self-help group participation. The network of church-affiliated clubs and groups in which many church members participate may afford opportunities for discussion of personal problems that concern them.

It is important to note that cultural incongruity and involvement in the Black church cannot be taken for granted as explanations for self-help group underrepresentation, especially in attempting to cope with problems in mental health. Broman (1987) reported that African Americans were less likely than Whites to seek help from a minister in response to a mental health problem. Supplemental analysis of the ECA data conducted for the present study produced a comparable finding—more help-seeking from a "religious figure" by Whites than Blacks. Although these data do not address the possibility of participation in church-related organizations—the most likely counterpart to self-help groups in providing face-to-face mutual assistance—they suggest a need for caution.

African-American underrepresentation in self-help groups also may result from lack of knowledge and lack of access. The availability of self-help groups and a perception of them as useful may have pervaded African-American communities less than society at large. This possibility suggests that organizations facilitating self-help group development and use ought to place greater emphasis on advertising in African-American communities.

Whether or not self-help groups are known in African American communities, they may not be readily at hand. That self-help groups should be located in communities hospitable to potential users was implied in the work of Humphreys and Woods (1994) mentioned earlier. In that study, the investigators found that African Americans living in African-American communities were more likely than African Americans living among Whites to attend Twelve Step groups following substance abuse treatments. Insofar as these groups were located in the Black community, they may have been more inviting to African Americans, perhaps partly through location and perhaps partly through a greater Black membership in the groups.

Greater attention should be given to creating chapters of established self-help groups in Black communities and devising formats that appeal to African Americans. Such an approach may include modification of belief systems and practices to incorporate the cultural outlook of African Americans. Such efforts should not preclude outreach into African-American communities by established groups.

The feasibility of such an effort and preliminary assessment of its potential for success can be seen in the success of Jason et al. (1988) in introducing self-help groups into inner city communities. There is reason to believe that public education and promotion of self-help groups, when conducted in a genuine spirit of collaboration with community leaders and institutions, can increase the availability of self-help groups to African Americans as well as African-American involvement. It appears that at least for some African Americans who are not now involved in self-help groups, this format for face-to-face mutual assistance would prove acceptable and possibility beneficial. More attention should be given to developing and evaluating strategies for increasing their participation.

REFERENCES

Antze, P. (1976). The role of ideologies in peer psychotherapy organizations: Some theoretical considerations and three case studies. *Journal of Applied Behavioral Science, 12,* 323-346.

Broman, L. (1987). Race differences in professional help seeking. *American Journal of Community Psychology, 15,* 473-489.

Camino, L. A. (1989). Nerves, worriation, and black women: A community study in the American South. In D. David & S. Low (Eds.), *Gender, health and illness* (pp. 203-222). New York: Hemisphere Publishing.

Cheung, F. K., & Snowden, L. R. (1990). Community mental health and ethnic minority populations. *Community Mental Health Journal, 26,* 277-291.

Gottlieb, B., & Peters, L. (1991). A national portrait of mutual aid group participants in Canada. *American Journal of Community Psychology, 19,* 651-666.

Hamilton, A. (1990). Self help and mutual aid in ethnic minority communities. In A. Katz & E. Bender (Eds.), *Helping one another: Self-help groups in a changing world.* Oakland, CA: Third Party Publishing.

Humphreys, K., & Woods, M. D. (1994). Researching mutual-help group participation in a segregated society. In T. J. Powell (Ed.), *Understanding the self-help organization: Frameworks and findings.* Thousand Oaks, CA: Sage.

Jason, L. A., Tabon, D., Tait, E., Iacono, G., Goodman, D., Watkins, P., & Huggins, G. (1988). The emergence of the inner city self help center. *Journal of Community Psychology, 16,* 287-295.

Jaynes, G. D., & Williams, R. M. (1989). *A common destiny: Blacks and American society.* Washington, DC: National Research Council National Academy Press.

Levy, L. H. (1976). Self-help groups, types and psychological processes. *Journal of Applied Behavioral Science, 12,* 310-322.

Levy, L. H. (1984). Issues in research and evaluation. In R. Gartner & F. Riessman (Eds.), *The self help revolution* (pp. 155-172). New York: Human Science Press.

Lieberman, M. A., & Borman, L. (1979). *Self-help groups for coping with crises: Origins, members, processes and impact.* San Francisco: Jossey-Bass.

Lieberman, M. A., & Snowden, L. R. (1994). Problems in assessing prevalence and membership characterisitcs of self-help group participants. In T. J. Powell (Ed.), *Understanding the self-help organization: Frameworks and findings.* Thousand Oaks, CA: Sage.

Maton, K. (1984). Fewer self help groups in cities: Why? *Network, 4,* 5.

Narrow, W. E., Regier, D. A., Rae, P. S., Manderscheid, R. W., & Locke, B. Z. (1993). Use of services by persons with mental and addictive disorders. *Archives of General Psychiatry, 50,* 95-107.

Neighbors, H. W., Elliott, K. A., & Gant, L. M. (1990). Self help and Black Americans: A strategy for empowerment. In T. J. Powell (Ed.), *Working with self help* (pp. 189-217). Silver Spring, MD: NASW Press.

Robins, L. N., & Regier, D. A. (1991). *Psychiatric disorders in America.* New York: Free Press.

Statistical Abstract of the United States. 1991. *The national data book.* Washington, DC: U.S. Department of Commerce, Bureau of the Census.

Snowden, L. R., & Cheung, F. K. (1990). Use of inpatient services by members of ethnic minority groups. *American Psychologist, 45,* 347-355.

5. Researching Mutual-Help Group Participation in a Segregated Society

KEITH HUMPHREYS
MICHAEL D. WOODS

The thesis of this chapter is that research on African-American mutual-help group participation must recognize that Black and White Americans are still largely segregated both culturally and geographically. Mutual-help[1] group participation has different meanings, predictors, and outcomes for African Americans and Whites. To develop this argument, analyses of data from an ongoing longitudinal study of the substance abuse treatment system and Twelve Step mutual-help groups that the first author is conducting with several collaborators are presented (Humphreys, Mavis, & Stöffelmayr, 1991a, 1991b, in press). In keeping with the theme of this volume, methodological issues that are of relevance when studying minority mutual-help group participation and mutual-help participation generally are given careful attention.

AUTHORS' NOTE: We thank Niall Bolger, Caroline Kaufman, Mellen Kennedy, Eric Mankowski, Ken Maton, Brian Mavis, Kristy Nielsen, Thomas Powell, and Julian Rappaport for their comments on earlier versions of this chapter. Address corresponsence to Keith Humphreys, Center for Health Care Evaluation, VA Medical Center, (152-MPD), 795 Willow Road, Menlo Park, CA 94025.

62

GUIDING FRAMEWORK

The main point guiding this analysis is that mutual-help groups are truly democratic institutions. That is, they are only what the community members who attend make them. Unlike the institution of psychotherapy, which has the homogenizing influence of a professional class, mutual-help groups are shaped enormously by the local ecology. National mutual-help organizations usually give a general structure for local chapters to follow, but these are not so restrictive as to prevent great variation in social environment, membership, and helping techniques from local chapter to local chapter (or within a chapter, from meeting to meeting depending on who shows up on a particular day). As communities vary demographically, economically, and culturally, so too will whatever mutual-help groups exist in them. Because mutual-help organizations are shaped so strongly by local community members, it makes no more sense to think of mutual-help organizations as monolithic entities than it does to believe that all Baptist churches, elementary schools, or PTAs are the same across communities.

In the context of this chapter, the implication of this point is that in a society where races are geographically and culturally segregated, mutual help will have an extremely different character across different racial groups. Thus findings from studies of mutual-help groups in White communities may not always generalize to mutual-help groups in racial and ethnic minority communities. Within Alcoholics Anonymous (AA), for example, research has shown that chapters of the organization differ across Native American (Jilek-Aall, 1981), Black (Caldwell, 1983), and Irish Catholic (Vaillant, 1983) communities. Given the high degree of control that members have over how a particular meeting is conducted, one cannot imagine how it could be otherwise; it would be illogical to expect different people and different subcultures to create identical social groupings. Thus, in a study of Black and White mutual help such as this, it is important to consider the differences between the lives and communities of Black and White Americans.

Although racial integration in America increased significantly in the 1960s and 1970s, Black Americans and White Americans are still largely segregated in a number of important ways. Analysis of census data undertaken by Farley (1985) shows that in the 25 cities with the largest populations of Black Americans, residential neighborhoods are still highly segregated. Typically, suburban areas are populated predominantly by Whites, and urban areas are populated predominantly by Blacks. Further, despite the *Brown v.*

Board of Education ruling, metropolitan school districts are still largely racially segregated (Farley, 1985). This geographical and educational separation reinforces economic and cultural differences between Black and White Americans. In many ways, Blacks and Whites still live in largely separate worlds within American society.

In the research program on the substance abuse treatment network in the State of Michigan that the first author and his collaborators are conducting, one can see support for Farley's observations and its effect on mutual-help organizations. The segregation of Black and White Americans is replicated in and reinforced by the professional substance abuse treatment system. Approximately three fourths of the Black persons who participate in this substance abuse research program live in Detroit. In this context, treatment agencies tend to be residential and employ large proportions of recovering staff and paraprofessionals. In central and western Michigan, predominantly populated by Whites, most treatment agencies are outpatient clinics that are highly professionalized and employ few or no recovering staff (Humphreys, Mavis, & Stöffelmayr, 1991b).

The implications of this bifurcation of professional services for Twelve Step programs are great. Urban residential agencies are frequently based on the Twelve Step philosophy and get high proportions of their clientele into mutual-help groups after treatment (Humphreys, Mavis, & Stöffelmayr, 1991b; Mavis & Stöffelmayr, 1989). Although outpatient agencies in small cities and towns are not free of Twelve Step influence (perhaps no American substance abuse agency is), they tend to be less enthusiastic about this approach (Mavis & Stöffelmayr, 1989), and few of their clients become involved in mutual-help groups after treatment (Humphreys, Mavis, & Stöffelmayr, 1991b). Thus professional attitudes and practices have an influence on attendance patterns and success levels of local Twelve Step groups, and these professional attitudes are predicted by the area in which the agency is located and the race and social class of its clientele.

These findings suggest that the ecology of race, professional attitudes and services, and geography all interact in a complex fashion to influence mutual-help participation. Yet very little is known about how these forces operate because most mutual-help research focuses heavily on the individual level of analysis (see Maton's chapter in this volume). The present study examines how these factors along with the individual differences of clients affect Black and White participation in Twelve Step groups after substance abuse treatment.

METHOD

Participants

The client sample consisted of 516 substance abusers who were treated at one of 22 agencies in the State of Michigan. These 516 persons were a subset of an initial sample of 726 consecutive admissions, the remainder of whom were not located at 1-year follow-up. This represents a 1-year follow-up rate of 71.1%. Those clients who were lost at follow-up were not significantly different, $p > .05$, from those who were found on age, education, race, gender, intake drug problem level, intake alcohol problem level, or intake psychological problem level. A description of the sample is presented in Table 5.1.

Professional staff members also contributed data to the study. The AA Beliefs Scale (see instruments section) was distributed to all 417 staff members at the 22 treatment programs. The completion rate was 72% ($n = 301$), and the refusal rate was 5% ($n = 22$), for a total response rate of 77%. The setting of the agency (residential or outpatient) was determined by looking at the agency's site license.

Instruments

The Addiction Severity Index (ASI; McLellan, Luborsky, Woody, & O'Brien, 1980) was administered by a trained assessor to all client participants at treatment intake. The ASI has excellent psychometric properties and provides problem severity scores (range 0-9) for seven different areas: medical, legal, family/social, psychological, drug, alcohol, and employment/support problems. One year after treatment intake, the assessor recontacted, where possible, the client and interviewed him or her again. At these interviews, the client also reported on any mutual-help group meetings that he or she had attended.

The AA Beliefs Scale (Mavis & Stöffelmayr, 1989) was distributed to all staff members at the agencies. This instrument is a 16-item checklist of Twelve Step beliefs (Cronbach's alpha = .88) that assesses how supportive each staff member is of the AA/NA approach (see appendix). Scores on the Beliefs Scale were averaged across staff members to produce one score for each agency.

Data Analysis

This study is intended to shed light on the factors that shape mutual-help involvement among African-American and White American substance abusers.

TABLE 5.1 Description of 516 Substance Abusers

Race	Gender	
267 White	367 men	
233 Black	149 women	
6 Native American		
10 Hispanic		

Education	Marital Status	
153 less than high school	73 married	
227 high school/GED	7 widowed	
115 some college	144 separated/divorced	
21 college graduate	292 single	

NOTE: Age: mean = 31.3 years, SD = 8.0 years

Consistent with the view that mutual-help groups are always influenced strongly by the local context, this analysis incorporates individual client clinical variables, variables relating to professional services and attitudes, and variables that tap ecological factors that influence both professionals and clients. The data analytic procedure employed is structural equation modeling with LISREL 7 (Jöreskog & Sörbom, 1988). Because structural equation models can be fit with almost any large data set given enough attempts, one should have theoretical or empirical rationales for why each variable was entered into the equation. Thus each variable is presented with both a description and a rationale for its use.

Client Clinical Variables

A frequent suggestion in the literature is that measures of clinical problem severity predict involvement in substance abuse mutual-help groups. In general, clients with more severe problems are thought to be more likely to attend a Twelve Step group (see Emrick, Tonigan, Montgomery, & Little, 1993; Humphreys, Mavis, & Stöffelmayr, 1991a). Whether such clinical variables have significant independent influence on mutual-help group attendance or are simply markers of more important factors (e.g., where the client obtained treatment) is open to debate. Therefore the model is fit with and without the clinical variables. From this point on, the model that includes individual clinical variables is termed *the full model* or *the complete model,* and the model that considers them in the correlation matrix but not in the estimation of path coefficients is called the *reduced* or *competing model.* The clinical problem measures used in this study are described below.

Intake-level substance abuse problem severity was measured using the ASI. As the ASI provides separate scores for alcohol and other drug use severity, the severity of the client's primary problem was used as a single substance-abuse severity score for each client. This variable was selected for several reasons. First, analysis of the 6-month follow-up data indicated that mutual-help group attendees had higher substance-abuse severity scores than did nonattendees (Humphreys, Mavis, & Stöffelmayr, 1991a). Second, persons with more severe problems are probably more likely to seek out additional aid, including mutual-help groups, after professional treatment than are those with less severe problems. Third, Twelve Step programs have a philosophy of recovery that emphasizes loss of control over substance abuse. Thus persons with more severe problems may more easily integrate into a mutual-help group because they find that Twelve Step programs provide a perspective on substance abuse that is consistent with their experience.

Intake-level psychological problem severity and family/social problem severity were also measured by the ASI. These variables were selected for reasons similar to those for substance abuse severity.

Attendance Variables

Mutual-help group attendance was measured dichotomously. Those who reported attending meetings in the month they were followed up were classified as mutual-help attendees. Those who had not were coded as not attending. Some would criticize reliance on self-report of mutual-help group attendance (e.g., Yeaton, in press), perhaps particularly because substance abusers have a reputation of not being honest. Contrary to this stereotype, extensive research shows that substance abusers give valid self-reports if they are drug free, assured of confidentiality, not cognitively impaired, and evaluated within a clinical or research setting (Polich, 1982; Sobell & Sobell, 1986). All of these conditions were met in the interviews, and further, the same assessor usually did all interviews with the same participant, building a sense of trust over time. Finally, the assessment team was racially diverse and most interviews were done by an interviewer of the same race as the client, which also promotes credibility and rapport.

Treatment Variables

A mean score on the AA Beliefs Scale was computed for each agency. This variable was selected because exposure to the Twelve Step philosophy when one is in a state of crisis (having just entered treatment) might prime an individual for future mutual-help group participation. In contrast, at an agency where the staff do not agree with Twelve Step principles, clients might come to understand their difficulties in ways that clash with Twelve Step groups (see Humphreys, 1993).

Treatment setting was determined by looking at the treatment agency's site license. This is a binary variable (coded 0 for outpatient agencies and 1 for residential agencies). This variable was selected because previous work shows that residential agencies have a very different organizational culture than do outpatient agencies, being much more congenial to Twelve Step groups and ideas (Mavis & Stöffelmayr, 1989). This variable was also selected because residential agencies are a more intense intervention. Exposure to the Twelve Step approach day and night in a residential agency may have a powerful transformative effect on substance abusers who are in a state of crisis, making them more likely to "convert" to the Twelve Step worldview.

Length of treatment was measured in months. This variable was selected because how long a client is exposed to an agency's view of substance abuse problems, whether pro-Twelve Step or not, may affect how well the Twelve Step philosophy is internalized.

Ecological Variables

The substance abuse treatment system has a strong relationship to another system that affects clients—the legal system. Thus legal problem severity was measured at intake. A dichotomous variable was also coded to reflect whether or not the client was pressured or forced to enter treatment by a judge or lawyer. Previous work suggests that clients who are in the treatment system due to legal pressure rarely are motivated to continue mutual-help activities after treatment is over (Humphreys, 1991).

For the final variable, a measure of the "racial fit" of the client to the community was developed. This variable was chosen because although many believe that African Americans do not participate in mutual-help groups, research conducted by the first author and his colleagues shows that they do (Humphreys, Mavis, & Stöffelmayr, 1991a, in press). One reason for this discrepancy could be that these studies encompassed more Black neighborhoods than is typical of mutual-help research. This suggests that the racial composition of the neighborhood mediates the mutual-help participation of different racial groups. People might be more likely to go to a mutual-help group if they live in an area where their own race predominates because mutual-help groups that also are composed primarily or entirely of people of their own race are readily available. Thus this variable was coded as *racial fit* if an African American was treated at an agency in Detroit or a White person was treated in an agency in central or western Michigan. The variable was coded as *no racial fit* if a White person received treatment in Detroit or a Black person received treatment in central or western Michigan. This is an imperfect measure but was the best available given the data. More sophisticated measures of racial fit are discussed in the concluding section.

Full Model

The full model is presented in Figure 5.1. All client clinical severity and ecological measures (substance abuse problems, psychological problems, family/social problems, legal problems, pressure from criminal justice system for treatment, and racial fit) are purely exogenous variables that predict mutual-help group attendance. One of the treatment measures (Twelve Step beliefs) is also purely exogenous. Treatment mode (residential or outpatient setting) influences mutual-help group attendance in a direct fashion and indirectly with length of treatment serving as a mediator variable.

Competing Model

Figure 5.2 shows the competing model. Other than having the paths between the client clinical problem variables and mutual-help attendance fixed at zero, it is identical to the full model.

RESULTS

Fitting the Models With and Without Interactions

The presence of binary variables (e.g., racial fit, mutual-help group attendance) precludes the use of estimation methods that assume multivariate normality among the observed variables. Hence unweighted least squares (ULS) estimation was used.[2] As the variables are on different scales, polychoric correlations were analyzed instead of covariances.

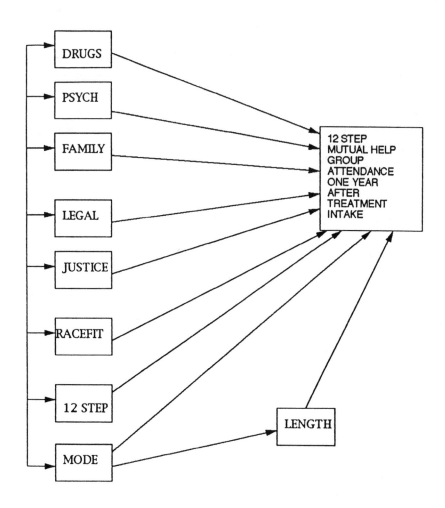

Figure 5.1. Full Model of Mutual-Help Attendance Predictors 1 Year After Treatment

NOTE: DRUGS = substance abuse problems at intake; PSYCH = psychological problems at intake; FAMILY = family/social problems at intake; LEGAL = legal problems at intake; JUSTICE = pressure from justice system for treatment; RACEFIT = local representativeness of client's race; 12 STEP = Twelve Step beliefs of agency staff; MODE = residential or outpatient setting; LENGTH = length of treatment.

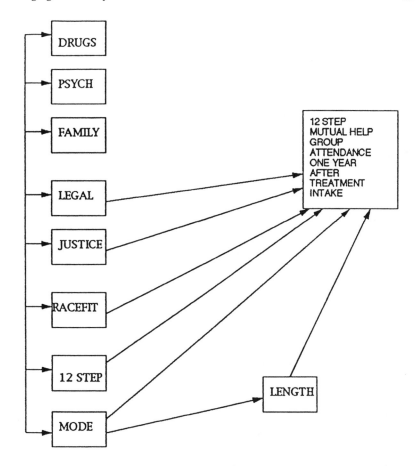

Figure 5.2. Reduced Model of Mutual-Help Attendance Predictors 1 Year After Treatment

NOTE: DRUGS = substance abuse problems at intake; PSYCH = psychological problems at intake; FAMILY = family/social problems at intake; LEGAL = legal problems at intake; JUSTICE = pressure from justice system for treatment; RACEFIT = local representativeness of client's race; 12 STEP = Twelve Step beliefs of agency staff; MODE = residential or outpatient setting; LENGTH = length of treatment.

Polychoric correlations among the variables in the White and Black subsamples are presented in Table 5.2. The descriptive breakdown for each of the variables in the model for the White and Black subsamples is presented in Table 5.3. The data on the 16 non-Black minority clients were not used in the LISREL model.

TABLE 5.2 Polychoric Correlations of Variables for Blacks and Whites

	Length	Self-Help	Drugs	Family	Psych	Justice	Legal	Mode	Twelve Step	Race fit
Length	—	.37	.03	.06	.06	.07	−.07	.00	−.07	.03
Self-help	.25	—	.03	−.07	−.08	−.27	−.26	.44	.03	.50
Drugs	−.05	.29	—	.27	.37	−.15	.13	.16	.14	.09
Family	−.03	.13	.28	—	.55	−.05	.20	−.02	.09	−.10
Psych	.00	.29	.36	.54	—	−.12	.09	.09	.05	.11
Justice	.06	−.24	−.33	−.32	−.42	—	.61	−.49	−.12	−.64
Legal	.02	−.08	.09	.04	−.05	.39	—	−.29	.05	−.51
Mode	−.20	.28	.48	.04	.10	.11	.24	—	.45	.80
Twelve Step	−.03	.02	−.10	.04	−.13	.12	−.04	.42	—	.21
Racefit	.05	−.12	−.19	−.12	−.15	.38	.26	−.56	−.15	—

NOTE: Whites are on lower left and Blacks on the upper right. Length = length of treatment; Self-help = attendance at self-help group (0 = no, 1 = yes); Drugs = substance abuse severity at intake; Family = family/social problems at intake; Psych = psychological problems at intake; Justice = entered treatment on pressure from lawyer or judge (0 = no, 1 = yes); Legal = legal problems at intake; Twelve Step = level of agreement with Twelve Step principles among agency staff; Mode = type of agency (0 = outpatient, 1 = residential); Racefit = similarity of client race to community race (0 = different, 1 = same).

The full and reduced models were each fit using a multisample approach, with race as the grouping variable. Specifically, a two-step procedure was implemented for each model. First, the models were fit with path coefficients constrained to be equal across the Black and White samples. Next, path coefficients were estimated separately for each race. This second step represents an interaction with race as the moderator. If there was no interaction effect, one would expect the constrained and unconstrained models to fit equally well.

Comparison of the fit of the full and reduced models (each with and without race interactions) is shown in Table 5.4. Whether we consider the full or reduced model, all indexes of fit suggest that the interaction model is superior (GFIs and R^2s are higher and RMSRs are lower).

Because correlations were analyzed and all the observed variables are not multivariate normal, the chi-square is interpreted as a goodness-of-fit measure rather than as a test statistic. (The p values for the tests therefore have no substantive meaning and are not reported.) The ratio of the chi-square to its degrees of freedom for the full interaction model, 46.97/14 = 3.36, is superior to that for the full no-interaction model, 135.37/24 = 5.64, as larger ratios indicate poorer fit. Similarly, the competing model with an interaction fits better than the competing model without an interaction, 3.98 versus 5.03.

TABLE 5.3 Comparison of White (*n* = 267) and Black (*n* = 233) Substance
              Abusers on Model Variables

Variable	Whites		Blacks	
	M	*SD*	*M*	*SD*
Length of treatment (months)	3.2	3.3	2.8	3.1
Intake substance abuse severity	4.6	1.6	5.0	1.4
Intake family problem severity	2.8	1.9	2.9	1.7
Intake psychological problem severity	2.9	2.1	3.1	2.0
Intake legal problem severity	2.1	1.7	1.6	1.7
AA beliefs of staff	11.3	1.7	11.3	0.9
	Percentage		*Percentage*	
Attending mutual help after treatment	31.8		33.9	
Criminal justice referral	48.7		24.2	
Residential treatment	31.8		63.5	
Living outside Detroit	92.5		24.9	

Therefore, one can argue persuasively that there is a substantial interaction effect for race in this sample. Substantively, this suggests that different dynamics underlie attendance patterns of White and Black substance abusers, even though their rate of attendance is comparable (see Table 5.3).

As for the comparison of the competing model with the full model (both with race interactions) the results are not as clear-cut. Because the chi-square statistics are not asymptotically correct, comparing competing models is something of a judgment call. The GFIs and R^2s for the reduced model are slightly less than those for the full model, and the RMSRs and ratio of the chi-square to its degrees of freedom for the reduced model are slightly greater than those for the full model. These data, in combination with a desire to err on the side of too much information rather than too little, led us to use the full model as the basis of our analysis. However, even in doing so we note that although clinical variables seem to contribute slightly to the prediction of mutual-help attendance, their importance does not seem to be as great as some commentators believe (at least not in this study).

White Mutual-Help Group Attendance

Within the White sample (*n* = 267), 85 persons (31.8%) were involved in mutual-help groups 1 year after treatment and 182 were not. The results of the estimation for the White sample are shown in Figure 5.3.

TABLE 5.4 Comparison of Fit of Full and Reduced Model With and Without a Race Interaction

	Full Model, Interaction	Full Model, No Interaction	Reduced Model, Interaction	Reduced Model, No Interaction
GFI White	.998	.991	.996	.990
GFI Black	.997	.990	.996	.991
RMSR White	.017	.036	.024	.038
RMSR Black	.020	.040	.025	.038
χ^2	46.97	135.37	79.63	135.85
df	14	24	20	27
χ^2/df	3.36	5.64	3.98	5.03
R^2 White	.36	.23	.30	.23
R^2 Black	.43	.35	.41	.36

NOTE: df = degrees of freedom; χ^2/df = ratio of chi-square to its degrees of freedom; GFI = goodness-of-fit index for indicated racial group; RMSR = root mean square residual for indicated racial group; and R^2 = proportion of variance in mutual-help attendance explained in indicated racial group.

Parameter estimates presented in Figure 5.3 are accompanied by asterisks to indicate significance at the .05 level, |T| > 2. Because the standard errors of these estimates are not asymptotically correct, the results of the significance tests should be interpreted with caution.

Of the individual clinical-level variables, only substance abuse severity at intake significantly predicted mutual-help group attendance. Contrary to expectation, more severe substance abuse problems predicted less mutual-help group involvement. One speculation that might help account for this surprising result is that persons with very high substance-abuse problems are more likely to relapse after treatment and therefore not get or stay involved with abstinence-focused Twelve Step groups.

All three of the ecological variables had significant influences on mutual-help group attendance. More severe legal problems and entry into treatment under legal pressure both were related negatively to posttreatment Twelve Step group involvement. Presumably, such persons had low internal motivation to enter treatment and thus vacated the substance abuse network at the earliest legal opportunity (i.e., when professional care ended).

Interestingly, racial fit was a strong, positive predictor of mutual-help group involvement after treatment. Whites in White areas are more inclined to attend a group than are Whites in Black areas. This finding is consonant with the argument that the dynamics of mutual help always reflect the larger

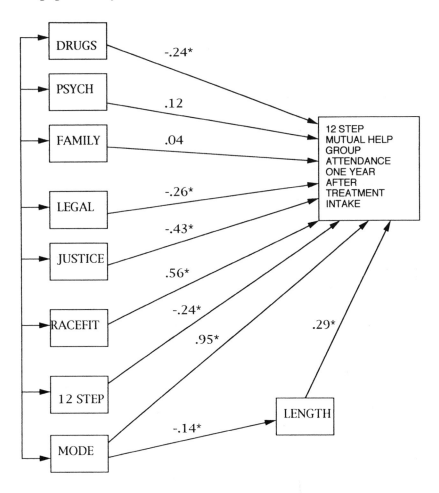

Figure 5.3. Mutual-Help Attendance Predictors Among 267 White Substance Abusers

NOTE: Path coefficients are printed just above their path. Higher scores on mode indicate residential treatment.
*p < .05; |T| > 2.

context. Just as some White people prefer to have White neighbors, so too might a White person choose not to attend meetings of a mutual-help group where most of the people are Black. Although Twelve Step groups try to minimize expressions of bigotry or discomfort with other races within the organization (Denzin, 1987), participants will inevitably reflect racial attitudes in the community because community members are what constitute any mutual-help group.

The treatment measures also had significant predictive effects on mutual-help group involvement. The direction of the effect indicates that Whites treated at residential agencies are much more likely to be involved in mutual-help groups after treatment than are those treated in outpatient settings. The magnitude of the effect of treatment setting on mutual-help group attendance is startling. However, it is believable if one considers the fact that most White clients receive treatment at outpatient clinics that put less emphasis on the Twelve Step philosophy and have fewer "recovering" persons on staff. In contrast, residential programs tend to endorse the Twelve Step approach and employ significant numbers of recovering counselors (Mavis & Stöffelmayr, 1989). Thus a White person who is treated at a residential agency receives a much higher exposure to the Twelve Step philosophy, relative to other White clients.

The negative effect of staff Twelve Step beliefs on mutual-help group attendance among Whites is also surprising. Yet an earlier study gives an indication of what the underlying process might be (Mavis & Stöffelmayr, 1989). In outpatient programs, which is where most White clients are treated, Twelve Step influence on treatment correlates strongly with client dissatisfaction with treatment. Mavis and Stöffelmayr (1989) suggest that there could be a negative reactive effect among certain outpatient clients, especially court referrals, who are strongly presented with the AA perspective. These clients might form a negative or rebellious attitude toward AA in treatment and thus not pursue mutual-help groups after treatment is over.

One must ponder the contrast between the finding that agencies that employ many recovering staff (usually residential agencies) are successful at getting White clients into mutual-help groups while at the same time the espoused Twelve Step beliefs of agency staff negatively predict involvement. Apparently, what moves clients to seek out Twelve Step programs after treatment is not having a clinician say that AA is good or that the Twelve Steps should be followed. Rather, just as the AA organization maintains, seeing another person live out and benefit from recovering principles is what makes mutual-help an attractive option. The findings here would suggest that professionals who wish to encourage clients to become involved in Twelve Step groups recognize that (to pinch a line from Synanon) if "you don't walk the walk, don't talk the talk."

To return to the discussion of Figure 5.3, length of treatment positively predicts Twelve Step involvement. The length of time a person spends in treatment is an indicator of how serious they believe their problem is, how motivated they are to seek help, and how receptive they are to aid. It seems that among White clients, those who desire extensive care from professionals are also more likely to get involved in mutual-help groups after treatment (a "help seeker" effect).

The indirect effect of treatment setting on mutual-help group attendance mediated by length of treatment is also worthy of comment. The direction of effect of a "higher score" on treatment mode (indicating residential care) on mutual-help group attendance is positive, but residential centers also have significantly shorter lengths of treatment, making the overall indirect effect negative, although nonsignificant, $t = .65$. In other words, the powerful positive influence of residential centers on subsequent mutual-help group attendance among Whites is attenuated somewhat by their tendency to treat clients for shorter lengths of time than do outpatient agencies. The White client most likely to attend a mutual-help group after treatment is therefore probably someone who has been treated for an extended period in a residential agency.

Although fitting a model is certainly a good sign that a research conceptualization has some merit, one might also consider how much variance in the variable of interest is explained by the model. The coefficient of determination for the mutual-help attendance variable is .36, indicating that slightly over a third of the variance in mutual-help group attendance is explained by these variables in this configuration. The amount of variance left unexplained suggests that this model be regarded as an interesting beginning rather than a definitive analysis.

Black Mutual-Help Group Attendance

Figure 5.4 presents the results of the model estimation for the 233 African-American substance abusers in the sample. Among African Americans, 79 persons (33.9%) were attending Twelve Step groups 1 year after treatment, whereas the remainder ($n = 154$) were not.

Within the Black sample, most of the tested paths were not significant (|T| < 2). Yet the nonsignificant findings are worthy of some attention because many of them occur on paths that were significant in the White sample.

The positive influences of family/social and substance abuse problems on mutual-help group attendance are in the expected direction but did not achieve significance. Surprisingly, psychological problems at intake were a significant negative predictor among Blacks of mutual-help involvement 1

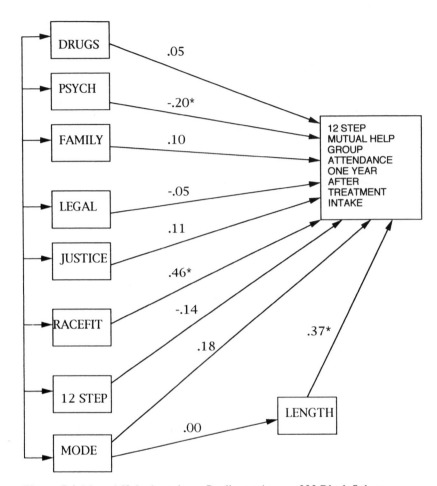

Figure 5.4. Mutual-Help Attendance Predictors Among 233 Black Substance Abusers

NOTE: Path coefficients are printed just above their path. Higher scores on mode indicate residential treatment.
*p < .05; |T| > 2.

year after treatment. This was not the case among Whites. Inspection of the distribution of psychological problems within race reveals that only the African-American sample had a bimodal distribution (i.e., Black clients tended to have either high or low psychological problems, whereas White clients were evenly distributed across psychological severity). African Americans with severe psychological problems might not feel comfortable or be fully accepted at Twelve Step meetings.

Among Whites, legal problems strongly predicted lack of mutual-help group involvement, but among Blacks they predicted nothing. As shown in Table 5.3, the legal system directs fewer Blacks to treatment than it does Whites. Why African-American clients who are referred to treatment by the justice system do not show the same aversion to posttreatment Twelve Step groups that White clients do is not clear. However, the first author's informal observations suggest one possible explanation. Disproportionate numbers of Blacks go to prison under War on Drugs law enforcement initiatives. Hence, by comparison to other Blacks who are substance abusers, a Black person who gets treatment via the courts might see him- or herself as relatively fortunate and therefore approach treatment with less resentment and hostility than would a White criminal justice referral (who presumably, compares him- or herself to White substance abusers who get away with it).

A notable similarity of Blacks to Whites is that the local racial context strongly influences their mutual-help group participation. Blacks in Detroit are more likely to go to mutual-help groups than are Blacks in predominantly White areas (central and western Michigan).[3] The implications of this finding for research are discussed extensively in the conclusion.

Although the pattern of results for Twelve Step beliefs and treatment setting for Blacks were in the same direction as for Whites, the results did not attain significance in the Black sample. However, length of treatment was a significant positive predictor of mutual-help group involvement for Blacks just as it was for Whites.

The model explains 43% of the variance in mutual-help group involvement, which is excellent, given that many of the paths are nonsignificant. This model appears to be a good beginning for understanding the factors underlying posttreatment mutual-help group affiliation among African-American substance abusers.

CONCLUSIONS

A multisample path-analytic model of posttreatment mutual-help group participation yielded different findings for Black and White substance abusers. Among Whites, a variety of individual, treatment, and ecological level variables were good predictors of mutual-help group attendance. Among

Blacks, only racial fit, psychological problems, and length of treatment had significant effects on mutual-help attendance 1 year after treatment. The most obvious conclusion that one can draw from these data is that findings from mutual-help research do not easily generalize across racial groups. As stated in the introduction, mutual-help groups are highly sensitive to the racial, psychological, and social environment in which they are situated. Therefore, it is reasonable to expect that as long as racial groups are largely separated, their mutual-help groups (even different groups within one organization) will be different.

The data presented here also show the impact of professionals on local Twelve Step groups. The type of treatment received, the beliefs of staff members, and the length of treatment all had significant effects on posttreatment mutual-help group attendance. All of these facets of treatment vary systematically with the race and social class of clientele, which suggests that studies of minority Twelve Step group participation should consider the local mental health system's attitudes toward both mutual-help groups and race. The only study of which the authors are aware that has been conducted along these lines revealed that treatment professionals were more likely to refer White clients to mutual-help groups than they were to refer minority clients (DenHartog, Homer, & Wilson, 1986). Other inquiries into this area could yield similarly interesting and important results.

That said, the authors do not mean to imply that substance abuse treatment professionals control who ends up in mutual-help groups. Many persons go to these groups without having been treated by professionals, and many persons who are referred to groups by professionals do not choose to go. Thus studies of minority mutual-help participation should consider factors influencing participation in addition to professional attitudes and practices. One of the variables that seems particularly important to consider is racial fit.

An interesting finding of this study is the role of racial fit in both Black and White mutual-help group participation. Whites are more likely to attend mutual-help groups in predominantly White areas, and Blacks are more likely to attend a group in predominantly Black areas.

In the future, more study of racial fit seems warranted. A rather crude measure of racial fit was employed in this study. Given that it revealed a powerful effect despite its imperfections suggests that more sophisticated measures of racial fit might show an even stronger effect on mutual-help involvement. A better way to measure this variable (which was beyond our means) is to use census tract data, which allows one to measure racial segregation neighborhood by neighborhood. Knowing both the location of members' residences and the location of groups might provide interesting information on how people select mutual-help groups. It may also be informative to visit neighborhood groups and determine their racial composition.

The finding that Blacks who live in predominantly Black areas are more likely to attend mutual-help groups than are Blacks who live in predominantly White areas provides a potential explanation for why it is so commonly believed that racial minorities do not participate in mutual-help groups. Our results suggest that in White areas (where research is frequently conducted) this pattern obtains. Yet in Black areas, where research is less frequently conducted, one sees high levels of participation by Blacks and low levels by Whites. Thus the common finding that mutual help is White says as much about where research is done as it does about mutual-help groups. Researchers who assert that mutual help is primarily or exclusively a White, middle-class phenomenon might be mistaking their own vantage point (which comes largely out of White, middle-class existence) for a universal quality of mutual-help organizations.

To rephrase the above issue in terms of base rates, it appears that many substance abusers prefer to go to meetings in areas where their own race is well-represented. Thus racial base rate information must be taken into account when planning and interpreting mutual-help research. Where the base rate of minorities in a community is low, there is a smaller pool of potential members and those potential members might be less likely to go than they would if their base rate was high. Once a critical mass is achieved (i.e., once there are enough people to support an all- or primarily minority mutual-help group) attendance should go up. Research that does not take such base rate information into account could mistakenly attribute low minority mutual-help group participation to the nature of the mutual-help organization studied rather than to the characteristics of the community in which the study was conducted.

In addition to conducting more mutual-help research in areas where there are a significant number of racial minorities, we could also expand our understanding of mutual-help participation by studying groups that deal with minority concerns. In the substance abuse area, there are dozens of studies of Alcoholics Anonymous that deal with the "White drug of choice" and hardly any of Narcotics Anonymous (Peyrot, 1985), which deal with drugs that are used more commonly by minority substance abusers. Again, one could make the argument that we are biasing our research in ways that overstate the "Whiteness" of mutual help. One can learn a great deal about minority mutual-help group participation if one looks in the right places (see the chapter by Nash & Kramer, this volume).

In this study, we examined minority mutual help by looking at organizations that were started by Whites and then spread to the Black community. Thus our study looked at mutual help through a White lens. Although we obviously think this approach has value, we at the same time believe it should be supplemented by studies of mutual-help organizations as they are created and defined by African Americans. There might be forms, purposes, and styles of mutual-help organizations in African-American communities that have no parallel in White society but nonetheless should be included under our conceptual and mutual-help research umbrella.

Our findings also show the value of studying mutual-help group participation using multiple levels of analysis, as suggested by Maton (this volume). A univariate difference that emerges in a simple contrast of mutual-help group attendees and nonattendees might disappear in a multivariate analysis. When we ignore the context that is formed by local professionals, ecological variables, and other systems (churches, legal) we might misunderstand our results and overgeneralize from them. In research on Twelve Step groups in particular, it is very important to study the context formed by local professionals because Twelve Step groups, unlike any other mutual-help organizations, have completely infiltrated the professional care system (Denzin, 1987).

One criticism that one could make of this study from an ecological perspective is that, although data at different levels were discussed, the level of statistical analysis was still the individual client. A fully developed ecological program on mutual-help attendance would include comparisons of agencies and of communities. This would require researchers to become familiar with more complex statistical procedures than were employed in this study. Particularly, hierarchical linear modeling procedures, which are currently being developed and promulgated, should be able to simultaneously estimate the effects of one level of analysis on another (e.g., the effects of communities on agencies and the effects of agencies on communities and clients). Although the structural equation modeling procedure used in this study yielded useful and interesting information, it was limited somewhat by the ability of the procedure to handle only one level of analysis at a time (as well as by the presence of nonnormal variables).

Before closing this chapter, we wish to take a few moments to discuss the politics of self-help group research with minority groups. Politics always shape how research is conducted and used, and mutual-help researchers who study minority organizations should be aware of the political implications of their work.

In an important contribution, Neighbors, Elliot, and Gant (1990) point out that some commentators fear that African-American mutual-help organizations will be used by conservative policymakers as a way of justifying a "pull yourself up by your own bootstraps" philosophy and an attendant cut in social services for Black Americans. One could add to this point the observation that many politically liberal academics and commentators (Rieff, 1991) are skeptical of Twelve Step programs for disenfranchised segments of the population because they seem to encourage self-involvement rather than political involvement and spiritual surrender rather than political empowerment.

The first response that should be made to these charges is that mutual-help groups are fundamentally democratic institutions in which people are viewed as being competent and intelligent. If we really believe that, it would be hypocritical to then say that we do not trust the decision of an African American, or a woman, or a Latino to join a mutual-help group. If we assume that mutual-help group members are competent to help themselves and each other, then we must also assume that they are acting responsibly and sensibly when they join a group.

Another point to consider is that even a sympathetic critic of American social policy would have to admit that social services provided to African-American communities have not been uniformly excellent, helpful, and welcome. To assume that more African-American mutual help and less professional services necessarily implies a lower quality of life for African Americans violates the assumptions of the mutual-help movement and buys into notions of "professional preciousness" (Sarason, 1972) which assume that the best of help only comes from a selected group of experts.

To endorse Twelve Step programs for Black Americans is not to imply that African Americans should hold themselves responsible for social inequities that contribute to their difficulties. As Neighbors et al. (1990) so cogently point out, taking responsibility for the solution of a problem is not the same as blaming oneself for the cause of a problem. This very distinction is in fact explicitly encouraged by Twelve Step groups, which do not hold substance abusers responsible for their "disease" but do hold them responsible for recovery. Implicit in Neighbors et al.'s article is the view that this is also an adaptive attitude for Black Americans to take toward racism in American society: that Blacks can hold the society responsible for racism while at the same time taking personal responsibility in their own lives for doing the best that is possible under the circumstances.

With regard to the discomfort of some commentators with the spiritual approach of Twelve Step groups of Black Americans, this attitude is probably more a reflection of the marked negative attitudes toward spirituality that are prevalent in social science and the mental health professions (see Bergin, 1991) than of any understanding of Black history. Religion and spirituality have been far from an opiate of Black masses. Religion has been the backbone of many Black political movements (Martin Luther King Jr.'s civil rights activities, Malcolm X's Nation of Islam, the Southern Christian Leadership Conference). Again, it is hazardous to interpret a phenomenon in one subculture from the perspective of another.

That (at least) two worlds, divided largely by race, exist in our society is a reality that we must always bear in mind in our research, especially so when we are studying minority mutual-help group participation. The racial divisions in our culture exert great influence not only on mutual-help groups, but also on mutual-help researchers and helping professionals. When we forget the racial context in which we work, we run the risk of mistaking our own biases for biases that are endemic to mutual-help groups.

The Twelve Step Belief Scale

Below is a list of beliefs or principles related to the treatment of alcoholism. Check any item which you think is true or which you might express to a client in treatment. Check as many as apply.

[ ] Alcoholism is an incurable, progressive, fatal disease
[ ] Avoid all chemical mood-changers
[ ] Go to AA meetings
[ ] Try not to test your willpower
[ ] Suspend judgment of yourself and of others
[ ] Be wary of drinking occasions
[ ] Share your experience, strength, and hope with other alcoholics
[ ] Try to turn your life and will over to a Higher Power
[ ] Practice rigorous honesty
[ ] Make regular use of prayer
[ ] Beware of phony pride
[ ] Read the AA message
[ ] When you are shaky, work with another recovering alcoholic
[ ] Take a searching and fearless moral inventory
[ ] Share your inventory with someone else
[ ] Remember that alcoholism is cunning and baffling

NOTES

1. A minor, but important, point in terminology is applied in this article. We believe we should use the term *mutual help* as much as possible when describing findings on minority participation. One reason for this is that it is simply a more accurate description of what happens in groups: People help each other. The second reason is that the term *self-help* can play into the wrong line of imagery—do it yourself, be a rugged individual, you are on your own, pull yourself up by your bootstraps, and so on. The power of mutual help in the Black community will not come from a series of individuals helping themselves but from everyone helping each other.

2. The recommended estimation strategy when there are ordinal (including binary) variables is to analyze the polychoric correlation matrix using weighted least squares (WLS) (Jöreskog & Sörbom, 1988). WLS uses as its weight matrix the inverse of the matrix containing asymptotic covariances of the polychoric correlations. This weight matrix can be obtained using PRELIS. However, the current version of PRELIS (PRELIS 1.12) contains a programming error that results in inaccurate weights when the sampling distribution of an observed variable is extremely skewed, as several were in the current study. The programmers at Scientific Software are planning to rectify this problem in PRELIS 1.20 (W. Wothke, personal communication, April 30, 1992). Because of the difficulties, ULS was used instead of WLS. ULS estimates are consistent and do not make distributional assumptions about the observed variables (Bollen, 1989).

3. When this finding was presented at the National Institute of Mental Health Workshop on Self-Help Research, one member of the audience suggested that racial fit was irrelevant and that this finding merely shows that urban Blacks are different from rural Blacks in terms of social class and social stability. Inspection of the data within the Black sample indicated that counter to this criticism, rural and urban Blacks were similar in terms of level of education, rate of unemployment, age, and marital status.

REFERENCES

Bergin, A. E. (1991). Values and religious issues in psychotherapy and mental health. *American Psychologist, 46,* 394-403.

Bollen, K. A. (1989). *Structural equations with latent variables.* New York: John Wiley.

Caldwell, F. J. (1983). Alcoholics Anonymous as a viable treatment resource for Black alcoholics. In T. D. Watts & R. Wright (Eds.), *Black alcoholism: Towards a comprehensive understanding* (pp. 85-99). Springfield, IL: Charles C Thomas.

DenHartog, G. L., Homer, A. L., & Wilson, R. B. (1986). *Cooperation: A tradition in action. Self-help involvement of clients in Missouri alcohol and drug abuse treatment programs.* (Available from Missouri Department of Mental Health, 1915 Southridge Drive, Jefferson City, MO 65102)

Denzin, N. K. (1987). *The recovering alcoholic.* Newbury Park, CA: Sage.

Emrick, C. D., Tonigan, J. S., Montgomery, H., & Little, L. (1993). Alcoholics Anonymous: What is currently known? In B. S. McCrady & W. R. Miller (Eds.), *Research on Alcoholics Anonymous: Opportunities and alternatives* (pp. 41-78). New Brunswick, NJ: Rutgers Center on Alcohol Studies.

Farley, R. (1985). Three steps forward and two back? Recent changes in the social and economic status of Blacks. *Ethnic and Racial Studies, 8,* 4-27.

Humphreys, K. (1991). *Factors predicting attendance at self-help groups after substance abuse treatment.* Unpublished master's thesis, University of Illinois, Urbana.

Humphreys, K. (1993). Psychotherapy and the 12-step approach for substance abusers: The limits of integration. *Psychotherapy, 30,* 207-213.

Humphreys, K., Mavis, B. E., & Stöffelmayr, B. E. (1991a). Factors predicting attendance at self-help groups after substance abuse treatment. *Journal of Consulting and Clinical Psychology, 59,* 591-593.

Humphreys, K., Mavis, B. E., & Stöffelmayr, B. E. (1991b, August). *Substance abuse treatment agencies and self-help groups: Collaborators or competitors?* Paper presented at the annual meeting of the American Psychological Association, San Francisco. (ERIC Document Reproduction Service No. ED 341 927)

Humphreys, K., Mavis, B. E., & Stöffelmayr, B. E. (in press). Involvement in mutual help groups one year after substance abuse treatment: Are twelve step programs appropriate for disenfranchised groups? *Prevention in Human Services.*

Jilek-Aall, L. (1981). Acculturation, alcoholism, and Indian-style Alcoholics Anonymous. *Journal of Studies on Alcohol, Suppl. 9,* 143-158.

Jöreskog, K. G., & Sörbom, D. (1988). *LISREL 7: A guide to the program and applications.* Chicago: SPSS.

Mavis, B. E., & Stöffelmayr, B. E. (1989, August). *Paraprofessionals, staff recovery status, and client satisfaction in alcohol treatment.* Paper presented at the annual meeting of the American Psychological Association, New Orleans.

McLellan, A. T., Luborsky, L., Woody, G. E., & O'Brien, C. P. (1980). An improved diagnostic evaluation instrument for substance abuse patients: The addiction severity index. *Journal of Nervous and Mental Disease, 168,* 412-423.

Nash, K. B., & Kramer, K. D. (1994). Self-Help for Sickle Cell Disease in African-American Communities. In T. J. Powell (Ed.), *Understanding the self-help organization: Frameworks and findings.* Thousand Oaks, CA: Sage.

Neighbors, H. W., Elliot, K. A., & Gant, L. M. (1990). Self-help and Black Americans: A strategy for empowerment. In T. J. Powell (Ed.), *Working with self help* (pp. 189-217). Silver Spring, MD: NASW Press.

Peyrot, M. (1985). Narcotics Anonymous: Its history, structure, and approach. *International Journal of the Addictions, 20,* 1509-1522.

Polich, J. M. (1982). The validity of self-reports in alcoholism research. *Addictive Behaviors, 7,* 123-132.

Rieff, D. (1991, October). Victims all? Recovery, codependency and the art of blaming someone else. *Harper's Magazine,* pp. 49-56.

Sarason, S. B. (1972). *The creation of settings and the future societies.* San Francisco: Jossey-Bass.

Sobell, L. C., & Sobell, M. B. (1986). Can we do without self-reports? *Behavior Therapist, 9,* 141-146.

Vaillant, G. (1983). *The natural history of alcoholism.* Cambridge, MA: Harvard University Press.

Yeaton, W. H. (in press). The development and assessment of valid measures of service delivery to enhance inference in outcome-based research: Measuring attendance at self-help group meetings. *Journal of Consulting and Clinical Psychology.*

6. Individual, Group Context, and Individual-Group Fit Predictors of Self-Help Group Attendance

DOUGLAS A. LUKE

LINDA ROBERTS

JULIAN RAPPAPORT

In the past decade, research on self-help has undergone a subtle but noticeable shift. Early work tended to frame self-help simply as an alternative to traditional treatment modalities, a "poor man's [sic] psychotherapy" (Leerhsen, Lewis, Pomper, Davenport, & Nelson, 1990, p. 51). Research of this type often focused on treatment efficacy (Bednar & Kaul, 1978; Garb & Stunkard, 1974; Lipson, 1982) and relationship to the professional service system (Borman, 1976; Hermalin et al., 1979; Levy, 1978). More recently, the focus has shifted toward viewing self-help as a social movement and self-help groups as settings that promote individual, interpersonal, and social change. This broader conception of self-help is not new (Katz, 1981, 1993; Killilea, 1976), but only recently has empirical work that

AUTHORS' NOTE: This chapter is based in part on a talk presented at the 1992 Self-Help Research Conference, sponsored by the Center for Self-Help Research & Knowledge Dissemination, Ann Arbor, MI. Support for this research came from an National Institute of Mental Health grant (MH37390) awarded to Julian Rappaport and Ed Seidman. All correspondence should be addressed to Douglas Luke, Michigan State University, Department of Psychology, 129 Psychology Research Building, East Lansing, Michigan, 48824.

is based on this broader social and ecological conception become more common.

For example, we are now starting to see in the literature empirical investigations of self-help groups as behavior settings (Luke, Rappaport, & Seidman, 1991), self-help groups as community settings that have a life cycle through time (Maton, Leventhal, Madara, & Julien, 1989), self-help groups as settings that shape the social networks of their members (Borkman, 1984), and self-help groups as settings that exist in a complex grassroots information and support system at the community, state, and national levels (Madara, 1986; Meissen, Gleason, & Embree, 1991). All of this work explicitly embraces an ecological framework.

The purpose of this chapter is to provide a further example of an ecologically oriented inquiry into self-help. Specifically, using survival analysis, this chapter presents data on how the individual characteristics, the group context, and the "fit" between a member and a particular self-help group can influence the subsequent participation of the member.

ATTENDANCE AND PARTICIPATION

There are both theoretical and applied reasons why examining attendance and participation patterns is important for understanding self-help. Although a number of theoretical frameworks have been proposed for self-help, no consensus has emerged concerning their acceptance. These approaches include organizational, reference group, social network, small-group dynamics, ideology, and behavioral change theories (Antze, 1979; Levy, 1976; Powell, 1987; Stewart, 1990).

These theories vary dramatically in the mechanisms for participant change that they propose. Different aspects of self-help organizations, groups, and meetings (e.g., membership requirements, roles of leaders, structure of the organization, behavioral expectations, rules for member relationships, connections with other service providers) all have varying roles to play. However, an implicit assumption that underlies each of these theories is the fundamental importance of participation. If persons are supposed to change as a result of their membership in a particular group, they must attend and become participants in that group. Thus no matter what mechanism of change we think is taking place, self-help participation is a vital aspect of the self-help process.

Understanding attendance and participation is also important for applied reasons. Anyone who has ever formed a self-help group, been involved with a self-help organization, or provided consultation or technical assistance to groups knows that member attendance and participation is always a critical issue at all stages of group development. This can take the form of public relations (how to let more people know about the group), recruitment (how to get more new people to attend), retention (how to keep them from dropping out), group division (there are too many people in the group), or participation (the same people always talk in the meetings).

Meissen et al. (1991) have provided data on the importance of attendance and participation to self-help organizations. They surveyed 90 different groups that were affiliated with a statewide self-help clearinghouse to find out about the most important needs and problems of each group. Responding to open-ended questions, 23.3% of the groups stated that lack of member participation was a major problem, second only to lack of public awareness (24.4%). When asked to rate the importance of 11 different common problems of self-help groups, recruitment of members was listed as the most serious problem.

The voluntary nature of self-help is an important factor that shapes attendance and participation patterns in self-help groups. Many, if not most groups have no specific requirements regarding length of involvement or rate of attendance. Although members are encouraged to attend regularly, they are free to attend in whatever pattern they choose. This is an important part of the empowering nature of self-help; participants have a great deal of control over the nature of their self-help experience.

However, this situation poses a potential dilemma for some self-help organizations. Many people choose to attend one or two meetings of a self-help group and never return. For example, in their 1989 survey, Alcoholics Anonymous (AA) (1990) reports that approximately a third of members attend only a few meetings, and that almost half of new members stop attending within 3 months. In point of fact, given the cross-sectional nature of their survey, it is likely that they are oversampling long-term members and that these numbers are underestimates.

From the perspective of the individual groups, this type of attendance pattern can be troubling. For many groups, attracting and keeping members is a difficult problem. Many of the individuals who attend only a meeting or two could benefit from longer involvement. As AA concluded, "We often say that no one gets to AA by accident, so the fact that we lose within three months half of those that begin our program may mean that we lose a great number of alcoholics who desperately need sobriety" (p. 5).

Although persons who attend only a few meetings can be troubling for the group, there might be very good reasons for their attrition. For example, people who attend once or twice might conclude that they would not benefit from the group. Or perhaps the group realizes that a particular member is not suitable and through either explicit or implicit means acts to prevent the member from returning.

This pattern of participation in which there is a high early attrition rate has been observed in many other types of mental health services (Gutfreund, Powell, & Luke, 1993). In fact, Phillips (1985, 1987) has stated that a "characteristic attrition curve," showing an initial high participation-attrition rate and negative acceleration asymptotically over time, is characteristic of all health service delivery systems (cf. Brown, 1989; Gill, Nolimal, & Crowley, 1992). It would not be surprising, then, to find a similar attendance pattern for self-help groups. However, simple statistical curves that describe overall group patterns often obscure interesting and important subgroup variations (Rapkin & Luke, 1993). Moreover, knowing that the characteristic attrition curve describes self-help group attendance is only a first step. What explains this phenomenon? Although we are starting to learn more about the factors that lead people to seek out self-help (Gidron, Chesler, & Chesney, 1991; Humphreys, Mavis, & Stöfflemayr, 1991; Levy & Derby, 1992; Powell, 1992), we currently know very little about what happens once a person has decided to attend a particular group. What type of person is most likely to contribute to this early high attrition rate? What group characteristics predict longevity in participation? What aspects of the initial meeting affect subsequent attendance? Why do some people never return after an initial meeting, whereas others become life-long members?

MEMBER-GROUP FIT

Person-environment fit is an important concept that plays a central role in environmental, ecological, organizational, and community psychology (Moos, 1987; Rappaport, 1977; Spokane, 1985). In this work, the degree to which there is congruence (fit) between a person and his or her environment is hypothesized to relate to a wide variety of psychological, behavioral, and social variables. We propose that member-group fit is an important factor in understanding self-help group participation patterns. A person who is quite similar to the other members of the group might experience more environmental press to "stay in," whereas a person who is very different will likely find more reasons to stay away. Although the mechanisms by which this occurs are difficult to observe, the results would be easy to assess. As long as it is possible to operationalize fit and to have reliable measures of attendance patterns, then it is a simple matter to test the relationship between fit and participation.

We have previously suggested that self-help participation can be understood using a two-stage model (Luke & Roberts, 1992). The first stage concerns the initial decision to return to a group after the first meeting or two. This stage can be simply modeled by examining the fit between the characteristics of the particular member and the group that the person first attends. If there is a good match between the group and the person, that person is more likely to decide to return. Once a person has decided to return (in effect, to become a member of the group), he or she enters the second stage of participation. Here, participation becomes an ongoing process that can be better understood by looking at the behaviors and experiences of the member in group activities. Persons who become involved in group activities, who share their personal experiences, who take on varying roles in the group and organization, and who become close to the other members are more likely to stay satisfied and involved with the group over a long period of time.

Although the data we presented supported this two-stage model, the concept of member-group fit was not fully articulated in our earlier work. In this chapter, we attempt to develop and elaborate three conceptualizations of member-group fit that could be relevant to the prediction of attendance duration.

There are a variety of ways of defining fit (see Gati, 1989, for a good overview of the conceptual and methodological issues involved with measuring person-environment fit). The following three ways of conceptualizing the match between a member and the group are certainly not exhaustive. They represent conceptually straightforward definitions that address disparate aspects of the context of self-help group participation.

First, any self-help group is designed for a specific type of person. This can be explicitly recognized, such as in groups that are open only to persons with particular disorders. Also, there might be implicit expectations, such as groups that tend to be made up of White, middle-class members. A person who first comes to a meeting and finds out that he or she is very different from the "typical" group member is finding out that he or she does not fit into the group very well. In this case, we would hypothesize that he or she would probably not attend the group as long as would another person who matches the group norm or ideal more closely. To assess this type of member-group fit, we use individual characteristics to predict participation patterns and compare our results to the characteristics of the "ideal" member the organization is attempting to attract and to the typical or average group member.

The second conceptualization of member-group fit focuses on the characteristics of the initial meeting a participant attends. Meetings can vary dramatically across time and across groups (in the case of a self-help organization). A meeting that is different from the ideal or normative meeting can affect how people perceive the group and organization. For example, if a particular meeting has a small turnout, and there is little interaction in the meeting because of the small size, a newcomer to the group might go away feeling that the group is cold and impersonal. Although individuals make up the group, the group is more than the sum of its parts, and attributes of the group per se—the *group context*—provide another data source for the prospective group member to evaluate with respect to fit. To assess whether these group context variables have an effect on participation, we will calculate group composition variables and use them to predict attendance patterns.

Finally, member-group fit can be conceptualized as the match between a participant and the other group members on any given characteristic. Unlike the previous conceptualizations, here we are able to assess fit directly rather than rely on inferences about fit. This type of fit can be operationalized straightforwardly by calculating indexes of *individual-group dissimilarity*. This is possible as long as characteristics are being measured of both the new member and the other members of the group at that meeting. For example, if socioeconomic status (SES) were assessed for everyone at a particular meeting, then a fit statistic could be calculated showing whether the new person was higher, lower, or about the same as the other members with regards to SES.

This fit statistic is essentially a measure of similarity or dissimilarity, and there are a myriad of ways of calculating it. The method chosen should depend on what you are trying to find out (see Gower, 1985, for a comprehensive overview of proximity measures; also see Skinner, 1978 for a good discussion of the conceptual issues involved in choosing the appropriate measure of similarity). In our case, we lack a theory of self-help group attendance that would suggest a fit statistic of a particular form. All other things being equal, then, we should choose a statistic that is simple and easy to understand.

Consider the earlier example of assessing fit using SES. A simple way to define fit is to say that the statistic should be small when a person is similar to the other members of the group and large when the person is dissimilar, regardless of direction. This is a nondirected measure of fit, in that the direction of the dissimilarity does not matter, only the absolute amount. For example, persons with much lower than average SES would be seen as just as dissimilar as those with much higher than average SES. A squared-Euclidean distance measure is the most commonly used statistic for a nondirected measure of fit.[1]

Each of these three methods of examining member-group fit (individual characteristics, group context, and individual-group similarity) allows for easy measurement and analysis. The more important question, however, is whether these different methods will result in finding out more about self-help participation than if we had simply chosen one of them. It is our hypothesis that each of these varying methods will tell us different things about the pattern of self-help participation over time.

METHOD

Background

The present study of self-help group participation is part of a large-scale evaluation project of GROW, Inc. (see Rappaport et al., 1985, and Roberts et al., 1991, for overviews of this project). GROW is an international self-help organization designed for persons with a history of serious mental illness or psychiatric hospitalization. GROW uses a Twelve Step program modeled after Alcoholics Anonymous. Most GROW groups meet weekly and are open to anyone. At any particular time, GROW groups will have members who are at varied levels of functioning. There are no attendance requirements, although members are encouraged to attend regularly. Also, new attendees are not considered official members until their third meeting.

Over a 27-month period, trained participant observers attended and collected data from 527 meetings of 15 different GROW groups in central Illinois. Most groups were observed either weekly or every other week. The average number of observations per group was 39, with a range from 17 to 71.

Participants

During the study, 861 different people were observed attending at least one GROW meeting. They ranged in age from 15 to 85 years, $M = 39$ years, and tended to be single (73%), White (97%), female (60%), and have some education beyond high school (60%). A little over half of the participants had at least one psychiatric hospitalization in the past, and approximately three quarters of the members had received formal inpatient or outpatient treatment for psychological problems.

To examine the factors influencing early attendance, only those persons attending their first meeting during the study observation period are included here. This results in a sample of 644 GROW attendees. Summary statistics indicated that approximately one third of this group would attend only one or two meetings, another third would attend for 3 to 4 months before dropping out, and the last third would attend for longer periods of time (note the similarity between these GROW attendance findings and those reported by AA, 1990, discussed earlier).

Measures

Attendance

Every person attending a GROW meeting during the 27-month observation period was given a unique identification number. This ID number was used to keep accurate attendance data. To increase reliability, the attendance data were collapsed into monthly time units. By aggregating weekly attendance data into monthly intervals, it is less likely that we would misidentify someone as a dropout when they simply attended a meeting that was missed. Because the focus of this study is attendance duration and not attendance rates, the monthly attendance data are coded in binary form. Thus, for each participant, we know for each month of the study whether that person attended at least one meeting or not.

The monthly attendance data are then used to determine the attendance duration for each member. This is calculated as the number of months from first date of attendance to either (a) the last date of attendance, if the member stopped attending before the end of the study, or (b) the last date of the study. Although it might seem that by including persons still attending GROW at the end of the study, we would bias the attendance results, that is not the case. In fact, it is necessary to include these cases (called *censored* cases) to accurately model attendance patterns. One of the strengths of survival analysis (see below) is its ability to produce unbiased models of event durations using censored cases (see Luke, 1993, for a discussion of the technical issues of survival analysis).

Member Characteristics

Every new GROW attendee was asked to fill out a short questionnaire called the Brief Screening Procedure (BSP). The BSP measured a small set of demographic and social/psychological functioning variables. These variables describe basic characteristics of members at the time they start attending GROW. The following variables from the BSP were included in this study: age; education level (1 = *some high school*, 2 = *high school graduate*, 3 = *some college*, 4 = *college graduate or more*); gender (1 = *male*, 2 = *female*); marital status (1 = *married or was married*, 2 = *never married*); work status (1 = *working*, 2 = *not working*); previous hospitalization (1 = *yes*, 2 = *no*); and functioning (1 = *disturbed*, 2 = *somewhat disturbed*, 3 = *adequate*, 4 = *good*). Some variables from the BSP were not used in this study because of low variability (e.g., race), or high similarity with other variables (e.g., SES correlated highly with education level).

Table 6.1 lists frequencies and descriptive statistics for the member characteristics. (The varying sample sizes are due to the fact that simple demographics were collected on nearly everyone, but some people did not fill out the full BSP.)

Analytic Strategy

Attendance duration is the primary dependent variable in this study. However, there are serious difficulties involved with analyzing duration or time-to-event data. Traditionally, duration data are described either by reporting the percentage of a sample that has responded by a particular time point or by reporting the average length of time to the event for the sample (Allison, 1984). In either case, these summaries are biased because in most situations there was a subgroup that had not responded by the (usually arbitrary) endpoint of the study.

To avoid these problems, we used survival analysis to predict attendance duration. Survival analysis is a set of techniques that has been developed to produce unbiased models of duration data (for a more thorough introduction to survival analysis, see Allison, 1984; Luke, 1993; Singer & Willett, 1991).

Survival Curves

The first step in a survival analysis is to examine the general survival and hazard curves for the entire sample. Figure 6.1 presents the survival curve

TABLE 6.1 GROW Member Characteristics

Variable	Frequency	Percentage
Age (*M* = 38.6, SD = 13.0)		
Education level (*M* = 2.7, SD = 1.0)		
Some high school	50	12.4
High school graduate	119	29.5
Some college	133	33.0
College graduate	101	25.1
Gender (*M* = 1.6, SD = 0.5)		
Male	239	38.3
Female	285	61.7
Marital status (*M* = 1.4, SD = 0.5)		
Currently or previously married	294	63.2
Never married	171	36.8
Work status (*M* = 1.5, SD = 0.5)		
Working	225	50.6
Not working	220	49.4
Previous hospitalization **(*M* = 1.5, SD = 0.5)**		
Yes	170	51.5
No	160	48.5
Functioning (*M* = 2.8, SD = 1.1)		
Disturbed	58	15.0
Somewhat disturbed	88	22.8
Adequate	101	26.2
Good	139	36.0

for the 644 people who first attended GROW during the observation period of the study. The survival curve shows the proportion of people still attending GROW from 1 to 27 months after joining. The shape of the curve (steep initial drop that quickly levels off) indicates that most people drop out of GROW very quickly. In fact, the graph shows that almost 40% of the participants stop attending GROW after only 1 month. The median survival time is 2.8 months.[2] (Given the GROW open meeting policy, it is likely that many of these early dropouts are persons who attend a meeting or two and decide that the organization is not appropriate for them.)

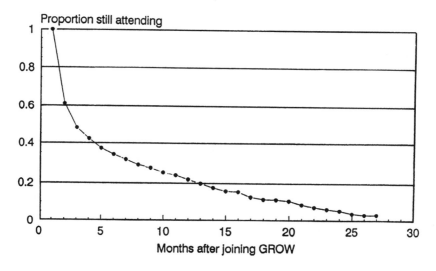

Figure 6.1. Estimated Overall Survival Function for GROW Data ($N = 644$)

Figure 6.2 presents the estimated hazard function for the GROW sample. The hazard curve shows the probability of dropping out of GROW for any particular month after joining. For example, the graph shows that there is approximately a 10% chance of dropping out after 4 months of attendance. The u-shaped curve of the graph (highlighted by the moving average line)[3] suggests that the probability of dropping out of GROW is high right after joining and after being a member for at least a year and a half. Between those times, the probability is a relatively low and stable 10%.

Analyses of Individual-Group Fit

The following analyses are concerned with showing how the fit between a particular member and the group that he or she first attends may (or may not) influence subsequent attendance duration. As discussed earlier, member-group fit can be conceptualized in different ways. In each of the following three sections, a set of variables relevant to each conceptualization is used to model attendance duration.

Individual Characteristics Model

A simple way to model member-group fit is to compare the individual member characteristics that predict attendance to the organizational ideal or

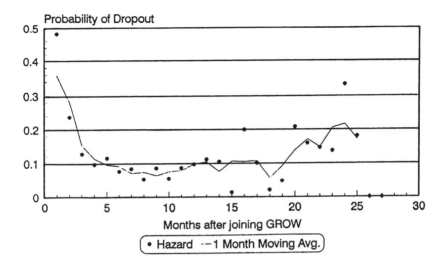

Figure 6.2. Estimated Overall Hazard Function for GROW Data ($N = 644$)

average. Thus if a first-time attendee is very different from the typical GROW member, there might be a variety of more or less explicit mechanisms that would act to keep the member from attending for very long. Note that with this model the composition of the particular group first attended is not considered at all.

Table 6.2 presents a Cox hazard model showing the effects of the set of individual member characteristics on the probability of dropping out of GROW (Cox, 1972). The results are interpreted in much the same way as multiple regression (Luke, 1993). The sign of the coefficients listed in column 2 indicate the direction of any effect. Positive coefficients increase the hazard function (probability of dropping out of GROW), thus decreasing survival time (duration of GROW attendance). The significance of the effect is listed in column 5. In this case, age, education, marital status, and functioning are found to have significant effects on the probability of dropping out of GROW. Individuals who are older, have more education, and have never been married are more likely to attend for longer periods of time (all have negative coefficients). Persons who are higher functioning, on the other hand, are more likely to drop out sooner (positive coefficient).

The last column in Table 6.2 is actually the most informative. It essentially is a measure of the effect size. The amount that this number deviates from 1.0 indicates the percentage change in the baseline probability of the hazard

TABLE 6.2 Hazard Model—Individual Characteristics Model ($n = 248$)

Variable	B	SE	B/SE	Significance	Exp(B)
Age	−.014	.006	−2.33	.022	.986
Education	−.150	.073	−2.05	.041	.861
Gender	.124	.152	0.82	.415	1.132
Marital status	−.512	.173	−2.96	.003	.599
Work status	−.019	.155	−0.12	.904	.981
Previous hospitalization	.126	.189	0.67	.504	1.134
Functioning	.183	.089	2.06	.039	1.201

rate for each unit change in the covariate. For example, the effect size for education is listed as .861. This means that for each positive change in level of education (e.g., from some high school to high school graduate or from high school graduate to some college) the probability of that person dropping out of GROW in any particular month is *reduced* by 14%, 1 − .861 = .139. In the case of functioning, each positive change in level (e.g., from adequate to good) *increases* the probability of dropping out by 20%, 1.201 − 1.00 = .201).

Figures 6.3, 6.4, 6.5, and 6.6 show subgroup analysis survival curves for each of the significant individual member characteristic variables. The graphs visually depict the impact of each variable on duration of attendance in GROW. Age has been dichotomized so that two different subgroups (young and old) can be compared.

In each case, the Mantel-Cox or Breslow tests indicate that the subgroup survival curves are significantly different from one another.[4] So, for example, Figure 6.3 shows that younger members are more likely to drop out of GROW sooner than are older members. Although with visual inspection the curves appear fairly close to each other, the subgroup differences are actually quite large. For example, consider the psychological functioning results depicted in Figure 6.6. After only 1 month, approximately 25% of persons rated as either very low or low functioning have dropped out of GROW. However, the dropout rate for persons with good or adequate functioning is 50%, double that of the lower functioning subgroups.

In sum, the people who are most likely to stay in GROW for more than a few weeks are older, educated, not married, and poorly functioning. For the most part, these are the people for whom GROW is intended. After all, high-functioning persons do not need GROW, and younger married persons often have other support resources available to them.

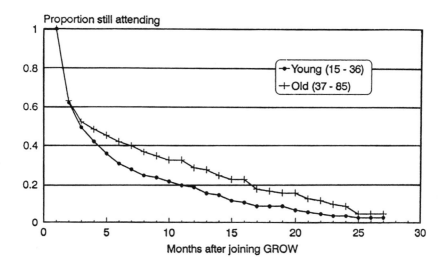

Figure 6.3. Subgroup Analysis: Duration of Attendance, by Age (*n* = 560)
NOTE: Mantel-Cox = 7.27, *p* = .007.

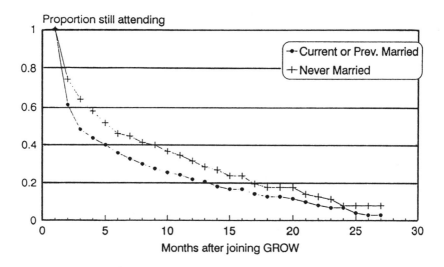

Figure 6.4. Subgroup Analysis: Duration of Attendance, by Marital Status (*n* = 467)
NOTE: Mantel-Cox = 7.02, *p* = .008.

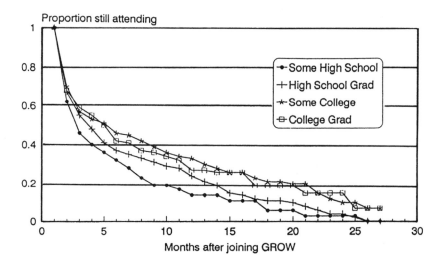

Figure 6.5. Subgroup Analysis: Duration of Attendance, by Education ($n = 403$)

NOTE: Mantel-Cox = 9.206, $p = .027$.

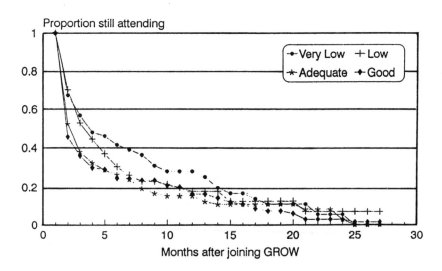

Figure 6.6. Subgroup Analysis: Duration of Attendance, by Psychological Functioning ($n = 388$)

NOTE: Mantel-Cox = 6.45, $p = .092$; Breslow = 13.27, $p = .004$.

TABLE 6.3 Hazard Model—Group Context Model ($n = 516$)

Variable	B	SE	B/SE	Significance	Exp(B)
Age	−.006	.011	−0.55	.570	.994
Education	−.097	.125	−0.78	.437	.907
Gender	.703	.323	2.18	.030	2.021
Marital status	−.176	.286	−0.62	.539	.839
Work status	.248	.249	1.00	.320	1.282
Previous hospitalization	−.230	.180	−1.28	.201	.794
Functioning	.056	.076	0.74	.459	1.058

Group Context Model

In the above model, the characteristics of the individual GROW members attending their first meeting were compared to the typical GROW member. Thus persons who were relatively high-functioning tended to drop out of GROW quickly. This is interpreted in the light that most GROW members have had a history of serious psychological and emotional problems; thus a high-functioning person does not fit into the GROW ideal.

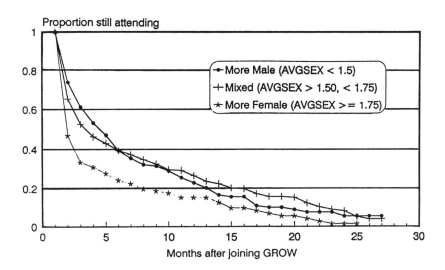

Figure 6.7. Subgroup Analysis: Duration of Attendance, by Group Gender ($n = 601$)
NOTE: Mantel-Cox = 16.00, $p = .0003$.

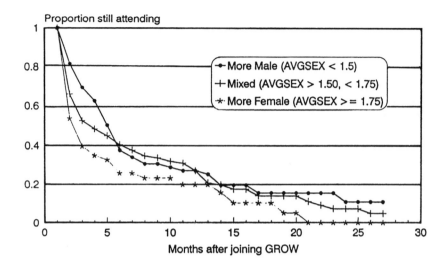

Figure 6.8. Subgroup Analysis: Duration of Attendance, by Group Gender—All Males ($n = 234$)

NOTE: Mantel-Cox = 4.55, $p = .103$; Breslow = 6.88, $p = .32$.

Instead of examining individual member characteristics, the effect of group context can be examined. Group context is defined as the average characteristics of all the members at a particular group meeting *except* for the person who is first attending. For example, if a person goes to a group where all the members are male and older, the group context is different than at a group meeting where the members are mixed in gender and age.

Table 6.3 presents the survival analysis results for these group context variables. Only gender shows a significant effect on attendance duration. The positive coefficient indicates that as a group changes from having more males to more females (average gender changing from 1.0 to 2.0), the individual member is more likely to drop out sooner. In other words, a GROW member is more likely to stay in GROW if the first meetings attended have more men in them.

In addition, the effect size is very large. A person is 102% more likely to drop out of GROW in any particular month if the first group attended was completely female as compared to completely male.

To examine this provocative finding in more detail, a variety of subgroup analyses were performed. First, Figure 6.7 presents a subgroup analysis

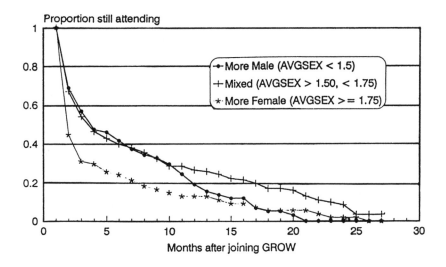

Figure 6.9. Subgroup Analysis: Duration of Attendance, by Group Gender—All Females ($n = 353$)

NOTE: Mantel-Cox = 12.91, p = .0016; Breslow = 15.50, p = .0004.

based on the variable AVGSEX. AVGSEX is the mean gender score for a particular attendee's first group meeting. This variable will range from 1.0 (all other group members are male) to 2.0 (all other group members are female). The median value of AVGSEX for all first meetings is 1.6, indicating that meetings typically have slightly more females than males in them. This variable was split into three categories: mostly male (AVGSEX < 1.5), mixed (1.5 < AVGSEX < 1.75), and mostly female (AVGSEX > 1.75).

The graph shows that after 1 month of attendance, over 50% of the persons who first attend group meetings that are mostly female have dropped out of GROW. This is compared to only 25% of persons who attend groups that are mostly male. However, this analysis ignores the gender of the person who is first attending these meetings. Perhaps men and women react differently to the varying gender mixes of the GROW meetings.

First, a Cox regression analysis was used to model the effects of Gender, AVGSEX, and the interaction of Gender by AVGSEX on attendance duration. If men and women react differently to varying gender mixes, that would show up in a significant interaction effect. However, the interaction term was nonsignificant.

TABLE 6.4   Median Survival Times—Member Gender by Group Gender
            Category

| Group Gender Category | Member Gender | |
	Males	Females
Mostly male (AVGSEX < 1.5)	5.01	3.71
Mixed (AVGSEX > 1.5, < 1.75)	3.57	3.50
Mostly female (AVGSEX > 1.75)	2.25	1.90

NOTE: AVGSEX is the mean gender score for a particular attendee's first group meeting.

As a further test, the subgroup analyses based on AVGSEX were repeated twice, once for male first-time attendees and once for female. Figures 6.8 and 6.9 present these survival analyses. Inspection reveals that there are, in fact, interesting differences in how men and women respond to the gender mix of initial meetings. In the early months, men seem to distinguish between meetings that are mostly male and mostly female (all three lines stay separated for the first 6 months). Women, on the other hand, primarily distinguish meetings that are mostly female, and this difference lasts for the first year after joining. Another interesting pattern is that the women who attend GROW for over a year are those that first attended mixed-gender meetings. This finding is strong and stable, lasting until the end of the study.

Another way to examine this effect is to consider the median attendance durations for the GROW members. Table 6.4 shows the median survival times for the men and women and the three different gender mixes. From the perspective of member retention, males who attend mostly male meetings are the most successful—over 50% of them attend for at least 5 months. Women respond most negatively to meetings that are mostly female. Median survival time is less than 2 months for this group.

Individual-Group Dissimilarity Model

Each of the previous two models was based on examinations of either individual member or group characteristics but not both. To directly assess member-group fit, we calculated a distance metric. This is relatively uncomplicated because member and group characteristics are assessed using the same variables. The most common measure of similarity is the squared-Euclidian distance, calculated by squaring the deviation of the individual member from the group mean for each variable:

TABLE 6.5 Hazard Model—Individual-Group Dissimilarity Model ($n = 210$)

Variable	B	SE	B/SE	Significance	Exp(B)
Age	−.012	.066	−0.18	.850	.988
Education	.026	.057	0.46	.640	1.027
Gender	−.265	.425	−0.62	.532	.767
Marital status	−.635	.327	−1.94	.052	.530
Work status	−.512	.399	−1.28	.195	.596
Previous hospitalization	.482	.213	2.26	.024	1.620
Functioning	−.069	.048	−1.44	.153	.933

$$dig = (x_i - X_{g-i})^2$$

(It is important to remember that the group mean is the average score for everyone at the particular meeting except for the member who is attending for the first time.) By squaring the deviation scores, the measure of similarity becomes nondirected: a person who is either higher or lower than the group mean will have a high distance score (and thus lower member-group fit).

Table 6.5 presents the results of the Cox hazard model for the dissimilarity measures. Previous hospitalization experience is significant and marital status is on the 0.05 cusp. These results indicate that in their first meeting, persons who have different hospitalization histories or a different marital status from the rest of the group have the shortest attendance durations.

DISCUSSION

As many have noted, self-help groups are settings that frame complex social systems (Luke et al., 1991; Maton et al., 1989). Persons come to these settings with many expectations and multiple goals. It is not unreasonable to assume that persons will continue to participate as long as those goals and expectations are being met. Given the complexity of self-help groups and the diversity of group participants, it is not surprising that we are only starting to understand the nature of self-help group participation.

This study represents a first step toward that understanding. Multiple conceptualizations of member-group fit were suggested to organize our attempt to identify predictors of self-help participation and attrition and

TABLE 6.6 Summary of Survival Results for Each Model

Model	Persons Most Likely to Drop Out
Individual characteristics	Younger, less educated, currently or previously married, high functioning
Group context	Members who attend meetings that are more than 2:1 female
Individual-group dissimilarity	Different hospitalization history, different marital status

preliminary support was found for their utility. Specific results are presented in the context of our discussion of three areas: the importance of multiple conceptualizations and operationalizations of member-group fit, the mechanisms of group entrance and maintenance, and the implications for policy and practice.

The Importance of Multiple Conceptualizations of Fit

From a methodological perspective, an intriguing finding from this study is that how you conceptualize member-group fit is critical. Each of the three different models yielded different survival results, suggesting that multiple types of member-group fit could be important in predicting attendance duration and attrition. Examining the individual characteristics of first-time GROW attendees revealed that those persons who were most like the typical GROW member (educated, older, not married, and low functioning) were most likely to return after the first meeting. Exploring the characteristics of the initial meetings suggested that the gender mix of the meeting was related to subsequent attendance patterns. Finally, calculating a direct person-group fit statistic allowed us to see how marital status and hospitalization history influenced participation patterns over time. In other words, a complete picture of how the context of the initial meeting influences subsequent participation can only be obtained by using multiple perspectives on the nature of member-group fit. Table 6.6 summarizes these results.

The importance of multiple measures and sources of information is almost a canard in the social sciences. However, the practice of including multiple measures in studies is often still the exception rather than the rule. Resource constraints are often the reason for this deficit. As we have demonstrated here, however, there are simpler ways to include multiple measures in a study. By postulating different definitions of important constructs, multiple perspectives can be included without expensive data collection methods. Here we proposed that the concept of person-group fit could be operationalized in three different ways. These were not simply different computational procedures. Rather, they were different ways to interpret person-group fit, each of which had a different computational formula.

Mechanisms of Group Entrance:
Evaluation and Gatekeeping

The above results make it clear that by examining a few characteristics of individuals in self-help meetings, we can discover a lot about subsequent attendance patterns. Furthermore, the match between a person who is attending his or her first meeting and the rest of the members at that meeting clearly affects the likelihood of returning after the initial meeting. However, no matter how interesting these results are, they shed little, if any, light on the mechanism of self-help participation. Our study is inherently exploratory. There are a number of intriguing possibilities that can be examined in future research.

Throughout this chapter, we have emphasized the concept of person-group fit as being critical for understanding how persons enter a self-help group setting and become a participating member. To the extent that a person and group match each other, that person is more likely to return and become an ongoing member.

How, specifically, might this work? Although there are any number of mechanisms that might be operating, there are two that we would suggest are important: individual evaluation and group gatekeeping. Individual evaluation is the process that persons who are first attending a group use to decide if the group will be worthwhile to them. Group gatekeeping, on the other hand, is the mechanism by which a group can either exclude or include potential members.

To illustrate these ideas, consider the previous results concerning the effects of gender mix on subsequent attendance. Both males and females are less likely to stay involved with GROW if the first meeting they attend is predominately female. For females, the effect is strongest for meetings that are more than 2:1 female to male. If the meeting is either predominately male or mixed, they are more likely to stay as members. Males, on the other hand, show a slightly different pattern. Males are most likely to stay in if the first meeting is predominately male and are most likely to drop out if the meeting is mostly female. Males' responses to mixed gender meetings is between these two extremes.

We do not have the data to know for sure what is going on here. However, given the strength of the finding and the fact that it was the only group characteristic that was related to attendance patterns, it is important to explore this further.

Psychologists, sociologists, and anthropologists have long noted that individuals (both women and men) in Western society evaluate male characteristics and activities more positively than female characteristics (see, e.g., Broverman, Vogel, Broverman, Clarkson, & Rosenkrantz, 1972; Miller, 1986; Reskin, 1988; Treiman & Terrell, 1975). It would not be surprising if potential GROW members exhibit these same biases. If this is true, then persons who first attend groups that are predominately female might evaluate these groups in a more negative light.

Group gatekeeping provides a different possible explanation. It is well-known that men and women form relationships differently and are different in group settings (Belenky, Clinchy, Goldberger, & Tarule, 1986). Men are often more instrumental, whereas women are more focused on relationship building and maintenance. Thus it is likely that the behavioral patterns in a self-help group meeting that is predominately female are different from those in a primarily male group. If that is the case, the group will be easier or harder to enter, depending on the gender mix. For example, a mostly female group might have a complicated relationship system that has been built up over time and hence might be more resistant to new members joining the existing community.

Again, it is important to note that given our data we cannot decide between either of these possible explanations. In fact, it could be that both of these mechanisms (or neither) are working at the same time. The effect of gender mix on participation undoubtedly will be an important topic for further research.

Policy and Practice Implications

As mentioned above, attracting and keeping members is an ongoing problem for many self-help groups. Understanding more about how persons come to groups, how they decide about whether to come back, and how groups act to welcome or bar new members is of obvious interest to those involved with self-help.

The specific relationships found in this study apply only to those GROW groups that we examined. However, there are a number of conclusions we can draw from this research that can apply generally to other self-help groups. We list these here in the form of a list of suggestions to group leaders, consultants, and members:

1. *First meetings are important.* It is clear that characteristics of the group and group members at the very first meeting can strongly affect later participation. Be aware of how your group appears to the newcomer and also how your group might react differently to different types of potential members.

2. *Be clear about who your group is for.* Every group is intended for certain types of people. Make sure that this is clear to potential members. If this is clear, the group will be able to focus more of its limited resources on persons who are appropriate members. A better person-group match from the outset will help to ensure higher participation rates.

3. *Find out more about why people are joining or not.* If you ask first-time attendees about their impressions, you might be able to discover important information about your group and the obstacles to becoming a group member. This can be done either informally by talking to the person or more formally with a questionnaire.

4. *Recognize the need for change.* If you discover a problem, it probably will not disappear until you do something about it. For example, GROW might decide to educate its members about how different gender mixes influence group meetings. Greater awareness could lead to fewer negative attendance effects.

As the self-help movement continues to grow and provide more settings for personal change in this country, more and more people will be making the decision to join a group. The more we know about self-help participation, the more we can help groups continue to provide a rich and rewarding experience for their members.

NOTES

1. If you were interested in not only the amount but the direction of the fit, you should calculate a directed fit statistic. Using the above example, a person with a higher than average SES would have a positive fit score, a person with a lower than average SES would have a negative fit score, and a person who is similar to the rest of the group would have a score around zero. The square root of the squared-Euclidean distance is a simple directed fit measure.

2. This median survival value is listed in the computer output. However, it can also be determined from the overall survival function graph (Figure 6.1). Draw a horizontal line from the 0.5 point on the Y-axis to the curve. At the point where the horizontal line hits the curve, draw a vertical line down from the curve to the X-axis. This point on the X-axis is the median survival time. In this case, the median value indicates that 50% of the GROW sample stopped attending within the first 2.8 months.

3. The moving average line is included in the graph simply to indicate the pattern of probability over time. It should not be interpreted as a fitted curve as in regression.

4. These are nonparametric statistics used to test the null hypothesis that there are no differences between subgroup survival functions based on single categorical predictors. The Mantel-Cox or simple log-rank test applies equal weights to every time period. The Breslow statistic, on the other hand, gives more weight to earlier observations, thus being less sensitive to later events (Norusis, 1992).

REFERENCES

Alcoholics Anonymous. (1990). *Alcoholics Anonymous 1989 membership survey.* New York: A. A. World Services.

Allison, P. D. (1984). *Event history analysis: Regression for longitudinal event data.* Beverly Hills, CA: Sage.

Antze, P. (1979). Role of ideologies in peer psychotherapy groups. In M. A. Lieberman & L. D. Borman (Eds.), *Self-help groups for coping with crisis: Origins, members, processes, and impact* (pp. 272-304). San Francisco: Jossey-Bass.

Bednar, R., & Kaul, T. (1978). Experiential group research: Current perspectives. In S. Garfield & A. Bergin (Eds.), *Handbook of psychotherapy and behavior change* (2nd ed., pp. 769-815). New York: John Wiley.

Belenky, M. F., Clinchy, B. M., Goldberger, N. R., & Tarule, J. M. (1986). *Women's ways of knowing.* New York: Basic Books.

Borkman, T. S. (1984). Mutual self-help groups: Strengthening the selectively unsupportive personal and community networks of their members. In A. Gartner & F. Riessman (Eds.), *The self-help revolution.* New York: Human Sciences Press.

Borman, L. D. (1976). Self-help and the professional. *Social Policy, 7,* 46-47.

Broverman, I. K., Vogel, S. R., Broverman, D., Clarkson, F. E., & Rosenkrantz, P. S. (1972). Sex-role stereotypes: A current appraisal. *Journal of Social Issues, 28,* 59-79.

Brown, K. P. (1989). *Patterns of individual psychotherapy utilization: A survival analysis of length of treatment.* Unpublished doctoral dissertation, Northwestern University.

Cox, D. R. (1972). Regression models and life tables. *Journal of the Royal Statistical Society, Series B, 34,* 187-202.

Garb, J. R., & Stunkard, A. (1974). Effectiveness of a self-help group in obesity control— Further assessment. *Archives of Internal Medicine, 134,* 716-726.

Gati, I. (1989). Person-environment fit research: Problems and prospects. *Journal of Vocational Behavior, 35,* 181-193.

Gidron, B., Chesler, M. A., & Chesney, B. K. (1991). Cross-cultural perspectives on self-help groups: Comparisons between participants and nonparticipants in Israel and the United States. *American Journal of Community Psychology, 19,* 667-682.

Gill, K., Nolimal, D., & Crowley, T. J. (1992). Antisocial personality disorder, HIV risk behavior and retention in methadone maintenance therapy. *Drug and Alcohol Dependence, 30,* 247-252.

Gower, J. C. (1985). Measures of similarity, dissimilarity, and distance. In S. Kotz & N. L. Johnson (Eds.), *Encyclopedia of statistical sciences* (Vol. 5, pp. 397-405). New York: John Wiley.

Gutfreund, J., Powell, T., & Luke, D. A. (1993). *Duration of participation in self-help, psychotherapy, and other problem-solving/self-improvement activities.* Unpublished manuscript.

Hermalin, J., Melendez, L., Kamarck, T., Klevans, F., Ballen, E., & Gordon, M. (1979). Enhancing primary prevention: The marriage of self-help groups and formal health care delivery systems. *Journal of Clinical Child Psychology, 8,* 125-129.

Humphreys, K., Mavis, B., & Stöfflemayr, B. (1991). Factors predicting attendance at self-help groups after substance abuse treatment: Preliminary findings. *Journal of Consulting and Clinical Psychology, 59,* 591-593.

Katz, A. H. (1981). Self-help and mutual aid: An emerging social movement? *Annual Review of Sociology, 7,* 129-155.

Katz, A. H. (1993). *Self-help in America: A social movement perspective.* New York: Twayne.

Killilea, M. (1976). Mutual help organizations: Interpretations in the literature. In G. Caplan & M. Killilea (Eds.), *Support systems and mutual help: Multidisciplinary explorations* (pp. 37-93). New York: Grune & Stratton.

Leerhsen, C., Lewis, S. D., Pomper, S., Davenport, L., & Nelson, M. (1990, February 5). Unite and conquer. *Newsweek,* pp. 50-55.

Levy, L. H. (1976). Self-help groups: Types and psychological processes. *Journal of Behavioral Science, 12,* 310-322.

Levy, L. H. (1978). Self-help groups viewed by mental health professionals: A survey and comments. *American Journal of Community Psychology, 6,* 305-313.

Levy, L. H., & Derby, J. F. (1992). Bereavement support groups: Who joins, who does not, and why. *American Journal of Community Psychology, 20,* 649-662.

Lipson, J. G. (1982). Effects of a support group on the emotional impact of cesarean childbirth. *Prevention in Human Services, 1,* 17-29.

Luke, D. A. (1993). Charting the process of change: A primer on survival analysis. *American Journal of Community Psychology, 21,* 203-246.

Luke, D. A., Rappaport, J., & Seidman, E. (1991). Setting phenotypes in a mutual help organization: Expanding behavior setting theory. *American Journal of Community Psychology, 19,* 147-167.

Luke, D. A., & Roberts, L. (1992, August). *A two-stage model of self-help group participation.* Paper presented at the annual meeting of the American Psychological Association, Washington, DC.

Madara, E. J. (1986). A comprehensive systems approach to promoting mutual aid self-help groups: The New Jersey Self-Help Clearinghouse Model. *Journal of Voluntary Action Research, 15,* 57-63.

Maton, K. I., Leventhal, G. S., Madara, E. J., & Julien, M. (1989). Factors affecting the birth and death of mutual-help groups: The role of national affiliation, professional involvement, and member focal problem. *American Journal of Community Psychology, 17,* 643-671.

McFadden, L. (1993). *Do birds of a feather flock together? The relationship between personal background characteristics and participation in a mutual help group.* Unpublished doctoral dissertation, University of Illinois at Urbana-Champaign.

Meissen, G. J., Gleason, D. F., & Embree, M. G. (1991). An assessment of the needs of mutual-help groups. *American Journal of Community Psychology, 19,* 427-442.

Miller, J. B. (1986). *Toward a new psychology of women* (2nd ed.). Boston: Beacon.

Moos, R. H. (1987). Person-environment congruence in work, school, and health care settings. *Journal of Vocational Behavior, 31,* 231-247.

Norusis, M. J. (1992). *SPSS for Windows: Advanced statistics, Release 5.* Chicago: SPSS.

Phillips, E. L. (1985). *Psychotherapy revised: New frontiers in research and practice.* Hillsdale, NJ: Lawrence Erlbaum.

Phillips, E. L. (1987). The ubiquitous decay curve: Service delivery similarities in psychotherapy, medicine, and addiction. *Professional Psychology: Research and Practice, 18*(6), 650-652.

Powell, T. J. (1987). *Self-help organizations and professional practice.* Silver Spring, MD: National Association of Social Workers.

Powell, T. J. (1992, August). *Predictors of participation in self-help groups.* Paper presented at the annual meeting of the American Psychological Association, Washington, DC.

Rapkin, B., & Luke, D. A. (1993). Cluster analysis in community research: Epistemology and practice. *American Journal of Community Psychology, 21,* 247-277.

Rappaport, J. (1977). *Community psychology: Values, research, and action.* New York: Holt, Rinehart & Winston.

Rappaport, J., Seidman, E., Toro, P. A., McFadden, L. S., Reischl, T. M., Roberts, L. J., Salem, D. A., Stein, C. H., & Zimmerman, M. A. (1985). Finishing the unfinished business: Collaborative research with a mutual help organization. *Social Policy, 16,* 12-24.

Reskin, B. A. (1988). Bringing the men back in: Sex differentiation and the devaluation of women's work. *Gender & Society, 2,* 58-81.

Roberts, L. J., Luke, D. A., Rappaport, J., Seidman, E., Toro, P., & Reischl, T. M. (1991). Charting uncharted terrain: A behavioral observation system for mutual help groups. *American Journal of Community Psychology, 19,* 715-737.

Singer, J. D., & Willett, J. B. (1991). Modeling the days of our lives: Using survival analysis when designing and analyzing longitudinal studies of duration and the timing of events. *Psychological Bulletin, 110,* 268-290.

Skinner, H. A. (1978). Differentiating the contribution of elevation, scatter and shape in profile similarity. *Educational and Psychological Measurement, 38,* 297-308.

Spokane, A. R. (1985). A review of research on person-environment congruence in Holland's theory of careers. *Journal of Vocational Behavior, 26,* 306-343.

Stewart, M. J. (1990). Expanding theoretical conceptualizations of self-help groups. *Social Science and Medicine, 31,* 1057-1066.

Treiman, D. J., & Terrell, K. (1975). Sex and the process of status attainment: A comparison of working women and men. *American Sociological Review, 40,* 174-200.

7. Narrative Studies, Personal Stories, and Identity Transformation in the Mutual-Help Context

JULIAN RAPPAPORT

Intrinsic to self-help research are a number of contradictions that have been troublesome for its advocates. Demands from the mutual-help community for collaborative and participant-based research is only the political side of the contradiction. As a practical matter, smart, sensitive, and politically astute researchers are increasingly able to enlist members of the self-help community and the consumer movement into the service of traditional research aims.[1] These alliances can be mutually beneficial, especially if the work provides the self-help community with needed resources. But at a deeper level, to understand the phenomenon of mutual help, theories and methods consistent with the experiences of the members are required (Department of Health and Human Services, 1988).

The narrative approach to understanding cognition, personality development, culture, and community is one that is emerging from several disciplines as a way to understand human experience, memory, and personal identity from the point of view of a person in social context (e.g., Coles, 1989; Gergen & Gergen, 1988; Howard, 1991; McAdams, 1993; Ross, 1989; Sarbin, 1986). In its simplest form, the narrative approach means understanding life to be experienced as a constructed story. The stories that people tell and are told are powerful forms of communication to both others and one's self. Stories order experience, give coherence and meaning to events and provide a sense of history and of the future. Some scholars go so far as to regard narrative as a root metaphor for psychology (Sarbin, 1986). Others see it as a means of socialization (Miller & Moore, 1989) or identity development (McAdams, 1993), as basic to human cognition and learning (Schank, 1990), or as a method for understanding individual language and lives (Labov, 1982; Mischler, 1986). For those interested in understanding communities, the narrative itself is sometimes viewed as the community (Bruner & Gofrain, 1984; Goldberg, 1982, 1987; Hauerwas, 1983).

For our present purposes, although more precise definitions have been suggested and debated (Brewer & Lichtenstein, 1982; Labov, 1982; LeGuin, 1990, pp. 37-45; Schank, 1990; Stein, 1982), it is sufficient to think of narratives and stories as interchangeable terms, used here in exactly the same sense that the terms are used in ordinary conversation. However, one useful convention is to refer to narratives when speaking at a community level of analysis and to stories when referring to the individual level of analysis— thus for convenience one can speak of community narratives and personal stories. Both can be subject to similar narrative analysis, and such analysis is a useful way to understand individual lives within their community contexts.

In whatever way one uses the terms, for those interested in the relationship between individual lives and the social processes of communities, narrative studies provide a powerful analytic and methodological tool. The thesis of this chapter is that narrative studies can also provide a conceptual framework and theory-driven methodology appropriate to the study of mutual help. Consistent with the mutual-help ethos, the narrative approach highlights the nature and functions of the community, the power of its narrative, and how it changes (and is changed by) the members' personal life stories. One advantage of this approach is that it makes the study of mutual-help organizations a specific example of the processes that can be shown to occur in the lives of people more generally. This way of understanding self-help, wherein membership in a mutual-help organization is viewed as joining and living in a community, is contrasted here with the more common view of self-help as an alternative treatment for a medical or psychiatric disorder. In addition to its usefulness for understanding, conceptualizing mutual-help organizations as narrative communities is one way for researchers to avoid the professional centrism that necessarily emerges from conceptualizing mutual-help communities as alternative treatments.

SELF-HELP AS AN ALTERNATIVE TREATMENT

A common way to think about mutual-help organizations is as alternative treatments for people with problems in living. Although this is not an unreasonable way to construe them, it is largely the result of mental health professionals' and social scientists' application of an implicit medical or human services model, defined more by the purposes of the professional community than by the contexts in which people live their lives. I am not simply referring here to notions of etiology or conceptions of problems in living as illness, disease, or social dysfunction. I am also concerned with that aspect of the medical-social service model that has to do with "style of delivery" (Rappaport & Chinsky, 1974) and its way of regarding people as recipients of services. As Ernest Kurtz (1992) recently put it, "Examining [groups such as] Alcoholics Anonymous under the heading of 'treatment' is like studying the formation pattern of bears flying South for the winter" (p. 397). Both bears and Canadian geese change their winter habits. Both Alcoholics Anonymous (AA) and alcohol treatment can benefit the lives of alcoholics, but to conclude that they are in the same category makes as much sense as concluding that the bears are the same as the geese.

Taken to an extreme, the recipient-of-services model tends to lead researchers to go so far as to suggest that we must, or lament that we cannot, randomly assign people to self-help groups, despite the fact that to do so would change the phenomenon we want to understand (Levy, in press). In the human services way of understanding the world, people are thought of as service seekers, and the alternatives available to them are viewed as treatments or programs. People are seen to join a program, benefit or not, and drop out or continue, in ways analogous to joining and dropping out of a medical or psychological treatment program. This approach is quite useful for mental health professionals, who can apply many of the research methods and ideas with which we are already familiar to what is now seen as simply a different form of treatment. Indeed, collaboration between mental health professionals and mutual-help organizations is probably facilitated by this way of thinking. Certainly, it can be an attractive way to garner the support of funding agencies that are used to thinking about illness and disease, treatments, and cures. However, as many who are a part of the self-help movement are aware, there is danger that the movement itself will be taken over by well-meaning professionals.

Being "taken over" has several meanings, ranging from the self-help community becoming dependent on professionals for resources through the powerful imposition of ways of thinking that are derived more from professional training than from experiential knowledge (Borkman, 1990). Professional training often disregards, despite the best of intentions, the self-help ethos (Riessman, 1985). Ironically, the self-help ethos often includes members' rejection of a view of themselves as recipients of services—an ascribed status granted to them by professionals. Their rejection of that status expresses itself in various ways that could involve the adoption of a new ideology and a transformation of identity, or sense of self, according to a narrative provided by the organization (Antze, 1976; Cain, 1991; Kennedy, 1991; Levine, 1988). Before further discussing some of the ways in which this transformation can be understood through narrative analysis, I present a summary of some of my own previous work as an example of the limitations in an alternative services model.

THE GROW STUDY:
ALTERNATIVE TREATMENT OR A NEW STORY?

I want to illustrate some of the limits of the alternative services model in part by reflecting on my own work with numerous colleagues studying one mutual-help organization for the mentally ill over a long period of time (see Rappaport et al., 1985, for the details of the research design and a description of the organization, GROW, Inc.). In various ways we have applied, not without benefit, a services model to this organization for people who have a lengthy history of seeking mental health services. We have found a number of interesting things, and I would like to review just a few of them that resulted from construing the organization as a provider of services and then trying to understand what we had found.

A logical question for a treatment agency is does it have an impact on its clients, based on their rate of attendance? Although one could not, in the absence of random assignment to control or comparison groups (an approach that violates the ethos of mutual help), demonstrate the effectiveness of the program as an alternative to other treatments, it would at least be logically consistent with an effective program to demonstrate that rate of attendance is related to improved functioning. One can also argue that many of the members of this organization have already had a long history with traditional treatments that have failed, and in a sense they constitute their own control group. Finally, it can be argued that because the members of this organization have not found, according to their own report, significant assistance from the professional services community, any assistance they find in a mutual-help organization extends the range of services to some people who would otherwise not be reached.

In one study, based on Douglas Luke's (1989) dissertation, we followed 115 GROW members over an average of 10 months. The multiple measures we used were classified into three groups: psychological, interpersonal, and community adjustment. A cluster analysis found that members could be classified into three types on the basis of their pattern of change on the measured categories: positive (improved), negative (got worse), or stable. Although the results are a bit more complicated, one way to characterize them is to note that dropouts were more likely to be in the negative change cluster. We also found that committed members, as opposed to those who attended less than once per month, were more likely to be classified as positive changers on at least one of the three measurement domains (78% vs. 50%). Committed GROW members were also found to be more likely to fall into the positive change cluster when the criterion was change on at least two of the domains.

It will be obvious to anyone with a passing knowledge of research design that Luke's (1989) findings might very well be due to a self-selection factor—those who liked what they were experiencing stayed in the organization and those who did not benefit dropped out. What we can say is that those who stayed and those who left did not look different at the outset and that those who stayed and showed improvement had the same history of dissatisfaction with professional services as did those who left. What we do not know from this work is why those who stayed and benefited found this mutual-help community to be one they decided to join. To anticipate a question that emerged later, one might ask, "Why did some people adopt the GROW story as their own?"

A second study was restricted to those GROW members who had a history of state hospitalization during the 32 months just prior to joining GROW (see Kennedy, 1989, for study details). They were individually matched (by use of a computer program blind to their ultimate positive or negative outcomes) with a sample of nonmembers on hospitalization history and demographics, including race, sex, age, marital status, total number of days in hospital prior to joining GROW, number of previous hospitalizations, community tenure, discharge region, diagnosis, legal status, and religion. Although the two groups had spent a similar number of days in the hospital during the 32 months prior to the date the member joined GROW (an average of 174 days vs. 179 days), during the next 32 months GROW members spent significantly less time in the hospital than did their nonmember counterparts (49 days vs. 123 days).

In addition to these outcome findings, we have carefully observed how the organization expanded in membership throughout the state (Zimmerman et al., 1991) and the nature of the verbal behavior during group meetings (Roberts et al., 1991). These studies have told us quite a bit about group variance and about behavior in the groups. They have also enabled us to characterize the GROW approach as creating new groups that provide their members with a niche, or a role. We have characterized our findings as demonstrating that GROW expands by the creation of underpersoned settings—that is, settings where there are more roles than people. Thus many members who typically have experienced most of their life as a receiver of help are now placed in the position of also being a giver of help. Again, to anticipate later thoughts, at the time we conducted this work we did not ask what effect joining a community in which the narrative includes stories about how members are both givers and receivers of help might affect the personal stories that people tell, nor did we inquire as to how those stories create a new identity.

LISTENING TO STORIES AS AN
ANTIDOTE TO PROFESSIONAL CENTRISM

Narrative analysis provides an alternative to the study of mutual help in a treatment and services paradigm. Rather than view people as help seekers obtaining services from an agency, albeit an agency staffed by nonprofessionals or peers, this way of conceptualizing self-help removes it from implicit or explicit comparison to treatment. By its very nature, applying narrative analysis is an antidote to professional hegemony. It forces us to ask questions, such as "Who has the right to speak for this person?" It requires us to learn about both the structure and content of the stories that people tell about their own lives and of the lessons they learn from their communities of membership. It highlights (albeit imperfectly) their views of themselves rather than emphasizing our views of them. Narrative studies is a theoretical framework that can be applied at multiple levels of analysis, that is, to understand the community as well as the individual. It can provide a link between individual identity development and cultural and community imperatives.

In addition to requiring us to listen more carefully to the voices of the members themselves, researching mutual help as "the stories people tell" has several advantages, not the least of which is to free the idea of mutual help from the stigmatizing implication that those who are involved in such organizations are more needy or less competent than those who are "on their own" or that the implicit standard for comparison is professional treatment. For example, in a recent study of over 800 professionals throughout the State of Illinois, my colleagues and I (Salzer, McFadden, & Rappaport, in press) found that, although professionals tended to see self-help groups in a positive light (well above the neutral point on a 7-point scale), regardless of their discipline and regardless of where they worked (in a community mental health center, a general hospital, or a state hospital), they always viewed professional groups as more helpful than self-help groups. We termed this attitude *professional centrism.* So long as mutual-help organizations are viewed as service agencies they will necessarily be considered second-rate because the standard for comparison will be limited to treatment outcome data as judged by the professional community rather than belonging and social identity as judged by the members themselves.

Despite a variety of rather interesting findings in our GROW project, we did not understand, from the point of view of the members, very much about how the organization worked its way into members' lives. When one has spent a dozen or so years talking with people in an organization and then looks at the reported findings expressed in the form of outcome variables and discrete behaviors, there is a very obvious gap in understanding. Our formal data simply did not capture the experience of the members. Despite our efforts to examine the processes of group behavior in some detail—including the members' perceptions of social climate (Toro, Rappaport, & Seidman, 1987) and of what they think is important about being in the groups (Roberts, 1987), their reports on questionnaires and our behavioral observations are quite distant from the ways in which the members experienced changes in themselves over time. It is only from conversations with individual members over a long period of time that I became convinced that many people have experienced a change in their social identity that is simply not captured well by the sort of data we have obtained. What we have lacked is a theory-driven methodology appropriate to the phenomena. One such theory is found in narrative studies.

A different, and less professional-centric, way to understand how the mutual-help organization shapes the identities of its members is to try to understand the organization's narrative about itself (the community narrative) and how that influences the personal life stories of the members. What is it about the GROW narrative that becomes incorporated into the personal life stories of those members who have decided to join the GROW community? How does it happen?

INFORMAL OBSERVATION OF COMMUNITY
NARRATIVES AND PERSONAL STORIES

My interest in narratives began with the serendipitous observation that the membership of the GROW organization—one that encourages cooperation with, but independence from, the professional caregiving network—often led people who had a history of serious and diagnosable psychological disturbance to tell very different stories about themselves than did their peers who continued to be treated under the care of professionals. In listening to personal stories, although each had its own life-course details, there was a striking cross-person similarity. What accounts for that similarity, I believe, is the well-developed narrative (identifiable in both written and verbal behavior) that defines the community. This narrative is very different from the one that defines the professional care community.

I have spent some 25 years doing research and talking to people with serious problems of the sort that get people labeled "chronic patients" (see Rappaport, Chinsky, & Cowen, 1971). But I have never before encountered the kind of personal conversion stories that many of the GROW members tell—stories in which one can hear echoed the formal ideas of the GROW organization. If one listens to the personal life stories told by many GROW members (often expressed in "personal testimonies" during formal meetings or in individual interviews), one hears people with a history of mental hospitalization who have come to see themselves as a part of what the community narrative refers to as a "caring and sharing" community of givers as well as receivers, with hope, and with a sense of their own capacity for positive change. People often describe their life in terms that characterize it as "before and after" GROW. Their personal stories are often consistent with the kinds of themes we had found in a content analysis of the organization's written material, which members use for discussion, study, and reflection (McFadden, Seidman, & Rappaport, 1992). In short, the personal stories of GROW members tend to reflect its community narrative. These personal stories are very different from those I had heard for so long from other patients under professional care for their mental illness. Typical professional patient stories often revolve around learning to see one's self as sick and dependent on medication to control behavior. Professional patients often hope for independent living, despite its loneliness, and see themselves as dependent recipients of services who have little to offer others.

While conducting the self-help research project I also observed in these organizations the sorts of functions that formal religious organizations serve for their members. Although I did not hypothesize, or even consider, such matters initially, I began to notice a similarity between how certain church members and mutual-help group members changed over time. This led to exploration, with a local religious leader, of the kinds of stories that people tell about their own life and the congruence between those stories and the church's communal narrative (Rappaport & Simkins, 1991). Both the patients and the church members tended to incorporate into their own life stories elements of their respective community narrative. It was at this point that I began to think that the phenomenon observed in two settings where I happened to be working might in fact be more general and that each of us might construct our personal life stories under considerable influence from the community narratives that operate in the settings to which we belong.

MUTUAL-HELP ORGANIZATIONS AS NORMATIVE NARRATIVE COMMUNITIES

The narrative framework views mutual-help organizations as one of a number of potential communities of membership available to people. An important characteristic of a community is that it has a narrative about itself and about its individual members. It often has a narrative about individual change and stability (Ross, 1989). In this sense, the mutual-help organization is a normative structure in social experience—not unlike families, religious organizations, political parties, labor unions, professional organizations, or other voluntary associations. The members are not clients getting services and therefore somehow different from the rest of us; rather, they are people living lives. Professional treatment is not necessarily the appropriate comparison group if one wants to understand such experiences.

Everyone has problems in living and everyone uses, for well or for ill, the available mediating structures for figuring out (constructing) answers to such questions as "Who am I?" "To whom am I connected?" and "Who can I hope to become?" By this reasoning, although they each have their own content domain, the same processes that operate in other community organizations—so as to facilitate or hinder identity development and transformation—also operate in mutual-help organizations. Such organizations are simply a special case of a more general phenomenon: The experience of identity formation and change takes place within a social context that contains community narratives that can be read, observed, communicated, or otherwise understood. These organizations might be better understood as voluntary communities rather than as social service agencies. When membership leads to significant change in a person's identity and behavior, it could be understood as a change in community of membership and lifestyle rather than as a "treatment outcome."

One advantage of this normalizing view is that it enables us to learn from a wide variety of research on social cognition, institutional processes, and individual identity development (Baumeister, Stillwell, & Wotman, 1990; Colby, 1982; Markus & Nurius, 1986; McAdams, 1993; Mumbry, 1987; Schank, 1990). It suggests that the same processes of identity construction that take place in schools, families, neighborhoods, churches, professional associations, clubs, or other voluntary organizations take place in mutual-help organizations. It does not set apart those who join mutual-help organizations as especially different. They are best understood as similar to other people who also continue to develop and change their individual identities in the context of social and community life throughout the life span.

The fact that people who join mutual-help organizations are often looking for an alternative or an addition to professional services or for a community of people with similar life experiences is no more or less important than someone else looking for a different church, transferring to a new college, seeking more schooling or employment training, joining a social or athletic club, or moving to a new neighborhood. These are *community joining acts* that have consequences for identity development and change (some of which will be self-imposed and some of which will be imposed by others) through the normal processes of social communication by means of shared narratives.

In this view, people who elect to join mutual-help organizations are not necessarily deciding to obtain a treatment, so much as making a decision that helps them to answer identity questions of the form "Who am I?" Indeed, people who join such organizations might be rejecting the paradigms of professional treatment as a way of life and the identity it has offered them as recipients of services. Similarly, those who leave an organization might not be dropouts as much as people who have decided that the organizational story does not match their own current or desired life story. That does not necessarily mean that they would not like to obtain services, but it often means that they are trying to figure out how to get what they need in a way that provides a more dignified sense of identity. This point of view suggests that the way that a mutual-help organization provides members with an identity is through the narrative it tells about the community of membership, about how members change, and that this narrative serves as a basis for change in one's personal identity story.

The general idea that personal stories are changed through experiencing a new communal narrative was anticipated by Antze (1976) and can be found in his notion of the mutual-help organization providing an "ideology." William James's (1902/1929) discussions of religious conversion are also pertinent, as is the work of modern anthropologists such as Cain (1991). But there is now a field of narrative studies that can serve as a basis for development of a much more detailed theory for exploring how the process of change in identity takes place in community contexts. One advantage of such theories is that they make the study of mutual-help organizations a specific example of processes that can be shown to occur for people in general. This means that the relatively small number of self-help researchers can benefit from work by many other researchers and that our work can contribute to understanding human functioning more generally.

NARRATIVE STUDIES:
COMMUNITY NARRATIVES AND PERSONAL STORIES

Although there is now a burgeoning area of thought that falls within the rubric of narrative studies, the notion that the community narrative and the personal life story are embedded in a mutual influence process requires further development. A community narrative is a story repeatedly told among many members of a setting. It can be told directly, as in face-to-face contact, or indirectly by means of written material, rituals, implicit expectations, shared events, and nonverbal behaviors. A setting can be a family, a neighborhood, or a social, religious, or business organization. One might also be a member of a psychological community (i.e., homeless persons or veterans of particular wars) or a member of the women's movement or of a professional community. One way to know if a setting is a community is to look for the presence or absence of shared stories. Sometimes, the community story will be written. In the modern world, people belong to many settings. How one's personal story is constructed and transformed by the multiple settings to which one belongs is an overarching question in understanding identity development in social context (Gergen, 1991).

Community narratives tend to be heavily invested with implicit as well as explicit meaning. A personal story is more private and more idiosyncratic. It serves the purposes of individual identity development, maintenance, and change. But it is also reasonable to expect that these levels of analysis are not entirely independent. Understanding the link between these two kinds of stories and the role they play in psychological, social, and behavioral change in the context of formal organizations is of concern to many disciplines. Understanding the basic mechanisms of personal and group identity in these contexts has important implications for the practical world of organizational management and development, as work, church, educational, and family environments play an important part in personal identity for most people.

This sort of work is pursued by scholars and scientists from many disciplines. The "narrative project" is one that both challenges and unites anthropology, psychology, sociology, literature and rhetorical studies, history, linguistics, and religious studies. By narrative studies I am referring to a broad range of ideas and methods that have developed around textual analysis of written or spoken language in ritual and everyday behavior along with general propositions, such as narrative is a "root metaphor" for human experience (Sarbin, 1986), people "live by" stories (McAdams, 1993), and "a community is its story" (Hauerwas, 1983). In a more applied context it has been argued that stories are a particularly powerful tool for teaching and moral development (Vitz, 1990) and that understanding clients' "narrative schemas" might be useful for psychotherapists (Howard, 1991) who are concerned with problems such as how to understand and help change the identity or sense of self of their clients (Russell & Van Den Broek, 1992). In most of this research, somewhat predictable by the discipline of the investigator, there is a tendency to emphasize either the cultural messages in the narratives of a community—without attention to individual differences among the members—or to emphasize the individual members' personal life stories without much attention to the common community narrative in which the person develops her or his own personal story. In few cases is any attention paid to how the community narrative becomes incorporated into the personal lives of individual people (an exception is the work of some developmental psychologists with children, e.g., Miller & Moore, 1989; Nelson, 1993).

Narrative studies provides a theoretical framework that can account for a variety of empirical facts and ways of thinking about self-help, with the advantage of not doing violence to the perspective of the members of such organizations or to the self-help ethos (Riessman, 1985) because it requires understanding the world from the point of view of the individual members and their community. We could be wrong—that is, as researchers we might misunderstand or misinterpret the people we are trying to understand, but the goal of such work is to understand what their stories mean to them. This research approach is similar to the one referred to by Denzin (1989) as the interpretive point of view.

The narrative project tends to be sensitive to the point of view of the people being studied. It also encourages a multiplicity of research methods. Stories have been proposed as "especially interesting prior experiences" basic to human memory and intelligence (Schank, 1990). The study of narratives ranges from very detailed textual analysis in linguistics (Labov, 1982) through very global conceptions of culture and myth by anthropologists (Bruner & Gofrain, 1984). It is often concerned with personality development and cognitive processes as well as with the contemporary uses of historical texts. Scholars and researchers, at whatever level of analysis, share the view that the study of narratives—their structure, function, and influence on our lives—is a powerful way to understand cognitive and social life, personality development and change (especially with respect to identity), and the power of community life.

NARRATIVE STRUCTURE, FUNCTION, AND CHANGE

Narratives (and stories) have certain structural features. These features include event sequences arranged in context over time. Thus they are different from abstract principles (rules) that tend to be acontextual and static. Narratives also serve certain functions: They communicate to members and others what the community is like, how it came to be that way, and (sometimes implicitly) what behavior is expected. Narratives are powerful devices for effective communication. Some scholars have suggested that the narrative is the defining characteristic of a community (Goldberg, 1982, 1987; Hauerwas, 1983).

Most psychologists who have studied narratives tend to be concerned with their structure, as in linguistic analysis, or with cognitive representation and memory. Sociologists and anthropologists tend to be more concerned with the functions of narratives and questions of meaning. It might be useful to link approaches around such questions as "How do people develop personal identity, and how do they change?" and "How does the mutual influence process of individuals in organizations operate in the realm of storytelling?" These sorts of questions apply to individual, organizational, and social change and have implications for psychological application to a wide range of contexts, including the special cases of people who seek assistance for problems in living and those who do so in the context of mutual help.

The view that mutual-help organizations can be understood as contexts for identity transformation is consistent with recent thinking about autobiographical memory. Although I am not now prepared to defend a particular model of the process, there are several general features of these sorts of theories and considerable empirical research that can be seen as consistent with the idea that self-help organizations can be viewed as a special class of communities in which an alternative identity is provided and that those who become embedded members do so by transforming their personal life stories so as to conform to the community narrative.

Nelson (1993), for example, in the context of children's development of autobiographical memory (personal stories), distinguishes between generic event memory, episodic memory, and autobiographical memory. Generic event memory is taken to be similar to what Schank and Abelson (1977) called scripts, that is, general outlines of common events, without specific details of time and place, similar in some respects to what is called semantic memory (Tulving, 1983). Episodic memory refers to specific times and places, although the exact times and places themselves need not be recalled. According to Nelson (1993), what matters is the sense that it happened at one particular time, as opposed to scriptlike memory that things of this sort happen "this way." More important for the present purposes is Nelson's argument that the development of autobiographical memory occurs in a social context and that this occurs through learning, most likely early in life, by talking about events with a caretaker, and by reinstatement (repeating the events). The more frequently an event is experienced the more it becomes scriptlike. But Nelson notes that this does not account for how single events become autobiographical, and she argues that the functional significance of autobiographical memory is sharing it with other people:

> Memories become valued in their own right—not because they predict the future and guide present action, but because they are shareable with others and thus serve a social solidarity function. . . . This is the social function of story-telling, history-making narrative activities, and ultimately all of our accumulated knowledge systems. . . . Once the autobiographical memory system is established it takes on personal as well as social value in defining the self. (pp. 12-13)

In other words, Nelson's model for the psychological and social origins of autobiographical memory is consistent with the view that personal stories are developed in a social context, that they serve social as well as personal functions, and suggests that a change in one's community of membership can be an important source of change in personal identity.

Schank (1990), a cognitive psychologist who studies artificial intelligence, has recently theorized that story-based knowledge expresses our points of view and philosophy of life and that it depends on telling. What we tell, he suggests, indicates our making of decisions about what to remember and that "listeners reveal, usually implicitly, which stories they want to hear" (p. 136). In his view, with respect to memory, the storytelling process requires one to make decisions about which episodes to relate and which to ignore. He argues that once composed, stories remain and indeed become shorter and more compact as they are retold: "Memory tends to lose the original and keep the copy" (p. 138). He argues that telling stories that express a lack of ability to cope (i.e., answering questions about the problem or about what sort of help one requires) might actually reinforce the kinds of problems people have. He suggests that it would be better (including in psychotherapy) to encourage people to tell stories that put themselves in a positive light.

Schank (1990) also makes an interesting proposition concerning how to deal with negative experiences. His view is that once told they can be forgotten, partly because the details will tend to be lost after a story is composed. Certain events that are very important to the person—he calls them situation-defining episodes—are likely to remain in memory if not told to another person. This is partly because one tends to look for other events to match to it. He suggests that untold stories can be troubling in part because if not expressed they can remain less coherent. Stories told only to oneself do not benefit from the modification and coherence required for a listener. Because important stories that were never told might have retained childish explanations, if they are not talked about they can remain accessible and continue to provide bad explanations for present events. But Schank predicts that given the nature of what he calls "memory organization packages" a story once told must be retold many times to remain a "findable memory structure." He suggests, therefore, that to maximize the likelihood of forgetting, a bad story should be told once and never again:

> The sooner you tell a story, the sooner you can begin to forget it—by never telling it again. If you want to remember the story, on the other hand, keep telling it. Telling stories is fundamentally a memory reinforcing process. The more you tell the more you remember. The areas you dwell on when you talk are the areas your memory wants to, and does, reinforce. (p. 141)

RETURNING TO SELF-HELP RESEARCH
WITH A NARRATIVE PERSPECTIVE

These notions of memory and storytelling explicated earlier in a theoretical context seem to have been acquired, albeit in less abstract terms, by many of the people I encountered in the GROW organization. In the course of our research analyzing group conversations, we found that when members were asked to rate how good (defined by an evaluation factor on a set of ratings) a particular meeting was, they tended to find those meetings in which there was a great deal of negative talk and a relatively large amount of personal questioning (defined by independent observations of verbal behavior) to be significant negative predictors of meeting quality. Clinical psychology graduate student observers, asked to rate the quality of a group meeting, however, gave significantly better ratings to meetings with more personal questions—exactly the opposite of the members themselves. When I presented this data to the GROW organization group leaders they were delighted. In a research feedback meeting with me they expressed, not without enthusiasm, that they were tired of being asked by doctors to tell bad stories about themselves and that they now saw GROW as doing the best for people when new stories about dealing with today's practical tasks of living were being told.

Mellen Kennedy is conducting a dissertation on this topic. She is interviewing members of GROW in an effort to understand more directly how they undergo the ideological transformation that she hypothesizes is a major factor in the organization's success. This kind of thinking seems consistent with the work of others who have more directly investigated stories in the mutual-help context. For example, Cain (1991) found that answers to the question "Who am I?" (Kuhn & McPartland, 1954), in which the respondent has 20 opportunities to answer the question, were more related to what she called the "AA identity" among members who had most closely adopted the AA story as a model for their own personal life story. In her view, "the AA story provides a general framework, of which the individual stories are specific examples" (Cain, 1991, p. 227). Similarly, Humphreys (1992) has identified five types of AA stories and demonstrated through interviews and textual analysis their multiple functions. He describes the "drunk-a-log" as a particularly important story that, among other things, transmits AA ideology into personal identity. Over time the drunk-a-logs are constructed so as to become more similar to those reported in the AA literature (Cain, 1991).

Many of the ideas presented here are the result of an ongoing seminar-research group convened at the University of Illinois. Our project, broadly conceived, is to consider how what we refer to as community narratives become embedded in the personal stories of individual people. This work has many facets to it. On the one hand, we are willing to assume that the content of a particular community's shared narrative is likely to be adopted by the members of the community. On the other hand, this assumption demands empirical demonstration, and a number of studies in a variety of settings have been conducted to provide it (Rappaport, 1992). However, what we want to know is not simply *if* the community narrative is adopted as a part of community members' personal stories but *how* it is adopted.

Asking how leads us to be concerned with questions of social cognition and social communication. That is, how does the external social world become a part of one's internal world? How do individuals come to understand themselves in the context of their communities of membership? Or, conversely, how does the community come to understand itself in relation to its members? We ask these questions with particular attention to the problem of identity. More precisely, how do the communal narratives available to any given individual become a part of his or her personal identity? Which narrative becomes the vehicle for transformation? Why does a particular narrative persuade some people and not others at a given time?

These are not new questions. They could be framed in terms of traditional research on socialization processes, but today, such questions are asked in a postmodern environment. It is now widely believed that personal reality is constructed (and therefore can be reconstructed throughout the life span) and that there is an iterative process between the internal and external. The way that we have begun to study this is to conduct research in which we spend time trying to explicate the details of the community narrative. This can be accomplished in a variety of ways, including extended observation of meetings, conducting focus groups, and detailed reading of available texts. It requires thick descriptions of organizational processes as well as detailed interviews with community members (e.g., Denzin, 1989; Lincoln & Guba, 1985; McAdams, 1990; Mischler, 1986) to explicate their individual life stories. It is in the search for relationships across these levels of analysis that the experience of participation in a mutual-help community can be explicated in ways that more closely approximate lived experience.

Opportunities for choice and change in identity are more available (see, e.g., Gergen, 1991). In such an environment, the narrative viewpoint is particularly appealing for several reasons.

1. Given acknowledgment of life-span opportunities for redefinition of self (and others), understanding what has been thought of as socialization requires a mechanism that can account for the subjective experiences of both stability and change (see, e.g., Ross, 1989). Asking people to tell their life stories provides a vehicle for the sharing of personal constructions in a way that is intuitively sensible to most people (see Coles, 1989). Almost everyone is able to describe, in some coherent story, who they are and how they have always been that way, yet are different than they used to be or will be at some future time (see Markus & Nurius, 1986, on possible selves). That is, everyone knows what a personal story is.

2. It is no accident that personal testimonies in both religious and self-help contexts have had such a powerful effect on people. Nor is it an accident that good advertising and journalism—the kind that attract readership—are often woven around particular stories of lives or that stories are often thought to be entertaining (Brewer & Lichtenstein, 1982). There are many other examples, all of which suggest that most people (including those who are the subjects of our research) think that telling stories about themselves and their communities of membership makes sense and is persuasive.

3. Narratives provide us with a vehicle, or a focal point, for examination of the nature and result of active constructivist processes. Narratives are assumed to be dynamic rather than stable. They are not defined by their text alone but must include their context. That is, every community narrative will be told in some context that will be a part of its meaning. Similarly, personal stories are told in particular contexts to make particular points to others or to one's self. They are acts of communication and self-definition.

4. Narratives are continuously constructed, and the process of storytelling is an active one from the viewpoint of both the teller and the listener.

5. The processes mirror themselves at different levels of analysis—thus allowing direct cross-level comparisons between individuals and larger units of analysis. Such processes lend themselves to cross-disciplinary study that draws from the understanding of many different methods and viewpoints—a distinct advantage at a time when all the major canons of logical positivism as the single acceptable philosophy of science and method are in serious retreat (Manicas, 1987, pp. 243-244).

6. It is rare to find a phenomenon of interest that so clearly cuts across the social and behavioral sciences and humanities. Although pursued by the various disciplines as a means to analysis and understanding per se, narrative studies also has profound implications for the world of action, including

practice in clinical and community psychology, applied social psychology, social work, psychiatry, and pastoral and other forms of counseling (see, e.g., Howard, 1991). Although this approach provides an interesting alternative theory for the professional practice of helping (Russell & Van Den Broek, 1992), it is especially useful for the field of self- and mutual help. Indeed, narrative studies can provide a basis for the long sought systematic theoretical and methodological approach appropriate to the study of self- and mutual help.

NOTE

1. The term *self-help* is used most often as a self-descriptor by members of the groups and organizations about whom this chapter is written. *Mutual help* is the term preferred by many researchers. In this chapter, I use the terms interchangeably. I personally prefer the term mutual help as a more precise descriptor of the hypothesized processes of shared responsibility. Theoretically, group and organization members are both givers and receivers of help, usually meeting face-to-face and engaging in interpersonal discourse in the absence of a designated professional responsible for the group by virtue of educational credentials. Although from my own technical research and academic perspective, self-help seems to convey a connotation of individualism that may not communicate the ethos of equalitarian mutuality and shared roles suggested by the term mutual help, my experience has been that many leaders of the organizations with whom I have worked prefer to be called, usually for practical reasons of public communication, members of self-help groups. The designation self-help group is widely understood in the popular media to refer to such organizations. The term *consumer* has been adopted by many such groups who see their role as advocating for both better professional services and greater independence and control over services.

REFERENCES

Antze, G. W. (1976). The role of ideologies in peer psychotherapy organizations: Some theoretical considerations and the three case studies. *Journal of Applied Behavioral Science, 12*, 323-346.

Baumeister, R. F., Stillwell, A., & Wotman, S. R. (1990). Victim and perpetrator accounts of interpersonal conflict: Autobiographical narratives about anger. *Journal of Personality and Social Psychology, 59*, 994-1005.

Borkman, T. (1990). Experiential, professional and lay frames of reference. In T. J. Powell (Ed.), *Working with self-help*. Silver Spring, MD: NASW Press.

Brewer, W. F., & Lichtenstein, E. H. (1982). Stories are to entertain: A structural-affect theory of stories. *Journal of Pragmatics, 6*, 473-486.

Bruner, E. M., & Gofrain, P. (1984). Dialogic narration and the paradoxes of Masada. In E. M. Bruner (Ed.), *Text, play, and story: The construction and reconstruction of self and society* (pp. 56-116). Washington, DC: American Ethnological Society.

Cain, C. (1991). Personal stories: Identity acquisition and self-understanding in Alcoholics Anonymous. *Ethos, 19*(2), 210-251.

Colby, B. N. (1982). Notes on the transmission and evolution of stories. *Journal of Pragmatics, 6,* 463-472.

Coles, R. (1989). *The call of stories: Teaching and the moral imagination.* Boston: Houghton Mifflin.

Denzin, N. K. (1989). *The research act.* Englewood Cliffs, NJ: Prentice-Hall.

Department of Health and Human Services, Public Health Service. (1988). *Surgeon general's workshop on self-help and public health* (HRSA, Bureau of Maternal and Child Health and Resource Development Publication No. 224-250). Washington, DC: U.S. Government Printing Office.

Gergen, K. (1991). *The saturated self: Dilemmas of identity in contemporary life.* New York: Basic Books.

Gergen, K. J., & Gergen, M. M. (1988). Narrative and the self as relationship. *Advances in Experimental Social Psychology, 21,* 17-56.

Goldberg, M. (1982). *Theology and narrative.* Nashville, TN: Abbington Press.

Goldberg, M. (1987). *Jews and Christians: Getting our stories straight.* Nashville, TN: Abbington Press.

Hauerwas, S. (1983). *The peaceable kingdom.* Notre Dame, IN: University of Notre Dame Press.

Howard, G. S. (1991). Culture tales: A narrative approach to thinking, cross-cultural psychology, and psychotherapy. *American Psychologist, 46,* 187-197.

Humphreys, K. (1992, May). Twelve step stories and transformations in personal epistemology. In J. Rappaport (Chair), *Community narratives and personal stories,* Symposium conducted at the annual meeting of the Midwestern Psychological Association.

James, W. (1929). *The varieties of religious experience.* New York: Modern Library. (Original work published 1902)

Kennedy, M. (1989, June). *Psychiatric hospitalizations of Growers.* Paper presented at the Second Biennial Conference on Community Research and Action, East Lansing, MI.

Kennedy, M. (1991, June). *Ideology and transformation in mutual help groups.* Paper presented at the Third Biennial Conference on Community Research and Action, Tempe, AZ.

Kuhn, M., & McPartland, T. S. (1954). An empirical investigation of self-attitudes. *American Sociological Review, 19*(1), 68-76.

Kurtz, E. (1992). Commentary. *Annual Review of Addictions, Research and Treatment,* 397-400.

Labov, W. (1982). Speech actions and reactions in personal narrative. In D. Tannen (Ed.), *Analyzing discourse: Text and talk* (pp. 219-247). Washington, DC: Georgetown University Press.

LeGuin, U. (1990). *Dancing at the edge of the world: Thoughts on words, women, places.* New York: Harper & Row.

Levine, M. (1988). An analysis of mutual assistance. *American Journal of Community Psychology, 16*(2), 167-188.

Levy, L. (in press). Self-help groups. In J. Rappaport & E. Seidman (Eds.), *Handbook of community psychology.* New York: Plenum.

Lincoln, Y. S., & Guba, E. G. (1985). *Naturalistic inquiry.* Beverly Hills, CA: Sage.

Luke, D. A. (1989). *The measurement of change in a self-help context.* Unpublished doctoral dissertation, University of Illinois, Urbana-Champaign.

Manicas, P. T. (1987). *A history and philosophy of the social sciences.* New York: Blackwell.

Markus, H., & Nurius, P. (1986). Possible selves. *American Psychologist, 41,* 954-969.

McAdams, D. P. (1990). Unity and purpose in human lives: The emergence of identity as a life story. In A. I. Rabin, R. A. Zucker, R. A. Emmons, & S. Frank (Eds.), *Studying persons and lives* (pp. 148-200). New York: Springer.

McAdams, D. P. (1993). *The stories we live by.* New York: William Morrow.

McFadden, L., Seidman, E., & Rappaport, J. (1992). A comparison of espoused theories of self and mutual help: Implications for mental health professionals. *Professional Psychology: Research and Practice, 23* (6), 515-520.

Miller, P. J., & Moore, B. B. (1989). Narrative conjunctions of caregiver and child: A comparative perspective on socialization through stories. *Ethos, 17,* 428-445.

Mischler, E. G. (1986). *Research interviewing: Context and narrative.* Cambridge, MA: Harvard University Press.

Mumbry, D. K. (1987). The political function of narrative in organizations. *Communication Monographs, 54,* 113-125.

Nelson, K. (1993). The psychological and social origins of autobiographical memory. *Psychological Science, 4*(1), 7-14.

Rappaport, J. (Chair). (1992, May). *Community narratives and personal stories.* Symposium presented at the annual meeting of the Midwestern Psychological Association.

Rappaport, J., & Chinsky, J. M. (1974). Models for delivery of service: An historical and conceptual perspective. *Professional Psychology, 5,* 42-50.

Rappaport, J., Chinsky, J. M., & Cowen, E. L. (1971). *Innovations in helping chronic patients: College students in a mental institution.* New York: Academic Press.

Rappaport, J., Seidman, E., Toro, P. A., McFadden, L. S., Reischl, T. M., Roberts, L. J., Salem, D. A., Stein, C. H., & Zimmerman, M. A. (1985). Collaborative research with a mutual help organization. *Social Policy, 12,* 12-24.

Rappaport, J., & Simkins, R. (1991). Healing and empowering through community narrative. *Prevention in Human Services, 10,* 29-50.

Riessman, F. (1985). New dimensions in self-help. *Social Policy, 15,* 2-4.

Roberts, L. J. (1987, May). *The appeal of mutual help: The participants' perspective.* Paper presented at the First Biennial Conference on Community Research and Action, Columbia, SC.

Roberts, L. J., Luke, D. A., Rappaport, J., Seidman, E., Toro, P., & Reischl, T. (1991). Charting uncharted terrain: A behavioral observation system for mutual help groups. *American Journal of Community Psychology, 19,* 715-737.

Ross, J. (1989). Relation of implicit theories to the construction of personal histories. *Psychological Review, 96,* 341-357.

Russell, R. L., & Van Den Broek, P. (1992). Changing narrative schemas in psychotherapy. *Psychotherapy, 29*(3), 344-354.

Salzer, M. S., McFadden, L., & Rappaport, J. (in press). Professional views of self-help groups: A comparative and contextual analysis. *Administration and Policy in Mental Health.*

Sarbin, T. R. (1986). The narrative as a root metaphor for psychology. In T. R. Sarbin (Ed.), *Narrative psychology: The storied nature of human conduct* (pp. 3-21). New York: Praeger.

Schank, R. C. (1990). *Tell me a story: A new look at real and artificial memory.* New York: Scribner.

Schank, R. C., & Abelson, R. (1977). *Scripts, plans, goals, and understanding.* Hillsdale, NJ: Lawrence Erlbaum.

Stein, N. L. (1982). The definition of a story. *Journal of Pragmatics, 6,* 487-507.

Toro, P., Rappaport, J., & Seidman, E. (1987). The social climate of mutual help and psychotherapy groups. *Journal of Consulting and Clinical Psychology, 55,* 430-431.

Tulving, E. (1983). *Elements of episodic memory.* New York: Oxford University Press.

Vitz, P. C. (1990). The use of stories in moral development: New psychological reasons for an old educational method. *American Psychologist, 45,* 709-720.

Zimmerman, M. A., Reischl, T. M., Seidman, E., Rappaport, J., Toro, P. A., & Salem, D. A. (1991). Expansion strategies of a mutual help organization. *American Journal of Community Psychology, 19,* 251-278.

8. Moving Beyond the Individual Level of Analysis in Mutual-Help Group Research: An Ecological Paradigm

KENNETH I. MATON

Mutual-help groups represent a fast-growing and increasingly important component of the natural helping and human services sectors in American society (Eisenberg, 1993; Jacobs & Goodman, 1989; Levy, in press; Maton, Leventhal, Madara, & Julien, 1989; Powell, 1987). Individuals who share a common problem or life situation come together in a group context to receive help, provide help, and influence laypersons and professionals in the larger community. To date, most mutual-help group research has been limited to research questions conceptualized and examined at the individual level of analysis, focused primarily on levels and correlates of member well-being. Although important, this focus on the individual as the primary unit of analysis and psychological variables as the primary domain of interest is unduly narrow and limiting. A fuller understanding of the individual-group-community-based phenomena of mutual help necessarily depends on conceptual frameworks and methodological approaches beyond those currently dominant in the clinical research tradition.

AUTHOR'S NOTE: This is a revised version of a paper presented at the Center for Self-Help Research & Knowledge Dissemination National Institute of Mental Health Funded Research Workshop at the University of Michigan, Ann Arbor, February 16-18, 1993.

   An ecological paradigm for mutual-help research represents one promising conceptual framework useful for expanding the focus of mutual-help research. Central to the social ecological paradigm is the assumption that social phenomena occur within and are shaped by a complex, interrelated network of factors that span multiple variable domains and levels of analysis. Taking this assumption seriously, an ecologically based understanding of mutual-help group phenomena requires research that encompasses multiple variable domains and multiple levels of analysis. Furthermore, an ecological paradigm points to multiple and reciprocal pathways of influence among variables and suggests a number of concepts and hypotheses from social ecological theory likely useful in understanding social phenomena. Such concepts and hypotheses include the importance of niche and fit, recycling of resources, temporal succession, and variation due to local conditions (cf. Kelly, 1966; Levine & Perkins, 1987).

   As a guide to ecologically based research in the mutual-help group area, Table 8.1 presents a selected listing of variable domains important in mutual-help group research, specified at three different levels of analysis. The first column presents variables conceptualized at the individual (group member) level of analysis. Within the variable domains at this level, specific variables refer directly to facets of a member's experience in a mutual-help group or encompass aspects of the individual's life beyond the group context. For instance, concerning the group per se, members will vary in their personal acceptance of the group ideology (ideology variable domain), sense of belonging (climate), involvement in various role capacities (structure), levels of providing and receiving help (helping mechanisms), duration of involvement (temporal), group-based changes in psychological and physical health (well-being), and perceptions of benefit and group satisfaction (appraisals). Independent of the group, individuals will vary in severity and time since onset of their problem (focal problem), personal beliefs, such as religiosity (ideology), community involvements (linkages), levels of life stress (stressors), family and friend support (resources), age and ethnicity (demographic), and overall well-being. Many of these individual-level variables have been studied in mutual-help group research.

   The second column presents variables conceptualized at the group level of analysis. Groups will vary in type of focal problem, ideology, leadership capability, and cohesion (climate), role differentiation and order/organization (structure), the type and frequency of helping mechanisms, external networks, and affiliations (linkages), internal and external stressors, tangible and systemic supports (resources), member turnover and group age (temporal),

TABLE 8.1 Mutual-Help Group Research Variables, by Variable Domain and Level of Analysis

Variable Domain	Individual	Level of Analysis Group	Community
Focal problem	Duration, severity	Type, nature	Prevalence, incidence
Helping ideology	Personal belief system	Group ideology	Professional, lay beliefs
Climate	Personality, belonging	Leadership, cohesion	Professional, lay attitudes
Structure	Nature/number of role involvements	Role structure, order/organization	Community, human services
Helping mechanisms	Coping style, help provision, receipt	Types, frequency, effectiveness	Types, accessibility
Linkages	Social network, friendships	Affiliations, networks	Referral networks
Stressors	Life stress, group stress	Internal stress, systemic stress	Social problems
Resources	Psychological, social, tangible	Tangible, systemic supports	Human service budgets
Temporal	Length of time in group	Member turnover, age of group	Population stability
Demographic	Gender, age, SES, ethnicity	Composition, size	Composition, size
Well-being	Behavioral, emotional, physical	Viability, stability	Epidemiology, life quality
Subjective appraisal	Perceived benefit, satisfaction	Systemic appraisals	Appraisals of groups

composition and size (demographic), viability and stability over time (well-being), and opinions concerning various lay and professional groups (appraisals). Although these variables have sometimes been the focus of theoretical work in the mutual-help group area, with the notable exception of group-helping mechanisms, they have rarely been the focus of empirical research.

The third column of Table 8.1 presents variables conceptualized at the community level of analysis. Within the variable domains at this level, specific variables might refer directly to the mutual-help group sector or refer to facets of the community independent of the group context. Concerning community variables related to mutual-help groups per se, communities will vary in lay and professional ideologies concerning various group focal problems (ideology), lay and professional attitudes to mutual help (climate), human services linkages to groups (linkages), and appraisals of specific groups. More generally, communities will vary in the prevalence of a given focal problem, accessibility and availability of various helping services (helping mechanisms), social problems (stressors), human service budgets (resources), population stability (temporal), size and composition (demographic), and community epidemiology and quality of life (well-being).

Consistent with an ecological paradigm, the variables listed in Table 8.1 will potentially be interrelated in complex and diverse ways. For instance, variables might influence each other either directly or indirectly (i.e., through an intermediate third variable). An example of indirect linkage would be the climate of a group influencing the length of member involvement, which in turn would influence the extent of impact on well-being over time.

Two variables might simultaneously and independently influence a third variable, or one of the two variables might moderate the effect of the other (i.e., at one level of the moderating variable, the second and third variables are related in one fashion, but at another level of the moderating variable they are related in a different fashion or not at all). An example of a moderating influence would be if group leadership capability were strongly related to group viability in groups that are loosely structured (e.g., rap groups), but group leadership capability and group viability were less strongly linked in groups that are highly structured (e.g., Twelve Step groups).

Pathways of influence can be unidirectional or reciprocal. An example of reciprocal influence would be if professional attitudes in a community affect the type and extent of linkages that groups develop with professionals, which in turn affect the attitudes of professionals.

Variables might be related quantitatively (more of one leads to more of the other) or qualitatively (a certain type of one leads to a certain type of another). Finally, pathways of influence can be within levels of analysis (individual, group, or community) or across levels of analysis. In the latter case, variables at a higher level of analysis will generally be expected to have a major influence on those at lower levels. However, under certain conditions, variables at lower levels can be expected to have an impact on those at higher levels as well. For instance, group ideology about the cause or means of dealing with a problem could affect the community—that is, widespread adoption of the ideology by helping professionals and laypersons; this appears especially likely when the current ideology is not particularly effective (e.g., as in the case of traditional clinical understanding and treatment of alcoholism; cf. Denzin, 1987).

A vast array of interesting mutual-help research questions can be generated from the variables presented in Table 8.1. By way of demonstration, four areas of research consistent with an ecological paradigm are discussed below. Each was generated by drawing on multiple variable domains and levels of analysis contained in Table 8.1 and, to some extent, by bringing to bear social ecological concepts and hypotheses. A number of specific hypotheses or variable pathways are generated for each research area, as depicted in Figure 8.1. The various arrows drawn in Figure 8.1 and discussed below reflect the diversity of possible types of variable interrelationships noted above (direct vs. indirect, main effect vs. moderator effect, quantitative vs. qualitative, etc.). The hypotheses and pathways discussed are not presented to convince the reader of their correctness or of their greater importance than other paths between variables not drawn; this is a task for future empirical research. Rather, the primary purpose is to demonstrate concretely the types of important mutual-help research hypotheses that can be generated from an ecological paradigm, moving beyond sole focus on the individual level of analysis.

FOUR MULTILEVEL,
MULTIDOMAIN RESEARCH AREAS

Group-Level Variations and Member Well-Being

Section 1 of Figure 8.1 depicts some of the variable domains and pathways through which group characteristics could influence individual well-being. Consistent with a social ecological paradigm, the underlying assumption is that individual groups will differ greatly on important group characteristics—and member well-being will vary accordingly.

The arrows leading from the group-level variables in Figure 8.1, Section 1, portray a number of different types of influence among variables. On the one hand, key group characteristics are shown as directly influencing individual-level variables (i.e., member experiences) within the same variable domain (cross-level-within-domain). Thus individual groups with more viable or better developed ideology, climate, structure, and helping mechanisms are, respectively, expected to have greater influence on their members' adoption of group beliefs (ideology), sense of belonging (climate), involvement in meaningful roles (structure), and receipt of help and support (helping mechanisms). In this sense, the group is the medium through which effective individual experiences (depicted in the left-hand column of the figure) occur.

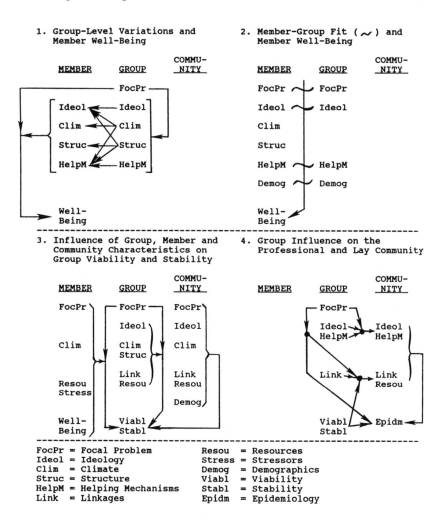

Figure 8.1. Four Mutual-Help Group Research Areas, by Variable Domain and Level of Analysis

In addition, cross-domain-cross-level paths of influence are depicted. Thus group climate and group structure are also shown as partial, *cross-domain* influences on individual beliefs (ideology) and receipt of help and support (helping mechanisms). Specifically, groups with more talented leadership and higher levels of cohesion (climate) and more viable role differentiation and order/organization (structure) will have members who are more open to and influenced by the group's ideology and helping mechanisms. This assumes that (a) a viable group climate and structure are preconditions for attracting, maintaining, and influencing members, and (b) independent of group ideology and helping mechanisms, each individual group will vary in the extent of its capability to develop viable climates and structures. In this sense, the group is not only the medium but also the context within which effective individual psychosocial change processes occur.

Additional types of variable interrelationships are reflected in the arrows leading from the group focal problem. On the one hand, the group focal problem is expected to directly affect other group characteristics. For instance, the likelihood and potential of a group to develop a high quality climate and a differentiated, viable structure will depend in part on the nature of the focal problem affecting members (e.g., physical health vs. addictions or life stress; see Maton, 1988). Group focal problem will also directly influence the nature of the group ideology (Antze, 1976) and the type of helping mechanisms (e.g., support vs. behavioral prescription) operative (Wollert, Levy, & Knight, 1982).

Furthermore, the group focal problem is expected to have moderating and direct effects on member well-being (combined arrow). The moderating influence stems from the assumption that, depending on the group focal problem, different types of member psychosocial experiences are expected to be important for well-being (e.g., in-group support vs. behavioral prescription vs. friendship development; Lieberman & Borman, 1979; Maton, 1989b). The direct influence stems from the assumption that different domains of well-being (e.g., depression vs. behavior change) will be affected in groups focused on different focal problems (Maton, 1989b).

Further delineation and theoretical justification of the pathways depicted in Figure 8.1, Section 1, are beyond the scope of the current chapter. It should be emphasized again, however, that the specific pathways offered are meant to be illustrative and suggestive, not exhaustive or definitive; other paths between group characteristics and member well-being could easily be generated. For current purposes, the important point is that groups will inevitably vary on important group characteristics linked to member well-being. Empirical research is needed to ascertain exactly which variations in group-helping ecology are linked to member well-being and how these patterns differ across theoretically important dimensions of the group focal problem.

Member-Group Fit and Member Well-Being

Person-environment fit theory asserts that individuals will be interested in, feel comfortable with, participate in, and benefit maximally in community settings or environments whose characteristics are well-matched to their own personal characteristics. Levine and Perkins (1987) applied the social ecological concept of person-environment fit to mutual-help groups. They noted that a process of *homogenization* inevitably occurs in groups, such that members with characteristics that fit are admitted to the group and others with different characteristics are effectively screened out. More generally, it can be expected that the greater the fit between an individual and a group, the greater the level of individual involvement in, and benefit from, the group.

Levine and Perkins illustrated the specificity of person-environment fit primarily with demographic examples, such as ethnicity, education, and social class. Empirical support for the importance of demographic fit is reported elsewhere in this volume by Humphreys and Woods, who found that the racial fit of the individual to the local community was an important predictor of involvement in substance abuse mutual-help groups: African Americans were more likely to attend substance abuse groups in primarily African-American neighborhoods than in primarily Caucasian areas, whereas the opposite was true for Caucasians.

In addition to demographics, a number of other variable domains also appear important for fit, including focal problem, ideology, and helping mechanism. These are included as part of the ecology of fit pathways depicted in Section 2 of Figure 8.1.

Concerning the focal problem, the more congruent the specifics of an individual's focal problem with those of other group members, the more likely group involvement and benefit will follow. For instance, in bereavement groups, the more closely the fit among members concerning the decedent's age (e.g., infant, teenager, adult) and the social context of death (e.g., accident or illness, homicide, suicide), the greater the fit. Similarly, individuals with belief systems compatible with those of a group's primary helping ideology, or coping styles compatible with the group's primary helping mechanisms, will more likely become involved and benefit from the group. For instance, individuals whose beliefs run counter to a major aspect of a group's helping ideology (e.g., concerning "a higher power," controlled drinking, importance of grieving) will likely not stay involved in that group very long or benefit extensively. Individuals who prefer to cope by sharing their feelings with others can be expected to fit to a greater extent in an emotional support-focused group than will individuals whose preferred coping style is keeping busy through involvement in instrumental tasks and activities.

The low levels of involvement of males, ethnic minorities, and lower socioeconomic-status (SES) individuals in most mutual-help groups might partly reflect a lack of fit due to personal belief systems and coping and partly a lack of comfort due to being "different" demographically. Interestingly, Alcoholics Anonymous (AA) is one mutual-help organization where males, lower-SES individuals, and minorities are more likely involved. Clearly, the specific types of individual and group characteristics relevant to fit in a given group will depend in part on the nature of the group's focal problem. This represents an additional and important focus of research in the ecology-of-fit research area.

Influence of Group, Member, and Community Characteristics on Group Viability and Stability

Based on a population-ecology-of-organizations model (cf. Maton et al., 1989), a mutual-help group can be viewed as an organizational entity that occupies a niche both in the community and in the health care and human services systems. The niche of the group is defined by the type of focal problem that members share and by the geographic and interorganizational environment in which the group is located. The internal characteristics of groups, the characteristics of members, and the external environments in which groups function are assumed to together influence the organizational life cycle, viability, stability over time, and population ecology (prevalence, rates of birth and death) of groups.

Section 3 of Figure 8.1 depicts some of the group, member, and community characteristics that likely influence group viability, stability (i.e., group disbanding), and population ecology. Concerning group-level characteristics, external group linkages represent one important factor important for group viability and population ecology. For instance, groups with greater systemic support, whether from affiliation with a national parent organization or from supportive local professionals, should be more viable. Thus a Compassionate Friends bereavement group might prove more viable, over time, than a local, unaffiliated, bereavement support group. Important domains of support available from such external linkages include established guidelines for group structure and activities, consultation, encouragement, and support for group leaders, and established recruitment channels and resources (e.g., via regional publicity, promotional materials, name recognition, and public legitimacy).

Group ideology, climate, structure, and helping mechanisms, consistent with the earlier discussion, can singularly and in combination also be expected to affect group viability. For instance, groups with low levels of role differentiation and in which leadership is limited to one key individual are more likely to disband over time (e.g., when the founding leader withdraws from group activity). In addition, the type of group linkages and characteristics linked to group population ecology, and their relative importance, will likely vary depending on the specific group focal problem. For instance, professional involvement may generally be facilitative of group viability for certain focal problems (e.g., child abusers, anorexia) and generally be disruptive of group viability for other focal problems (e.g., former psychiatric patients, victims of incest).

Concerning community characteristics, a number of different variable domains can be expected to influence group population ecology. Communities or regions with more positive lay and professional attitudes to mutual help (ideology) and more human service outreach activities (including self-help clearinghouses) directed at supporting groups can be expected to have more group births and fewer group deaths. The accessibility of professional help, level of neighborhood problems (e.g., personal safety at night), and community demographics (population age, SES, stability) will also likely be linked to group prevalence and birth and death rates, although the specific relationship will likely depend on the specific focal problem under consideration. For instance, addictions and other behavior control groups might be disproportionately present in urban, rural, and ethnic minority communities, whereas life stress groups might be disproportionately present in suburban and higher SES communities. Finally, there is likely to be a direct link between the types of focal and social problems prevalent in a given region (e.g., rates of mental illness, unemployment rates, rates of physical disability), and the relative prevalence of corresponding groups for that specific focal problem.

Concerning member characteristics, member personality, psychosocial resources, and well-being appear especially likely to have an impact on group viability. For instance, characteristics of the group leader(s), including severity of focal problem and personality, could influence longer-term viability through their impact on group climate, capability to weather group crises, and perceived legitimacy and access to community referral sources. A certain level of personal psychosocial resources and of well-being among a core group of members is similarly necessary to generate a group climate capable of attracting and maintaining members over the longer term. Generally speaking, the personal characteristics of members can be especially important in affecting the initial establishment and longer-term viability of groups that lack established helping ideologies, parent organization or agency staff backup, and preestablished legitimacy in the lay and professional community.

Group Influence on the Professional and Lay Community

Consistent with an ecological perspective, mutual-help groups can be expected to influence the larger community and human services systems of which they represent a constituent part. Three potential domains of community impact include lay and professional ideologies, human service referral networks, and community epidemiology. In each case, the extent and nature of influence may be expected to vary across focal problem types. Section 4 of Figure 8.1 depicts these pathways of group influence in the community.

Lay and Professional Ideologies. Tenets of mutual-help ideology concerning a focal problem, over time, are likely to influence both laypersons' and professionals' perspectives on the nature and means of coping with the problem. There are numerous routes of influence, including media, direct personal experience in a group, conferences and workshops, and professional training curricula. To date, perhaps most notable in this community domain has been the diffusion of AA ideology concerning the nature of alcoholism and the importance of reliance on a "higher power" and abstinence for coming to terms with the problem.

Referral Networks. The levels and sources of human services referrals to groups vary by focal problem and community. In part, this variation could be due to the viability and population ecology of groups in a region, the extent of group outreach, and the attitudes of key professionals and human services policymakers.

Community Epidemiology. The rates of disorder in a community can be affected by mutual-help groups through both direct and indirect pathways. Over time, groups can directly reduce the incidence and prevalence rates of a disorder by directly helping individuals who currently have, or in the future would otherwise have developed, a psychological, behavioral, or physical problem or illness. In addition, groups, over time, can indirectly influence prevalence and incidence rates by altering lay and professional ideologies and helping modalities.

Generally speaking, communities or geographical regions with more mutual-help groups, more viable groups, and groups that have been operative a longer period of time would be expected to register the greatest group impact on community characteristics. However, as discussed earlier, community characteristics themselves will influence the viability and population ecology of groups. Delineating the reciprocal influence of these factors represents a major challenge for research in this area.

THE DESIGN OF ECOLOGICALLY
BASED RESEARCH STUDIES

To adequately carry out ecologically based research in the research areas discussed earlier and related areas, researchers will need to modify their standard research approaches. Three modifications appear especially important: routinely obtaining data that span multiple variable domains and levels of analysis; examining complex interactions among variables, including cross-domain and cross-level interactions; and using combined ethnographic-quantitative research methods. Each of these is discussed below.

Obtaining Data That Span Multiple
Variable Domains and Levels of Analysis

Central to the ecological framework and the research areas presented earlier is the interplay and interdependence among factors that span variable domains and levels of analysis. For research to describe and examine mutual-help phenomena across these multiple domains and levels of analysis, at least two special design considerations are apparent: obtaining a large enough sample of groups (or communities) so that the group (community) level of analysis can be examined in the design and using measures that are appropriate and valid for each variable domain and level of analysis under study.

Sampling. Most mutual-help research studies to date have been limited to members of one or a handful of chapters or groups from a single mutual-help organization. This is sufficient for analyses at the individual level but insufficient for analyses at the group level. To accomplish the latter, using at minimum a sample of 8-10 groups and ideally much larger samples of groups appears necessary. Depending on the location of the researcher and the specific groups being studied, researchers might need to extend their sampling universe beyond their immediate geographic community to the surrounding county or region.

When comparisons across multiple focal problems are included in a study, careful attention will need to be paid to obtaining groups for each focal problem type from comparable types of communities. In addition, in comparative studies, groups representing at least three different types of focal problem should ideally be sampled (e.g., substance abuse, life stress, and physical illness groups). This allows meaningful examination of differences due to the focal problem, and at the same time allows enhanced confidence in the generalizability of findings in those variable domains where differences are not expected or found.

Measures. Mutual-help research to date has generally incorporated reliable and valid measures of well-being (individual level), helping mechanisms (individual and group level), and social climate (group level). With a few exceptions, self-report measure have been used. There is a great need for researchers to adopt or develop measures to assess variable domains beyond the few just noted, especially non-self report measures at the group and community levels of analyses. In some cases, measures developed for the study of other types of community groups or organizations could be used or adopted for mutual-help research.

As Tebes and Kraemer (1991) have argued, it is important for mutual-help research to go beyond psychology's traditional sole reliance on quantitative measures by including qualitative measures as well. Qualitative measurement approaches include interviewing, observation, and review of archival records. Qualitative measurement allows holistic, multifaceted descriptions of numerous components of group or community environments in a way impossible in a quantitative study focused on a limited number of discrete variables.

Cross-Domain and Cross-Level Interactions

An ecological paradigm for mutual-help research assumes that in many cases the relationship between any two variables will depend in part on the moderating influence of additional variables. Traditionally, such moderating effects are examined by testing for statistically significant interactions. Consistent with the interrelationships among variables depicted in Figure 8.1, both cross-domain-within-level and cross-domain-cross-level interactions are potentially important foci for ecologically based data analysis. The discussion below of these interactions focuses primarily on the group and individual levels of analysis.

Cross-Domain-Within-Level Interactions. Researchers should routinely look for interactions (i.e., moderating effects) among variables included in their studies. Given the tremendous differences in the needs of individuals with different types of problems, the group focal problem is especially likely to figure in interactions with a diversity of variables from other variable domains. For instance, Maton et al. (1989) found interactions of focal problem and group linkages in a study of group births and deaths. Behavior control groups (e.g., alcoholism, overeating) not affiliated with a national parent organization were much more likely to disband over time than were life stress (e.g., bereavement, divorce) or medical (e.g., physical illness) groups similarly not affiliated with a national parent organization. On the other hand, behavior control groups that were affiliated with a national parent organization were neither more or less likely to disband than were life stress or medical groups that similarly were affiliated with a national parent organization. Interactions involving group ideology, helping mechanisms, climate, structure, and resources should also be examined for various criterion measures.

Cross-Level Interactions. Cross-level interactions are not generally examined in psychological research but are directly implicated in an ecologically based approach. Statistical tests of group level-by-individual level variable interactions generally involve giving the same score (e.g., a group mean or group dummy coded score) to each group subsample in a regression analysis while retaining individual scores on the other predictor variable and the criterion variable. To date, two studies reporting cross-level interactions have been reported in the mutual-help literature. Maton (1989a) found that recently bereaved (high-stress) members of highly cohesive (high-support) Compassionate Friends groups reported greater well-being than did recently bereaved members of lower cohesion (low-support) groups, whereas the well-being of less recently bereaved members (low-stress) did not vary across high versus low-cohesion Compassionate Friends groups. Maton

(1989b) found that group friendship development was positively related to group satisfaction for a group focal problem characterized by high levels of social network disruption (multiple sclerosis) but not for two focal problems characterized by lower levels of social network disruption (overeating, death of a child).

Descriptive Analysis. Possible moderating effects can be explored through other means than direct statistical tests of interaction. In quantitatively focused research, analyses can be run separately for groups of two different types or at two different levels on a continuum and the extent of differences in findings compared using (commonsense) descriptive rather than statistical methods. In qualitatively focused research, qualitative analysis can be used to discover and delineate differential patterns of relationship among variables in different types of groups (or communities).

Combined Ethnographic-Quantitative Methods

The ethnographic tradition in anthropology and sociology has as its primary goal the understanding of the worldviews, values, language, and practices of members of a culture markedly different from that of the researcher. The methodology is based on an extensive period of fieldwork in which, to the extent possible, the researcher lives and participates in the culture or subculture under investigation. Extensive observation, in-depth interviews of members (inhabitants) and key informants, and archival analysis represent the major research tools used. Extensive field notes are recorded. Descriptive and theoretical understanding emerge from and are continually deepened and revised as part of an ongoing, integrated process of qualitative data collection and analysis (Denzin, 1989; Fetterman, 1989).

To the extent that a given mutual-help group subculture is different from that of the mainstream human services and social science culture, an ethnographic approach appears to hold great benefit. Among the major strengths of the ethnographic method for mutual-help research are the potential for understanding a group's *subjective culture, thick description,* and *grounded theory.* Subjective culture refers to members' subjective view of social reality, including assumptions about causality, core values, and meanings attributed to the focal problem and group events. Careful observation over time combined with in-depth interviewing will allow some entry into the subjective world of participants in this distinct cultural milieu. Similarly, sustained observation allows the in-depth identification and description (thick description) of key aspects of group life and the different contexts and forms in which they occur. Finally, through ongoing qualitative analysis of relationships among facets of subjective culture, behavior, and context, the ethnographer is uniquely able to generate theoretical ideas concerning processes, theories that are "grounded" in the realities of the local group culture (cf. Glaser & Strauss, 1968).

For ecologically based research, an ethnographic methodology presents unique advantages, given its capability to generate hypotheses involving multiple domains and levels of variables to describe individual, group, and community factors affecting group phenomena and to enhance confidence that the culture of the group is not being systematically misrepresented or distorted due to the biases of mainstream scientific approaches. Two recent examples of ethnographic research in the mutual-help area are Klass's (1992) 10-year participant observation study of a chapter of Compassionate Friends and Zimmerman et al.'s (1991) direct observation study of the development of new GROW groups in various communities throughout Illinois.

The source of the primary strength of ethnographic methodology—reliance on the investigator as "human instrument"—is also the source of its primary weakness. When combined with traditional quantitative methods in an ongoing research study, however, the respective strengths of each can be capitalized on and their respective weaknesses offset (Maton, 1993). As noted above, ethnographic methodology allows constructs and theory to be grounded in members' cultural experience and facilitates an in-depth understanding of context. Quantitative field research allows systematic comparisons across individuals and groups, general theory development, and replication of findings. The use of either methodology alone results in serious research limitations. However, for research consistent with an ecological paradigm, a combined ethnographic-quantitative methodology appears optimal, in that multiple variable domains and levels of analysis can be meaningfully and carefully examined and maximal research understanding of these nontraditional community settings obtained.

The time and resource costs of combining an ethnographic approach with traditional quantitative field methodology, of course, can be substantial. Also, there could be logistical and pragmatic problems, including obtaining group permission for the extended involvement of an ethnographer in the group. However, if the researcher approaches a group in a collaborative fashion, obtaining permission to use a combined methodology is likely feasible in many cases.

CONCLUSION

The thesis of this chapter is that mutual-help group research needs to move beyond the individual level of analysis in conceptualizing important research questions and designing field studies. An ecological approach to mutual-help phenomena is helpful in moving the field in this direction, as it takes as given that examining multiple variable domains and levels of analysis is a precondition for valid understanding. Taking an ecological perspective seriously in generating research questions and designing research studies presents research design challenges, some of which are discussed earlier. However, our commitment to good science and to the current and future well-being of mutual-help groups requires us, in collaboration with other social scientists and with the groups themselves, to forthrightly address the challenges and incorporate the insights of the ecological perspective in our work.

REFERENCES

Antze, P. (1976). The role of ideologies in peer psychotherapy organizations: Some theoretical observations and three case studies. *Journal of Applied Behavioral Science, 12,* 323-346.

Denzin, N. K. (1987). *The recovering alcoholic.* Newbury Park, CA: Sage.

Denzin, N. K. (1989). *The research act* (3rd ed.). Englewood Cliffs, NJ: Prentice-Hall.

Eisenberg, D. M. (1993, January 28). 10% in U.S. sought "unconventional" medical care: 1990 survey finds alternative therapy often was used without telling primary physician. *Washington Post,* p. A13.

Fetterman, D. M. (1989). *Ethnography: Step by step* (Applied Social Research Methods Series, Vol. 17). Newbury Park, CA: Sage.

Glaser, B. G., & Strauss, A. (1968). *The discovery of grounded theory.* Chicago: Aldine.

Humphreys, K., & Woods, M. D. (1994). Research mutual-help group participation in a segregated society. In T. J. Powell (Ed.), *Understanding the self-help organization: Frameworks and findings.* Thousand Oaks, CA: Sage.

Jacobs, M. K., & Goodman, F. (1989). Psychology and self-help groups. *American Psychologist, 44,* 536-545.

Kelly, J. G. (1966). Ecological constraints on mental health services. *American Psychologist, 21,* 535-539.

Klass, D. (1992). Religious aspects in the resolution of parental grief: Solace and social support. In K. I. Pargament, K. I. Maton, & R. E. Hess (Eds.), *Religion and prevention in mental health: Research, vision, and action* (pp. 155-177). New York: Haworth.

Levine, M., & Perkins, D. V. (1987). *Principles of community psychology: Perspectives and applications.* New York: Oxford University Press.

Levy, L. H. (in press). Self-help groups. In J. Rappaport & E. Seidman (Eds.), *Handbook of community psychology.*

Lieberman, M. A., & Borman, L. D. (Eds.). (1979). *Self-help groups for coping with crisis.* San Francisco: Jossey-Bass.

Maton, K. I. (1988). Social support, organizational characteristics, psychological well-being, and group appraisal in three self-help group populations. *American Journal of Community Psychology, 16,* 53-77.

Maton, K. I. (1989a). Community settings as buffers of life stress? Highly supportive churches, mutual help groups, and senior centers. *American Journal of Community Psychology, 17,* 203-232.

Maton, K. I. (1993b). Towards an ecological understanding of mutual-help groups: The social ecology of "fit." *American Journal of Community Psychology, 17,* 729-753.

Maton, K. I. (1993). A bridge between cultures: Linked ethnographic-empirical methodology for culture-anchored research. *American Journal of Community Psychology 21,* 701-727

Maton, K. I., Leventhal, G. S., Madara, E. J., & Julien, M. A. (1989). Factors affecting the birth and death of mutual help groups: The role of national affiliation, professional involvement, and member focal problem. *American Journal of Community Psychology, 17,* 643-671.

Powell, T. (1987). *Self-help organizations and professional practice.* Silver Spring, MD: National Association of Social Workers.

Tebes, J. K., & Kraemer, D. T. (1991). Quantitative and qualitative knowing in mutual support research: Some lessons from the recent history of scientific psychology. *American Journal of Community Psychology, 19,* 739-756.

Wollert, R. W., Levy, L. H., & Knight, B. G. (1982). Help-giving in behavioral control and stress coping self-help groups. *Small Group Behavior, 13,* 204-218.

Zimmerman, M. A., Reischl, T. M., Seidman, E., Rappaport, J., Toro, P. A., & Salem, D. A. (1991). Expansion strategies of a mutual help organization. *American Journal of Community Psychology, 19,* 251-278.

9.   Roles for Mental Health Consumers in Self-Help Group Research

CAROLINE L. KAUFMANN

Present efforts to remodel the mental health system focus on involvement of consumers and family members in the design and delivery of hospital and community-based care. Through these efforts, the concept of "empowerment" has emerged as one key issue. However, the concept of empowerment has more salience as political rhetoric than as human experience. In general, it connotes a transfer of power from providers of mental health services to the consumers of those services. In the conduct of research on self-help groups, investigators have entered into relationships with consumers that fall outside of the customary roles. Recent experiences in consumer participation have resulted in expanded influence and control among service recipients. Historically, the mental health consumer's role in research has been a powerless one, and debate has focused on mechanisms to protect psychiatric patients from abuse in biomedical and behavioral research. Only recently have there been concerted efforts on the part of the

AUTHOR'S NOTE: This chapter was prepared for presentation at an invited conference on Self-Help and Mental Illness at the Center for Self-Help Research, University of Michigan, Ann Arbor, February 16-19, 1993. Work for this chapter was supported in part by grants from the National Institute of Mental Health, Clinical Services Research Branch (MH45218), and the Substance Abuse Mental Health Service Administration, Center for Mental Health Services (MH47686). Copies are available by contacting Dr. Kaufmann at WPIC 3811 O'Hara Street, Pittsburgh, PA. 15212, Phone: 412-624-0880, FAX: 412-624-0672. Comments are welcome.

research community to involve consumers in the design, implementation, and dissemination of research. With these initiatives come new problems in renegotiating the rights and duties of investigators and consumers.

This chapter examines the emerging roles of mental health consumers in self-help group research. The examples presented here are taken from empirical studies of self-help groups in social and vocational programs.[1] These instances are examined with respect to prior understanding of traditional role relationships. The objective is to generate a working typology of the new roles that are developing from a more empowering approach to consumer participation in mental health services research.

BRIEF OUTLINE OF ROLE THEORY

A role is a set of expectations for behavior that members of a group impose on others. It usually involves some rule or norm as a prescription of how an individual should behave socially. Norms are classified as either rights or duties. For example, based on Parsons's (1964) classic definition of the "sick role," a person with an illness has the right to be excused from his or her normal social obligations and a duty to try to get well. Normative expectations of what a person ought to do are summary judgments based on experience. They are cognitive devices used to code our perceptions of social life—a social cognition shaped from experience. We construct a heuristic for what to expect and act on our heuristic expectations (Simon, 1979). We are much more likely to sanction the person violating our expectations than to change our expectations to fit what the person is doing. If we have a set of expectations about how we and others are supposed to behave, we can make judgments about what to do and what to expect from others.

Without norms and compliance to normative expectations, human behavior would be extremely complex and unpredictable. However, compliance with norms becomes problematic in times of social change when people enter into new relationships and engage in new behaviors (Barber, 1971). In the relationship between researchers and other human beings, there is an established set of expectations in the natural and social sciences that are being tested in the area of self-help group research. In this chapter, I discuss six roles for mental health consumers in self-help group research: subject, informed participant, key informant, adviser, research assistant, and co-investigator. The roles are presented in a rough order of the degree of involvement of consumers in the actual research process. At issue currently

Role	Right to:	Duty to:
Subject	Protection from harm	Voluntary or involuntary compliance with data collection procedures
Informed participant	* Full information disclosure regarding nature of study, risks, benefits, and alternatives * Make decision to consent or refuse in a noncoerced circumstance	* Voice decision to consent or refuse * Demonstrate competence to make this decision
Key informant	* Privacy * Feedback and validation	* Speak from experience
Adviser	* Participate in decisions relevant to self/group interests	* Consult with the investigator(s) as needed
Research staff	* Prevailing wage for work * Protection under current fair labor practices	* Perform tasks as specified by the job * Follow a chain of command
Researcher	* Pursue areas of scientific inquiry * Access information relevant to the research area * Publish results based on standards of peer review	* Follow the protocol * Demonstrate fiscal accountability * Adhere to guidelines for protection of human subjects * Report all results to parties responsible for the financing and conduct of research

Figure 9.1. Typology of Consumer Roles in Research

is the set of rights and duties that defines the new roles that emerge from changing relationships of consumers to the provider system of care. Figure 9.1 illustrates some of the emerging roles and possible rights and duties that might be imposed on role incumbents. The remainder of the chapter presents empirical examples from current research projects. This discussion should be viewed as a first step to the construction of an expanded heuristic framework for consumer roles in self-help group research.

CONSUMER AS THE SUBJECT OF OBSERVATION

In traditional scientific study, the role of the subject is determined by the researcher. In simple observational studies, the investigator makes minimal intervention on the person who is identified as the subject of scientific study. The subject is assumed to be passive in the face of observation, and his or her behavior is presumed to be independent of the act of observation. The purpose of inquiry is defined as acquisition of basic information so that the researcher can extract more generalized statements about the subject based on observation. The parameters of the inquiry are defined exclusively by the investigator.

Classical psychiatry and psychology offer many examples of this role. The basic observational studies of Kraepelin and Bleuler on schizophrenia began with the observers' detailed clinical records of institutionalized patients (Colp, 1989). Both Kraepelin and Bleuler were primarily concerned with detailed observations of the natural course of a disease. The patients they observed were all institutionalized for long periods of time. The observers could not readily describe the behavior of a person with schizophrenia without also describing a person who experienced long-term institutionalization. It has been argued recently that the poor outcomes they described were partly a result of the conditions in psychiatric asylums of the 19th century. Furthermore, the downward course of schizophrenia has now been modified by improved medical and social treatment (Strauss, 1987).

A Right to Protection, a Duty to Comply

From a historical perspective, the rights of a subject in an observational study are limited to protection from harm arising directly or indirectly from his or her role as subject. Assuming that the observation involves no material risk of physical injury or death, the potential harm to subjects in such studies is assumed to be minimal. Subjects must not have effective treatment withheld solely because they are subjects in an observational study (Public Health Service, n.d.).

The role of subject entails a limited set of duties, including passive cooperation with data collection procedures. The subject in naturalistic experiments is assumed to be uninvolved and, for the most part, unaware of the fact that he or she is being observed. Further, the act of observation is assumed to have no effect on the behavior observed. Psychiatrists in the 19th century paid relatively little attention to the rights of the subjects of their inquiries because there were few, if any, standards to allow psychiatric patients to make choices. Very little in the way of nonconsensual observation and research is permitted by current standards. Although some investigators accept the subject's appearance at the clinic as evidence of willingness to participate in a research project, such passive assent is not consistent with current scientific standards. Contemporary investigators are required to obtain consent from patients who are presented in case studies or other clinical investigations.

The mechanisms for obtaining consent from subjects in observational studies are not always apparent to the subjects themselves. For example, individuals admitted for inpatient treatment at psychiatric teaching hospitals are asked to sign a release form giving the investigator permission to observe and record information from direct observation, clinical records, or both. If the patient chooses not to sign such a form, then the investigator is not permitted to use any information about that individual. These procedures are policed by an institutional review board (IRB), which examines all research protocols for their potential abuse of human subjects. Review of psychiatric records for research purposes is regulated by the same mechanisms. Collection of data from patients' charts requires prior review by an IRB with assurances of confidentiality. From the point of view of investigators and many IRBs, chart review studies pose minimal or no risk to individual patients or subjects. Patients are often asked to sign general consent forms that give permission to staff to review their records for purposes of clinical studies.

The role of IRBs in protecting consumers who volunteer as subjects in research is essential to assuring that subjects' rights are upheld. The membership of these boards is composed of professionals with experience in service delivery, research, and administration. By virtue of experience, the review boards have more in common with the investigators than with the subjects. The standards for protection of human subjects are developed within the research community and scrutinized by a system heavily dependent on peer review (e.g., see *Guidelines for the Use of Human Subjects in Psychosocial Research*, 1992).

The balance between the right to protection from harm and passive compliance with unobtrusive observation shifts when the research enterprise is taken out of the clinical domain. Researchers in self-help groups have encountered situations where self-help group members regard the collecting of information about their groups as intrusive and inherently harmful. In a recent example, the directors of consumer-run drop-in centers refused to allow a research team to obtain any information about psychiatric diagnoses or treatments from its members (Kaufmann, Ward-Colasante, & Farmer, 1993). The reasons for their refusal were not adequately addressed by traditional assurances of confidentiality and individual anonymity. The directors were concerned that the act of collecting data about psychiatric diagnoses violated their political stance against psychiatric labeling. They were deeply concerned that the researchers might regard them as "cases" or "mental patients" and thereby promote their stigmatization. In addition, they objected to any counting procedures that would require them to become "full of red tape." These directors, who were innovators in local and state mental health planning, felt that the very act of research and the counting and measuring involved would force them to become more like provider agencies and compromise their status as nontraditional programs. This example illustrates how the act of observation—however unobtrusive it might appear from the researcher's perspective—casts the subject in a relationship that might not be acceptable to the leaders of the group. This is particularly an issue in self-help group research when the group has established itself in political opposition to a professional system.

In such a context, the agreement to become the "subject of observation" conflicts with the expressed needs of group members to establish their identities independent of professionals. The solution for the researcher requires a compromise in the type of information collected, a compromise made difficult due to the demands of the research endeavor. The researcher is limited to collecting data that is agreeable to the subject regardless of how unobtrusive the data collection procedures appear to be. For individual self-help group members, compliance with data collection might reinforce their feelings of resentment that professionals have access to information from psychiatric records. The issue of access to information is central in brokering differences in power between researchers and self-help group members.

THE CONSUMER AS INFORMED PARTICIPANT

With the advent of federal guidelines for the protection of human subjects and a well-established body of tort cases and statutory regulations, the role of a subject in research has changed significantly (Kaufmann, 1983). The doctrine of informed consent specifies a broad set of parameters for the relationship between researchers and subjects. The requirement of informed consent developed out of a recognition of inequality in that relationship. The basic elements of informed consent to research include information disclosure by the investigator, freedom of choice for the consumer (also termed voluntariness), and competence on the consumer's part to make a decision (Meisel, Roth, & Lidz, 1977).

Under current standards, the assumed unequal distribution of knowledge between the subject and the investigator requires the investigator to disclose information to the subject before asking him or her to consent. Disclosure requirements include information about the risks and benefits of participation in research as well as the alternatives available should the individual decide not to participate. The researcher is the first person to decide what information should be disclosed, subject to IRB review. It is not uncommon for a review board to require the investigator to make more extensive disclosure, particularly regarding risks (Benson, Roth, Appelbaum, & Lidz, 1988).

All consents to research studies require the participant to sign a form describing the nature of the study, its risks, benefits, and alternatives before enrolling in the research. The consent form must contain language explaining that participation in the research project is voluntary and that the individual can withdraw from the study at any time without jeopardizing his or her treatment. This means that the individuals must be in a position to make a free choice whether to participate in the research.

Freedom of choice assumes a range of options for mental health consumers that might be illusory, given the restricted access to services that many consumers perceive. In some cases, consumers see consent to participate in an experimental study as a means to demonstrate their cooperation with staff or as a way to get access to preferred treatment. Some bioethicists have argued that it is likely impossible to obtain informed consent from persons in institutional settings because they have very limited choices and might see compliance with any request from authority figures as mandatory rather than volitional (Bentley, 1991).

The informed consent model assumes that investigators and professionals have an extensive knowledge of ethical issues in research and are able to judge the pertinence of information to a subject's decision to consent or refuse research. The competence of individuals to weigh the information presented and make a reasonable decision is usually determined by the investigator. Should the investigator have any reason to question a subject's competence to consent or refuse to participate in research, a proxy decision maker would be selected to make the decision in place of the subject. The willingness of investigators to find a research subject competent to consent or refuse to participate in research is partly a function of the degree of risk to which the subject is potentially subjected should he or she consent. Thus a person would be held to a lower standard of competence to consent to a study requiring only questionnaires than to one requiring a surgical proce- dure. In the case of questionnaire studies, the subjects need only show up for the interview and be able to sign the consent form. For a study in which the subject risks potential serious harm, a higher standard for competent consent is required.

Individual Versus Corporate Consent

Informed consent implies a relationship between the individual partici- pant and the researcher that unfolds in a face-to-face interaction. Researchers tell participants as much as possible about the study, and the participant decides to participate based on what has been presented. The individual person makes his or her own decision to consent or refuse. In self-help group research, the consent sought is more often a corporate one, requiring a consensual agreement to participate on the part of the group as a whole as well as individual members. Researchers may well find that while adhering strictly to informed consent requirement with individual participants, they have failed to adequately address the informational needs of the group.

Addressing this issue requires the researcher to establish multiple avenues for communicating information about the research. For example, in a recent empirical study of outcomes of self-help group participation, the author obtained consent from individual participants at the time of each individual assessment. When the researcher had any contact with the self-help group members or attended group meetings, she obtained permission from those present in the group. She also held regular open meetings with all members who had contact with the study and explained the nature of the research project, as well as its risks, benefits, and alternatives. This process of group disclosure was helpful in maintaining a working relationship with those involved in the self-help group. However, it did not guarantee access to all meetings or prevent misunderstandings among the researchers and the self- help group members.

In one instance, the author sought and obtained prior verbal consent from a group of individuals to tape-record their conversation. Several days later, when the researcher appeared at the meeting with a tape recorder, three members who had given prior consent complained about the tape recorder, although they did not ask the researcher to stop the taping. A few days after the meeting, the researcher received a phone call from one group member complaining about the taping. This member further remarked that "everybody" in the group was upset about the tape recording. The researcher returned to the group the following week and presented the tape to them for their disposal. She made no use of the recorded conversation. In this example, the researcher felt that the relationship established with the group was both important and sufficiently compromised by the data collection procedures to indicate withdrawal of individual and group consent. This example illustrates the fluid nature of informed consent, particularly evident in self-help group research. Individuals might make a decision in isolation that they would wish to change in a group context. In such an event, the researcher must be willing to negotiate and renegotiate the relationship and permit both individuals and groups to withdraw consent at any time and for any reason. The researcher is required to comply with the wishes of the individual and the group regarding the initial decision to consent and any subsequent decisions that affect participant involvement in the research process.

THE ROLE OF KEY INFORMANTS

In qualitative research and cultural anthropology, the researcher often relies heavily on information obtained from key informants. These are individuals who are themselves members of a group and can provide detailed information about group behavior, norms, and activities based on their personal experiences. A good example of consumers used as key informants is found in the work of Estroff (1981) in the book *Making It Crazy*. In this work, Estroff carefully defines her role as an investigator independently of those of consumer and provider in the health care system and establishes confidential relationships with consumers as research subjects.

Estroff explains herself to consumers as someone who is interested in how they live but who is not there to give them treatment or advice. Estroff's data are based largely on her field notes of conversations and experiences she had as an observer at one community mental health program. Her use of questionnaire data is limited to one interview using a community adjustment survey instrument. In using the survey, she expresses concern over how the consumers might view the questionnaire because it connotes the types of objective questions about their personal experiences that they are frequently asked to answer by providers in the mental health system. Estroff's concern here is that the survey questionnaire will change the quality of her relationship with the consumers and destroy some of the natural rapport she established through her months of field observation.

Speaking from Experience

The key informant is important in sensitizing researchers to pertinent issues in the lives of consumers and establishing the validity of research measures (Lipson, Meleis, & Afaf, 1989; McNabb, 1990; Weiss, 1992). Consumer involvement in the development of research protocols and questionnaires through the use of key informants helps to shape the quality of inquiry so that it has relevance to the daily lives of people receiving mental health services. In this role, the consumer has a duty to speak from experience. For example, in the self-help research project noted above, this researcher observed a drop in the number of women attending self-help group meetings over an approximate 2-year period of observation. When the researcher presented this observation at a general meeting, several women stated that they got together in a small group every week, but they did not call this a self-help group meeting. They then discussed among themselves whether their gathering should be considered a self-help group meeting and asked the researcher to give them a working definition of a self-help group. The researcher provided them with the criteria published by a self-help clearinghouse. After a brief discussion, the members decided that the women's meeting was a self-help group and asked that the researcher include their meetings in the observations. This example embodies the problem of self-definitions of self-help groups. It might be that the researcher imposes a priori definitions of a self-help group that do not incorporate members' concepts of the phenomenon.

Reliance on experience has dramatic implications for the field of self-help group research. If the researcher enters the field with preestablished definitions of self-help, he or she could miss important instances of peer support activities. In studies of self-help among ethnic groups, particularly those in the African-American community, some researchers have suggested that there is a paucity of self-help group activities. However, individuals might be actively engaged in peer mutual support that is organized around extended families, neighborhoods, and churches. Participants might not label such activities as self-help, although the affiliations meet all criteria that define a self-help group. Key informants are central to the process of identifying the phenomenon for researchers when instances of self-help are present but called by other names.

The Right to Feedback and Validation of Findings

The rights of a key informant include a right to feedback and validation of the research findings. Powell and Cameron (1991) describe a series of discussions between researchers and self-help group members in which the members voiced concerns that their interests were not well-represented in a project specifically devoted to the study of self-help. The call for studies of outcomes and efficacy may challenge the value of self-help group participation. In contrast, studies descriptive of group process and members' self-perceptions of the effectiveness of self-help group participation are more likely to be self-validating.

Our first study of self-help groups among people with severe mental illnesses is currently in the stage of data analysis and reporting (Kaufmann, Schulberg, & Schooler, in press). The first report from this study deals with the overall low rates of participation in a random sample of people with no prior experience of self-help groups. The major finding from this study is that rates of participation in self-help group activities are low compared to use of professional mental health care among people with psychiatric diagnoses, such as schizophrenia or major affective disorders. This finding is supported by at least one well-designed national survey of self-help use among people in treatment for various psychiatric illnesses (Narrow, Regier, Rae, Manderscheid, & Locke, 1993).

The problem from the researchers' point of view was how to reconcile this empirical finding with the large number of people present at self-help group meetings during the course of the research project. We began by asking each of the outreach workers to report on how many people they had contacted and whether any of these potential new recruits actually showed up at a meeting. The outreach workers noted that they had a great deal of trouble reaching people, and when they did, very few ever came to a meeting. One outreach worker had made three visits to a prospective new member and eventually convinced him to come to the place where the self-help group met. The researcher discussed the experiences of the outreach workers in the context of the findings on participation rates. This discussion grounded the abstraction of participation rates in self-help groups in the concrete experiences of the members. The members agreed that there were many people whom they knew as friends who could benefit from the self-help groups but chose not to join.

ADVISERS IN DESIGN AND IMPLEMENTATION

Most researchers interested in self-help establish collaborative relationships with identified leaders. The collaboration allows both the researchers and the consumers to specialize in what they know best. Researchers focus on the technical details of research design, funding, and implementation. Consumer leaders focus on rallying support for the project among their peers and advising the investigator on directions the research should take. For such a collaboration to be sustained, both the researcher and the consumer must acknowledge their unique contributions to the research project and be willing to strike compromises when possible. A few examples from the self-help research projects in Pittsburgh are offered as illustrations of consumer-researcher collaboration.

Our first project was designed as a clinical trial of the effects of self-help group participation for people with long-standing mental illness. A sampling frame was established based on the population of all persons who were in active treatment at a local community mental health center and who had a diagnosis of schizophrenia, schizoaffective disorder, or major mood disorder. Potential subjects also had to be adults, native speakers of English, and have no major physical disability or sensory impairment. Approximately 200 individuals were excluded from the eligible sample due to prior exposure to the self-help group experience.

Although the exclusion of existing self-help members makes very good sense from the standpoint of research design, it raised serious questions from those members of the self-help group who were ruled ineligible for the study. The researcher had asked for the members' help in designing and implementing the study, and the members ran the self-help group meetings to which the research subjects were referred. However, these members felt left out of an important part of the research because they were not subjects themselves.

To address this issue, the researcher and self-help members held a series of meetings to discuss their views of the research project and the ways in which they wanted to be involved. One key issue was money. Research subjects were paid $35 for the research interviews but were not paid for going to self-help groups. Although $35 is not a great deal of money, it was significant enough to raise questions from the members and to represent their feeling of exclusion from the project. By mutual agreement, we developed a consumer monitoring system whereby the self-help group members recorded attendance at group meetings and reported back to the research project. Also, the researcher asked consumers to volunteer as daily quality assurance reporters and group secretaries. Members participated in a brief training program and were given a small financial compensation as volunteers to the research project for each form they completed. The amount of compensation represented their bus fare and the cost of a light lunch for the days they volunteered for the research project. The consumer self-reported data on the content of the self-help groups provided qualitative detail about meetings from the members' point of view. This added depth to the research data and also enlisted the members in the daily operation of the research project.

A second example is taken from the Self Help Employment Center Project, funded by the Substance Abuse and Mental Health Services Administration, Center for Mental Health Services (Ward-Colasante, Kaufmann, Roth, & Cook, 1990). In this project, the researchers involved consumers directly in the earliest stages of the design of the project. Through a series of meetings, the project formed a consumer advisory group that developed into the Quality Assurance (QA) Committee at the Employment Center. This group meets twice a month and monitors program quality. Members serve as volunteers and receive the equivalent of bus fare and lunch for the days they perform QA functions. The QA group reviews the content of the programs and monitors attendance. When attendance at particular groups drops, the QA group advises staff on ways to promote attendance. They have drafted suggestions for groups and activities that are being incorporated into the daily program activities and are recruiting members to positions of leadership in the self-help group meetings.

An important feature of the advisory role is that there be a majority of consumers on the advisory groups. This serves to avoid tokenism and enhances the ability of consumers to gain support from one another in revising the research programs. It is also important that the researchers meet regularly with the consumer advisers to apprise them of progress and provide guidance as to how flexible (or inflexible) the research protocol is. In the case of the Employment Center project, consumer involvement is a key factor in the original request for proposals and has been maintained throughout the implementation of the grant.

CONSUMERS AS RESEARCH STAFF

This is a somewhat problematic role, depending on the qualifications and responsibilities of the position. The most immediate difficulty involves a loss of freedom on the consumer's part when he or she joins the research staff as a paid employee. Consumers who have learned effective techniques in professional relationships as advocates have to acquire new skills as employees. In one published example, the former president of a statewide consumer network had been accustomed to contacting top policymakers by phone to discuss advocacy issues. This same person experienced difficulty accepting the fact that he could not do this after he accepted a paid job as an employee of a mental health agency (Paulson, 1991). It is important for consumers and researchers to acknowledge the limits imposed in accepting a role as a paid staff person. Consumers likely experience a loss of authority and influence when they move from the role of adviser to one of employee.

In return, consumers hired as members of a research staff have a right to be paid the prevailing wage for their work. This becomes problematic if the person's salary is partly determined by professional credentials. Particularly in a university setting, staff salaries are determined by professional training and experience. Some universities require a bachelor's degree for any person hired as a research associate. People without this minimal level of formal education might be hired as research assistants or lower level nonprofessional staff members, but they have difficulty being recruited to more advanced positions regardless of their experience (Garrard, Husman, Mansfield, & Compton, 1988). The solution is to draft a policy of equivalency of training and experience which will assure that workers doing equivalent work are paid equivalent salaries.

In the self-help projects, we have hired consumers both as paid workers and as volunteers. These relationships are sometimes problematic, however. For example, in one instance, a consumer who had served as both a key informant and later as an adviser to the research project expected to be given a paid job once funding was obtained. The researcher did not know about this expectation and was surprised to learn that the former adviser was now hostile to the project. The basic issue was that the consumer believed that the money for the research project was to be used to pay directly for consumers to run support groups. The fact that the National Institute of Mental Health (NIMH) earmarked the majority of funds to pay for research angered the consumer, who now felt cheated by the researcher.

In another instance, this researcher sought to hire the consumer as a paid staff person. However, all the jobs with the research project required literacy skills that the consumer did not have. The situation became more complex because the consumer did not disclose that she could not read or write. This was particularly difficult because the bulk of the material explaining the research project was in the form of written materials, charts, and graphs. The researcher was unaware that the consumer did not understand written material and continued to show the consumer literature and written illustrations for review. This is an example of a problem arising from breaks in communication and lack of complementary expectations between researchers and consumers. Consumers who fill one role in a research project quite well might not be suited to others.

A positive example from the same project is the use of consumers as outreach workers to increase subject participation in self-help groups. There has been at least one report in the literature of problems arising from the use of lay interviewers in psychiatric research (Turnbull, 1988). In one study, this researcher created a set of paid part-time jobs to be filled by members of the self-help groups. These individuals were hired by the university and given training in telephone survey techniques and procedures to assure confidentiality. The outreach workers then were given a list of individuals who had consented to participate in the research project and had been invited to join a self-help group. The outreach workers called each consenting participant to explain the self-help group activities and invite the subject to join. Outreach workers also offered to meet the subject at his or her home or other convenient location and go with him or her to the first self-help group meeting. Four such outreach workers were employed: two for each of the self-help groups participating in the study. All of the outreach workers completed a 2-day training session and signed a confidentiality statement required of all members of the research staff. The outreach workers met weekly with the researcher and passed on any information about future attendance.

Both the researcher and the direct care staff were concerned that the outreach workers would become involved in potential emergency situations or other circumstances of high risk. The workers appeared less concerned over emergencies than over the possibility of being treated rudely over the phone by a person they did not know. This problem was addressed by having all outreach workers call from either the research office or from one of the drop-in centers during times when a staff person was available. Outreach workers were instructed to notify a staff person immediately if the research subject sounded or appeared upset, cried, or threatened to harm others or him- or herself. Over the course of a 6-month period, no such instances occurred. However, all persons in the outreach position reported having at least one unpleasant phone conversation. The researcher discussed each instance in detail with the worker and offered assurance that negative comments from some subjects should not be taken personally. The research staff provided support and reassurance and were immediately available to the outreach workers during their scheduled hours of work.

CONSUMERS AS RESEARCHERS

Several recent examples of consumers as researchers demonstrate the blending of roles for researchers and consumer advocates.

The community support programs (CSP) initiatives for research and demonstration at the federal level all entail significant consumer involvement in research design. Researchers are funded because they demonstrate competence in the design and conduct of the project, not by virtue of their experiences as former mental patients or psychiatric survivors. The credentials needed for the consumer movement do not necessarily overlap with those needed to be a researcher. Researchers draw expertise from their academic training at universities; consumers receive advanced degrees from the "school of hard knocks." There is nothing in the training or experience of a researcher that uniquely qualifies him or her as a consumer. Nor is there anything in the background of consumers, per se, that qualifies them as researchers.

There is a potential for misunderstanding of the role of research in consumer advocacy. The primary purpose of research is to produce empirical results that indicate the effects of interventions. Such information can then be used to develop better programs. However, the nature of the improvement will be responsive to consumer desires only insofar as consumers are directly involved in the development of the research agenda and its implementation. The objectivity of the investigation might be questioned when the roles of consumer and researcher are combined. However, similar issues arise when physicians and other health care providers combine treatment and research on their patients and clients.

In conditions of scarcity, there is likely to be competition between service providers and researchers for funding. Currently, the NIMH funds researchers and is precluded from allocating funds for the provision of services not essential to the conduct of the research. The Substance Abuse Mental Health Service Administration (SAMHSA) does have some authority to fund demonstration projects with strong research components, but the combination is difficult. Like oil and water, research and service delivery do not mix well. The consumer as researcher might be confronted by findings that do not support popular opinion.

CONCLUSION

Role relationships between consumers and researchers have traditionally defined consumers as the objects of scientific inquiry and clinical intervention. With the development of guidelines for the protection of human subjects in biomedical and behavioral research, a new standard for rights of subjects has been developed. However, requirements for informed consent limit applications to the more involved roles developing out of recent experiences with participatory research strategies, particularly in the area of self-help group research.

The new roles emerging from the consumer advocacy and community mental health movements develop out of shifts in power made concrete by changes in priorities for funding research. The newest research initiatives from the SAMHSA and the CSP programs involve consumers directly in the design and implementation of research. This movement goes beyond informed consent and the protection of human subjects to the incorporation of consumer experiential knowledge as a basis for inquiry and understanding of mental illness and its treatment. The expanded roles of consumers in self-help group research presents a challenge to traditional research approaches based on informed consent.

NOTE

1. All examples referring to individuals are masked to protect privacy.

REFERENCES

Barber, B. (1971). *Stability and social change*. Boston: Little, Brown.

Benson, P. R., Roth, L. H., Appelbaum, P. S., & Lidz, C. W. (1988). Information disclosure, subject understanding, and informed consent in psychiatric research. *Law and Human Behavior, 12*, 455-475.

Bentley, K. J. (1991). Voluntary recruitment of psychiatric patients for clinical research. *International Journal of Mental Health, 20*, 94-104.

Colp, R. (1989). Psychiatry: Past and future. In H. I. Kaplan & B. J. Sadock (Eds.), *Comprehensive textbook of psychiatry, Vol. 5*. Baltimore, MD: Williams & Wilkins.

Estroff, S. E. (1981). *Making it crazy*. Berkeley: University of California Press.

Garrard, J., Husman, W., Mansfield, C., & Compton, B. (1988). Educational priorities in mental health professions: Do educators and consumers agree? *Medical Education, 22*, 60-66.

Guidelines to the use human subjects in psychosocial research. (1992). Pittsburgh, PA: University of Pittsburgh Press.

Kaufmann, C. L. (1983). Informed consent and patient decision-making: Two decades of research. *Social Science and Medicine, 17,* 1657-1664.

Kaufmann, C. L. (1993). Reasonable accomodation to mental health disabilities at work. *Journal of Psychiatry and Law, 21,* 2, 153-174.

Kaufmann, C. L., Schulberg, H. C., & Schooler, N. R. (in press). An experimental study of self help group participation among people with severe mental illness. *Human Health and Prevention.*

Kaufmann, C. L., Ward-Colasante, C., & Farmer, J. (1993). Development and evaluation of drop-in centers run by mental health consumers. *Hospital and Community Psychiatry, 44,* 675-678.

Lipson, J., Meleis, G., & Afaf, I. (1989). Methodological issues in research with immigrants. *Medical Anthropology, 12,* 103-115.

McNabb, S. L. (1990). The uses of "inaccurate" data: A methodological critique and applications of Alaska Native data. *American Anthropologist, 92,* 116-129.

Meisel, A., Roth, L. H., & Lidz, C. W. (1977). Toward a model of the legal doctrine of informed consent. *American Journal of Psychiatry, 134,* 285-289.

Narrow, W. E., Regier, D. A., Rae, D. S., Manderscheid, R. W., & Locke, B. Z. (1993). Use of services by persons with mental and addictive disorders: Findings from the National Institute of Mental Health Epidemiologic Catchment Area program. *Archives of General Psychiatry, 50,* 95-107.

Parson, T. (1964). *The social system.* Glencoe, IL: Free Press.

Paulson, R. I. (1991). Professional training for consumers and family members: One road to empowerment. *Psychosocial Rehabilitation Journal, 14,* 69-80.

Powell, T. J., & Cameron, M. J. (1991). Self-help research and the public mental health system. *American Journal of Community Psychology, 19,* 797-805.

Public Health Service. (n.d.). *Protection of human subjects.* Bethesda, MD: Office for Protection from Research Risks, National Institutes of Health.

Simon, H. A. (1979). *Models of thought.* New Haven, CT: Yale University Press.

Strauss, J. (1987). *Psychosocial treatment of schizophrenia: Multidimensional concepts.* Lewiston, NY: Huber.

Turnbull, J. E. (1988). Who should ask? Ethical interviewing in psychiatric epidemiology studies. *American Journal of Orthopsychiatry, 58,* 228-239.

Ward-Colasante, C., Kaufmann, C. L., Roth, L. R., & Cook, M. (1990). *The Self Help Employment Center Project* (MH No. 47686). Rockville, MD: Substance Abuse and Mental Health Services Administration.

Weiss, C. I. (1992). Controlling domestic life and mental illness: Spiritual and aftercare resources used by Dominican New Yorkers. *Culture, Medicine, and Psychiatry, 16,* 237-271.

10.   The Naturalistic Paradigm as an Approach to Research With Mutual-Help Groups

MELLEN KENNEDY

KEITH HUMPHREYS

THOMASINA BORKMAN

T he positivist and postpositivist paradigms (Guba, 1990b) have been and continue to be the explicit and implicit approaches underlying the study of mutual-help groups, just as they have been the dominant paradigms in much of the behavioral and social sciences. In this chapter we argue that positivist paradigms are limited and inappropriate for studying many facets of mutual-help groups. We then present an alternative paradigm which has its own assumptions, criteria, and methods—naturalistic inquiry—as a guide for some research on self-help groups. After reviewing the advantages of using the naturalistic paradigm in mutual-help research, we provide practical guidelines for applying it to two areas of research: the problem resolution of participants in mutual-help groups and the process of transformation in worldviews among members of mutual-help groups. In the con-

AUTHORS' NOTE: This chapter grew out of a symposium at the Fourth Biennial Meeting of the Society for Community Research and Action in Williamsburg, VA, June, 1993. We would like to acknowledge and thank the other panel members and audience of the symposium for their contributions to the discussion and development of ideas reflected in this paper.

clusions, we summarize the challenges and advantages of adopting the naturalistic paradigm for research with mutual-help groups.

Before introducing and evaluating research paradigms, a definition of paradigm is in order. Mitroff (1974), following Kuhn, defines paradigm as an accepted framework that provides relatively clear-cut guidelines for all facets of scientific activity.

> It specifies the problems that will be worked on, the methods that will be used in working on them, the basic vocabulary that will be used for describing (recognizing) scientific problems, and above all, a common language, process, or medium for resolving the inevitable disagreements or disputes that arise among scientists, data, and theories. (p. 257)

A paradigm is a holistic framework with interrelated assumptions, concepts, and methodologies, not just a method, such as participant observation. Thus efforts to equate qualitative methods and the naturalistic paradigm are simplistic and misleading. In fact, while emphasizing qualitative methods, the naturalistic paradigm can and does use quantitative methods also.

THE POSITIVIST AND POSTPOSITIVIST PARADIGMS AND THEIR CRITICS

Positivism and postpositivism (a modified version of positivism) hold that reality exists out there and is subject to fixed natural laws and mechanisms. Positivism holds that it is possible and essential for the inquirer to adopt a distant, noninteractive posture by which the researcher's values and other confounding factors will be excluded from influencing observation. Postpositivism recognizes that pure objectivity is impossible but believes that objectivity can only be approximated and should be retained as a regulatory ideal (Guba, 1990a). The classic randomized experimental-control design with experimenter manipulation of variables is the methodological exemplar for positivism. The goal is to verify hypotheses and to test context-free theories. Postpositivism modifies methodologies by adding studies in natural settings using more qualitative methods and grounded theory and reintroducing discovery (not just verification) into the research process (e.g., Tebes & Kraemer, 1991). These additions are to help offset the perceived imbalances in the positivist paradigms between rigor and relevance, precision and richness, and elegance and applicability.

Across disciplines the positivist paradigms are under sustained criticism. The ideal of the detached researcher objectively collecting data has long been discredited in the physical and natural sciences (Lakoff & Johnson, 1980). In contrast to the myth of the detached observer, Mitroff (1974) showed that physical scientists were passionately committed to their pet theories and hypotheses.

> All the behavioral evidence I am aware of suggests that all observation by anything resembling human observers is mediated by their entire past behavioral and physical history, their current emotional state, their feelings and aspirations. In a word, all observations are observer dependent, dependent on the complicated and highly partial mental states of some observer. (Mitroff, 1974, p. 256)

Because of such criticism of the positivist paradigms, alternative paradigms are being explored vigorously in sociology (see Strauss & Corbin, 1990), psychology (see Gergen, 1985), education (see Lincoln & Guba, 1985), and other social and behavioral sciences, even economics, the queen bee of quantitative behavioral science (see Lavoie, 1990).

Given that part of the overall landscape of social science includes critiques of positivism and consideration of alternative paradigms, it seems appropriate to relate these issues to the context of self-help/mutual-aid research. Egon Guba (1990b), a major proponent of the naturalistic paradigm (Lincoln & Guba, 1985), has argued that all research paradigms are being challenged and clarified and therefore are evolving; none of the present paradigms will win out: "Rather, it is to take us to another level at which all of these paradigms will be replaced by yet another paradigm whose outlines we can see now dimly, if at all" (Guba 1990a, p. 27). Guba invites us to enter into a dialog about research paradigms, and in this chapter we extend the same invitation specifically to mutual-help researchers.

To understand the role of various paradigms in mutual-help research it is useful to review the history of how groups have been conceptualized. Research on mutual-help or self-help groups in the 1990s has been growing in amount, sophistication, and understanding (Borkman, 1991). We now know that these groups are much more complex, multidimensional, and diverse than was initially thought. In the 1970s these groups were patronizingly dismissed by some professionals as "hand holding" or "huddle together" groups (Sagarin, 1969) or were equated with professional group therapy (Hurvitz, 1974; Lieberman & Bliwise, 1985). Positivistic methodologies such as treatment effectiveness research with randomized assignments to experimental-control groups were touted as ideal designs which were unachievable in practice. Some enterprising psychologists created artificial groups (almost in the laboratory), labeled them self-help groups, and compared their outcomes with the equally artificially contrived control groups (see Jensen, 1983). In the 1980s, more workers have shown how self-help groups differed from formal human services systems (Riessman, 1990). For example, Twelve Step groups have been shown to have sophisticated ideological underpinnings which are not immediately apparent without in-depth understanding of them (Bateson, 1971; Kurtz 1982).

Current research is conceptualizing mutual-help groups as "communities of interest" (Borkman, 1990; Gidron & Chesler, in press) or "communities of belief" (Kennedy & Humphreys, in press), rather than as alternative human service systems. Many groups are autonomous social worlds coexisting amicably within mainstream society but with their own language, customs, beliefs, and social networks. The culture creating and transmitting aspects of groups is being explored, including how groups develop and use specialized experiential knowledge of their common problem (Schubert, 1991). Mutual-help groups construct their own cultural ideas including worldviews or subcultures that are often discrepant in certain ways from professional ideas (see Borkman, 1990; Humphreys, 1993b) or from their equivalent in mainstream society.

Accompanying the shift to conceptualize mutual-help groups as culture-transmitting entities, there is a reexamination of appropriate approaches for studying them. Even the "liberal" postpositivistic paradigms that use a variety of qualitative methods to situate the groups contextually are inadequate and limited.

THE ALTERNATIVE NATURALISTIC INQUIRY PARADIGM

We present the naturalistic inquiry paradigm as an appropriate alternative to positivistic or postpositivistic paradigms for studying mutual-help groups. The assumptions and criteria for adequate research in the naturalistic inquiry paradigm (as summarized in Table 10.1), as well as its methodological techniques for gathering and analyzing data, map well onto the culture-creating features of voluntary, community-based, naturally occurring mutual-help groups.

Assumptions of the Naturalistic Paradigm

We first describe the major assumptions of research of the naturalistic paradigm, based on the work of Guba and Lincoln (Guba, 1990a; Guba &

TABLE 10.1 Differences Between the Positivistic and Naturalistic Paradigms

	Paradigm	
Assumptions about	Positivist	Naturalistic
Reality	Single, tangible, convergent, reducible	Multiple, intangible, divergent, holistic
Researcher/ respondent relationship	Independent, objective	Interdependent
Relation of values to inquiry	Value-free	Value-bound
Nature of truth statements	Context-free generalizations, nomothetic statements, focus on similarities	Context-bound, idiographic statements, focus on differences
Criteria for judging	Internal validity External validity Reliability Objectivity	Credibility Transferability Dependability Confirmability
Additional criteria for naturalistic paradigm		Fairness Authenticity

Source: Based on Guba & Lincoln, 1983; Lincoln & Guba, 1986.

Lincoln, 1983; Lincoln & Guba, 1985). The naturalistic paradigm assumes that objectivity is impossible because the human observer perceives and interprets the world through a set of lenses based on upbringing, cultural heritage, values, social position, and experiences, as explained in foregoing quote by Mitroff. Thus, social "reality" is constructed by the observer, usually in interaction with other human beings (Berger & Luckmann, 1967). Observations are inherently value-laden (Howard, 1985). Research, therefore, is always influenced by the values of the researcher and those being researched, including the values inherent in the setting. The choice of research problem, the theory that frames the research, and the methods of inquiry are bound by the researcher's values as well.

The question of what is the nature of social reality is answered relativistically; that is, there are multiple realities in the form of "multiple mental constructions, socially and experientially based, local and specific, dependent for their form and content on the persons who hold them" (Guba, 1990a, p. 27). Social reality is therefore assumed to be complex, constructed, and changing rather than simple, concrete, and static. As opposed to a single objective "truth," the naturalistic researcher seeks multiple viewpoints on a phenomenon. The interpretations and meanings of people's social worlds are the focus of naturalistic inquiry.

The naturalistic paradigm assumes that all aspects of the phenomenon under study are interdependent and mutually interacting so that the determination of linear causality is impossible and inappropriate. The intent of naturalistic inquiry is not to generate causal models but rather to thickly describe (Geertz, 1973) the setting, people, processes, and the meanings and interpretations people have of their world. Similarly, the goal in naturalistic research is not to generate "universal" all-encompassing theories but to explore and describe phenomena within a specific context, in this case mutual-help groups. Accordingly, the research produces idiographic statements rather than broad generalizations.

If all observers are constructing their own version of social reality and the researcher's version is not inherently superior to that of the observed, the hierarchical position of the researcher in relation to the "subject" of research becomes inappropriate. The conceptual and practical walls between researcher and subject are thus removed. Naturalistic researchers accept that they will affect and be affected by the people and the group and that this engagement produces a fuller understanding of the group rather than a necessarily biased one.

Criteria for Judging Naturalistic Research

Because the naturalistic paradigm has a different set of assumptions, it follows that the criteria for judging naturalistic studies are also different from those used in the positivist paradigm. In this chapter we simply summarize these criteria in order to alert the reader to these differences. We refer the reader particularly to the work of Lincoln and Guba (Guba & Lincoln, 1983; Lincoln & Guba, 1986) for in-depth discussion. In the positivist paradigm, the main concern has been to assure the rigor of a study with the criteria of validity, reliability, and objectivity. In the naturalistic paradigm the concept of rigor is replaced with that of trustworthiness, and the criteria for testing for trustworthiness are different than the criteria associated with the positivist paradigm. In the naturalistic paradigm, rather than internal validity, researchers are concerned with meeting the criterion of credibility through having extended engagement in the field, using triangulation, and performing negative case analysis. Rather than external validity, naturalistic researchers address the criterion of transferability. Through thick description of the setting, the organization, and so on, they allow the reader to assess the transferability of findings to other contexts. Rather than emphasizing reliability and objectivity, naturalistic researchers are concerned with the criteria of dependability and confirmability. The empirical materials gathered through observation, interviews, and conversations are organized, and these materials as well as the written product are subjected to an audit by an external auditor (Lincoln & Guba, 1986).

In addition, naturalistic studies must meet the criteria of fairness and authenticity, which are unique to the naturalistic paradigm (Lincoln & Guba, 1986). Because multiple realities, values, and beliefs exist in every setting, the criterion of fairness is addressed by attempting to determine the diverse views, values, and experiences and to provide a balanced presentation of them. The naturalistic criterion of authenticity refers to the implications and educative impact of the study itself. Naturalistic researchers are concerned with the effectiveness of the study in raising the awareness of members of the setting and of readers of the study as well (Lincoln & Guba, 1986). In summary, the adequacy of a naturalistic study is assessed with the criteria of credibility, transferability, dependability, confirmability, fairness, and authenticity, rather than with those criteria appropriate for research in the positivist paradigm.

THE ADVANTAGES OF NATURALISTIC INQUIRY WITH SELF-HELP GROUPS

One of the main advantages of naturalistic research is that its assumptions are consonant with the setting of mutual-help groups. As we begin to see self-help groups as complex communities of interest or belief, multiple constructions of the social reality of the group become apparent. Each member holds his or her own construction of reality and personal story. What occurs in a group is not unidimensional, but rather complex and varied. With a naturalistic approach, these different perspectives and different voices in a setting are sought and valued. The approach liberates researchers from the tyranny of the mean score by allowing them to explore the entire distribution of experiences, including unusual cases. It emphasizes describing and conveying the complexity of a group, including minority or marginalized experiences. The naturalistic paradigm reflects this complex and multifaceted representation of reality and thus is congruent with the characteristics of the phenomenon of self-help groups.

The naturalistic approach also provides an understanding of the processes by which a group functions by allowing researchers the opportunity to see groups as members do. Naturalistic researchers try to render the interpretations of the setting held by the members themselves, which opens up new areas of inquiry. Work in the area of mutual-help storytelling and worldview transformation would not have appeared out of a positivist approach because these elements of mutual-help are not likely to be known to outsiders (Antze, 1976; Cain, 1991; Humphreys, 1992; Humphreys & Kennedy, 1993; Kennedy & Humphreys, in press).

Another advantage of naturalistic research is its potential for yielding a product that promotes experiential understanding of mutual help. A trademark of naturalistic research is the thick, descriptive texts that are generated, relying heavily on the voices, accents, and feelings of the people in the setting. This kind of engaging text provides an experiential bridge for the reader, which is accessible to the ordinary reader and is particularly useful for the reader unfamiliar with mutual-help groups. In reading the research report, mutual-help group members can recognize their group and their experience.

Another advantage is the potential for empowerment that this approach holds. Researchers are attempting to understand the group from the members' perspectives rather than testing their own a priori theories. Thus in a naturalistic study, the group members are active participants in the research process. The involvement of group members includes a shared control of the direction of the project. This control is enhanced by the fact, as indicated above, that the mutual helpers themselves can usually understand the report of a naturalistic project in a way they usually cannot understand a multivariate statistical analysis of their organization.

APPLICATIONS

Thus far we have described the philosophical underpinnings of the naturalistic paradigm and detailed its advantages as an approach to mutual-help research. Because for many researchers an understanding of the philosophy of science behind research paradigms is not sufficient for appropriate translation into methods, we turn now to a discussion of the practice of naturalistic inquiry. Naturalistic inquiry usually involves the study of a naturally occurring setting or phenomenon, as opposed to experimental control and manipulation. Naturalistic researchers are usually engaged in fieldwork in this setting over an extended period of time as opposed to conducting a single observation or incident of data collection. The naturalistic project is by design emergent and does not necessarily proceed linearly, because it is discovery oriented rather than purely theory driven. The focus of the naturalistic project is on understanding and describing the experiences of the people in the setting. Methods typically associated with the naturalistic paradigm have included participant observation, in-depth interviewing, life history, ethnography, and case study to name a few.

To become a competent practitioner of naturalistic inquiry the researcher should become familiar with the discourse from disciplines that have long traditions of naturalistic research (e.g. sociology, education, anthropology). Naturalistic research requires learning a new vocabulary and way of looking at the research enterprise. This entails becoming familiar with a different knowledge base, learning a different set of skills and methods across the entire enterprise of research including fieldwork, data collection and analysis (for useful starting points, see Burgess, 1984; Charmaz, 1983; Chesler, 1991; Denzin, 1990; Denzin & Lincoln, 1994; Fielding & Lee, 1991; Glaser & Strauss, 1967; Goetz & LeCompte, 1984; Jacob, 1987; Lincoln & Guba, 1985; Miles & Huberman, 1994; Spradley, 1979, 1980; Strauss & Corbin, 1990; Taylor & Bogdan, 1984; Werner & Schoepfle, 1987; Whyte, 1991). A distinct challenge of naturalistic research is that it requires a different kind of writing than that practiced in writing positivist reports. There have been a number of very helpful resources, particularly in recent years, to guide a researcher in this process (Atkinson, 1991; Lincoln & Guba, 1990; Richardson, 1990; Wolcott, 1990).

Although calls for naturalistic and qualitative research have been made and applauded in the self-help area for 20 years, few studies of this sort have actually been conducted. To help alleviate this problem, we will now give specific ways that the naturalistic paradigm can be and has been used in the study of mutual-help groups. Because there is not sufficient space to discuss the many possible topics, we have narrowed our discussion to two specific areas of mutual-help research: the effects of group participation on problem resolution and the experience of worldview transformation.

Problem Resolution

Although self-help members themselves have no doubt that their programs are helpful, policymakers and many social scientists have great interest in the question of outcomes or "Does self-help really work?" Thus, numerous studies have attempted to determine if self-help groups help resolve the problems they address (e.g., Does Take Off Pounds Sensibly result in weight loss?, Does Narcotics Anonymous help people stop using drugs?, etc.). Naturalistic research takes a different approach to these issues than have some controlled experiments which used random assignment to study the effectiveness of groups (e.g., Levitz & Stunkard, 1974).

The naturalistic approach to studying the effects of the group on the problems of its members is to collaborate with group members in trying to understand how they think the group benefits them. In cases where the naturalistic researcher has experienced the problem or status addressed by the group, he or she gains further information on outcome by joining the group, participating in it actively, and thereby experiencing the phenomenological and behavioral changes that "regular" members do.

Because social reality is constructed, naturalistic researchers view any question about the effectiveness of a group as being subjective, value laden, and representing someone's interests. The question of effectiveness could not be asked in naturalistic research, free of a description of the interests and characteristics of the inquirer, putting that person or organization on an equal footing with self-helpers who believe their group works. For example, a naturalistic researcher who was studying an antipsychiatry mutual-help organization for former mental patients could ask any number of questions such as:

In the opinion of local mental health professionals, does this group make patients less trusting of their psychiatrists?

Do policymakers who want rates of mental health service utilization to drop think this group is effective because it reduces hospitalization rates and thereby saves money?

Do the people who participate in the group feel it helps them, and if so how?

From a feminist perspective, does this mutual-help group give sufficient opportunities for women members to lead meetings?

Obviously, the list of potential questions is extensive. The obligation of the naturalistic researcher is not to consider every question of effectiveness but to explicitly identify the value-laden nature of whichever questions and ways of studying the group's ability to resolve problems is employed. No univocal verdict on the group's ability to resolve the problems of members would be offered. Each interested party would get their say. Each person's opinion would be represented as the subjective viewpoint of an interested party, not as truth.

An example of the redefinition of problem resolution comes from self-help groups for people who stutter. In the 1970s early self-help groups for people who stutter tried the problem resolution approach of many speech therapists who believed the outcome of speech therapy was fluency. But members had multiple experiences being fluent only in the therapist's office or for a few months after completing therapy. The self-help group gradually redefined problem resolution as (a) being comfortable talking although disfluent and (b) expanding, not restricting their life goals and activities, although they sometimes stuttered (Borkman, 1979, 1993).

Part of identifying the subjective viewpoints that define what is good or bad about a group is for researchers to be forthcoming with their own subjectivity. In studying the effectiveness of a mutual-help group, the researcher's general attitudes about self-help are important to detail. For example, in his ethnographies of Alcoholics Anonymous (AA), Denzin (1987) states clearly that he is "pro-Alcoholics Anonymous." Similarly in studying Adult Children of Alcoholics mutual-help groups, Humphreys (1993c) stated that although he did not believe the organization was above criticism, his general evaluation of the people who participated in the group was very positive.

Another important task for naturalistic researchers who study a group's effect on the problems of its members is to explore the diversity of outcomes experienced by members. To avoid the confirmatory bias, it is important that researchers actively seek out cases where any general hypotheses do not apply. This negative case analysis is part of doing naturalistic research competently (Lincoln & Guba, 1986). If 24 members of a 25-member self-help group for bereaved parents come to feel a new sense of faith but the 25th member becomes depressed at the cruelty of the world, each type of change should receive full and careful attention. Or if the researcher believes that a group is more helpful for older people than younger people, it would be important to interview an older person who was not helped by the group and a younger person who was helped by it a great deal. Thus rather than imposing a single outcome standard that may not fit the setting, the naturalistic researcher illuminates the diverse effects self-help has on participants.

Finally, to ensure that information on how groups help their members is understood in its context, a naturalistic researcher describes the context of the groups studied in great detail ("thickly"). Many commentators have noted that within particular self-help organizations, the diversity among chapters is increasing. For example, in studying AA in one community, Keith

Humphreys noted that some meetings focused entirely on how to control cravings to drink whereas others dealt with spiritual and philosophical concerns of alcoholics who had been sober for many years. A naturalistic study would include a description of these kinds of differences across group meetings. Characteristics such as the physical setting, the town in which the meeting was held, who attended, the length of time and intensity of participation of members, the format, the size of the group, and the gender, racial, and age composition of the members, just to name a few important features, would be included in the report. This enables the reader to understand the specific context of problem resolution of group members in that study.

Worldview Transformation

Most mutual-help research does not do justice to the aspect of self-help that many members consider to be of paramount importance: the group's teachings and how members absorb and apply them (Antze, 1976). Through their participation in the group, members are exposed to new interpretations of the world, which affect how they view their relationships, themselves, their problem, and their spirituality (Kennedy & Humphreys, in press). One logical undertaking of self-help research that is still clearly incomplete is understanding such changes.

One of the reasons worldview transformation has such a small place in the research literature relative to its importance to self-helpers is that it is nearly impossible to study with positivist methods and paradigms. Worldview transformation cannot be experimentally manipulated, and because members typically experience it as intensely meaningful and important, they are often unwilling to reveal their experience to emotionally detached investigators. The positivist tenet that understanding a phenomenon is in an oppositional relationship with engaging it deeply and personally can be easily discredited by attempting to study worldview transformation under such a standard. One mutual-help researcher, Norman Denzin (personal communication, July 5, 1993), has noted that many AA members have now developed catch phrases to answer questions from curious outsiders, including academics. According to Denzin, "I don't know—it just does" is becoming a common response to the question "How does your organization really work?" As shown in Denzin's ethnographies (1986, 1987), AA members actually often have quite elaborate theories as to how AA works, but they, like many self-helpers, are not interested in making them known to unsympathetic or insensitive observers.

In contrast, if researchers are willing to give up methodological and personal control and engage group members in a collaborative, mutually open fashion, a great deal about worldview transformation can be learned. Rudy (1986) used a naturalistic approach to study changes in worldview of AA members. Through participant observation and in-depth interviews with AA members, he studied the processes involved in identifying oneself as a member of AA and as an alcoholic. He paid particular attention to the testimonies of AA members and to how new members are exposed to and sometimes assimilate the identity of alcoholic and the beliefs of AA that are reflected in that understanding of themselves.

For a number of years, a mutual-help organization for chronic mental patients (GROW) has collaborated with researchers at the University of Illinois on a series of research projects (Rappaport et al., 1985). One of these studies was a naturalistic project undertaken by Kennedy (Kennedy & Humphreys, 1993). Kennedy spent several years attending meetings of GROW, participating actively in the organization and becoming friends with members. Over this period she developed initial ideas about how members experienced changes in their worldviews over time, largely by hearing members' testimonies. With the consent of highly involved members of the group, Kennedy then created a transcript of each member's story of transformation. The transcript was given to the member so that the GROW member could comment on and have control over how the information was presented. Kennedy and the GROW members thus shared control and negotiated the final version of the transcript. Through this process Kennedy's initial ideas were refined to better map the phenomenology of the members. Kennedy subsequently identified similarities and differences in worldview change across the members with whom she collaborated. Although a positivist might criticize such an approach and perhaps label it as "going native," other approaches would not have accessed worldview changes of group members. If the goal of social science is understanding the phenomenon, then Kennedy's naturalistic approach was clearly the appropriate paradigmatic choice.

Cain (1991) conducted a naturalistic study of worldview transformation that emphasized the role of personal stories in mutual-help groups (see Humphreys, 1993a; Rappaport, this volume). She immersed herself in the personal stories told in AA's Big Book, eventually delineating a prototypical story. She subsequently asked AA members with varying levels of experience in AA to tell her their personal stories of recovery. She did not try to direct the process of their storytelling. She then showed that those who had more AA experience told personal stories that were more similar to the prototypic AA form. Thus she argued that storytelling is a way that AA members incorporate the AA worldview and the identity of "alcoholic" into their consciousness.

No research paradigm is perfect for the study of all problems, but the naturalistic paradigm has unique contributions to make both to the study of worldviews and other culturally created knowledge as well as outcome or problem resolution. We turn now to some concluding remarks on the naturalistic paradigm in mutual-help research.

CONCLUSIONS

The naturalistic approach is not a panacea. Among the challenges in conducting naturalistic research is the necessity for adequate training. For many researchers, their training has had primarily if not solely a positivistic bent. Without adequate study and training one can easily and unknowingly bring the blinders of the positivist research paradigm into a naturalistic project.

A naturalistic approach may present the researcher with ethical issues and dilemmas quite different than those encountered in the positivist approach. The concepts from the ethical armament of the positivist paradigm—informed consent, researcher detachment, confidentiality, and avoidance of harm—leave the researcher unprepared for the complexity of naturalistic work. These concepts were developed and are appropriate for experimentation on human subjects. For example, in a naturalistic study of a mutual-help group an informed consent form could be seen by group members as odd, unnecessary, or even alarming (Lykes, 1989). When naturalistic researchers become members of the group, the ethical norms of that community apply to them as well as to other members. They are seen as having responsibility and obligations to others in the group and to the organization of the group itself. Thus naturalistic research has developed alternative concepts and constructions of ethical issues in naturalistic research (Flinders, 1992) that address the complexity of ethical dynamics in fieldwork.

Because of the immersion of researchers in the group and the open-endedness of inquiry, researchers will discover unanticipated information which will sometimes present ethical dilemmas. In a positivist research approach, this is less likely to occur because the data collection instruments specify and limit the kinds of information obtained and to an extent protect researchers from awareness of certain aspects of the setting.

A final challenge of naturalistic research is the emotional and professional vulnerability that researchers may experience in order to be truly immersed in a mutual-help group which they also study. In fieldwork, the approach requires that researchers be able to endure uncertainty and ambiguity. Researchers need to be patient and tolerant of the inherently uncontrollable nature of real world phenomena. These aspects can be problematic for researchers on a strict time line or needing to respond to committees or funders.

In addition, because researcher detachment is so highly prized in academia, naturalistic researchers may be accused of going native or of practicing substandard research. A clear and strong command of the assumptions of the naturalistic paradigm is necessary in order for researchers to argue and explain their methods and choices. The methods, although seemingly flawed or inadequate when judged by the assumptions of the positivist paradigm, are actually sound and follow quite logically from the naturalistic paradigm. An implicit assumption here is that researchers must also understand the positivist paradigm (often better than its proponents) in order to argue effectively for how and why their approach differs.

In closing, we are encouraging researchers interested in mutual-help groups to consider the informed use of naturalistic inquiry. This includes awareness of the challenges of this kind of work as well as its many potential benefits. In our own work we are finding that the benefits of the approach certainly counterbalance the difficulties entailed, particularly when researchers undertake a project with an understanding of these difficulties. Use of the naturalistic approach will not solve all problems in mutual-help research but it will provide a rich description of the varied experiences of group members, address the agenda of empowerment in the research process, yield an accessible and engaging product, and promote an understanding of the processes active in groups from members' perspectives.

REFERENCES

Antze, P. (1976). The role of ideologies in peer psychotherapy organizations: Some theoretical considerations and three case studies. *Journal of Applied Behavioral Science, 12,* 323-346.

Atkinson, P. (1991). Supervising the text. *Qualitative Studies in Education, 4,* 161-174.

Bateson, G. (1971). The cybernetics of "self": A theory of alcoholism. *Psychiatry, 34,* 309-337.

Berger, P., & Luckmann, T. (1967). *The social construction of reality.* New York: Doubleday.

Borkman, T. (1979). *Mutual self-help groups: A theory of experiential inquiry.* Unpublished manuscript, National Institute for on Alcohol Abuse and Alcoholism.

Borkman, T. (1990). Experiential, professional and lay frames of reference. In T. J. Powell (Ed.), *Working with self-help* (pp. 3-30). Silver Spring, MD: NASW Press.

Borkman, T. (1991). Introduction to the special issue (on self-help groups). *American Journal of Community Psychology, 19,* 643-650.

Borkman, T. (1993, December). *The evolution of worldviews about stuttering in a self-help group.* Paper submitted to the Social Movement Section of the American Psychological Association.

Burgess, R. G. (1984). *In the field: An introduction to field research.* London: George Allen & Unwin.

Cain, C. (1991). Personal stories, identity acquisition, and self-understanding in Alcoholics Anonymous. *Ethos, 19,* 210-253.

Charmaz, K. (1983). Grounded theory method: An explication and interpretation. In R. M. Emerson (Ed.), *Contemporary field research: A collection of readings* (pp. 109-126). Boston, MA: Little, Brown.

Chesler, M. A. (1991). Participatory action research with self-help groups: An alternative paradigm for inquiry and action. *American Journal of Community Psychology, 19,* 757-768.

Denzin, N. K. (1986). *The alcoholic self.* Newbury Park, CA: Sage.

Denzin, N. K. (1987). *The recovering alcoholic.* Newbury Park, CA: Sage.

Denzin, N. K. (1990). *Interpretive biography.* Newbury Park, CA: Sage.

Denzin, N. K., & Lincoln, Y. S. (Eds.). (1994). *Handbook of qualitative research.* Thousand Oaks, CA: Sage.

Fielding, N. G., & Lee, R. M. (1991). *Using computers in qualitative research.* Newbury Park, CA: Sage.

Flinders, D. J. (1992). In search of ethical guidance:Constructing a basis for dialogue. *Qualitative Studies in Education, 5,* 101-115.

Geertz, C. (1973). *The interpretation of cultures.* New York: Basic Books.

Gergen, K. J. (1985). The social constructionist movement in modern psychology. *American Psychologist, 40,* 266-275.

Gidron, B., & Chesler, M. (in press). Universal and particular attributes of self help: A framework for international and intranational analysis. In *Prevention in Human Services.* New York: Haworth.

Glaser, B., & Strauss, A. (1967). *The discovery of grounded theory.* Chicago: Aldine.

Goetz, J. P., & LeCompte, M. D. (1984). *Ethnography and qualitative design in educational research.* Orlando, FL: Academic Press.

Guba, E. G. (1990a). The alternative paradigm dialog. In E. Guba (Ed.), *The paradigm dialog* (pp. 17-27). Newbury Park, CA: Sage.

Guba, E. G. (Ed.). (1990b). *The paradigm dialog.* Newbury Park, CA: Sage.

Guba, E. G., & Lincoln, Y. S. (1983). Epistemological and methodological bases of naturalistic inquiry. In G. F. Madaus, M. Scriven, & D. L. Stufflebem (Eds.), *Evaluation models: Viewpoints on educational and human services evaluations* (pp. 311-333). Boston: Kluwer-Nijhoff.

Howard, G. (1985). The role of values in the science of psychology. *American Psychologist, 40,* 255-265.

Humphreys, K. (1992, May). *Stories and personal transformation in Alcoholics Anonymous.* Paper presented at the meeting of the Midwestern Psychological Association, Chicago.

Humphreys, K. (1993a). Expanding the pluralist revolution: A comment on Omer and Strenger. *Psychotherapy, 30,* 176-177.

Humphreys, K. (1993b). Psychotherapy and the Twelve Step approach for substance abusers: The limits of integration. *Psychotherapy, 30,* 207-213.

Humphreys, K. (1993c). *World view transformation in Adult Children of Alcoholics mutual help groups.* Unpublished doctoral dissertation, University of Illinois, Urbana.

Humphreys, K., & Kennedy, M. (1993, June). The function and power of stories in mutual help groups. In M. Kennedy (chair), *Communal narratives: The functions of storytelling in diverse settings,* Symposium conducted at the fourth biennial meeting of the Society for Community Research & Action, Williamsburg, VA.

Hurvitz, N. (1974). Peer self-help psychotherapy groups: Psychotherapy without psychotherapists. In P. I. Roman & H. M. Trice (Eds.), *The sociology of psychotherapy* (pp. 84-138). New York: Jason Aronson.

Jacob, E. (1987). Qualitative research traditions: A review.*Review of Educational Research, 57*(1), 1-50

Jensen, P. S. (1983). Risk, protective factors and supportive interaction in chronic airway obstruction. *Archives of General Psychiatry, 40,* 1203-1207.

Kennedy, M., & Humphreys, K. (1993, June). *Promises and perils of naturalistic research with mutual help groups.* Paper presented at the fourth biennial meeting of the Society for Community Research & Action, Williamsburg, VA.

Kennedy, M., & Humphreys, K. (in press). Understanding worldview transformation in members of mutual help groups. In *Prevention in Human Services.* New York: Haworth.

Kurtz, E. (1982). Why A.A. works: The intellectual significance of A.A. *Journal of Studies on Alcohol, 43,* 38-80.

Lakoff, G., & Johnson, M. (1980). *Metaphors we live by.* Chicago: University of Chicago Press.

Lavoie, D. (Ed.). (1990). *Economics and hermeneutics.* London: Routledge.

Levitz, L. S., & Stunkard, A. J. (1974). A therapeutic coalition for obesity: Behavior modification and patient self-help. *American Journal of Psychiatry, 131,* 423-427.

Lieberman, M., & Bliwise, N. G. (1985). Comparisons among peer and professionally directed groups for the elderly: Implications for the development of self-help groups. *International Journal of Group Psychotherapy, 35,* 155-175.

Lincoln, Y. S., & Guba, E. G. (1985). *Naturalistic inquiry.* Newbury Park, CA: Sage.

Lincoln, Y. S., & Guba, E. G. (1986). But is it rigorous? Trustworthiness and authenticity in naturalistic evaluation. *Naturalistic Evaluation, 30,* 73-84.

Lincoln, Y. S., & Guba, E. G. (1990). Judging the quality of case study reports. *Qualitative Studies in Education, 3,* 53-59.

Lykes, M. B. (1989). Dialogue with Guatemalan Indian women: Critical perspectives on constructing collaborative research. In R. K. Unger (Ed.), *Representations: Social constructions of gender* (pp. 167-185). Amityville, NY: Baywood.

Miles, M. B., & Huberman, A. M. (1994). *Qualitative data analysis: An expanded sourcebook.* Thousand Oaks, CA: Sage.

Mitroff, I. (1974). *The subjective side of science.* New York: Elsevier.

Rappaport, J. (1994). Narrative studies, personal stories, and identity transformation in the mutual-help context. In T. J. Powell (Ed.), *Understanding the self-help organization: Frameworks and findings.* Thousand Oaks, CA: Sage.

Rappaport, J., Seidman, E., Toro, P. A., McFadden, L. S., Reischl, T. M., Roberts, L. J., Salem, D. A., Stein, C. H., & Zimmerman, M. A. (1985). Collaborative research with a mutual help organization. *Social Policy, 15,* 12-24.

Richardson, L. (1990). *Writing strategies: Reaching diverse audiences.* Newbury Park, CA: Sage.

Riessman, F. (1990). Restructuring help: A human services paradigm for the 1990s. *American Journal of Community Psychology, 18,* 221-230.

Rudy, D. R. (1986). *Becoming alcoholic: Alcoholics Anonymous and the reality of alcoholism.* Carbondale: Southern Illinois University Press.

Sagarin, E. (1969). *Odd man in: Societies of deviants in America.* Chicago: Quadrangle.

Schubert, M. A. (1991). *Investigating experiential knowledge in a self-help group.* Unpublished doctoral dissertation, George Mason University, Fairfax, VA.

Spradley, J. P. (1979). *The ethnographic interview.* New York: Holt Rinehart & Winston.

Spradley, J. P. (1980). *Participant observation.* New York: Holt Rinehart & Winston.

Strauss, A., & Corbin, J. (1990). *Basics of qualitative research.* Newbury Park, CA: Sage.

Taylor, S. J., & Bogdan, R. (1984). *Introduction to qualitative research methods: The search for meaning.* New York: John Wiley.

Tebes, J. K., & Kraemer, D. T. (1991). Quantitative and qualitative knowing in mutual support research: Some lessons from the recent history of scientific psychology. *American Journal of Community Psychology, 19,* 739-756.

Werner, O., & Schoepfle, G. M. (1987). *Systematic fieldwork: Vols. 1 and 2.* Newbury Park, CA: Sage.

Whyte, W. F. (Ed.). (1991). *Participatory action research.* Newbury Park, CA: Sage.

Wolcott, H. F. (1990). *Writing up qualitative research.* Newbury Park, CA: Sage.

11. The Self-Help Clearinghouse: A New Development in Action Research for Community Psychology

GREGORY J. MEISSEN

MARY L. WARREN

S elf-help clearinghouses have developed to facilitate awareness of and use of self-help groups. The self-help clearinghouse can be defined as an interface between self-help groups and other organizations, populations, professionals, and the public. Although the functions of self-help clearinghouses vary, they generally offer some combination of the following services: compilation and distribution of self-help group listings, information and referral to groups, technical assistance to existing groups, assistance to persons starting new groups, public awareness, professional education, and research related to the nature and effectiveness of self-help groups (Borck & Aronowitz, 1982; Madara, Kalafat, Miller, 1988; Meissen, Gleason, & Embree, 1991; Wollert, 1987, 1988). The President's Commission on

AUTHORS' NOTE: Work for this chapter was supported in part by grants from the Kansas Health Foundation and the National Institute of Mental Health and was first presented at a National Institute of Mental Health-sponsored workshop on Advances in Self-Help Group Research held at the Center for Self-Help Mental Health Research and Dissemination, Ann Arbor, Michigan. Thomas Powell, Director of the Center for Self-Help Mental Health Research, provided useful suggestions on earlier drafts, as did other participants at the research workshop.

Mental Health (1978) specifically recommended the development of self-help clearinghouses. *Healthy People 2000,* the National Health Promotion and Disease Prevention Objectives published by the U.S. Department of Health and Human Services (DHHS), includes the establishment of statewide self-help clearinghouses in at least 25 states as one of its year 2000 goals (DHHS, 1990). There now are about 50 self-help clearinghouses in the United States, including a number of statewide clearinghouses and two national ones. There are several self-help clearinghouses in Canada, as well as in a number of countries outside of North America.

Lewin's (1946, 1947) thinking regarding action research has served as a model for many profitable adaptations and elaborations (e.g., Campbell, 1972, 1974; Fairweather & Tornatzky, 1977; Ketterer, Price, & Polister, 1980; Tolan, Keys, Chertok, & Jason, 1990) which have been applied to numerous social problems and organizational settings (e.g., Cowen, Gesten & Weissberg, 1980; Monahan, 1980). The action research concepts of collaboration, acquisition of theoretically driven practical knowledge, organizational feedback, intervention, and evaluation provide a framework for understanding how researchers, self-help clearinghouses, and self-help groups can collaborate to advance the understanding and the effectiveness of self-help groups and of clearinghouses.

Community psychology has historically struggled with the application of rigorous methodology developed for laboratory and clinical settings to complex, multivariate community-based research questions (Campbell, 1972; Tolan et al., 1990). The complexity is increased by an action research perspective, which includes collaboration with consumers/participants of the research (Rappaport, 1990). Many of these same issues apply to research involving self-help groups. A more profitable and less confining perspective on community-based research has begun to emerge, one that does not abandon community psychology's strong commitment to rigorous methodology but does encourage a research focus on the construction of knowledge and of understanding: "The value of research knowledge, then, is in its descriptive richness, explanatory utility, and conceptual robustness, rather than in its situational independence, ability to provide a general fact, and generalizability of results" (Tolan et al., 1990, p. 7). This perspective encourages qualitative, historical, and anthropological approaches at different levels of analysis and seems particularly appropriate considering the nature of self-help groups, the need for close collaboration with group members, and the difficulty of conducting traditional outcome research with self-help groups. Self-help clearinghouses have more to contribute to research from this perspective because they possess a working understanding of many different types of groups and operate as an interface between self-help groups and other entities in the community. Clearinghouses also will be more likely to participate in research that actively provides information and that improves their ability to serve self-help groups.

THE SELF-HELP CLEARINGHOUSE
AS METHODOLOGICAL INVENTION[1]

The self-help clearinghouse can be viewed as a *methodological invention* that can address some of the practical and methodological difficulties of conducting self-help group research, in part through the opportunity which it offers to access large numbers and diverse samples of self-help groups for research purposes. Self-help clearinghouses have routine contact with self-help groups, which produces established, mutually beneficial relationships with groups. The success of a clearinghouse is based on understanding, and being invested in, the needs of the self-help groups in its geographic area (Meissen, Gleason et al., 1991). This combination of access to groups and concern about their well-being can make possible high-quality research that is sensitive to the needs and the autonomy of self-help groups.

Early research on self-help groups focused on descriptions of group function, attempts at group typologies, and anecdotal accounts of positive outcomes for members (Katz, 1981; Levy, 1984). Recent research has been more quantitative in nature, and a number of outcome studies have been conducted, many with methodological strengths (Medvene, 1987). Some researchers have suggested that outcome studies of self-help groups have been overemphasized and that quasi-experimental and qualitative studies are important in order to provide more in-depth understanding of the nature of self-help groups and why people find them beneficial (Borkman, 1990; Riessman, 1992). There are many important research questions related to the nature and use of self-help groups that should be pursued, especially since it is likely that self-help groups will be in greater use in the future (Eisenberg, et al., 1993; Jacobs & Goodman, 1989; Powell, 1987). Even though research related to self-help groups has increased in sophistication and volume, the extent of such research is still quite limited, considering the number of people involved in groups and the extent to which self-help groups have become a part of human services (DHHS, 1988; Eisenberg et al., 1993; Levy, in press). Self-help clearinghouses can be viewed as methodological inventions that enable one to specifically address many of the most serious methodological problems of conducting research with self-help groups.

Overcoming the Research Problem
of the Definition of a Self-Help Group

One continuing problem in self-help group research involves the operational definition of a self-help group. Self-help groups are defined most commonly as being cost-free, member governed, and peer led and made up of people who share the same problem or situation. Despite the self-help label, the assistance provided is best described as mutual help or mutual assistance (Levine, 1988). Self-help clearinghouses implicitly define a self-help group as one which is in their database of groups. For example, in order to be listed in the Self-Help Network of Kansas database, a group has to meet the following criteria: (a) composition of members who share a common situation or problem; (b) mutual-assistance orientation—members helping members as the primary form of assistance; (c) no user fees or fees for professional service. Groups charging a fee, including fees on a sliding scale, are not included. At the same time, it is common for groups to collect small voluntary contributions for basic group needs (e.g., refreshments, newsletter costs, chapter dues to their national organization). Although about 43% of the groups in our database ask for small contributions, a great majority of them are peer-led groups and all of them are based in mutual assistance.

There are many groups of peers who share a common problem in which professionals are involved in some leadership role. These groups with professional involvement make up about 30% of our database (Meissen, Gleason et al., 1991; Meissen, Warren, Volk, & Herring, 1992). The roles of these professionals range from being quite unobtrusive (e.g., "on call" liaison from a local agency, telephone contact person for referral) to being in charge of the group as part of one's job description at a local agency sponsoring the group (Meissen et al., 1992). At the same time, the nature of the help provided in these groups is mutual assistance, access to the group is free of charge, and the group is made up of people who share the same problem. Our experience in making over 30,000 referrals to groups over the past 5 years is that persons seeking a self-help group are concerned about finding a cost-free group of peers who share the common problem; they usually are not concerned about the level of professional involvement. Most self-help clearinghouses include in their database groups which have professional involvement because it is better to refer to such a group based in mutual assistance than to not refer a person to a group at all.

One critical issue when conducting research is to provide an explicit operational definition of a self-help group and of the specific type of group to be included in the sample, a task more difficult than many researchers initially expect. The primary advantage of accessing a self-help clearing-house database in terms of definitional issues is that a sample of groups that conform with the operational definition outlined for the research can be obtained. In this way, researchers can develop explicit operational defini-tions for inclusion of specific types of groups in a particular study and draw a sample based on that operational definition. For example, we have recently drawn a random sample of peer-led groups that do not have a Twelve Step philosophy in order to study the phenomenon of leader burnout. Profession-als in leadership positions in self-help groups were not included in the sample because their roles in working with people typically are broader and more varied, which theoretically could impact burnout in different ways. Groups with a Twelve Step orientation were not included because their traditions typically prohibit formal leaders, with the work of the group spread among the membership. A sample large enough to draw legitimate conclusions can be obtained while the researcher is still able to select the types of groups that make the best theoretical sense for the research questions being asked.

Improving Methodological Rigor

There are some special methodological difficulties involved in self-help group research which explain, in part, the relative paucity of such research, especially funded research (Levy, 1984, in press). Although essential to optimizing internal validity, it is impossible to randomly assign individuals to self-help group and control conditions without compromising the nature of the phenomena being evaluated. Although positive outcomes have been found through studies in which individuals were randomly assigned to self-help group and to control conditions (e.g., Barrett, 1978; Marmar, Horowitz, Weiss, Wilner & Kaltreider, 1988; Speigel, Bloom, Kraemer & Gottheil, 1989), the groups constructed were likely to be fundamentally different in some important ways from naturally occurring self-help groups. It has been theorized that one of the components of self-help groups respon-sible for positive outcomes is that members are attracted to a particular group and to its existing members, that they voluntarily join, and that they purpose-fully maintain their affiliation with the self-help group. This produces a unique helping situation for each self-help group, based in large part on the individuals who make up the group and their personal interactions and relationships. This lack of uniformity of self-help groups even occurs across groups which are affiliated with national self-help organizations (e.g., Alcoholics Anonymous [AA], Compassionate Friends) and which follow the same basic philosophy (e.g., Twelve Steps and Twelve Traditions). Conducting research with existing groups that involves intervention or intrusive data collection also can alter the natural functioning of the groups, distorting the data obtained, but more importantly it can risk the autonomy of the group and can jeopardize what is helpful to the members of the groups being investigated (Borkman, 1990; Levy, 1984).

Although collaboration with self-help clearinghouses cannot solve the intractable issues that undermine the internal validity of traditionally designed outcome studies of self-help groups, collaboration with self-help clearinghouses can positively impact these methodological problems. It is important that outcome studies with constructed groups of peers be continued (e.g., Speigel et al., 1989). Clearinghouses already assist in the development of many new groups every year, and thus they may have more experience related to the development of new groups than do researchers working independently of a clearinghouse. Self-help clearinghouses can assist researchers to make the constructed groups more closely simulate naturally occurring self-help groups, particularly by promoting peer leadership in these experimental groups.

The need to go beyond effectiveness studies of self-help groups is important if a more complete understanding of the nature and usefulness of such groups is to be obtained. Collaboration with self-help clearinghouses provides greater ability to conduct internally valid nonoutcome, nonintervention research, as one can randomly assign groups to conditions because of access to a large number of groups. For example, a recent study was conducted to determine how receptive AA contact persons were toward individuals with a mental illness, and more specifically to assess the relative impact of the label of mental illness and the beliefs the label activates compared to the influence of the symptomatic behavior of mental illness (Herring, Nansel, & Meissen, 1992; Meissen, Herring, & Powell, 1993). In order to make these comparisons, 100 AA groups were randomly assigned to one of four conditions: (a) mental illness label, mental illness symptomatic behavior; (b) mental illness label, physical illness symptomatic behavior; (c) physical illness label, mental illness symptomatic behavior; and (d) physical illness label, physical illness symptomatic behavior. Through telephone interviews, these labels and behavioral descriptions were presented in the form of a vignette. AA contact persons were asked a series of questions about how the person described in the vignette would fit into their group. Receptivity by AA contact persons generally was positive for all conditions. The label of mental illness, however, produced a significantly more negative response than did the label of physical disorder. The data obtained have been useful in better understanding how mental health consumers might best approach AA groups (Meissen et al., 1993). Many other research questions can be approached in a similar manner by randomly assigning self-help groups to nonintrusive experimental conditions. Such research would provide a better understanding of the nature of groups and of how best to access them for populations presently underserved by self-help groups.

Improved Generalizability of Research Findings

Much of the research on existing self-help groups also suffers from problems related to external validity, primarily because it is difficult to obtain representative samples of self-help groups or of group members, or representative samples of specific types of self-help groups (e.g., bereavement groups, health groups). There are very few studies of self-help groups that have been able to obtain representative samples of the domain of self-help groups in a specific geographic area, much less representative samples on a national level. In fact, there has been little research to establish basic demographic information about the broad range of self-help groups or their members. Empirical information documenting such basic information about the nature of self-help groups, such as the range of leadership styles or the guiding philosophy of groups, also is lacking. Although a number of typologies of self-help groups have been hypothesized, the typologies have not been based on representative samples of actual self-help groups. The practical issues of obtaining samples of self-help groups or of group members are profound compared to access to research participants for studies of other helping interventions, such as group or individual therapy or case management. Most self-help groups, by their very nature, are not affiliated with professionals, agencies, or other institutions from which members can be recruited. That the philosophy of some groups does not allow or encourage participation in research also contributes to this difficulty. However, representative samples across the broad range of self-help groups and specific subsets of self-help groups can be obtained through self-help clearinghouses.

COLLABORATION GUIDED
BY SOCIAL EXCHANGE THEORY

Collaboration between researchers and consumers has become a critical component of contemporary research on community-based issues (Rappaport, 1990). Adapting a social exchange model, as Dillman (1978) did for survey research, provides advantages in defining and understanding the potential collaborative relationships between researchers, self-help clearinghouses, and self-help groups. Dillman conceptualized the relationship between survey researchers and survey participants as one in which the perceived cost of participation in the survey must be minimized, the perceived rewards for participation must be maximized, and trust must be established so that participants believe the rewards will be forthcoming (Dillman, 1978). Following Rappaport's (1990) insight that collaborative research must "begin before the beginning," self-help clearinghouses already have established mutually beneficial relationships with self-help groups upon which one may build successful research collaboration:

> We believe the high participation rate reflects the credibility our project achieved within the community by providing consultive and informational services through our clearinghouse to self-help groups and community residents at the same time that we were pursuing a research mission. (Wollert, 1986, p. 68)

Consciously taking into account the costs and benefits of the stakeholders will increase the likelihood of successful collaborative research.

Clearinghouse Costs and Benefits

From a social exchange perspective, self-help clearinghouses have much to gain by engaging in collaborative research with self-help groups. Research, particularly evaluation research, can increase the credibility of clearinghouses. Professionals would view the activities of the clearinghouse, and self-help groups in general, in a more positive light if information could be provided that documents the impact of clearinghouse activities and the usefulness of self-help groups. To make the most accurate referrals to self-help groups, it is important to keep the clearinghouse database current, a difficult task considering the constant changes that occur in groups. Research projects which require contact with groups can include questions that update the clearinghouse database or provide information relevant to self-help clearinghouse policy. Positive personal contacts with group leaders

and members also would be useful in developing and maintaining relationships and in providing information to groups. Funding for collaborative
research can also enhance overall clearinghouse operations. At the same
time, there are tangible and intangible costs incurred by clearinghouses
engaged in research. One of the potential inadvertent negative consequences
to clearinghouses is loss of credibility with groups if the research or researchers turn out to be insensitive to group needs.

Self-Help Group Costs and Benefits

As with participants in survey research, the rewards for self-help groups
and members are often less tangible and personal than are those for the
researcher. Consequently, from a social exchange perspective it is important
that the research be relevant to and have the potential to provide information
useful to self-helpers, self-help groups, or persons wishing to access a group.
It is critically important that participants understand how the research will
contribute and believe the research will be useful. Contributing to a "greater
good" can be a powerful incentive to participate in research (Dillman, 1978).
We have found that group members and leaders are interested in participating
in research projects, in part, because they understand explicitly how the data
will be helpful to self-help groups. They also trust that we will use the results
in a way that is helpful to groups, based on past displays of dedication to
self-help approaches. Response rates for surveys conducted through the
Self-Help Network have ranged from 90% for a random sample of self-help
group leaders to a 65% response rate for a sample of AA group contact
persons. The costs involved for groups have been kept to a minimum (e.g.,
20-minute phone interview) in certain cases. At others times, the costs have
been higher (e.g., group time to complete a questionnaire). In a true experiment that included a condition in which students attended a number of
successive group meetings, members were asked to teach the students about
self-help (Sanders & Meissen, 1992). Actively involving self-helpers in the
development of research ideas has been an important part of making sure a
project will produce useful information. A research advisory committee
made up of self-helpers, researchers, and clearinghouse staff can be helpful
to ensuring that the needs of groups are taken into consideration.

Researcher Costs and Benefits

The benefits to researchers interested in self-help groups in many ways
are the most obvious. Collaboration allows data collection from repre-

sentative samples to answer important research questions and to guide future research and intervention. Collaboration also provides for better understanding of self-help groups and has the potential to improve internal and external validity. There are costs to researchers that are not so obvious. Collaboration almost always produces compromise. Researchers risk the loss of exclusive control over research design and over optimal time lines. Often, data beyond the original research questions are needed to provide direct benefits to groups, and it takes some time to gain the trust of particular groups and group members. "Questionnaires were distributed only after positive working relationships were established with the members of the various groups . . . after about five group meetings as nonparticipant observers" (Wollert, 1986, p. 68). Clearinghouse staff generally will want to go slower, to proceed more cautiously, and to elevate concerns related to the needs of groups and their relationship with groups over research issues.

THEORY-GUIDED PRACTICAL
KNOWLEDGE THROUGH ACTION RESEARCH

The acquisition of theoretically driven practical knowledge through the action research concepts of needs assessment, organizational feedback, intervention, and evaluation provide a framework, consistent with the social exchange approach discussed above, for understanding how self-help clearinghouses can become methodological inventions. This framework is also useful in reviewing past research conducted in collaboration with self-help clearinghouses and in outlining important areas of future research.

Needs Assessment

One of the most advantageous research projects for self-help clearinghouses is a needs assessment of the groups in their database. With so many groups that are all so different, it is difficult to know what activities clearinghouses can provide that would be most beneficial. From an action research approach, a needs assessment provides important feedback concerning the direction and nature of activities that can be available for groups through a self-help clearinghouse. For example, prior to a needs assessment conducted through the Self-Help Network of Kansas, we presumed that problem members would be a prevalent concern and that overinvolvement of professionals was a widespread problem (Meissen, Gleason et al., 1991). We also had assumed that leader workshops were needed, that a library of self-help materials would be useful, and that group leaders would desire networking with other leaders. These presumptions concerning needs and problems were based primarily on day-to-day experiences with a nonrepresentative set of group members and leaders. Through an empirically sound needs assessment of a representative sample, we found instead that recruiting new members, keeping new members, getting members to regularly attend meetings, getting members to share the work, and lack of public awareness were considered the most important problems facing the group (Meissen, Gleason et al., 1991). Related to these concerns was the associated problem of overworked and tired group leaders. These issues centered around maintaining the viability of the group through continued flow of new members and keeping members involved and invested in the group. The problems are interconnected and of the type Sarason (1978) saw as intractable, because they are tied to the very essence of self-help groups. In the tradition of action research, these results were interpreted in light of guiding theory and then shared with participant groups for further feedback before being sent to all groups in our database. This personal contact followed by feedback from the needs assessment has produced some consciousness raising among groups (Marti-Costa & Serrano-Garcia, 1983). Many groups believed their needs to be unique when in fact most were commonly shared and were related to group survival.

Knowledge for Understanding

As outlined by Maton (this volume), there is much to learn about the complex phenomenon of self-help groups at the individual level (e.g., member, leader), group level, and community level (e.g., group interactions with local organizations). Wollert has conducted a number of studies through a self-help clearinghouse that obtained useful knowledge and understanding about groups and their relationships to other organizations. In one experiment, Wollert (1988) randomly assigned members of sexual assault self-help groups to communications training in addition to their self-help group. He found increases in communication abilities for the experimental condition and suggested that self-help groups could provide opportunities for problem-specific training useful to members. Wollert (1986) also assessed the psychosocial helping processes in a heterogeneous sample of 21 self-help groups, attempting to understanding the patterns of helping exchanges among members and how they might be affected by organizational variables of the groups. In a related study, he found that self-help groups emphasized supportive and expressive approaches to helping, often avoiding more confrontational techniques (Wollert, Levy, & Knight, 1982). These studies, guided by theory, were primarily focused on group-level variables that provided useful information to clearinghouses while elevating current knowledge about self-help groups.

Research to understand self-help group leadership is important because a group's functioning is affected by the those in leadership positions. The likelihood that the group will disband also is higher when leader turnover occurs. Leaders are the primary contact between self-help groups and clearinghouses. To understand the antecedents and predictors of leader burnout, the Self-Help Network conducted a study of 200 randomly selected self-help group leaders (Meissen et al., 1992). Guided by role theory and past research on burnout, we found that role ambiguity, inaccurate perceptions of leader role by members, activities related to member recruitment and retention, and lack of shared leadership were related to leader burnout. The information and insights obtained in this study were disseminated to self-help groups. A second leadership study that more specifically focuses on burnout and type of leadership style is being conducted to advance our understanding of leader burnout, and provide groups with information on how to prevent it (Volk & Meissen, 1993). Self-help clearinghouses are in a particularly advantageous position to provide information to groups about developing shared leadership, planning for the succession of leaders, and preventing leader burnout.

Clearinghouses can act as a useful interface between self-help groups and other populations and organizations. In a study that highlights the potential of collaborative research at a community level, Maton, Leventhal, Madara, and Julien (1989) examined organizational variables that affected the birth and death of self-help groups. They found that one important factor in the survival of groups involved affiliations with outside resources. Having a local professional attend meetings or affiliating with a national self-help organization provided outside resources for the group and was thought to be in part responsible for the extended survival of groups. At the same time, it was found that groups with both a local and a national affiliation had higher odds of disbanding (Maton et al., 1989). There could be an optimal level or combination of outside support for groups. Different types of support also could affect different problems and needs. It was also found that life stress groups had higher rates of disbanding than did medical groups (Maton et al., 1989). Greater member and leader turnover was thought to occur in the life-stress groups due to the less chronic nature of the focal problem of the group. This type of information is particularly useful for clearinghouse policy development and for work with self-help groups.

Clearinghouses also act as an interface between self-help groups and the professional community. Clearinghouses often engage in professional education activities and make many referrals to self-help groups through professionals. Approximately 15% of our referrals are provided to professionals who are seeking a self-help group for someone with whom they are working. The attitudes of professionals toward self-help groups has been investigated, but typically not from a self-help clearinghouse perspective. Consequently, two surveys of professionals and graduate students in social work and psychology were conducted by the Self-Help Network (Gleason, 1988; Meissen, Mason, & Gleason, 1991). These studies, guided by Fishbein and Ajzen's (1975) Theory of Reasoned Action, illustrated the positive attitudes and behavioral intentions toward self-help groups that professionals and graduate students had, but they also revealed a certain lack of understanding and knowledge about self-help. For example, participants believed that all potential roles for professionals involved in self-help were quite appropriate, including group leader and group therapist. Their unqualified acceptance of all possible roles suggests a somewhat naive "any help is good help" view of professional involvement with groups. It also was found that professionals believed they should be consulted prior to client involvement with a self-help group, that self-help works best in conjunction with therapy, and that self-help dealt with the superficial aspects of problems. It appears that the positive attitudes and beliefs of many professionals also are nested in a theoretical framework based on expert power and traditional roles (Lieberman & Borman, 1979; Toro et al, 1988). Based on these findings, the professional workshops and educational activities we offer on an ongoing basis were enhanced, and a special research project was developed to provide information and experiential opportunities regarding self-help groups for professionals, especially medical professionals.

The studies described above were theory based, conducted through self-help clearinghouses, and provided feedback useful to self-help groups. Some have precipitated interventions and policy changes within clearinghouses, highlighting the importance of the feedback, intervention, and evaluation components of the action research model.

Feedback, Intervention, and Evaluation

Unlike other research areas and organizational settings in which an action research perspective has been applied, developing interventions with self-help groups can be difficult pragmatically and ethically. At the same time, the information obtained in an action research program can be provided to groups without intervention, and clearinghouses can actively develop and evolve policy in response to empirical information obtained in theory-driven studies. Based in part on the results of the needs assessment of self-help groups and the leadership surveys described above, the Self-Help Network developed a project to create new roles and linkages for experienced self-help group leaders in rural communities, to increase the access and effectiveness of rural self-help groups (Warren & Meissen, 1992). The Self-Help Network works with these experienced leaders in order to develop better public and professional awareness of available self-help groups, and it provides requested assistance to groups in rural communities. A qualitative research project to analyze the social networks and social exchanges of these experienced self-help group leaders has provided a better understanding of how they and their local self-help groups fit into the larger health care system in rural communities (Nansel, Warren, Sanders, & Meissen, 1993).

At a community level, results of clearinghouse surveys of psychologists and social workers described above led to an experiment designed to increase knowledge of and appropriate interactions with available self-help groups by medical personnel (Meissen, Sanders, & Gleason, 1990). In this action research project, Physician Assistant students were randomly assigned to a health-related self-help group practicum or to a nursing home practicum. The self-help groups were asked to teach students about self-help groups during their semester of attendance. Intentions to interact and to refer to self-help groups were significantly greater for those students in the self-help practicum compared to the nursing home practicum. Of the 16 recommendations from the Surgeon General's workshop, professional training regarding self-help was the No. 1 priority (DHHS, 1988). Involving self-help groups and members in this training effort is potentially empowering, is likely to produce partnerships based on mutual respect, and is a wise use of the expert resources that groups can provide to the professional community. Self-help clearinghouses are in a particularly advantageous position to coordinate and conduct research on this type of activity because of their ongoing relationships with both professionals and groups and their values based on respect for the autonomy of self-help groups.

An excellent example of clearinghouse services evaluation that fits into the action research framework was conducted by Wollert et al. (1987). They evaluated the information and referral functions and the technical assistance functions of a clearinghouse. Their research resulted in a number of alterations of policy and practices. Procedures for data collection were altered, classification of groups was revised, and more complete data were obtained about area self-help groups. Other research projects also were facilitated through this evaluation. Other evaluation opportunities of related self-help programs and organizations are available through self-help clearinghouses, especially in the area of self-help and mental health. Because of extensive prior work with area self-help groups for mental health consumers, the Self-Help Network was approached to conduct an evaluation of an after-hours peer counseling and self-help drop-in center designed to reduce inappropriate psychiatric use of emergency rooms (Chacon et al., 1993). The Network also has just begun a 3-year statewide research project funded by the National Institute of Mental Health (NIMH) that focuses on the impact of self-help groups and self-help organizations for consumers of psychiatric services and their families. An important goal of this research is to understand how self-help groups and organizations interact with the formal health and mental health care delivery system and how to include greater number of families and consumers in self-help groups.

Future Research Through Self-Help Clearinghouses

Over most of the past decade the orientation of the Self-Help Network has evolved from concentrating on individual self-help groups to viewing the clearinghouse as an interface between self-help groups and other organizations, populations, and the public. As we have grown into being a statewide clearinghouse and have become much better at identifying self-help groups for our database, it has become clear that there are too many self-help groups and too few staff, an insight not unlike Albee's (1968) conclusions regarding individual psychotherapy approaches and mental health personnel power. The results of research have been the primary influence in the evolution toward this interface role. We learned that groups, in general, do not want or need assistance inside their groups but do desire and consider useful activities that affect the relationships between groups and other organizations and populations—what Seidman (1988) termed the mesosystem level of analysis. The interface between self-help groups and other community entities is an area of future research that is most promising, but one which in many cases will require the kind of collaboration with self-help clearinghouses discussed in this chapter.

Studies of Representative Samples of Self-Help Groups. Many researchers and theorists interested in self-help have called for research on self-help groups to determine such basic demographic and descriptive information as gender, age, and race of members, number of members, average attendance, and so on (e.g., Jacobs & Goodman, 1989; DHHS, 1988). There is also a need to better understand group-level characteristics such as the guiding philosophy of the group, nature of leadership, and the nature of affiliations and interactions with other organizations and populations. A multisite study using self-help clearinghouses, each taking representative samples of groups from their databases, would provide this information in an externally valid manner. More in-depth studies of specific subsamples of groups also would provide essential data for the improved understanding of self-help groups. When conducting these in-depth studies of specific subsamples of groups, qualitative and rigorous case studies approaches could be used, as described by Yin (1989). Expanding this to a multisite approach, the development of common data collection instruments shared by a number of clearinghouses used to collect routine group information also could provide much important data about the nature and characteristics of self-help groups. Similar procedures could be developed for those who receive referrals from self-help clearinghouses (Wollert, 1987). All clearinghouses obtain data of this type, but the fact that all collect somewhat different information does not allow comparison or merging of these data for research purposes.

Research on Public and Professional Awareness of Self-Help Groups. Although there have been a number of studies on professional attitudes toward self-help, there have been virtually no studies of a representative sample of the general public regarding their attitudes, beliefs, and knowledge regarding self-help groups or their past and present use of groups. Research regarding how to increase the public's knowledge about self-help groups and how to access groups would be useful to clearinghouses and service providers. Considering that clearinghouses have spent years attempting to impact public and professional awareness and would be a primary user of the information obtained, they would be logical partners in this type of research. The first step in any public health approach to increasing services is to elevate the public's consciousness regarding the availability of the service. Clearinghouses also could conduct research on the reactions of professionals who actually use a clearinghouse to find groups for their clients and on how their experience influences future referrals and dissemination of information to fellow professionals.

Research on the Increased Use of Self-Help Groups. An important area of collaborative research that would benefit self-help groups and clearinghouses involves issues of access to and use of groups by those presently underserved by self-help groups. Like many other public health issues, creating awareness and facilitating the use of potentially helpful treatment and preventive interventions by persons with health and mental health concerns is a major difficulty. Self-help clearinghouses, in the role as an interface between self-help groups and those subpopulations, can participate in important ways to promote action research that would encourage affiliation by those subpopulations who underuse self-help groups.

Research aimed at understanding how to increase participation of minority and ethnic groups is important, as they are underrepresented in self-help groups and have traditionally had less access to traditional forms of care. That self-help groups are cost-free could be a particularly attractive feature. Clearinghouses would be a logical collaborator in such research because of their interest in increasing referrals to groups and their existing relationships with community organizations that serve minorities. Some promising research by Medvene and Lin (1993) found that increased membership in National Alliance for the Mentally Ill (NAMI) groups by Hispanic parents was in part generated by linking access to NAMI groups with mental health agencies already familiar to family members. This approach appeared to work well in recruiting at least one hard-to-reach population. Replicating this organizational approach across other hard-to-reach populations provides many collaborative research opportunities. In another study with action implications for self-help clearinghouses, it was found that when African Americans and Whites first attended an AA group that consisted primarily of members of the same race, they were significantly more likely to continue membership than those whose first meeting was dominated by the other race (Humphreys & Woods, this volume).

It is generally assumed that the elderly are not as active in their use of self-help groups as younger persons. At the same time, there is reason to believe that many would benefit greatly from membership in a self-help group. As the number of elderly increase, especially in rural areas, self-help groups could be an important health resource. Research analyzing how best to approach the elderly in terms of the use of self-help groups would be useful to clearinghouses and others who work with elderly populations. Many elderly also suffer from chronic conditions and will need to engage in long-term self care while adjusting to a different set of life conditions. The use of self-help groups has recently been documented as an attractive "alternative therapy," outside of traditional health care settings (Eisenberg et al., 1993). Conducting research focused on efforts to increase use of self-help groups by persons with chronic conditions could produce important benefits and potential health-care savings. Understanding how to facilitate use of self-help groups through hospitals and medical settings is an important topic for research in which self-help clearinghouses would be particularly useful.

Another underserved population for all types of health and mental health care are those in rural areas. In many ways self-help groups have been considered primarily an urban phenomenon, because the population in cities is large enough to sustain groups of people who share the same specific situation or problem. At the same time, self-help clearinghouses often are faced with large but sparsely populated rural areas in which people desire access to self-help groups. It seems that self-help groups would be a natural extension of the kind of mutual support among community members that often characterizes rural areas. Research on the development and promotion of less homogenous groups would be useful (e.g., instead of a breast cancer group, a cancer group for women). Action research projects linking self-help groups with existing rural organizations like rural hospitals and the rural extension service could potentially increase the number and use of rural self-help groups.

CONCLUSIONS

Viewing the self-help clearinghouse as a methodological invention in action research for community psychology highlights the advantages of conducting research through a self-help clearinghouse. This setting allows the use of a broad range of methodologies from a variety of research and policy perspectives. From a public health perspective, it is considered important to conduct comprehensive studies of the nature and characteristics of self-help groups and of their members. Experimental and quasi-experimental outcome studies still need to be pursued, but should be complemented by a wide range of both quantitative and qualitative studies of the nature and usefulness of self-help groups. From a health service policy view, it is important to understand how to attract subpopulations of persons presently underserved by self-help groups and to conduct research on how groups can most effectively be used as part of a comprehensive, integrated health and mental health care delivery system without losing autonomy. This research agenda can best be achieved by collaboration between self-help clearinghouses, self-help groups, and researchers.

NOTE

1. The term *methodological invention,* along with other useful comments, was suggested by Clayton Alderfer, Editor of the *Journal of Applied Behavioral Science.*

REFERENCES

Albee, G. (1968). Conceptual model and manpower requirements in psychology. *American Psychologist, 23,* 317-320.

Barrett, C. J. (1978). Effectiveness of widows' groups in facilitating change. *Journal of Counseling and Clinical Psychology, 46,* 20-31.

Borck, L. E., & Aronowitz, E. (1982). The role of a self-help clearinghouse. *Prevention in Human Services, 1,* 121-129.

Borkman, T. (1990). Self-help groups at the turning point: Emerging egalitarian alliances with the formal health care system? *American Journal of Community Psychology, 18,* 321-332.

Campbell, D. T. (1972). Reforms as experiments. In C. H. Weiss (Ed.), *Evaluating action programs* (pp. 187-223). Boston: Allyn & Bacon.

Campbell, D. T. (1974). *Qualitative knowing in action research.* Paper presented at the American Psychological Association, New Orleans.

Chacon, S., Sanders, L., Jones, P., Meadows, S., McNally, K., & Meissen, G. J. (June, 1993). *Collaborative research between a consumer operated center and a self-help clearing- house.* Paper presented at the 4th Biennial Conference on Community Research and Action, Williamsburg, VA.

Cowen, E. L., Gesten, E. L., & Weissberg, R. P. (1980). An integrated network of preventively oriented school-based mental health approaches. In R. H. Price, P. E. Polister, & R. F. Ketterer (Eds.), *Evaluation and action in the social environment* (pp. 173-210). New York: Academic Press.

Department of Health and Human Services, Public Health Service. (1988). *Surgeon general's workshop on self-help and public health* (HRSA, Bureau of Maternal and Child Health and Resource Development Publication No. 224-250). Washington, DC: U.S. Govern- ment Printing Office.

Department of Health and Human Services (1990). *Healthy People 2000: National health promotion and disease prevention objectives* (DHHS Publication No. [PHS] 91-50213). Washington, DC: U.S. Government Printing Office.

Dillman, D. A. (1978). *Mail and telephone surveys: The total design method.* New York: John Wiley.

Eisenberg, D. M., Kessler, R. C., Foster, C., Norlock, F. E., Calkins, D. R., & Delbanco, T. L. (1993). Unconventional medicine in the United States: Prevalence, costs, and patterns of use. *New England Journal of Medicine, 328,* 246-252.

Fairweather, G. W., & Tornatzky, L. G. (1977). *Experimental methods for social policy research.* New York: Pergamon.

Fishbein, M., & Ajzen, I. (1975). *Belief, attitude, intention, and behavior: An introduction to theory and research.* Reading, MA: Addison-Wesley.

Gleason, D. F. (1988). *Mental health professionals' beliefs and practices toward self-help groups.* Unpublished master's thesis, Wichita State University, Wichita, KS.

Herring, L., Nansel, T., & Meissen, G. J. (1992, April). *The receptivity to mental health consumers by nonmental health self-help groups.* Paper presented at the Annual Conference of the Southwest Psychological Association, Austin, TX.

Humphreys, K., & Woods, M. D. (1994). Researching mutual-help group participation in a segregated society. In T. J. Powell (Ed.), *Understanding the self-help organization: Frameworks and findings.* Thousand Oaks, CA: Sage.

Jacobs, M. K., & Goodman, G. (1989). Psychology and self-help groups: Predictions on a partnership. *American Psychologist, 44,* 536-545.

Katz, A. H. (1981). Self help and mutual aid: An emerging social movement. *Annual Review of Sociology, 7,* 129-155.

Ketterer, R. F., Price, R. H., & Polister, P. E. (1980). The action research paradigm. In R. H. Price, P. E. Polister, & R. F. Ketterer (Eds.), *Evaluation and action in the social environment* (pp. 1-15). New York: Academic Press.

Levine, M. (1988). An analysis of mutual assistance. *American Journal of Community Psychology, 16,* 167-188.

Levy, L. H. (1984). Issues in research and evaluation. In A. Gartner & F. Riessman (Eds.), *The self-help revolution* (pp. 155-172). New York: Human Science Press.

Levy, L. H. (in press). Self-help groups. In J. Rappaport & E. Seidman (Eds.), *Handbook of community psychology.*

Lewin, K. (1946). Action research and minority problems. *Journal of Social Science, 2,* 34-46.

Lewin, K. (1947). Frontiers in group dynamics: Part II, Social planning and action research. *Human Relations, 1,* 143-153.

Lieberman, M. A., & Borman, L. D. (1979). *Self-help groups for coping with crisis: Origins, members, processes, and impact.* San Francisco: Jossey-Bass.

Madara, E., Kalafat, J., & Miller, B. M. (1988). The computerized self-help clearinghouse: Using "high tech" to promote "high touch" support networks. *Computers in the Human Services, 3,* 39-54.

Marmar, C. R., Horowitz, M. J., Weiss, D. S., Wilner, N. R., & Kaltreider, N. B. (1988). A controlled trial of brief psychotherapy and mutual-help group treatment of conjugal bereavement. *American Journal of Psychiatry, 145,* 203-209.

Marti-Costa, S., & Serrano-Garcia, I. (1983). Needs assessment and community development: An ideological perspective. *Prevention in the Human Services, 2,* 75-88.

Maton, K. I. (1994). Moving beyond the individual level of analysis in mutual-help group research: An ecological paradigm. In T. J. Powell (Ed.), *Understanding the self-help organization: Frameworks and findings.* Thousand Oaks, CA: Sage.

Maton, K. I., Leventhal, G. S., Madara, E. J., & Julien, M. (1989). Factors affecting the birth and death of mutual-help groups: The role of national affiliation, professional involvement, and member focal problem, *American Journal of Community Psychology, 17,* 643-671.

Medvene, L. J. (1987). *Selected highlights of research on effectiveness of self-help groups.* Los Angeles: California Self-Help Center, UCLA.

Medvene, L. J., & Lin, K. M. (1993). *Recruiting Mexican-Americans to participate in family support groups.* Paper presented at the 4th Biennial Conference on Community Research and Action, Williamsburg, VA.

Meissen, G. J., Gleason, D. F., & Embree, M. G. (1991). An assessment of the needs of mutual-help groups. *American Journal of Community Psychology, 19,* 427-442.

Meissen, G. J., Herring, E., & Powell, T. J. (1993, June). *Effects of label and behavior of mental health consumers on acceptance in AA groups.* Paper presented at the 4th Biennial Conference on Community Research and Action, Williamsburg, VA.

Meissen, G. J., Mason, W. C., & Gleason, D. F. (1991). Understanding the attitudes and intentions toward mutual-help of future professionals. *American Journal of Community Psychology, 19,* 699-714.

Meissen, G. J., Sanders, L., & Gleason, D. F. (1990, October). *Mutual-help training for medical personnel: An action research approach.* Paper presented at the Annual Ecological Community Psychology conference, East Lansing, MI.

Meissen, G. J., Warren, M. L., Volk, F., & Herring, L. (September, 1992). *A survey of leadership roles in self-help groups.* Paper presented at the International Conference on Self-Help, Ottawa, Canada.

Monahan, J. (1980). The role of research in changing the legal system. In R. H. Price, P. E. Polister, & R. F. Ketterer (Eds.), *Evaluation and action in the social environment* (pp. 211-229). New York: Academic Press.

Nansel, T. R., Warren, M. L., Sanders, L., & Meissen, G. J. (1993). *A qualitative study of the SHAL Project: Self-help group leaders in newly developing roles.* Paper presented at the 4th Biennial Conference on Community Research and Action, Williamsburg, VA.

Powell, T. J. (1987). *Self-help organization and professional practice.* Silver Springs, MD: National Association of Social Workers.

President's Commission on Mental Health. (1978). Report. Washington, DC: U.S. Government Printing Office.

Rappaport, J. (1990). Research methods and the empowerment social agenda. In P. Tolan, C. Keys, F. Chertok, & L. Jason (Eds.), *Researching community psychology* (pp. 51-53). Washington, DC: American Psychological Association.

Riessman, F. (1992, September). *Self-help redefined.* Paper presented at the International Conference on Self-Help/Mutual Aid, Ottawa, Canada.

Sanders, L., & Meissen, G. J. (1992, April). *An evaluation of a peer counseling program: Feedback for effectiveness.* Paper presented at the Annual Conference of the Southwest Psychological Association, Austin, TX.

Sarason, S. B. (1978). The nature of problem solving in social action. *American Psychologist, 33,* 370-380.

Seidman, E. (1988). Back to the future, community psychology: Unfolding a theory of social intervention. *American Journal of Community Psychology, 16,* 3-24.

Speigel, D., Bloom, J., Kraemer, H., & Gottheil, E. (1989). The beneficial effect of psychosocial treatment on survival of metastatic breast cancer patients: A randomized prospective outcome study. *The Lancet, 12,* 888-891.

Tolan, P., Keys, C., Chertok, F., & Jason, L. (1990). *Researching community psychology.* Washington, DC: American Psychological Association.

Toro, P. A., Rieschl, T. M., Zimmerman, M. A., Rappaport, J., Seidman, E., Luke, D. A., & Roberts, L. J. (1988). Professionals in mutual-help groups: Impact on social climate and member's behavior. *Journal of Consulting and Clinical Psychology, 56,* 631-632.

Volk, F., & Meissen, G. J. (1993, June). *Self-help leadership activities as predictors of burnout.* Paper presented at the 4th Biennial Conference on Community Research and Action, Williamsburg, VA.

Warren, M. L., & Meissen, G. J. (1992, September). *Rural self-help associate leadership project.* Paper presented at the International Conference on Self-Help, Ottawa, Canada.

Wollert, R. W. (1986). Psychosocial helping processes in a heterogeneous sample of self-help groups. *Canadian Journal of Mental Health, 5,* 63-76.

Wollert, R. (1987). Human services and the self-help clearinghouse concept. *Canadian Journal of Community Mental Health, 6,* 79-90.

Wollert, R. (1988). Self-help clearinghouses in North America: A survey of their structural characteristics and community health implications. *Health Promotion, 2,* 377-386.

Wollert, R. W., Levy, L. H., & Knight, B. G. (1982). Help-giving in behavioral control and stress coping self-help groups. *Small Group Behavior, 13,* 204-218.

Wollert, R., & The Self-Help Research Team (1987). The self-help clearinghouse concept: An evaluation of one program and its implications for policy and practice. *American Journal of Community Psychology, 15,* 491-508.

Yin, R. K. (1989). *Case study research: Design and methods.* Newbury Park, CA: Sage.

12. Self-Help for Sickle Cell Disease in African-American Communities

KERMIT B. NASH

KATHRYN D. KRAMER

It is widely acknowledged that the growing self-help movement is a force within the traditional health care system in the United States (Katz & Bender, 1990; Kurtz, 1990). Today, almost every conceivable health and social problem is addressed. However, Hamilton (1990) noted that the spread of self-help groups has not reached disadvantaged minority groups. Although underrepresented in well-known groups, such as Alcoholics Anonymous (AA) and Parents Anonymous, this study demonstrates that self-help groups do exist in the African-American community.

Because data are virtually nonexistent on mutual-help groups primarily serving African Americans, this qualitative study was undertaken to determine the location, structure, and function of groups helping individuals affected by sickle cell disease (SCD), an illness that, in the United States, primarily affects African Americans. SCD is a degenerative genetic disorder without a cure. With this disease, the red blood cells become sickle shaped and do not move through the capillary system. These malformed cells clog at the joints, preventing an adequate flow of oxygen throughout the body.

AUTHORS' NOTE: Many thanks to Amy Powell and Michelle Hughes for their contributions to this manuscript. This study was funded by the Heart, Lung, and Blood Institute of the National Instiues of Health (Grant No. 5P60 HL28392-10).

This causes excruciating pain, organ damage, and eventually death. One in 400 African Americans is affected by SCD. Sixteen percent of those affected will die before the age of 10, with the highest rate of mortality occurring in the first 5 years of life (Serjeant, 1985). SCD is the most common genetic disorder affecting a single population in this country (Consensus Conference, 1987). However, among the general population, few are aware of SCD or the existence of self-help groups to help individuals affected by it.

This chapter presents some results from a 5-year formative evaluation study on sickle cell self-help groups. This study is the first known to focus exclusively on self-help groups for African Americans with a genetic condition. The outcomes of this research provide an opportunity to discuss the participation of African Americans in the self-help movement. Although in-depth analyses of this research are under way, some preliminary findings are reported here. Two data sets are explored and discussed, allowing two levels of analyses to be undertaken: group and individual. Group-level data are from 123 groups across the United States. Individual-level data come from members of a subset of those groups (61 adults in 15 groups).

The first year of this research project was devoted to locating SCD groups in the United States. A combination of personal, telephone, and mail contacts were made to relevant individuals and organizations (e.g., SCD clinics and hematology departments in hospitals). The first mail survey was distributed to 429 parties; response rate was 33.1%. Throughout the year, telephone and personal contacts with prospective group leaders and members were made by researchers and the principal investigator. This combined networking approach continues today and is largely responsible for the successful recruitment efforts of the project.

On a yearly basis, SCD group information is compiled, published, and distributed in a directory.[1] By distributing the directory, a service is provided to the community as 54.3% of the groups ($n = 57$) reported that they had used the directory to refer members to other groups. In addition, the directory simultaneously serves as a recruitment tool. Forms are provided in the directory and are used to notify the researchers of new groups or any changes in the status of existing groups (i.e., groups becoming defunct or changing leadership). In addition to the initial mail surveys to locate the names and addresses of groups and the distribution of the directory, telephone and mail surveys with groups leaders have been conducted on a yearly basis. Through combined recruitment methods, 74 groups were located in 1988. Today, 134 groups are known to exist in 31 states, the District of Columbia, and one province in Canada (see Figure 12.1). Of the 134 groups, 123 group leaders

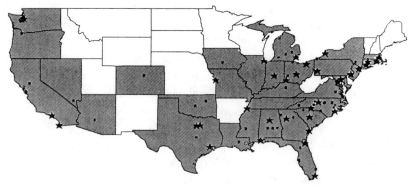

LEGEND

■   One group in the area
★   More than one group
    in the area

134 groups in 31 states and
Washington, D.C. (and Canada)

August, 1992

Figure 12.1. Sickle Cell Mutual-Help Groups

provided in-depth information on group structure and function (91.8% response rate).

In addition to group-level data on all known SCD groups, four interrelated studies have been conducted. First, 61 members of 15 SCD groups in 11 states and the District of Columbia primarily serving adults were recruited to provide data on their experiences with SCD and with the groups. The adult study was a longitudinal design with three data collection periods. Second, individual data were collected from 79 members of 13 SCD groups in 11 states serving parents of children with SCD. The parent study had two data collection periods. More recently, data were collected from 79 adolescents participating in 12 SCD groups in 10 states and 1 province in Canada. Due to the timing of the implementation of the adolescent study, only one data collection was possible. In addition, a quasi-experimental study targeting adolescents in SCD groups was implemented. Analyses compare the results of three different group models and a control group. Analyses are under way and results from these data sets are forthcoming.

For the purpose of this presentation, data are presented at the group level for 123 groups. Results include the location of SCD groups, information regarding group structure and function, a description of group activities and special features, a discussion of leadership patterns and professional involvement, and a measure of how well group leaders think the groups are functioning.

METHOD

Sample and Variables

Across all of the studies (i.e., adults, parents, and adolescents), individual-level data have been collected from approximately 247 group members from 41 groups across the United States. However, for the purposes of this presentation, preliminary results from 61 adults with SCD (members of 15 groups in 10 states and the District of Columbia) are provided. At the individual level, questions were asked regarding members' experiences with the mutual-assistance group and their experiences with SCD. Variables addressing experiences with the group were travel distance to meeting site and mode of travel, length of attendance, reasons for attending group, and group activities. Variables addressing experiences with the disease were physical symptoms, psychological symptoms, psychosocial interferences (e.g., interferences in leisure activities, work, school, relationships, daily activities, and finances), and health service use (e.g., frequency of medical visits, emergency room visits, and hospitalizations). Due to the high prevalence of depression among this sample, the variables focusing on the experiences of the disease (e.g., physical and psychological symptoms associated with SCD, psychosocial interferences associated with SCD, and health service use) and length of time in the group were used in a correlation model. This exploratory model might contribute to a better understanding of the reasons why individuals join SCD self-help groups and what groups are doing to address those needs.

Questionnaires

Questionnaires were adapted from a variety of instruments used in self-help and sickle cell research. Focus groups and pilot testing of the instruments were conducted in the initial phases of questionnaire development. In addition, the CES-D, a standardized scale to measure the presence of depressive symptomatology, was employed. The CES-D was developed by the Center for Epidemiological Studies, National Institute of Mental Health (NIMH), and was designed to measure depressive symptomatology in the general population (Radloff, 1977). The internal consistency of the instrument is .85 in the general population.

RESULTS

Structure and Function of 123 SCD Groups

An examination of SCD group membership (defined as regular participants at meetings) showed that the 123 groups could be categorized in four distinct groupings: 52.8% ($n = 65$) were organized for adults and children with SCD and their significant others; 18.7% ($n = 23$) were organized for parents of children with SCD; 16.3% ($n = 20$) were organized for adults with SCD; and 12.2% ($n = 15$) were organized for adolescents with SCD.

Across all groups, the average group size was 11 regular group members (SD = 6.8). Consistent with the female and male composition reported for other mutual-aid groups, there were more females than males attending the groups, with a ratio close to 2:1.

The age of the groups varied considerably, ranging from newly formed groups to those that had been in existence for as long as 23 years. The results show that 20% of the groups have existed for more than 10 years. The median age of the groups was 4 years, with a mean age of 6.2 years. Using self-report data on age of group, birth rates were calculated. These rates reflect the number of new groups that start or form each year. Rates were calculated from our yearly records since 1988. Preliminary results suggest that new SCD groups are forming at a rate of 13.4% per year.

As a measure of the general activity level of the groups, all 123 groups reportedly had met in the previous year. Most of the groups met monthly (54.9%), another 12.3% met twice a month, 5.8% met twice a week, and 1.6% met weekly. In addition, group leaders reported their perceptions of how well the groups were functioning (see Figure 12.2).

Group Leadership. Professionals were involved in the formation of 86.7% ($n = 104$) of the groups. However, it appeared that the role of professionals in the groups changed as the groups evolved. At the time of the interview, 27.3% of the groups ($n = 33$) were still led by a professional, 38.8% ($n = 47$) were co-led (leadership was shared between a member and a professional), 29.8% ($n = 36$) of all groups were member led with no professional involvement,

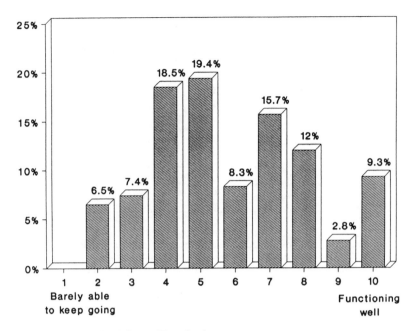

Figure 12.2. Perceived Group Functioning

and 4.1% ($n = 5$) had no specific leader. Overall, 66.1%, or 80 groups, still had some level of professional involvement in the leadership of the groups.

Special Features of Groups. Group leaders were asked to identify the special features that were associated with the group's activities (see Table 12.1). More than half of all of the groups in the study reported engaging in the following special features: advocating for changes (57.9%, $n = 70$), providing speakers for other groups (57.0%, $n = 69$), having a phone help system (55.8%, $n = 67$), providing transportation for other members to group meetings (52.9%, $n = 64$) and having a buddy system (50.4%, $n = 61$).

Supportive Role and Activities of Group Members. Group leaders also reported the supportive role and activities of group members (see Table 12.2). More than 80% of all of the groups in the study reported that group members gave advice to one another (95.9%, $n = 116$), talked about things that cause stress on the family (95.1%, $n = 116$), talked about very personal feelings (91.0%, $n = 110$), listened to experts talk about SCD (88.3%, $n = 96$), learned how

TABLE 12.1 Percentages of Groups Reporting Special Features

Special Feature	Number	Percentage
Advocate for changes	70	57.9
Speakers for other groups	69	57.0
Phone help system	67	55.8
Transportation to meetings	64	52.9
Buddy system	61	50.4
Newsletter	44	36.4
Fund-raising for members	41	33.9
Baby-sitting/meetings	26	21.5
Fund-raising for hospital	23	19.0

TABLE 12.2 Percentages of Supportive Roles and Activities of Group Members

Supportive Roles and Activities	Number	Percentage
Give advice to one another	116	95.9
Talk about things that cause stress on the family	116	95.1
Talk about very personal feelings	110	91.0
Listen to experts talk about sickle cell disease	96	88.3
Learn how to deal with emotional issues	107	87.7
Talk about how to recruit new members	99	81.1

to deal with emotional issues (87.7%, $n = 107$), and talked about how to recruit members (81.1%, $n = 99$).

Individual Member Demographics

The following demographic variables were collected on group members: sex, race, age, marital status, education, income, and employment status. These statistics are reported below and are summarized in Tables 12.3 and 12.4.

Sex, Race, Age, and Marital Status. Across all mutual-assistance groups in this sample, more females (62.3%, $n = 38$) than males (37.7%, $n = 23$) chose to participate in the group meetings. Again, this is a familiar pattern among mutual-assistance groups. The overwhelming majority of this sample was African American (96.7%, $n = 59$). However, 1 person self-identified as Hispanic (1.6%) and 1 as "other" (i.e., mixed race) (1.6%). The mean age of

TABLE 12.3 Comparison of Characteristics of 61 Adults in 15 Sickle Cell
Disease Groups With All African Americans

Sickle Cell Disease Members	Number	All African Americans Percentage	Percentage
Marital status			
Married	15	24.6	43.6
Single, never married	27	44.3	37.1
Separated	7	11.5	
Divorced	9	14.8	10.8
Widowed	2	3.3	8.6
Sex			
Female	38	62.3	
Male	23	37.7	
Race			
African American	59	96.7	
Hispanic	1	1.6	
Other	1	1.6	
Income (in dollars)			
0-14,999	34	55.7	42.4
15,000-24,999	7	11.5	19.1
25,000-34,999	11	18.0	13.5
35,000 and over	4	14.8	25.0
Age (in years)			
Range	19-68		
Mean	36.6		
SD	10.6		

the group members was 36.6 years (range: 19-68 years of age). Only 24.6%
($n = 15$) of the sample were married at the time of the interview. The
remainder of the sample were either single and never married (44.3%, $n =$
27), separated (11.5%, $n = 7$), divorced (14.8%, $n = 9$), or widowed (3.3%,
$n = 2$). As compared to the general population of African Americans, this
sample was less likely to be married (24.6% vs. 43.6%) (U.S. Department
of Commerce, 1992).

Education, Income, and Employment Status. The mean educational level
(number of years of school completed) of the group members was 13 years

TABLE 12.4 Educational Attainment of Adult Group Members ($n = 61$) and All African Americans

Group Members	Number	All African Americans Percentage	Percentage
Less than high school	1	1.7	15.2
Some high school	5	8.3	18.0
High school graduate	23	38.3	37.7
Some college/technical	20	33.3	17.5
College graduate	7	11.7	11.5
Range (years)	8-17		
Mean (years)	13		
SD (years)	10		

(range: 8-17 or more years of education). Almost half of the sample (48.3%, $n = 29$) had completed 12 or fewer years of education; 16.7% ($n = 4$) completed 17 or more years of education (postbaccalaureate). Interestingly, this sample tends to be more highly educated than the general population of African Americans. A much larger percentage of individuals in SCD groups went beyond a high school education (61.7% vs. 29.0%) (U.S. Department of Commerce, 1992).

Household incomes of the sample varied. Only 8.2% ($n = 5$) reported annual incomes of $45,000 and over. More than half (55.7%, $n = 34$) reported incomes of less than $14,999. This is more than among the general population of African Americans, where 42% have annual incomes below $15,000 (U.S. Department of Commerce, 1992).

In terms of employment status, 45% ($n = 27$) of the sample classified themselves as disabled. Another 38.3% ($n = 23$) were employed. Of those employed, 17.4% ($n = 4$) worked part-time (i.e., less than 30 hours per week), 47.8% ($n = 11$) worked full-time (40 hours per week), and 34.8% ($n = 8$) worked more than 40 hours per week.

Group and Personal Experiences

The majority of the sample lived within 10 miles of the meeting site (73.8%, $n = 45$), and most drove their own car to the meeting site (71.7%, $n = 43$) or carpooled (13.3%, $n = 8$). Very few participants used public transportation (6.7%, $n = 4$) or walked (5.0%, $n = 3$) to the meetings.

TABLE 12.5 Reasons for Participation ($n = 61$)

Reason for Participation	Number	Percentage
Help improve health care of people with sickle cell disease	55	90.2
Learn more about sickle cell disease	53	86.9
Give support to members	53	86.9
Get support	47	77.0
Raise money for causes	35	57.4
Make new friends	30	49.2
Learn how to solve personal problems	29	47.5
Have a safe place to express feelings	29	47.5
Have social activities to attend	29	47.5
Have a sense of belonging to a group	26	42.6

There were many reasons listed by the sample for participation in group meetings (see Table 12.5). More than 75% of all participants indicated that they attended the group to help improve the health care of people with SCD (90.2%, $n = 55$), learn more about SCD (86.9%, $n = 53$), to *give* support to other group members (86.9%, $n = 53$), and to *get* support from other group members (77.0%, $n = 47$). Other frequently endorsed reasons for participating in the groups were to raise money for causes (57.4%, $n = 35$), to make new friends (49.2%, $n = 30$), to learn more about how to solve personal problems (47.5%, $n = 29$), to have a safe place to express feelings (47.5%, $n = 29$), to have social activities to attend (47.5%, $n = 29$), and to have a sense of belonging to a group (42.6%, $n = 26$).

In addition to seeking help from the mutual-assistance groups, other help-seeking behaviors were reported among the sample. For example, 24.6% ($n = 15$) reported that they also sought help from the clergy and the same number, 24.6%, sought help from psychotherapists (i.e., psychiatrists, psychologists, and social workers). The majority (67.2%) still sought help mostly from family and friends.

Psychological Distress. In an attempt to examine the severity of distress that group members experienced, physical and psychological symptoms were measured at two different data points (T1 and T2) using the CES-D. Results of the CES-D at T1 showed that among the 61 individuals in the sample, 45% were clinically depressed (scored at 36 and above on the scale). At T2, 33.3% were clinically depressed. By combining the T1 and T2 samples, a larger sample was obtained ($n = 85$) (i.e., there was attrition from T1 to T2 and new subjects were recruited at T2). Further analysis with 85 individuals showed that 33.3% of the total sample of adults still were reporting symptoms of clinical depression.

By examining length of time that members were in a group to variables that could be signs of psychosocial distress, an exploration of potential benefits of group participation can be made. Group participants were asked to indicate how often (*never, almost never, sometimes,* or *very often*) they felt that sickle cell disease had interfered with the following: money or finances, job, job tasks, school activities, social activities, church activities, hobbies, physical activities, daily tasks, self-care, and relationships.

The Pearson correlation coefficients are shown in Table 12.6 for the following variables: interference variables, including interference with leisure activities, daily activities, work, school, relationships, and finances; SCD symptoms and psychological symptoms; and health service use (e.g., frequency of hospitalizations, emergency room visits, and doctor visits). Further analysis incorporating the CES-D data into the model is under way.

CONCLUSIONS

This study demonstrates that African Americans are joining self-help groups throughout the United States and the number of mutual-help groups increases yearly. Individual participants in the groups of this study were heterogeneous with regard to demographic characteristics. However, as compared to the general population of African Americans, this sample was less likely to be married (24.6% vs. 43.6%) and slightly more likely to be in the lowest income bracket (U.S. Department of Commerce, 1992). About 56% of this sample had incomes below $15,000, whereas 42% of all African Americans fall in this income category. Interestingly, this sample tends to be more highly educated than the general population of African Americans. A much larger percentage of individuals in SCD groups went beyond a high school education (61.7% vs. 29.0%). Although the higher education of the participants is not consistent with the lower reported incomes, one possible explanation is that individuals with SCD have depressed earnings due to chronic disabilities. Furthermore, among those with SCD, those with higher educations are more likely to seek help from mutual-help groups. Still, the demographic profiles of this sample would suggest the broad appeal of

TABLE 12.6 Correlation of Length of Membership With Psychosocial Interferences, Physical and Psychological Symptoms, and Health Services Use

	Time in Group
Interference total	−.31[a]
Interference with	
Leisure activities	−.23
Daily activities	−.22
Work	−.32[a]
School	−.08
Relationships	−.30[a]
Finances	−.23
Symptoms total	−.32[b]
Physical	−.19
Psychological	−.37[b]
Health services use	
Frequency of:	
Hospitalizations	.09
Emergency room visits	.10
Medical visits	.19
$n = 57$	
Range = 1/2-13 years	
Mean = 5.2	
SD = 3.2	

a. $r \geq .26, p < .05$.
b. $r \geq .32, p < .01$.

self-help groups for persons within the African-American community when the group is relevant to their needs and generally accessible.

An important question remains to be answered: Are SCD groups readily available to the population of individuals affected by the disease? Unfortunately, data on the location of individuals with SCD are unavailable. Only some states have recently made newborn screening programs mandatory. Although the distribution of groups and persons affected by SCD cannot be compared, this study suggests that living close to the meeting (i.e., generally within 10 miles of the meeting site) and having transportation are critical factors to consider when organizing groups.

Another important consideration is the possible prevalence of depression among group members with SCD. Data from the CES-D showed that many of the individuals in this study were experiencing significant symptoms of depression. Based on the norms reported by Comstock and Helsing (1976) on the CES-D for African Americans, more individuals in this sample were clinically depressed (45% at T1 and 33.3% at T2) than are African Americans in the general population (26.4%). Clearly, these individuals are seeking help through mutual-help groups. The supportive activities of the groups, such as giving advice to one another, talking about family stressors, talking about personal feelings, listening to experts, and learning about how to deal with emotional issues, suggest that groups are functioning in a way that addresses psychosocial needs of some of the group members.

In addition to intrapersonal needs, more than 80% of the members in this study wanted to join groups to help improve the health care of people with SCD, to learn more about SCD, and to give support to members. These proactive functions show a desire among group members to help others. Therefore, a balance between proactive and supportive roles would appear critical among SCD groups.

As group leaders examine the potential characteristics of members and address group activities that might meet those needs, another important factor to consider is how the leadership patterns may affect the particular group. Other researchers have explored these issues. Yoak and Chesler (1985) have suggested that shared leadership among members and professionals is vital to adequate health service delivery and growth and stability of health-related groups. Maton, Leventhal, Madara, and Julien (1989) reported that groups that had strong local professional support and were unaffiliated with national organizations were less likely to disband. Among SCD groups, professional involvement in the formation and continued operation of groups remained high. Findings would suggest that professional involvement in SCD groups is in part responsible for the continued growth of the groups. The trend might also be related to the general growth of the mutual-help movement in this country and the coalition of individuals affected by SCD.

This study also explored the relationship among long-term group participation and psychosocial benefits. Correlations suggest that some individuals benefit psychosocially if they remain in the group for a number of years. As previously stated, those who had been group members the longest reported fewer psychosocial interferences and psychological symptoms. Length of time in group was not associated with the physical symptoms associated with the disease or the patterns of health service use. Again, with a genetically based disorder, physical symptoms and service use would be less likely to respond to supportive interventions. However, another explanation for the results is that those individuals who remain in the group are those who have received the greatest benefits. Individuals who do not perceive the group as beneficial would likely drop out of the group and thus are not represented in the sample. A prospective longitudinal study matching members and non-members could shed light on these issues and address how individual groups can become more homogeneous over time.

It should be noted that the research design employed in this study limits the interpretations and generalizations that can be made regarding these findings. Even though these correlations suggest benefits from long-term participation in the groups in this sample, questions remain for researchers. For example, who benefits, and how do those individuals differ from those who drop out of groups or never join? Due to the methodological constraints of the research design employed in this study, the above questions cannot be answered. However, the findings are compelling and lay the foundation for future research questions and hypotheses regarding positive outcomes for African Americans in self-help groups (best addressed in prospective longitudinal designs).

It is hoped that the information reported in this chapter will contribute to the awareness of the existence of self-help groups among African Americans and help dispel the myth that African Americans do not gravitate to groups. Clearly, this is not the case. It seems more likely that there are some individuals (regardless of race) who do not gravitate to groups. Mutual-aid groups are not a panacea for all. It would seem that the question for any group has to do with "goodness of fit" between the individual's needs and the benefits provided by group participation (Maton, 1989). Group modalities can be appropriate and beneficial for some individuals but not for all. Determining those that would benefit most from mutual-aid participation would be a critical area of research for the future.

Qualitative analysis is an important first step to a program of research. This approach provided the information needed to establish the existence, structure, and function of mutual-aid groups among African Americans in the United States. In addition, the research at the individual level is critical to enhance our understanding of the reasons for group participation. Therefore, it is hoped that this chapter will stimulate further mutual-help research with minority populations and encourage the formation of groups among diverse cultures.

NOTE

1. The *National Sickle Cell Mutual Help Directory* is available from the Psychosocial Research Division of the Duke-UNC Comprehensive Sickle Cell Center (physically located at the University of North Carolina). Address: CB No. 3560, UNC, Chapel Hill, NC 27599.

REFERENCES

Comstock, G., & Helsing, K. (1976). Symptoms of depression in two communities. *Psychological Medicine, 6,* 551-563.

Consensus Conference. (1987). Newborn screening for sickle cell disease and other hemoglobinopathies. *Journal of the American Medical Association, 258,* 1205-1209.

Hamilton, A. (1990). Self-help and mutual aid in ethnic minority communities. In A. Katz & E. Bender (Eds.), *Helping one another: Self-help groups in a changing world.* Oakland, CA: Third Party Publishing.

Katz, A., & Bender, E. (Eds.). (1990). *Helping one another: Self-help groups in a changing world.* Oakland, CA: Third Party Publishing.

Kurtz, L. (1990). The self-help movement: Review of the past decade of research. *Social Work with Groups, 13*(3), 102-115.

Maton, K. (1989). Towards an ecological understanding of mutual-help groups: The social ecology of "fit." *American Journal of Community Psychology, 17,* 729-753.

Maton, K., Leventhal, G., Madara, E., & Julien, M. (1989). Factors affecting the birth and death of mutual-help groups: The role of national affiliation, professional involvement, and member focal problem. *American Journal of Community Psychology, 17,* 643-670.

Radloff, L. (1977). CES-D Scale: A self-report depression scale for research in the general population. *Applied Psychological Measurement, 3,* 385-401.

Serjeant, G. R. (1985). *Sickle cell disease.* New York: Oxford University Press.

U.S. Department of Commerce, Bureau of the Census. (1992). *Statistical abstract of the United States.* Washington, DC: U.S. Government Printing Office.

Yoak, M., & Chesler, M. (1985). Alternative professional roles in health care delivery: Leadership patterns in self-help groups. *Journal of Applied Behavioral Science, 21,* 427-444.

13. Identifying the Experiential Knowledge Developed Within a Self-Help Group

MARSHA A. SCHUBERT

THOMASINA BORKMAN

Although experiential knowledge is one of the criteria for defining self-help groups, there has been a dearth of research dealing with it. It is an amorphous, changeable entity which does not lend itself to traditional research methodologies; nor does it lend itself to generalization. Yet, it distinguishes self-help groups from other types of helping bodies, and it is highly valued by those who participate in those groups (Hasenfeld & Gidron, 1993; Humphreys, 1993; Powell, 1990).

The purpose of the study described here was to identify the experiential knowledge of a group and to assess its value to the group members relative to other forms of knowledge. To that end, the study was planned and carried out in close collaboration with group members using participatory action research (PAR) methodology (Borkman & Schubert, in press; Chesler, 1991); thus, it was designed to provide group members with information they wanted in addition to meeting the researcher's goals. This chapter describes the concept of experiential knowledge, the PAR process by which the study was done, and selected findings of that study.

AUTHORS' NOTE: We thank Maria Parisi, Aina Stunz, Tom Powell, and other reviewers, as well as Timothy Schubert, for their help with this chapter.

227

EXPERIENTIAL KNOWLEDGE

Experiential knowledge is information and wisdom gained from lived experience (Borkman, 1976). Borkman identifies two critical components of her concept of experiential knowledge. The first of these is the type of information upon which experiential knowledge is based consisting of the wisdom and know-how gained through reflection upon personal lived experience.

Although there will be variations because of specific circumstances, the experiences of members of a group are likely to be more or less representative of others who face the same problems or situations. When they pool their information in the group, individuals begin to see common elements in both problems and attempted solutions while recognizing the uniqueness of their own situations. Hence, experiential knowledge tends to be specific, pragmatic, and somewhat idiosyncratic.

The second component is belief in the validity and authority of the knowledge gained from an experience. Persons must believe that the knowledge obtained from their experiences has value and is worth sharing with others. Such sharing enables members of a group to define more clearly the problem they are facing and to evolve guidelines for dealing with it. Groups develop a model or template of experiential knowledge that has evolved within the group (Borkman, 1990). The template facilitates the sharing of the knowledge with newcomers to a group and/or with others interested in starting a group. Thus, Alcoholics Anonymous (AA) has developed its Twelve Steps and Twelve Traditions as part of its knowledge for coping with alcoholism (Kurtz, 1979).

Alternative Types of Knowledge

Another approach to delimiting the concept of experiential knowledge is to examine alternative types of knowledge. Borkman (1990) described two. One she termed "lay knowledge" or information about a problem or procedure which is learned incidentally. This is knowledge that has been gained through information handed down from generation to generation, from the mass media, through common sense or logic, or secondhand from scientists or professionals.

Professional knowledge is the second type. Borkman has defined it as "information, knowledge, and skills developed, applied, and transmitted by an established specialized occupation" to those who have fulfilled the requirements of a profession (Borkman, 1990, p. 6). Compared to experiential knowledge, it is analytical, grounded in theory or scientific principle, and abstract. After working in their fields for some time, professionals add to their knowledge and understanding of the problems faced by their clients, but unless they too have the problem(s), their perspectives remain based on their training and in research.

In addition to understanding the distinctions between these types of knowledge, researchers must be aware that people may possess two or all three types of knowledge in some area. For example, a professional counselor in a substance abuse program may also be a recovering alcoholic in AA.

To identify knowledge as one type or another, researchers need to consider its source, its use, its perceived validity, and its context. The context in which experiential knowledge exists includes the group's background and composition as well as its information-sharing activities. The experiential knowledge of a self-help group is a distinctive product of the group, including the interaction of self-helpers and professionals who work in the field in which the problem lies, whether or not professionals participate in the group. Thus, factors such as the age of the group, its leadership, its attitude toward professionals, its goals, and its information-sharing activities are all important to the investigator interested in experiential knowledge.

PARTICIPATORY ACTION
RESEARCH METHODOLOGY

Chesler (1991) described participatory action research (PAR) as particularly appropriate for studying self-help groups. In it, persons being researched become co-investigators and co-creators of the process in partnership with the researcher. The researcher contributes specialized knowledge of research techniques and concepts whereas members provide experiential knowledge of their problem, solution(s), and group operations. In this study, there was constant interaction between the researcher (Schubert) and the group members who actively participated in the research process. Schubert's goals included not just adding to professional knowledge in the literature but also concretely aiding the group in improving its functioning (the action part of PAR) by feeding back results that increased their knowledge of their group. PAR shares many commonalities with collaborative research (Rappaport et al., 1985) and action research (Lavoie, 1984) which are strategic for studying self-help groups.

Participatory action research is a two-way street—one that sometimes takes unexpected turns. Past PAR yielded cases in which there were unanticipated benefits of concepts, distinctions, or other findings that the typical "objective" researcher would have been unlikely to discern. This very situation occurred in this study. A major finding of the study, namely the distinction between specialist and generalist professionals, was made because of the collaboration between group leaders and the researcher (Schubert).

In this study, all the collaborators were parents of children with the Gifted and/or Talented/Learning Disablities (GT/LD) characteristics and had attended meetings regularly for at least 2 years; four had served the group as officers. Although these group members generally endorsed the idea of generating new knowledge about self-help groups and were willing to assist someone they considered a colleague and/or friend, their major rationale for agreeing to the study was that its outcomes would support their goals of increasing membership and providing appropriate information.

Once they decided to support the study, the self-helpers willingly assisted in a number of ways (see Borkman & Schubert, in press, for more discussion of the participatory process of this research). They spent hours conferring with Schubert, making telephone calls, critiquing the survey instrument, and so on. The core group was supplemented at times by four or five others who assisted in making follow-up telephone calls and sharing copies of notes from meetings and other materials. They asked for frequent progress reports and made suggestions on ways to facilitate the pace of the work.

A Self-Help Group for Parents

The focus of the study (Schubert, 1991) was a self-help group created by parents of children who were both intellectually gifted and/or talented (GT) and learning disabled (LD). Federal legislation mandates a free, appropriate public education for any U.S. student with a disability; state laws and school district policies must reflect this requirement. As a result agencies, school districts, and colleges have developed identification and assessment procedures and educational programs to provide required services. In addition, many school districts have implemented methods to identify and serve GT students who are intellectually gifted and/or talented. Parents of students who have both GT/LD characteristics often encounter problems in obtaining these educational services, and both they and their children become increasingly frustrated with the public schools and discouraged by the difficulties such students experience in that environment. In addition, they very often face difficulties in the home environment because of behaviors related to the GT/LD combination as well as because of the school-related stress.

The self-help group for parents/guardians of GT/LD children was formed in 1987 by two women: a parent of two children diagnosed as GT/LD and a teacher (Schubert) who worked professionally with such students. The goals of this group were to provide families with information and support, to increase educators' awareness of the GT/LD population and its problems, and to pressure local schools into providing appropriate services for GT/LD children. To meet these goals, the leadership of the group constantly monitored the sign-in list of attendees, noted areas of concern and questions raised at meetings, and kept abreast of changes in laws and policies.

Over a 3-year period, the group's mailing list grew from 18 to 249. Although official members paid dues to support the group's newsletter, library materials, and refreshments, anyone who wished to attend a meeting was welcome. Registration lists show that attendance averaged 25 to 30 people and ranged from 15 to nearly 100. The group seemed to evolve into a drop-in group; except for the officers and a few faithful others, most people attended only when a meeting was of interest to them and/or when they felt the need for assistance.

The monthly meetings were held in a local school in Fairfax County, Virginia, and scheduled to begin at 7 p.m. They began with an informal sharing time when people were introduced to each other, had a chance to talk and ask questions, registered, looked over available materials, and/or had some refreshments. Next came a planned program of some sort—a presentation by a professional working in a field related to the problem, a panel discussion of parents and/or students, small-group discussions of some aspect of the problem, a video, and so on. Any relevant announcements also were made at this time. The meeting ended by 9:30 p.m. and was followed by more informal chatting and consulting.

Although most members were parents/guardians, the group stipulated that all officers had to be parents/guardians of children with GT/LD problems. There was some distrust of professionals similar to that found in some self-help groups (Chamberlin & Rogers, 1990; Kurtz, 1985, 1990; Suler, 1984). Professionals who worked with these children (e.g., teachers, counselors, psychologists, social workers) were welcome at meetings and sometimes were asked to give presentations to the group. Professionals who did present information at meetings were questioned extensively, often asked to justify or validate their information, and at times disputed and told that they were in error. New information obtained from these professionals was scrutinized by individual members, compared with their own experiences and knowledge, and discussed with others. That which was found congruent with their own knowledge or which was found helpful when implemented and/or modified was shared with others and became part of the group's knowledge. Therefore, in this particular group, professional knowledge could be a source of experiential knowledge, not because of the authority of the professional who presented it, but because of the validating experiences of audience members.

THE RESEARCH PROCESS

The work began with the creation of a case study description of the group based upon memories of old-timers in the group and upon written materials, including newsletters and notes taken by as many people as would share them. The description of the group provided earlier came from this activity. This, coupled with the assistance of the collaborators and the Schubert's own years of experience with individuals with GT/LD characteristics, enabled her to recognize the issues around which the group had developed a knowledge base and to identify information-sharing activities which disseminated that knowledge.

How Is Experiential Knowledge Transmitted in the Group?

Given the "positive learning spiral" described by Borkman (1979), logically the body of knowledge used by a group at any given time would be reflected in its literature, topics of conversations at gatherings, content of sharing activities, and the wisdom of old-timers and/or leaders of the group. Observation of the parent group suggested that experiential knowledge was shared in several ways. One of the most popular was that of small-group conversations before and after meetings. These often began when one person asked another a question. Soon others interested in the topic would join these two individuals and would contribute what they knew. Because the meetings were usually designed with some sort of presentation, the interactions between audience and presenters were also a source of data. These parents did not sit quietly and take in information; they questioned, debated, offered examples, challenged and/or supported speakers, whether those speakers were professionals, self-helpers, or even a panel of their own members or of students who were GT/LD.

Individuals also had access to telephone numbers of volunteers who offered to share their knowledge—generally the officers of the group and a professional who worked with these students in the local school district; these individuals kept notes of their conversations to assist in planning future programs, to record areas in which additional information was needed, and to note concerns of the group's members. For this study, Schubert and her collaborators agreed that the single best source of data was the personal interactions in the group and the single best means of data collection was note taking by Schubert and other members who had volunteered their help. These notes included brief summaries of conversations before and after the actual meetings, notations of topics of telephone conversations when people called asking advice or sharing some aspect of the problem, questions asked during presentations, remarks made during sharing sessions, and ideas for future programs. Many of the members took notes during meetings, a fact which paid double benefits: first, some of them made their personal notes available to Schubert, and second, no one paid much attention to anyone who took notes during meetings.

What Is the Group's Experiential Knowledge?

In a sociological (not philosophical) sense, experiential knowledge about helping a GT/LD child consists of the statements, stories, or narratives reflecting some aspect of an individual's experience that she or he values and trusts as knowledge. To an uninvolved observer, much experiential knowledge may sound like or appear to be small talk or everyday conversation.

Five examples of experiential information and know-how that were specifically shared in the parent group follow. As is apparent from the examples, experiential knowledge is concrete, pragmatic and contextual.

Joyce told me that her son's seventh-grade teacher lets students use calculators, so in my last teacher conference I insisted that my fifth-grader be allowed to use one. His teacher said that she couldn't let him because when he got to the middle school, he would be totally lost. That's when I told her that seventh grade teachers let some kids use calculators. Having that specific example made all the difference. She wasn't happy, but she finally agreed. Now I'm looking for more examples of modifications teachers make for our children.

Bobby brings home four or five assignments a night. So does his younger brother, Todd. But Todd can finish his in about an hour, usually. Bobby—who's a smart boy—used to take hours and hours. He never had any time for anything else, just homework. He was depressed. I was depressed. His dad was depressed. Finally, my husband and I decided that it was just too much. We tried to talk to his teachers, but we didn't get anywhere. So then we decided that the world wouldn't end if he didn't do all that homework. We decided 2 hours a night was enough for all of us. And you know what? His grades are just about as good as they were before, and everybody's frustration levels are better.

That presenter we had last month made logical sense, so I tried that calendar organization idea with Barbara. Boy, was that a waste of time. If she were organized enough to use it, she wouldn't need it. We'll have to simplify it a lot if we use it.

I used to go to those annual school meetings all by myself and nod my head and sign what they told me. I was overwhelmed. Now I know better. After listening to some of you, I'll never go by myself again, and I'll be sure I make a list of my questions.

You can spend $700 at that clinic for testing if you want to, but the school doesn't have to use that information once you have it. Take it from me and my empty pocketbook.

Change in Experiential Knowledge Over Time

In working with the group over the years, Schubert realized how its knowledge had changed. When the group first began, for instance, many of the parents who attended meetings "knew" that they would not get appropriate educational services for their children from the public school system. They came to meetings looking for alternative ways to help their children and often to vent their frustration and hostility. Over time, as members shared ways in which their children received special education services and as school district employees talked with them, members of the group came to realize that the school district was not denying services. Instead, in most cases, the difficulties lay within the local school building where educators did not recognize these students and did not know how to serve students with GT/LD problems. By the group's 4th year, the focus on this issue had changed from blaming the school district for its perceived inadequacies to finding ways to obtain appropriate services for students in accordance with the policies of the school district. The group's experiential knowledge base reflected this change; it included: schools where modifications had been tried and were successful; specific academic modifications which were (or were not) helpful; and the names and professional titles of people who could and would assist them. It also included suggestions for working with educators in local schools who seemed unwilling to make needed adaptations for these special children. If, in years to come, appropriate educational services are routinely provided for these students, the group's knowledge base should change to emphasize other issues which would be of more concern at that point; until then, however, this issue will in all probability continue to be a central focus of the group.

Newcomers often came believing that the services their children needed could not or would not be provided, just as many of the original members did. At meetings, they would hear how others had obtained services and then go to their schools armed with that knowledge. Many times they were successful in getting some changes made; sometimes they were not. In any case, their knowledge base was modified and became more consistent with that of the group—that services could be and should be provided, but that often parents had to fight local school personnel to get those services.

Individuals may not be aware of changes such as these in their knowledge and/or attitude or even what they do or do not "know" about a specific topic or problem until they are asked. They also may not realize how or if their experiential knowledge base differs from that formed by the unspoken general consensus of the group. Research can help articulate that knowledge and thus facilitate its sharing—but only with the help provided by knowledgeable members of the group who understand the issues and processes that created that knowledge.

What Are the Topical Areas of Experiential Knowledge?

The next stage of the study was that of looking for patterns within the collected qualitative data. This began with a content analysis of the notes and records described above, using the technique of coding described by Bogdan and Bliken (1982). The combination of participant observation notes, telephone messages, and copied group documents yielded approximately 300 pages of typed material. This data did not include any notes taken on actual presentations by professionals or members, but only those made on questions, comments, discussions, and conversations with attendees— occasions which provided opportunities for the sharing and developing experiential knowledge. Schubert reviewed this material line by line, using the margin area to list topics or content. This process, combined with her familiarity with the group and with these types of students, soon suggested several coding categories or topic areas. Schubert's goal was to devise a set of categories so that each example of experiential knowledge would fit into only one of the coding categories and so that the number of items in the "miscellaneous" category was markedly fewer than any of the others. Despite making several attempts to group examples of experiential knowledge into mutually exclusive and exhaustive categories, she was unsuccessful until she consulted with three officers.

The result of this process was the group of eight topical areas of experiential knowledge shown in Table 13.1.

The miscellaneous category contained items which were shared at only one or two meetings and/or which arose once or twice in conversations between the self-helpers. These miscellaneous topics did not seem to arise spontaneously, but rather to be tied to a program, presenter, or attendee of a specific meeting.

Once the data had been coded and indexed, Schubert made a list of items grouped by the eight categories. She then talked with four members to see if they agreed that these categories were relevant to the task at hand, to ask if others should be added, and so on. Generally these people were very satisfied with the list, but two had suggestions. First, the parent founder recommended that the proposed survey include data about private as well as public school enrollment and about parent comfort levels in talking to professionals. The then-president of the group suggested that the proposed questionnaire include more about how parents got along with professionals, especially public school educators. She felt that the results would show a difference in people's attitudes toward those educators and professionals who served these students as private practitioners. These last comments eventually led to one of the major findings of the study.

Survey of the Usage and
Value of Experiential Knowledge

At this point, Schubert had developed topic areas of experiential knowledge. The next step was to design a survey instrument which would verify that the topical areas did encompass that knowledge base and that group members valued the information in that base.

Schubert prepared a draft of a questionnaire with items that reflected the content of the topical areas. This was then reviewed by her collaborators and by other researchers who had used questionnaires in their own work with self-help groups. The instrument was revised to incorporate most of their suggestions, including the addition of items to gather information requested by members. These included such items as the attendees' level of experience in dealing with the GT/LD problem and reasons for attending or not attending meetings; relationships between group members and professionals; the value placed on different types of knowledge; and representative items from the categories as shown in Table 13.1.

One area of interest was primarily to see how these self-helpers valued experiential knowledge compared to professional or lay knowledge. Respondents were presented with hypothetical situations and asked to indicate the person they would most likely consult (e.g., professionals with specialized knowledge, general educators, parents who had a child with similar problems, or close friends or family members).

The questionnaire was mailed to every person/couple who had been registered as having attended a meeting of the parent group between 1987 and 1990. Thus, the population was self-selected, as it has been in many other studies (e.g., Jacobs & Goodman, 1989; Powell, 1985). As in the Hinrichsen, Revenson, and Shinn (1985) study, the population included people who became group members in addition to those who shared the problem of concern to the group but chose not to join. This approach provided two logical groups for comparison. Two hundred forty-nine questionnaires were mailed out with a cover letter explaining the project and a return envelope. Several members of the group provided telephone follow-up assistance. A total of 181 questionnaires, 73% of the population, were returned, a rate above what Warwick and Lininger (1975) state is an appropriate level of response for a questionnaire. Of the 64 official dues-paying members, all but two responded, a rate of 97%.

Results Verifying Topical Areas

The responses from the survey instrument had two forms: Likert-scale ratings and narrative information volunteered by respondents. In all, 88 people included narrative information ranging from a few words to a four-page handwritten letter. These comments usually qualified an answer in some way (i.e., "My answer would be different for private professionals than for the schools.") Analysis of this data revealed that all responses could be categorized into the eight topical areas. Further, it indicated that respondents were aware of changes in both their attitudes and the knowledge based upon their experiences.

Both the responses to the Likert-like items and the comments reflected parent awareness and concern about items dealing with the difficulties inherent in rearing a child who is GT/LD. They also indicated that many

TABLE 13.1 Examples of Experiential Knowledge and Related Survey Items by Topical Area

Topical Areas of Experiential Knowledge	Examples of Experiential Knowledge	Items by Topical Area
Understanding GT/LD problem	Newsletter items and program topics on Attention Deficit Disorder (ADD)	Is impulsive and acts without thinking
	These students seem so disorganized. Why can't they remember things like bringing a pencil to math without being told everyday?	Is forgetful and disorganized
Concerns about their own GT/ LD children	He needs to use the special ed class, but he won't go. He says he can do it by himself—that he's not a baby.	Denies having problems; doesn't want any special help
	She's always in trouble and it's never her fault. The world—including me— is out to get her. If only she could hear herself!	Misreads social cues; says inappropriate things
Impact on the family	His dad and I seem to constantly fight about how much help to give our son. He says I give Tommy the answers, but I don't.	My spouse and I disagree about the best way to deal with our GT/LD child(ren) and related problems
	Our daughter spends hours and hours on homework every night. And so do I. When do we all get a break?	My spouse or I have to spend large amounts of time disciplining GT/LD child(ren) or helping with homework
Concerns about getting appropriate help for children from schools	Programs on school screening procedures and special education programs	Understanding school screening and/or placement procedures
	No one in Joanne's school is willing to admit that a child can be both gifted and disabled—unless she's Helen Keller!	School personnel were unaware of existence of GT/LD syndrome and its effects on GT/LD students

people felt the group was beneficial to them for the reasons which embraced the items in the section on benefits of the group. These results, combined with the fact that no new topical areas had emerged, confirmed the hypothesis

TABLE 13.1 Continued

Topical Areas of Experiential Knowledge	Examples of Experiential Knowledge	Items by Topical Area
Concerns about getting help from private sources	Our son's high school-age tutor helped him more than the psychologist who charged $50 an hour! After we spent all that time and money for a private assessment, the school told us they'd never heard of the clinic and that they legally had to do their own	Our family resources are strained because of the money and time spent for private assessment, remediation, and so on School personnel seemed reluctant to use information obtained from private practitioners
Concerns about ways to provide practical help for GT/LD children	Programs and newsletter items on study skills When my son was bringing home a lot of Fs, I called the special education teacher and she helped us get him back on track using an assignment notebook that we checked every night	Is forgetful and disorganized I didn't know who to contact at the school when my GT/LD child was having trouble
Benefits of the parent group	I never knew how much I knew about all this until I started talking to someone else School people listen to me a lot better when they realize I know my rights	Being able to help other parents of GT/LD students Learning my rights as a parent
Miscellaneous	Children with Tourette's Syndrome usually have tics and often have outbursts of profanity	IBM now has more educationally oriented programs than it used to

sis that the content analysis had delineated vital topics of the experiential knowledge of this self-help group.

Difference in Use and Value of Knowledge for Types of Attendees

To further investigate aspects of the group's use of experiential knowledge, factors such as length of time in the group, professional experience with the problem, and so on were related in a statistical analysis. In this study, Schubert identified several pairs of subgroups, including:

1. professionals and nonprofessionals in the fields directly related to working with individuals with GT/LD problems
2. old-timers and newcomers to the group
3. infrequent and frequent attendees
4. members of other groups for parents and members of this group only
5. parents who had dealt with the problem for years and those who had just begun

T-tests were conducted to evaluate comparisons between these subgroups. Although differences often were not significant at either the .10 or the .05 level, patterns did emerge from the data analysis which supported the concept of experiential knowledge as a distinctive and changing entity. For example, as might be expected, parents of younger children and/or those with the newer diagnoses of GT/LD appeared to be more actively seeking information and help than their counterparts, who should have accumulated experience and information upon which to draw. Newcomers to the group and/or frequent attendees both responded more favorably to items related to the value of the group than did their counterparts. Surprisingly, however, professionals in the field who were also parents of these children rated the group more favorably than parents who were not, despite the knowledge and resources one would expect the former to have.

SUMMARY OF THE FINDINGS

After final analysis of the qualitative and survey data including the input from group members and advisors, Schubert (1991) concluded the study had yielded major findings in these areas:

1. the identification of topical areas of the experiential knowledge base for the group
2. the value of that knowledge
3. attitudes of self-helpers toward professionals in the field
4. empowerment

The Experiential Knowledge Base of the Group

One of the most valuable outcomes of the study was a framework which articulated and organized the experiential knowledge of the group into eight categories, with the primary one being the understanding of the problem itself. Members of the group, especially those new to the problem, were interested in learning as much as possible about the GT/LD interactions and the results of those interactions between GT/LD individuals. They wanted to know what was "normal" for those afflicted with the problem, what might be expected. They also wanted information about those topics which seemed highly related to the GT/LD syndrome, such as Attention Deficit Disorder and problems in developing social skills. Parents and professionals alike often addressed the problems of students' low self-esteem and very poor organizational skills. Second, they wanted to explore the possible effects of the condition upon their own children. In a sense, they wanted to separate the child from the problem in order to see both more clearly and to make better judgments related to discipline and expectations. Thus, they explored issues such as accountability for his/her own actions, expectations for the future, and ways to recognize giftedness or talents.

Another topic area is the impact on the family. Family members were usually aware that the GT/LD child was often a source of stress within the family itself. Discussions often included such things as changes in family routines and/or relationships since the child began school, financial demands because of diagnostic and/or remedial treatments (including, in some cases, medications), ways in which different family members responded to the child and his or her needs, and ways in which the child resembled one or more older relatives. Stress between spouses often arose based upon the manner in which each reacted to the child and his/her problem, the solutions selected for difficulties related to the problem, and accusations of blame. In addition, there was often stress between/among siblings and/or parents and siblings because of competition for family resources, including adult attention and money. In some cases, even the extended family was involved due to lack of understanding of the problem and/or disagreement over the best manner in which to deal with the child.

Group members were also aware of the fact that legislation existed to provide needed services for handicapped learners. They were concerned about getting appropriate help for their children from schools and private sources. Many of those at meetings came to discover just what was included in that legislation and how the local school district was interpreting its legal obligations. They wanted to know what their rights were, what they could expect and/or demand of the schools, and how to be sure the schools were meeting the needs of the children. In addition, they often exchanged names of people in the district who could be helpful to a parent, they translated the bureaucratic jargon used in assessment data and documents for each other, and they gave each other advice on the best way to approach required meetings between school personnel and parents. They further discussed the pros and cons of different kinds and levels of special education services and possible consequences of having a child in specific education programs.

Group members also offered each other many practical suggestions for dealing with aspects of the GT/LD problem. For example, they talked about ways in which general educators had modified materials and/or procedures in order to help a child demonstrate or gain knowledge. They discussed the use of technology to compensate for poor academic skills and means of obtaining access to computers, taped books, and so on. They talked about their experiences with various professionals, the cost of their services, and the results. They explored ways of helping children get organized and deal with homework. They identified resources within the community, such as the parent center run by the schools, which had been useful to them. Pragmatic suggestions like these always seemed welcome.

Information about the benefits of the group was also shared. Members expressed their relief at not being the "only one" with the problem. Many expressed their gratitude for specific help or ideas they had obtained through the group. Some stated that they had not realized how much they knew about the topics until they had a chance to talk to someone else about some aspects of the GT/LD problem. Quite often, when a person had a problem which seemed particularly difficult, others would provide support and encouragement, such as, "I know it's hard, but you can do it. I did."

Value of Experiential Knowledge Versus Lay Knowledge

The results of the questionnaire, particularly the handwritten comments, indicated that group members valued experiential knowledge highly. As shown in Table 13.2, when respondents were given problematic situations and a choice of whom to turn for assistance, they chose experienced parents (42%) most often and much more often than those with lay knowledge— either generalists (such as public school personnel, 12%) or family and friends (6%).

TABLE 13.2 Choices for Advice and/or Support from Different Sources

| Issue Addressed by Hypothetical Situation | Experienced Parents | Number of Times Selected | | |
		Specialists	General Educators	Friends and Family
GT or LD placement?	70	83	17	4
Peer relationships	90	58	15	12
Easing family stress	58	84	3	21
Private sources of help	80	65	27	10
Practical suggestions	53	80	38	5
Helping child adjust to LD program	79	50	28	5
Total choices	430	420	128	57
	(41.5%)	(40.5%)	(12.0%)	(6.0%)

Attitudes Toward Professionals

As noted before, the parent group in this study resembled many other self-help groups in one respect—a wariness or distrust of professionals. Although professionals were invited to speak and to attend meetings, they were excluded from leadership positions. On the other hand, one finding of the study was that the respondents to the survey valued generalist professionals (in this case, usually public school personnel and family physicians) and specialists (usually private practitioners such as psychologists or psychiatrists) differently. (See Table 13.2.) When given problematic situations, they selected specialist professionals (41%) as a source of help far more often than generalist professionals (12%). In addition, their written responses on the questionnaire indicated that parents are more comfortable talking and working with specialists. The value of the professional knowledge held by specialists was also evident in the format of their meetings; the programs often consisted either of presentations by specialists or of panels or small groups of members. This distinction between generalists and specialists in related professions has not been apparent in literature on self-help groups, but it is likely to be valuable in evaluating or reassessing relationships between self-helpers and professionals.

Empowerment

Experiential knowledge empowered some members of the parent group. Several parents commented that the group had enabled them to meet professionals on a more equal basis and/or encouraged them to take an active role in conferences and educational placement decisions regarding their children. They became more comfortable working with professionals who in turn work with their children, and they were less intimidated by professionals or those in the school system for declaring a child eligible for services. One parent wrote that he did not know how much he actually knew about children with GT/LD problems in the schools until he listened to others at a meeting. He wrote that another parent was having a problem almost exactly like the one he and his wife had had the previous year and that suddenly he realized, "I knew what I was talking about." Even newcomers to the group have experiential knowledge which can be developed and shared with others.

CONCLUSION

This study was valuable in several ways. The PAR methodology was a fruitful strategy for identifying the experiential knowledge which the group had developed. The self-helpers' active participation in the research process helped ensure that the results of the study were trustworthy and authentic. Another positive outcome of their participation was that the research produced information which the group wanted as well as that of more interest to the authors. When the results were given to the leaders, they gained some ideas for increasing the attractiveness of its programs for members and potential members. Just as experiential knowledge empowers its individual owners to stand up for their rights vis-à-vis others, the PAR methodology entails a process that provides empowering information to the self-help group to improve its organization and to advocate for its needs in the community.

A valuable substantive outcome of the study was the identification of the experiential knowledge about parenting/guiding GT/LD children through their educational process that the group had developed over time. A framework within which the knowledge could be categorized was developed; the knowledge produced by the group could be coded into one of eight topical areas. The topical areas dealt with the definition of the problem and its immediate impact on the child(ren) and family, and the ways to obtain help to ameliorate the problem(s) from the schools and private sources. There was a miscellaneous category of one-of-a-kind issues or idiosyncratic concerns of individuals. Through the results of a survey questionnaire to all attendees to the group, these eight categories were shown to be exhaustive in encompassing the topical areas of experiential knowledge developed by the group.

From a cultural perspective these eight topical areas of experiential knowledge and the subtopics under them compose the worldview of the group. The worldview of self-help groups and individual self-helpers is currently emerging as a fruitful area of theory and research with which to understand them (Kennedy and Humphreys, 1993; Rappaport, this volume). This chapter has focused on the group's knowledge about its formulation of the GT/LD problem and means of obtaining help to resolve it. The parent group reported here works closely with a variety of private professionals and with school-based professionals to obtain help for their children; thus, knowledge of how to access the local system of professional help is an important part of their worldview. This situation is somewhat different from many Twelve Step and other self-help groups, in which the primary means of resolving the problem is done by the individual within the group, rather than relying extensively on external professional experts; in such cases, it is less likely that the group's worldview contains so much on accessing local systems of help.

The finding that self-helpers valued the professional knowledge of specialists as highly as they did the experiential knowledge of veteran parents is significant. Moreover, the self-helpers welcomed professionals as presenters or attendees but prohibited them from being officers of the group, thereby showing some wariness and distrust of them. These findings show that the issue of the self-helpers' relationships with professionals is much more multifaceted and complex than is often found in the literature, although some observers deal with the complexity (Kurtz, Mann, & Chambon, 1987; Powell, 1990).

Finally, the study was valuable in revealing why experiential knowledge is so difficult to research empirically. Being concrete, personalized, and pragmatic means that much experiential information appears to the uninvolved observer as small talk or everyday conversation that can easily be dismissed. Much of it is expressed as personal stories or narratives (Rappaport, 1994). Furthermore, it is not neatly packaged in third-person abstractions, as is much professional knowledge. It also seems as if the relevance and usefulness of the information is not immediately obvious to the uninvolved observer, who neither has the problem nor often comprehends its impact on parents and their children.

This study demonstrated the utility of the PAR methodology in empirically researching experiential knowledge. Hopefully, this study will pave the way for many more empirical studies researching experiential knowledge.

REFERENCES

Bogdan, R. C., & Bliken, S. K. (1982). *Qualitative research for education: An introduction to theory and methods*. Boston: Allyn & Bacon.

Borkman, T. (1976). Experiential knowledge: A new concept for the analysis of self-help groups. *Social Science Review, 50,* 445-455.

Borkman, T. (1990). Experiential, professional and lay frames of reference. In T. J. Powell (Ed.), *Working with self-help* (pp. 3-30). Silver Spring, MD: NASW Press.

Borkman, T. (1979). *Mutual self-help groups: A theory of experiential inquiry.* Rockville, MD: National Institute on Alcohol Abuse and Alcoholism.

Borkman, T., & Schubert, M. A. (in press). Participatory action research as a strategy for studying self-help groups internationally. In F. Lavoie, T. Borkman, & B. Gidron (Eds.), Special Issue on International and Intercultural Self-Help, *Prevention in Human Services.*

Chamberlin, J., & Rogers, J. A. (1990). Planning a community-based mental health system: Perspective of service recipients. *American Psychologist, 45,* 1241-1244.

Chesler, M. (1991). Participatory action research with self-help groups: An alternative paradigm for inquiry and action. *American Journal of Community Psychology, 19,* 757-768.

Hasenfeld, Y., & Gidron, B. (1993). Self-help groups and human service organizations: An interorganizational perspective. *Social Service Review, 2,* 217-235.

Hinrichsen, G. A., Revenson, T. A., & Shinn, M. (1985). Does self-help help? An empirical study of scoliosis peer support groups. *Journal of Social Issues, 41*(1), 65-87.

Humphreys, K. (1993). Psychotherapy and the Twelve Step approach for substance abusers: The limits of integration. *Psychotherapy, 30,* 207-213.

Jacobs, M. K., & Goodman, G. (1989). Psychology and self-help groups: Predictions on a partnership. *American Psychologist, 44,* 1-10.

Kennedy, M., & Humphreys, K. (in press). Understanding worldview transformation in members of mutual help groups. In F. Lavoie, B. Gidron, & T. Borkman (Eds.) Special issue on international self-help. *Prevention in Human Services.*

Kurtz, E. (1979). *Not God: A history of Alcoholics Anonymous.* Center City, MN: Hazelden.

Kurtz, L. F. (1990). The self-help movement: Review of the past decade of research. *Social Work with Groups, 13,* 101-115.

Kurtz, L. F. (1985). Cooperation and rivalry between helping professionals and A.A. members. *Health and Social Work, 10,* 104-112.

Kurtz, L. F., Mann, L. B., & Chambon, A., (1987). Linking between social workers and mental health mutual aid groups. *Social Work in Health Care, 13,* 69-78.

Lavoie, F. (1984). Action research: A new model of interaction between the professional and self-help groups. In A. Gartner & F. Riessman (Eds.), *The self-help revolution* (pp. 173-82). New York: Human Sciences.

Powell, T. J. (1985). Improving the effectiveness of self-help. *Social Policy, 16*(2), 22-29.

Powell, T. J. (1990). Self-help, professional help, and informal help: Competing or complementary systems? In T. J. Powell (Ed.), *Working with self-help* (pp. 31-49). Silver Spring, MD: NASW.

Rappaport, J. (1994). Narrative studies, personal stories, and identity transformation in the mutual-help context. In T. J. Powell (Ed.), *Understanding the self-help organization: Frameworks and findings.* Thousand Oaks, CA: Sage.

Rappaport, J., Seidman, E., Toro, P., McFadden, L., Reischel, T., Roberts, L., Salem, D., & Zimmerman, M. (1985). Collaborative research with a mutual help organization. *Social Policy, 15*(3), 12-24.

Schubert, M. A. (1991). *Investigating experiential knowledge in a self-help group.* Unpublished doctoral dissertation, George Mason University.

Suler, J. (1984). Role of ideology in self-help groups. *Social Policy, 14*(3), 29-36.

Warwick, D. P., & Lininger, C. A. (1975). *Sample survey.* New York: McGraw-Hill.

14. Twelve Steps for Everyone? Lesbians in Al-Anon

CHRISTINE FLYNN SAULNIER

The Alcoholics Anonymous (AA) Twelve Step program has been adapted for many different problems and populations, with varying success. Some believe the program was designed for and best serves the needs of a select group: mainstream, heterosexual, white men. A recurring criticism is that the program does not always meet women's needs, in part, because it reinforces traditional roles, unsuited to the current reality of women's lives. One way of studying the flexibility of the Twelve Step program in regards to women is to examine a version originally designed with women in mind: Al-Anon.

Believing that it would be instructive to look at a population of women who are unlikely to be comfortable with traditional definitions of men and women, the author conducted an ethnographic study of a lesbian Al-Anon group. Research questions included: How flexible is the Twelve Step program? Do members attempt to alter the program to meet their needs, or conform to it, or both? How successful are the adaptations and what is the price of conformity?

Background

There is dissension among feminists about the utility of Twelve Step programs. Some point to the programs' accessibility, especially when compared to the often expensive treatment found in medical establishments. Others have suggested that using Al-Anon or other AA-modeled programs to address addiction is dealing with an essentially political issue in a personal, victim-blaming way (Herman, 1988; Tallen, 1990). Concomitantly, division exists in Al-Anon concerning the suitability of a feminist presence. This chapter presents the findings of research conducted in the late summer and autumn of 1991, when the author examined an Al-Anon meeting which had a clear feminist leaning. This meeting for lesbians was influenced by feminist ideals, which were prominently featured but not always welcome.

The development of interest in alcoholism among lesbians has received some attention (cf. Hastings, 1982; Herman, 1988; Saulnier, 1991) but the involvement of lesbians' partners and family members has been ignored. Indeed, very little has been written about Al-Anon generally. It appears that nothing at all has been written about lesbian Al-Anon. This study will help fill that gap.

To place this study in its proper context, it is important to know the history of Al-Anon and something about lesbian participation in it. Lesbians have joined Al-Anon and other Twelve Step programs in large numbers. With the popularity of recovery groups, the emergence of negative attitudes toward the bar culture and the closing of lesbian bars, these programs became a significant source of socialization and support for lesbians (Ginsberg, 1989). But lesbian Al-Anon did not simply emerge from the gay civil rights efforts of the 1980s. Although newly found lesbian political identity contributed to the structure of lesbian Al-Anon, the growth and changes within Al-Anon as a whole must also be considered to understand the findings of this study. A brief review will also help clarify which concepts have a long history in the program and which are unique to this meeting.

The Al-Anon Families

Al-Anon began when wives of alcoholics gathered to play cards while their husbands were at meetings. These informal social gatherings were, in effect, the first Al-Anon meetings. The family groups, initially called the Alcoholics Anonymous Auxiliary, (Jackson, 1954) grew until, in 1986, there were 27,201 Al-Anon Family Groups registered.

Bailey, in her 1965 study of Al-Anon, found that the majority of members defined alcoholism as a combined mental and physical illness, accepting the AA/disease model. Martin (1989) suggested that Al-Anon's prohibition against questioning the conceptualization of the alcoholic as diseased contributes to an atmosphere of passivity and acceptance of the alcoholic's behavior. Martin's view seems to be supported by Al-Anon's stance that "marriage vows mandated loyalty through sickness and health, and indeed alcoholism is a sickness," (Ablon, 1974, p. 35) and the program's conviction that if a woman changes her own thinking and behavior, things will improve.

A more positive function of the disease concept however, is that it allows the woman to live with her husband's alcoholism without feeling she has to do something to stop or control it (Martin, 1989). When Martin examined Al-Anon's manual, she found that members were conceived of in relation to the alcoholic, rather than in their own right—an understandable occurrence, as the formation of the organization was based on that relationship.

The emphasis in Al-Anon is on acceptance of, typically, the wife's situation as God's will, and recognition of her powerlessness. Martin noted that it was a generalized powerlessness to which Al-Anon members referred, rather than the emphasis in AA, initially at least, to powerlessness over alcohol. The Al-Anon member was taught to keep the focus of her growth on herself, defining feelings like fear and resentment as faults rather than normal responses to the disruption of life experienced in relation to the alcoholic (Martin, 1989).

More than half of Al-Anon members have alcoholic parents (Ablon, 1974). It is not surprising, therefore, that Al-Anon has been greatly affected by a closely related, often intertwining phenomenon: the Adult Children of Alcoholics (ACOA) movement. The movement exists within and alongside of Al-Anon. In some instances, ACOA meetings are clearly labeled, and a distinction is made between them and Al-Anon meetings. Although at one time seen as a separate program, ACOA ideas are now incorporated into Al-Anon literature and into some Al-Anon meetings.

In 1988, Robertson devoted a chapter of her study of AA to the families of alcoholics, focusing primarily on the growing ACOA movement. She defined it as related to but separate from Al-Anon and AA. Robertson examined the high level of anger found in meetings of ACOA and contrasted ACOA's emphasis on expression of anger with the search for serenity more often found in Al-Anon.

After attending 12 sessions of an Al-Anon meeting, specifically an ACOA meeting, and interviewing 14 members for her dissertation, Cutter published a brief report on her findings. She noted remarkably little focus on problems related to alcohol. Emotional and relationship problems were the major concerns of members, followed by interest in how the Al-Anon program works and concern with issues from childhood (Cutter & Cutter, 1987).

Collet (1990) reported that ACOA borrowed the disease metaphor whole-sale from AA. Recall that AA describes alcoholism as a progressive, fatal disease that can never be cured but only arrested through abstinence. "This metaphor is now widely applied: to compulsive spending, sex, gambling, overeating, and 'codependence' . . ." (Collet, 1990, p. 28). Although some ACOAs still maintain separate groups, many now attend Al-Anon meetings. In November 1989, 1,900 Al-Anon groups specifically for ACOAs were registered (Collet, 1990).

A concept central to the Al-Anon program is detachment. In 1978, Reddy and McElfresh detailed the concept as it is used in Al-Anon. They suggested that the notion underlies all of the Al-Anon program. The term is defined as an avoidance of oversensitivity, acceptance of powerlessness, the setting of limits with an alcoholic, and avoidance of confrontations: "The true meaning of detachment is to let go (of) the behavior and drinking of the alcoholic and separate from them as a person" (Reddy & McElfresh, 1978, p. 30).

Others who have had considerable impact on Al-Anon are the advocates of the idea of codependence. The notion of codependence is related to the concept of detachment. As with ACOA, a disease model has been incorpo-rated into the codependence movement and subsequently, the Al-Anon program (Peele & Brodsky, 1991). Codependence has been described as a "personality disorder seen in people with a spectrum of stressful life expe-riences . . . (including) those who have been touched directly or indirectly by alcoholism" (Cermak, 1984, p. 38). Called variously an innate trait, a learned social role, and a disease (Asher, 1988), codependence was first used to describe partners "addicted" to rescuing and caretaking alcoholics (Stephanie Brown, as quoted in Asher, 1988). "That people who live with the alcoholic are also sick is fast becoming another taken-for-granted component of the . . . (disease model) ideology" (Asher, 1988, p. 332).

Krestan and Bepko (1990) explored the development of the concept. They acknowledged the relief of pain reported by many members of Twelve Step programs, yet they described the focus on codependence as an unproductive mythology "about our hope for redemption from our common human wound-edness" (p. 217). They located the roots of the codependence concept: (a) in sexist political ideology—that is, focus on the alcoholic husband left the wife appearing stronger than is generally acceptable— and (b) in the advent of family systems theory. They argued that family systems theory focuses on participation in problems by family members, thus laying the groundwork for the wife to be diagnosed as pathological and ultimately restoring the traditional balance of power (Krestan & Bepko, 1990).

The growing acceptance by lesbians of Twelve Step ideology can be seen in the flourishing of lesbian AA. In the 1980s the National Council on Alcoholism (NCA) recognized lesbian alcoholics as a subpopulation in need of treatment. Lesbian popular culture reflected the growing concern with alcohol in books, songs, music festivals, and newsletters. By the late 1980s the lesbian press started to respond with serious (and humorous) questions about the place of the recovery industry and the recovery movement in lesbian lives (Saulnier, 1991). Concern was expressed about the utility of the powerlessness model for women, particularly for lesbians (Herman, 1988). Differences between men giving up male power and women giving up female power and the contribution of the powerlessness model to women's continued subordination were explored (Johnson, 1989).

The following report describes an Al-Anon group. It reviews the meanings of detachment and codependence for members of this group. It discusses the struggle to include feminism in a traditional Twelve Step program and summarizes the problems women encountered in negotiating conflicts between the two.

METHODS

Design

This was an ethnographic research project using a case study design. A lesbian Al-Anon meeting cannot be seen as a typical Twelve-Step meeting. Its uniqueness is directly related to its utility, however: "A single case can . . . demonstrate that its features are possible and . . . must be taken into account in the formulation of general principles. . . . Representativeness is of no importance" (Platt, 1988, p. 11).

Three basic research methodologies were used: participant observation, interviews, and review of organizational literature. The researcher attended 12 lesbian-only Al-Anon meetings, functioning as a peripheral membership researcher (Adler & Adler, 1987). The mixed strategy of investigation, referred to as triangulation of data, consisted of the following:

1. Observations were conducted throughout the meetings. The researcher came early on some occasions and stayed late on others, to observe before and after meeting activities. Engagement in Al-Anon activities was minimal. The researcher's participation in customary readings occurred only upon

specific request. The three business meetings that transpired during the study period were observed. Very brief notes were taken on occurrences. Notes were expanded on and occurrences described in depth, usually within hours after the close of the meetings.

2. Informal relationships were developed with key informants, members who had participated in Al-Anon for various lengths of time ranging from several months to 8 years. Frequently, clarifying questions taken from study of notes or occurrences at a given meeting were asked. The researcher also engaged in informal conversations with key informants prior to or following meetings.

3. Three semistructured interviews with two key informants were conducted. Questions were drawn from study notes which had been analyzed prior to the interviews. Two of the interviews were conducted in person, one over the telephone. Interviews differed, as they reflected growing understanding of the program and unanswered questions from meetings. Very abbreviated notes were written during the interviews. The notes were fully transcribed within hours.

4. To study the history, approved Al-Anon literature, including pamphlets and books, was examined. Key informants provided the history of the specific Al-Anon meeting under study.

5. For comparison with other meetings, the author drew on her familiarity with AA and attended one lesbian and gay meeting in the same area as the meeting under study. She also went to one "beginner's" lesbian-only meeting. Additionally, she consulted with a colleague who was engaged in a similar ethnographic study of a Cocaine Anonymous meeting for African Americans in the area.

Participants

The meeting that was studied has been in existence for 8 years. Until 2 years ago, the meeting regularly attracted 50 women. When the study began, about half that many were attending. All regular attendees were White. Two African American women attended occasionally. Most members appeared to be in their thirties and forties. A few were younger. Two were probably in their fifties. Middle-class women predominated.

Data Analysis

Very brief notes were taken on occurrences at meetings. Sometimes notes were jotted during the meetings. More often they were hastily written on trips to the women's room or in the car after the meeting ended. Notes were expanded on and occurrences described in depth, usually within hours after the close of the meetings. During the interviews, very abbreviated notes were written. The notes were fully transcribed within hours. The full data set consisted of 132 pages of typed notes. All notes were maintained on a microcomputer, in chronological order. A standard word processing program provided sufficient flexibility for data storage and retrieval.

In qualitative research, "the complex data interpretations and the data collection are guided by successively evolving interpretations made during the course of the study" (Strauss, 1987, p. 10), so that the separation of data collection from analysis is somewhat inaccurate. Themes were systematically constructed using coded chunks of transcripts and field notes which were categorized by topic, with categories being suggested by the data itself (Weis, 1985). Descriptive codes, interpretive codes, and explanatory codes, which are retrieval and organizing devices, were used to cluster segments relating to the particular theme (Miles & Huberman, 1984).

Data were coded following a scheme described by Anselm Strauss (1987):

> *First,* the raising of *generative questions* is essential to making distinctions and comparisons. . . . *Second,* the researcher [made] a number of . . . linkages among the "discovered" (created) concepts. . . . *Third,* the theory [was] verified, because of the provisional linkages . . . during the succeeding phases of inquiry. . . . *Fourth,* the *relevance of the coding* to the real world of data [was] linked with . . . the examination and collection of new data. . . . *Fifth* . . . integration . . . [determination of] which dimensions, distinctions, categories, linkages are 'most important' . . . *Sixth,* theoretical ideas [were] kept track of, and continuously linked and built up by means of *theoretical memos* [which are] examined and sorted. (p. 17-19, italics in original).

FINDINGS

Names of all participants were changed to protect confidentiality. The names used in this report are those assigned by the author. The framework in which the findings are presented has three main sections: (a) program structure and personal story development, (b) the meanings and use of detachment and codependence conceptions, and (c) the modifications of program structure.

Members discuss their state of mind upon entering the program and attempt to make sense of their histories as well as their current pain. They use program sayings[1] and concepts, along with the Twelve Steps, to guide them. Members of this group travel in multiple worlds within the larger system of Twelve Step programs and negotiate meaning, define function, and use program concepts in ways which are particular to them. Negotiating "multiple membership," not in the sense of belonging to more than one Twelve Step program (although many do), but rather in the sense of coexisting identities within the single program, seemed to be the most challenging aspect of lesbian Al-Anon membership. Although there is naturally some overlap in categories, members attempt to define (a) Al-Anon's separate identity from AA, (b) their lesbian identity in a heterosexual program, and (c) their feminist identity within the Twelve Step movement.

Al-Anon Program Structure and Personal Story Development

The following description of the Al-Anon meeting and the changes which occurred with membership is ordered along the lines often presented at both AA and Al-Anon "speaker" meetings:

1. the way life was experienced prior to coming to Al-Anon
2. the occurrences in Al-Anon that seemed to affect life and the member's perception of it
3. the resulting perceptual and behavioral changes, or, in Twelve Step movement language: what it was like, what happened, and what it's like now

What It Was Like

Penny cried through her first 6 months in Al-Anon. She talked about how she used to focus so much on being a conduit for the activities and needs of others, she lost sight of herself and didn't know herself at all. Helena said that she hated herself when she came to Al-Anon, that she had been "in absolute despair." Using a movie screen as a metaphor, she said that before recovery, her disease had not only covered the entire screen but had gone off the screen, couldn't be contained or represented on it. "Now," she said, "there is a rim around the reflection of my disease on the screen."

Like AA, Al-Anon retains the concept of "hitting bottom." It is believed that until one has suffered sufficiently, one will not be ready for help. Each person must hit bottom in terms of lifestyle and despair before Al-Anon will be of help. There are "high bottoms" and "low bottoms," however. Some people hit bottom with their personal lives, social lives, and jobs or careers still intact. *Bottom* seems to be defined in terms of angst and a sense of inability to cope with life in those cases.

Women discuss bottom in terms of ineffective personal relationships. Allowing another person, especially the partner, to be the central figure in a relationship is considered a very serious problem. Some define their personal bottom in terms of physical violence carried over from childhood into adulthood: Edwina talked about how she used to be "beaten up" when she was little and then became involved in battering relationships as an adult. She sought help in a shelter for battered women, but when she left the shelter, she found she was being self-abusive. Al-Anon taught her how to stop that cycle. As Cutter (1985) noted, the theme of abuse in childhood seems to be common in Al-Anon.

Estee told a story about her grandmother having agreed to care for her during the week when she was a child. Estee went home to her parents on weekends and for the summer. She had lived with her grandmother and grandfather for the first year of her life. She said that her mother's having left her there day and night for 9 months explained her current inability to trust and her constant fear of abandonment. It was striking how negatively she perceived her grandparents' involvement in her upbringing. She did not present this as an extended family or as having multiple adults available to her, but as abandonment by her mother.

But complaints were not all of negligible problems. Many of the women told stories of serious neglect, of broken bones ignored, of injuries and illnesses in need of medical attention being left untreated. One told of her veterinary father, who stitched her split lip without anesthetic to save the $16 it would have cost to have a physician do it. Another talked about suicide. She said she'd been coming to Al-Anon for 7 years—since she was 19—but hadn't felt this bad since she arrived. She said she contracted with her therapist to not commit suicide but she came to the meeting to get whatever help she could.

What Happened

The concept of rebirth is strong. At "birthday" meetings, members describe themselves in terms of their time in Al-Anon, and birthday cards, as well as lavender chips denoting the number of years "old" each member is, are presented at the end of the meeting.

Members devoted a considerable amount of time and attention to emotional healing or emotional recovery from the pains of a difficult childhood or young adulthood. Tam said her fears that someone would be angry with her for hurting herself were changing to concern for her own pain and injury. Not everyone met with instant or even rapid emotional healing, however. Estee said she had been told that she needed to allow herself to feel her bad feelings in order to feel the good, but that after several years in the program, all she'd experienced so far was pain.

At times, a connection was drawn between the concept of anonymity and a notion of self-sufficiency. The presentation of anonymity may call up images of separation, loneliness, and lack of membership in a group. The interpretation of anonymity by some members of this group may help to explain why talk of alcohol and alcoholics was seldom heard in meetings. Penny explained that guarding anonymity of an alcoholic[2] meant, to her, to not talk about the individual. It is particularly important in lesbian Al-Anon she said, "since everybody knows everybody and no matter who you talked about, it wouldn't really be anonymous because everyone would know who you were talking about."

Collet (1990) found that Al-Anon members used concepts borrowed from Alice Miller's writings and often spoke of "re-parenting the inner child." Paying attention to one's inner child as a method of refocusing on oneself and healing from early emotional scars was a technique used by some members of this group. Quint often brought stuffed animals to meetings, indicating that was one way in which she was caring for her child self. References to the inner child were common, women reporting, for example, that they "learned in Al-Anon to focus on myself and to listen to my inner child."

Many women mentioned therapists, but not all agreed with the widespread use of psychotherapy:

> I think in conjunction with Al-Anon it can be good. There's a lot of skepticism about therapy in general and I share it—the idea of paying someone to listen to you . . . but these are very damaged people often, and therapy can be helpful.

Helena said fall is a rough time of year for her. It is the anniversary of her mother's hospitalization and death from alcoholism. The one major holiday which occurred during this study was Thanksgiving. Two women talked about the impact their years in Al-Anon had on holiday celebrations. One said that she was going to have dinner with her brothers. Because her parents are dead, it is especially important for the siblings to spend the holiday together to preserve a sense of family, she felt. She had prepared her brothers for her early departure from the festivities, however, saying that she would only be there for a couple of hours. She expected all the brothers to be "drunk and horrible," and she didn't want to be there when they were. If she didn't plan her departure in advance, there would be a scene about leaving early. She was pleased with the progress she'd made in arranging to meet her needs by leaving when the drinking got out of hand.

She did not seem to have seriously considered staying away from the celebration or demanding a more sober holiday. This seems to support Martin's (1989) finding that there may be "implicit social sanctions (in Al-Anon) against women expressing anger or making demands that tax someone else" (p. 26). The solution, in keeping with Al-Anon philosophy, was to change her behavior but to make no demands on the alcoholics to change theirs.

What It's Like Now

It was in the birthday meetings especially that women tended to focus on how life changed since joining Al-Anon. In one such meeting, speakers discussed the current year as distinct from previous years, reporting that they had expected life to get easier but that it hadn't, and they were still working very hard to take care of themselves.

On Helena's birthday, she explained that Al-Anon has "given me back my feelings. It doesn't fix everything," she said, "but it gives me the tools to deal." She said the lessons she learned were several: that Al-Anon offered hope and enlightenment; that she doesn't "have to take any crap from anyone anymore;" that she can value herself more and have some hope; and that she is "not as terrible or as wonderful as I thought I was." Tam was proud that she "shows up for myself" and says what is on her mind.

Not everyone who attends meetings regularly reports an ease at putting their own needs first, however. After implying that her now-frail mother had been abusive years ago, Rachel talked about her skin crawling at the thought of hugging her ailing mother. She said that when she went home for the holidays, she would be expected to provide physical care for her. The thought made her physically ill. Yet she planned to go. She seemed to be asking members for support with bearing her tribulations rather than for help with changing her behavior.

One evening, Tam suggested that having a sense of humor, playing with toys like a child, and paying attention to one's inner child were helpful in the process of recovery. After presenting a quite humorless talk, she suggested the use of humor in recovery as the topic for the evening. The group had considerable difficulty with it. Most of the women who spoke addressed humor, but all the remaining speakers talked about the darker side of humor, several saying that their humor consisted of sarcasm and biting remarks intended to hurt other people. Becky said that humor and fun were difficult for her to defend to herself as worthwhile activities. No one talked about enjoying her sense of humor. It was striking how much misery was contained in the attempt to deal with humor. Even those who had been "in recovery" for several years struggled. This is in contrast to Ablon's (1974) findings that members of the groups she observed were often cheerful and joking.

When asked about this, one of the interviewees said:

> That's what's missing: humor. Like in AA, people seem to have a sense of humor. Giving up drinking forces you to look at the fact that your lifestyle wasn't OK. It gives you a perspective that allows you to laugh. They don't laugh much in Al-Anon.

The times when women did laugh in meetings seemed significant, however. For example, there was some laughter when someone spoke about being unable to distinguish healthy boundaries between people from walls that keep people distanced. At other times, women smiled or laughed when someone spoke of self-limiting behaviors, nodding in apparent understanding and identification. It seems that with the prohibition against "crosstalk,"[3] such laughter was one of the few ways individuals joined together in some sense of "groupness," responding jointly to someone's comments. The lack of groupness or community perceived by the researcher may be better understood when one examines the concepts of detachment and codependence as discussed in this meeting.

Detachment and Codependence

A central notion in the Al-Anon recovery process is detachment. It was described as the ability to care for someone without allowing one's emotional states to be influenced by others' problems. Members often described themselves or their "failure to detach" as codependent behavior. Detachment was seen as a tool for addressing the tendency toward codependence and as a means of refocusing on oneself, rather than focusing on a partner or family member. When they discussed detachment, women often seemed to add a notion of distancing and a lack of what might be considered normal caregiving. Patty believed that, "In a perfect world, women would seek detachment from outcomes, not people." She did not see detachment as conflicting with caregiving or caring however: "It doesn't mean we don't care about people."

Quint drew a connection between learning how to detach and learning how to be "real." She explained, "if you are unable to detach, you are unable to be yourself." She described Al-Anon meeting rooms as "real rooms." Sounding like a recitation from the children's storybook. *The Velveteen Rabbit* (although the stuffed animal in her lap that night was a skunk), she said that "Once you wake up and be real, you're aware—and real."

Helena reported that Al-Anon has taught her to not be so other-focused. She said she still had trouble, though. Recently she was at a women's concert and was thinking, "if only _____ were here. She'd enjoy it so much." Later she decided, "But *I'm* here. Why not enjoy the concert *myself?*" Her wish to have someone she cared about share her pleasure in a concert was presented as focusing on another rather than herself. Positive use of the program philosophy was described as being able to forget about the person she was missing and focus only on herself and her pleasure in the concert. Self-sufficiency was often presented as the ideal.

Olna told a story about a friend of hers who was very ill and had been hospitalized for several weeks. She had visited him that day and discovered that he was getting much better and could go home soon. She also discovered just that day that another long-time friend of hers was in a Twelve Step program, and they had had a wonderful conversation, such as they'd never been able to have before. The problem in detachment was that she was in a very good mood that night but was concerned that her happiness seemed too dependent on other people. It was only because things were going well for others in her life that day that she felt like this. What if all was not well with them? Would she be miserable? She needed to learn to have her happiness depend on herself rather than on what was going on with those around her, she felt.

Becky's notion of detachment was suggestive of a cocoon, separating herself from her surroundings. She said, crying, that listening to the testimony of Clarence Thomas during the U.S. Supreme Court nomination hearings brought up her own history of sexual abuse. She told of having a dream about being raped and described how it was followed the next day by a disturbing incident in a park. A man there was playing his radio very loudly, and she found it distracting. She was unable to concentrate on anything but how distracting this man was. Several times he went into the bushes and she didn't know "whether he was urinating, masturbating, or what he was doing," but she was disturbed by it. She ended her story by framing her distraction in terms of an inability to detach, indicating that she should have been able (despite the hearings, her personal history, the dream, and the intrusion of this man's music) to ignore him and concentrate on her own reasons for being where she was.

Tam seemed bewildered by the concept. She said that she often gets confused by the word *detachment* and wasn't always sure when she was sticking up for herself and when she was "failing to detach." Sissy had an easier time understanding and using the term. She had a background of Buddhist practice which lent

> a better feel for the idea of detachment . . . If I'm OK I can keep my feet easier. It's also easier for me to experience 'cause I live with kids. I have to apply it, I can't get caught up in all their dramas.

Codependence was also a confusing concept sometimes. When asked about the term and its place in Al-Anon, Sissy said:

> I have a hard time with it. There are lots of assumptions about what it is and people talk about it assuming everyone is thinking the same thing, that everyone knows what it is and is working on it . . . It's considered a "disability" but it's not very well defined.

Although most women spoke of codependence as a problem which an individual exhibits in relation to another, Sissy applied the concept to the program as a whole: "the concept (of) Al-Anon as auxiliary led to the concept of codependence."

Modifications of Program Structure

Separate Identity from AA

It was important to members to distinguish Al-Anon from AA. Unlike the Al-Anon meeting Cutter attended (reported in Cutter & Cutter, 1987), where recovering alcoholics identified themselves as such, here women were reminded at the beginning of each session that those who were members of other programs should not mention them "to avoid confusion." Ablon (1974) also noted this prohibition in the meetings she attended.

The women struggled with a general distinction between their program and AA: "People still have issues about Al-Anon having been started as an auxiliary to AA." "There are not such clear-cut rules for who is in Al-Anon. It's not like other Twelve Step groups where you give up a substance or a particular behavior;" and the more specific distinction between lesbian and other Al-Anon; "It is a Twelve Step meeting like any other yet this is a lesbian meeting and it's distinctively lesbian. Sexuality issues might still come in and be seen as very appropriate to discuss."

There seems to be some resentment of the special place of the alcoholic and her/his problems in the Twelve Step movement. Penny complained of the alcoholic being the "star" and insisted on the need for recognition of the seriousness of the problems experienced by people in Al-Anon. She worried about whether AA members took Al-Anon and "our disease, which is just as deadly," as seriously as they took alcoholism or if they were less concerned about the "whiners," as Al-Anon members are sometimes called.

It seemed that success in Al-Anon was not easy to define either:

> I've struggled with that. I went to a gay and lesbian conference and ended up in a lot of AA-sponsored stuff and in AA meetings. I don't have a drinking problem but I was struck by the clear breaking point that alcoholics have. They know when they quit drinking. There is no clear breaking point in Al-Anon. For people in Al-Anon there is only continual struggle.

One of the clearest factors distinguishing Al-Anon from AA was the lack of attention to alcohol. There was confusion about the place of alcohol in the lives of Al-Anon members and about discussing alcohol and alcoholics in meetings. Alcohol was seldom discussed by this group. Only once did a member mention that she was learning how to identify an alcoholic. Occasionally indirect references were made to people with alcoholism. Some women reported having siblings or parents who are alcoholic. Others said that all their lovers had been alcoholics but that after coming to Al-Anon, the women they chose as lovers are sober or not alcoholic at all.

At one meeting, the speaker said that neither of her parents had a drinking problem, nor did her lover. If fact, she'd discovered that only about one quarter of the members of Al-Anon were involved with an alcoholic. Two other members confirmed this, saying that few people were in Al-Anon because they were involved with alcoholic: "The focus isn't on alcohol anymore, especially for people from dysfunctional families, especially in this meeting." This lack of a focus on alcohol-related problems corroborates Cutter's finding that only 17% of the problems mentioned in an Al-Anon group she studied concerned alcohol (Cutter & Cutter, 1987).

Lesbians in a Heterosexual Program

Focus on lesbianism was mixed. At times women argued strongly for a lesbian identity to the meeting. At other times, there was concern about overemphasis on a "special interest" population.

Sexuality was only occasionally discussed openly, but there was sometimes a dating atmosphere in the meetings and discussion of dating problems was sanctioned. Because the meeting was all lesbians, there was no need to guard against use of unacceptable pronouns when talking about dates, lovers, or partners. It was permissible, for example, to lament a broken date with a "cute, hot, sexy woman," apparently without offending members.

One interviewee said, "Women go (to this meeting) looking for a partner." Another said that "all the women in this meeting are potential partners" and that "it might be hard to talk about things you might not want a potential partner to know right away." Although, it was not always the case, the pairing off of women after the meeting was, at times, striking.

Concern was sometimes expressed openly about the place of lesbians in the larger AA/Al-Anon organization. In a business meeting, Penny told about a trip she had taken recently during which she relied on information provided by the International Advisory Committee (IAC), a group of lesbian and gay AA members who compiled a directory of lesbian and gay meetings all over the world. She had found it invaluable and wanted the organization to be supported by this group.

Penny asked the business meeting participants to donate money from the group to IAC. The debate which ensued covered concern about whether IAC included Al-Anon or was limited to AA, whether Al-Anon should develop its own organization of lesbians and gays, if Al-Anon would forever be playing catch up to AA, if it was proper for a portion of the money to be taken out of the general collection, or if a separate cup should be put in the "7th tradition" basket, clearly labeled IAC, as sometimes happened for hospitals and institutions (H & I).[4]

When asked why people couldn't lobby for IAC to become part of the AA/Al-Anon establishment, the response was that IAC was a special interest group and its guide denoted specifically lesbian and gay meetings. The meetings were not supposed to be listed as such in an Al-Anon directory. Women's groups and men's groups were listed separately as were Spanish-speaking groups. Lesbian and gay meetings, however, were considered special interest.

Feminists in AA/Al-Anon

Undoubtedly, not everyone in the meetings would define herself as a feminist. Some felt strongly that feminism held too much sway in this group. Others felt it was too often lost, but all seemed to agree feminism was present. Members sometimes found creative ways to incorporate current feminist notions into Al-Anon. Although dissension did exist, there was little disagreement over "feminization" of spiritual concepts, for example.

Politics and Political Activism

The place of politics and political issues was also contested.[5] Feminists have tended to focus on what is seen as a false division between personal and political lives (Echols, 1989). Power imbalances in personal relationships and in access to resources are prime feminist foci. Interestingly, the concept of empowerment, in the sense of having control over one's life, was seldom given air in these meetings, as it is in contrast to the principle of acceptance of powerlessness: "There is no control to be had over my life," said one member.

Political power, when it was discussed, did not seem to be valued. One woman said that the best response to the worsening impact of the Reagan-Bush era was to recognize her desire to change the situation as one of her character defects. It would be better, she maintained, to come to the understanding that she was "powerless over the economy and needn't get tied up in knots about it." Another woman commented, "Justice is not what recovery is about."

When asked how feminists who tend to have a "personal is political" belief system, determine what is "political" and not OK to talk about in meetings, one informant responded that

> there *is* much more political discussion in these meetings because they are lesbians meeting. They don't make an issue out of political topics though. There is no proselytizing. Women just discuss political issues in terms of how they affect them personally.

The focus was on the impact that political forces have on the individual. The concept of the political power of a collective of individuals was not discussed.

Members' responses were complex, however. Not all attention was deflected from larger issues. For some, political issues and political activism seemed to be important. Nor did Al-Anon membership necessarily preclude participation in politics—even if it meant missing a meeting. When attendance dropped sharply one week, a member mentioned that the women who were missing were probably at the AB101 demonstrations. (AB101 was a lesbian and gay rights bill, vetoed by California Gov. Pete Wilson the day before the meeting.) Members sometimes held contradictory notions about political activism and change. When asked how acceptable it is to miss a meeting for a political event, one informant said "totally," and indicated that she had done so. Yet this same woman said in a meeting later on that week, "What I can't change is everything and everyone else. What I can change is me. End of list."

Religion/Spirituality

When Edwina first came to Al-Anon, she thought of god as "a big man in the sky." She wasn't interested. She'd had enough of male images and decided it was time to create her own. She settled "on a big round roly-poly goddess with fat arms" that Edwina could "crawl up into to be comforted." Then she decided that at her age (43) she needed something a little different. Her image of god was evolving into an internal concept. She drew on herself and what was inside her for guidance.

Al-Anon presents itself as a spiritual rather than a religious program, as does AA. But the distinctions can often be cloudy. There are cautions in the literature against discussing specific religious tenets, yet disagreements arise and people quote their clergy and religious leaders and critique both the religions they were raised in and the religious bent they perceive to be present in AA and Al-Anon. Participation in prayer was announced as optional in this meeting, yet lack of participation was suspect. Women especially reacted against what they described as patriarchal versions of god and religion. In times of extreme stress, however, like many others, they tried to understand how religion or spirituality could help them cope.

The female pronoun was typically used to refer to god and references to deities in the Twelve Steps and Traditions were changed to female. Several women mentioned interest in ancient goddess religions and some practiced New Age versions of goddess worship.

Not surprisingly, there was concern about the Twelve Step movement's incorporation of The Lord's Prayer. Helena told participants in a business meeting that district gatherings close with The Lord's Prayer. There was "a woman at district who started organizing about getting rid of it." Helena said the woman had written up a statement and distributed it at the conference, asking those in agreement to bring it back to their groups. Helena was concerned about whether she should let members know she had a copy of the statement, because it was "not conference approved literature," and there had been "quite a stink" about the statement being circulated at the conference because it wasn't approved.[6] The statement complained about the use of a Christian prayer in Al-Anon and said that the writer felt "oppressed and alienated by religious prayers." The objection was that, " 'The Lord's Prayer' specifically addresses a paternal Deity who dwells in a particular place called heaven." The problem had been solved in the lesbian group by eliminating the prayer. It was decided that flyers should be made available to members who requested them, but not placed on the literature table.

Prayer in one form or another is present in all meetings. This group opened its meetings with the Serenity Prayer and closed with the Closing Prayer. There were mixed reactions to the researcher's lack of participation in them. She was considered suspect by at least one member and congratulated by another. When she stepped back from the circle as a prayer was about to begin, saying, "I don't pray." Yvonne exclaimed:

> I'm so glad you said that! I've noticed that you don't pray and I think it should be optional, but it isn't really, is it? Everyone does and there's pressure on people who don't. It was worse when the meetings all ended in The Lord's Prayer and it's horrible when you go to a different meeting and they still use it and say "he" for god.

Yvonne said she felt affirmed when someone indicated they do not pray.

The difficulty some of these women mentioned with spirituality was also noted by Cutter, who found that although 13% of her participants mentioned that Al-Anon and its spirituality helped them, half found that it was the last part of the program they understood, describing it as the most difficult part, the hardest thing, and threatening (Cutter & Cutter, 1987).

Gender, Sexual Violence, and Feminism

It is not unusual to hear complaints about the sexism of Al-Anon and AA. Penny said she still reacts strongly and negatively to the "sexist language and old-fashioned notions" incorporated into Twelve Step programs. Betty said she finds the Twelve Steps too male oriented. She said that it was only after participating in a group which was rewriting the Steps that she'd been able to come back to Al-Anon.

Sexual violence was a recurring theme in the meetings. During the Clarence Thomas Supreme Court nomination hearings, Sissy said she found the news offensive. She described a personal experience of sexual harassment in which a co-worker had made frequent sexual comments and had pushed her into a corner saying that he wanted to "stick" her. She wondered how any woman, including heterosexual women, could find that concept appealing. To her it sounded like, "I want to knife you . . . beat you . . . punch you."

But opposition to the presence of feminism and feminist ideas in the meetings was also in evidence:

> Personally, I think it gets in the way. I don't want to sound too rigid but I do think that people should take the program as they find it. If it's not what they want, there are plenty of other programs available these days, I don't think we need to be changing the gender of god all the time. I find it distracting.

And concerning the tension between being feminist and keeping to the Al-Anon structure and tradition, she said:

> I've been wondering about that . . . I sometimes feel funny when people change the words to the Steps and Traditions. I was raised Catholic so the references are familiar to me. I left the church because I didn't agree with it. I think the same should hold for Al-Anon. Take it or leave it. People can do it as it's written or strike out on their own.

Moving On

Attendance at this group's meetings dropped off considerably, from about two dozen in the late summer to less than a dozen when winter started. Patty reported that "It used to be 50 women every week. For the last couple of years it was only half that though. All meetings are dwindling these days. It's happening in AA too." She supposed that there were so many competing programs now that women were finding help in other places.

A phone call to Al-Anon World Service Office in New York confirmed Patty's impressions, For the first year, Al-Anon growth virtually stopped. Although the "Cooperation With the Professional Community Administrator" was not willing to go so far as to say membership was down, she did say that the number of Al-Anon groups did not grow at the same rate this past year as it had in the 1970s and 1980s. The number of groups stayed the same or at most had a small increase.

Sissy's concern, though, was with this meeting. This group discourages newcomers, she believed. "How is Al-Anon ever going to survive if it cuts itself off from newcomers and visitors? That's part of the problem with that meeting." But perhaps the meeting was more successful than members realized, particularly if Sissy was correct that "people stop coming when they get better, too. When they get better they don't feel the need to go to Al-Anon. Their lives are better, so what's the point?"

Limitations

The study is limited in several ways, the most obvious being that this is a lesbian-only group. Otherwise, the group composition was very similar to that described by Ablon (1974): all regular attendees were white; middle-class women predominated; most were in their thirties and forties. There are advantages and disadvantages to having conducted the study primarily in the autumn. The number of holidays make this an atypical period, yet it provided the opportunity to explore the women's responses to family holiday functions.

This meeting was one of many Al-Anon meetings in the area. It was chosen because it is the sole officially designated lesbian-only meeting. There may be other lesbian Al-Anon meetings with different norms and functions. Finally, activities outside of meetings were not studied. Since "fellowship"—that is, frequent phone calls, support, and involvement in each others' lives—is generally considered to be a major component of recovery in Twelve Step programs, this is a serious limitation.

Given the problems in validity noted in the literature on qualitative research, every effort has been made to use members' own terms and definitions (Kirk & Miller, 1990). This is, however, the author's interpretation of the understanding of some members. It cannot reflect Al-Anon as a whole or lesbian Al-Anon in general.

CONCLUSIONS AND SUGGESTIONS
FOR FURTHER RESEARCH

Lesbian involvement in Al-Anon seems to have followed on the heels of lesbians' concern with the place of alcohol in their lives. The lesbian Twelve Step movement has functioned as a way of defining oneself within a community of similar others, as a means of finding a lesbian place in a heterosexual world and a feminist place in AA, and, not to be underestimated, an alternative source of socializing and perhaps a place to meet a life partner. "Women go there looking for a partner and when they find someone and start a relationship they stop coming." Cutter also noted the prominence of socializing as a factor in members' improvement (Cutter & Cutter, 1987).

Al-Anon functions as a place to heal from wretched histories and a means for understanding and explaining the past. For some, solutions to grim problems are sought. For others, the issues presented seemed less momentous. Perhaps those women were looking primarily for somewhere to belong. The need for belonging, for a place to be acknowledged and accepted as lesbians, was reflected in the careful maintenance of a lesbian focus in meetings. The presence of so many women who report that alcoholism had not affected their lives directly may be indicative of a lack of alternatives for those who need support.

The concept of codependence seemed to be a troubling one for some of the women in this group.

> The codependence label is antineedy, antidependent; it's very isolating and it reinforces all the problems Adult Children bring with them from their childhoods. It encourages rejecting others, being unkind and ungiving, and it's antagonistic to good, healthy altruism. (Brown, as quoted in Collet, 1990, p. 28)

According to Krestan and Bepko (1990):

> If the [codependence] movement perpetuates an illusion of perfectibility by suggesting that if one recovers perfectly then one has painless relationships, it simply maintains . . . a false belief in the value of total independence and autonomy and fails to recognize the need for healthy interdependence. (p. 229)

What we find is that Al-Anon promotes a view of women and their relationships to other people and to society that sometimes compels members to struggle against their personhood and humanity. Lesbian Al-Anon members sometimes attempt to conform to the Al-Anon program. At other times they adapt the program to meet their needs. Sometimes the modifications required by lesbians, feminist or not, did not come easy. Al-Anon was, after all, designed for wives, always in relation to men.

Although men were not the focus in this group, the old idea still was reflected in resentment of the alcoholic's centrality. Often definitions of the Al-Anon members problems were residuals of conservative formulations about wives of alcoholics. As these women struggled to maintain a separate identity from AA, to maintain a lesbian and feminist integrity within Al-Anon, a rigid structure and system of rules was spelled out. But such rigidity may contribute to the demise of such groups.

Despite valiant attempts to merge the concepts, there exists an inherent contradiction between attending a program based ultimately on the alcoholism of another person and maintaining a sense of detachment. However, detachment was at the nexus of independent self-sufficiency and attempts to understand the impact of another's problems on the self, and so may have served to bridge that contradiction for these women.

A number of questions remain for future researchers to explore:

How are the notions of detachment and codependence understood and put into action by other members of Al-Anon?

Do these notions facilitate or interfere with bonding?

Do lesbians find suitable partners in Al-Anon?

And if, when they feel healed, they no longer come to Al-Anon, where do they find connections?

What is the state of alternative forms of organized support and socialization for lesbians seeking help with problems?

We need to know more about the function and impact of Al-Anon and of feminist alternatives for women seeking group support and assistance for dealing with their socialization needs as well as their problems.

NOTES

1. Some sayings are borrowed from AA: "Easy Does It," "One Day at a Time." Others appear to be unique to Al-Anon: "There are no victims, only volunteers."

2. Tradition Eleven states, "Our public relations policy is based on attraction rather than promotion; we need always maintain personal anonymity at the level of press, radio, and films."

3. "Crosstalk," defined as commenting on, questioning, or talking to someone who "shared" (spoke in the meeting), was not allowed, although commenting on something said by one of the birthday speakers is acceptable.

4. Members of a group make a commitment to attend and chair meetings in hospitals, residential settings, prisons, and so on. Support for literature, coffee, and other items needed at the H&I meetings comes from a separate collection jar, typically included in the basket which is passed at the chairperson's weekly "home" group.

5. The Twelve Step programs are all bound by the same Traditions. Tradition Ten prohibits inclusion of political issues in the program: "Alcoholics Anonymous has no opinion on outside issues; hence the AA name ought never be drawn into public controversy." The

explanation of this tradition indicates that the Washingtonians, a precursor of AA, became involved in the abolition movement to the detriment of that organization (Alcoholics Anonymous World Service, 1969).

6. Approval occurs upon review for concordance with the Al-Anon program and philosophy. Once it has been sanctioned it carries a notation signifying Al-Anon endorsement. If conference approved, the literature can be displayed at meetings.

REFERENCES

Ablon, J. (1974). Al-Anon family groups: Impetus for learning and change through the presentation of alternatives. *American Journal of Psychotherapy, 28*(1) 30-45.

Adler, P., & Adler, P. (1987). *Membership roles in field research.* Newbury Park, CA: Sage.

Alcoholics Anonymous World Service. (1969). *Twelve steps and twelve traditions.* New York: Alcoholics Anonymous Publishing.

Asher, R. (1988). Codependency: A view from women married to alcoholics. *The International Journal of the Addictions, 22*(4), 331-350.

Bailey, M. (1965). Al-Anon Family Groups as an aid to wives of alcoholics. *Social Work, 10*(1), 68-74.

Cermak, T. (1984). Children of alcoholics and the case for a new diagnostic category of codependency. *Alcohol Health and Research World, 8,* 38-42.

Collet, L. (1990, January/February). After the anger, what then? ACOA: Self-help or self-pity? *Networker,* pp. 22-31.

Cutter, C. (1985). *How do people change in Al-Anon? Reports of Adult Children of Alcoholics.* Doctoral dissertation, Brandeis University, the Heller Graduate School for Advanced Studies in Social Welfare.

Cutter, C., & Cutter, H. (1987). Experience and change in Al-Anon Family Groups: Adult children of alcoholics. *Journal of Studies on Alcohol, 48*(1), 29-32.

Echols, A. (1989). *Daring to be bad: Radical feminism in America: 1967-1975.* Minneapolis: University of Minnesota Press.

Ginsberg, R. (1989). An age of contrasts. *Bay Area Career Women Newsletter, 9*(3), 1-10.

Hastings, P. (1982). Alcohol and the lesbian community: Changing patterns of awareness. *Drinking and Drug Practices Surveyor, 18,* 3-7.

Herman, E. (1988, Summer). Getting to serenity: Do addiction programs sap our political vitality? *Outlook,* pp. 16-21.

Jackson, J. (1954). The adjustment of the family to the crisis of alcoholism. *Quarterly Journal of Studies on Alcohol, 15,* 562-586.

Johnson, S. (1989). *Wildfire.* Albuquerque, NM: Wildfire Books.

Kirk, J., & Miller, M. (1990). *Reliability and validity in qualitative research.* Newbury Park, CA: Sage.

Krestan, J., & Bepko, C. (1990). Codependency: The social reconstruction of female experience. *Smith College Studies in Social Work, 60*(3), 216-232.

Martin, J. (1989). *The evolution of Al-Anon: A content analysis of stories in two editions of its "Big Book."* Unpublished manuscript.

Miles, M., & Huberman, M. (1984). *Qualitative data analysis.* Beverly Hills, CA: Sage.

Peele, S., & Brodsky, A. (1991). *The truth about addiction and recovery.* New York: Simon & Schuster.

Platt, J. (1988). What can case studies do? In R. Burgess (Ed.), *Studies in qualitative methodology, 1,* 1-23.

Reddy, B., & McElfresh, O. (1978). Detachment and recovery from alcoholism. *Alcohol Health and Research World, 2*(3), 28-33.

Saulnier, C. (1991). Lesbian alcoholism: Development of a construct. *Affilia: Journal of Women and Social Work, 6*(3), 66-84.

Strauss, A. (1987). *Qualitative analysis for social scientists.* Cambridge, UK: Cambridge University Press.

Tallen, B. (1990). Twelve Step programs: A lesbian feminist critique. *NWSA Journal, 2*(3) 390-407.

Weis, L. (1985). *Between two worlds: Black students in an urban community college.* Boston: Routledge & Kegan Paul.

Williams, M. (1981). *The velveteen rabbit: How toys become real.* Philadelphia: Running Press.

15. Understanding Self-Help Groups

J. B. KINGREE

R. BARRY RUBACK

S elf-help groups target people who are motivated to cope more effectively with problems related to a particular negative status. These groups have proliferated in recent years, serving more people and addressing many types of status-related problems (Jacobs & Goodman 1989; Powell, 1987). This proliferation is expected to continue for several reasons, including the general—but largely untested—assumption that self-help groups promote well-being (Levy, 1979; Riessman, 1986).

Presumably, self-help groups promote well-being through multiple psychological processes, including encouraging participants to adopt more positive and adaptive perceptions of themselves and their problems (Lieberman, 1979). However, these processes have usually been inferred piecemeal from various social psychological theories and have not been sufficiently tested through empirical studies. Thus, whether these processes actually operate in a self-help group context and how they could be tied together in a theory of self-help group affiliation remain unclear.

The relative dearth of empirical attention to these processes is due partly to the organizational structure and culture of self-help groups. To facilitate membership, many self-help groups are structured to protect the anonymity and confidentiality of participants, thereby making it difficult for researchers to document the effects of individual involvement. Moreover, to encourage participatory democracy, many self-help groups are decentralized and thus lack the formal leadership that could assist in research activities such as subject recruitment. Furthermore, the spiritual and religious underpinnings of these groups produce members who distrust, and are reluctant to participate in, scientific research.

This dearth is also due to obstacles in conducting experimental investigations of self-help group processes. Asking whether a certain process is affected by self-help groups is a causal question that is best answered through experimental analyses. However, service research is not often amenable to such analyses, largely due to ethical concerns about withholding services from persons in control groups. Thus, the obstacles to rigorous research with self-help groups may have discouraged researchers from investigating their effects.

Of course, such obstacles should not preclude all efforts to examine the hypothesized processes, for some of these processes could be inferred from alternative methodologies. As a first step, careful measurement of individual levels of self-help group affiliation and specific psychological processes would allow for determining whether such affiliation is positively or negatively related to the processes.

This chapter discusses a research program on self-help group processes that is presently under way at Georgia State University. The aims of the research program include providing conceptual and methodological frameworks for examining hypothesized self-help group processes. For the most part, the theories that guide this examination have been generated by social psychologists for the purpose of understanding how people interpret and respond to their experiences. Because they consider the impact of groups on individuals, social psychological theories offer cogent frameworks for examining how self-help groups affect these interpretations and responses.

At present, the research program consists of three studies. The first study examined differences in self-perceptions and well-being in children of alcoholics (COAs) as a function of their prior affiliation in self-help groups. These self-perceptions included status embracement and status-based self-stigmatization. Because participants came from a college population, potential confounds such as age and educational level—which have not been controlled in previously published studies (e.g., Kashubeck & Christensen, 1992)—were held constant here. The second study, which also involved COAs, replicated and extended the first by testing whether the same self-perceptions as well as attributions for personal problems were linked to self-help group affiliation. The third study further expanded the research program by investigating all of these self-perceptions and processes in a treatment sample of substance abusers.

In the remainder of this chapter, we first discuss hypotheses concerning relations between self-help group affiliation and the social cognitions, as well as between the social cognitions and well-being. This discussion is followed by overviews of the methods and findings in the three studies. The chapter concludes with a discussion that summarizes the findings, identifies limitations in the three studies, and raises important questions that should be addressed in future research.

CONCEPTUAL FRAMEWORKS

Status Embracement

Self-Help Group Involvement and Status Embracement. Involvement in self-help groups probably affects multiple self-perceptions. For example, self-help groups targeting a particular status may promote embracement of that status. To embrace a status is to make it central to a self-concept. People who embrace or strongly identify with a particular status are also likely to incorporate this status in their self-evaluations. In other words, they tend to be self-schematic with respect to this status, and thus the status influences how they view themselves (Jones et al., 1984).

Regarding the relation between self-help group affiliation and embracement of the status targeted by the group, theorists have made apparently conflicting predictions. On the one hand, some have predicted that self-help group affiliation leads people to embrace the status targeted by the group (Jones et al., 1984; Powell, 1987). Accordingly, these theorists have argued that greater status embracement occurs through exposure to self-help group ideologies emphasizing how participants' life circumstances result from their statuses (Antze, 1979). In addition, these theorists have maintained that greater status embracement also stems from affiliating with persons who share that status, for this affiliation promotes perceptions of these others as an in-group, and a status is more likely to be embraced when others who share the status are perceived as an in-group (Crocker & Major, 1989).

On the other hand, other theorists have predicted that associating with persons through self-help groups actually reduces how salient the targeted status is for participants (Gibbons, 1986; Jones et al., 1984). Accordingly, these theorists have argued that any individual's status is less prominent in settings where many persons share it than in settings where relatively few persons share it (McGuire, McGuire, Child, & Fujioka, 1978). Because people should be less likely to embrace a status when it is not salient to them, this position implies that self-help group affiliation lessens, rather than increases, status embracement. Thus, a discrepancy seemed to exist regarding the effects of in-group affiliations on status embracement. We believed that whether these affiliations lead to more or less status embracement would be conditional on the context in which the affiliations occur. When the context emphasizes the specific status, the salience of the mutually held status should be enhanced. In fact, most self-help groups emphasize the status of participants, partly by using the status as a framework for explaining the participants' life circumstances and partly by encouraging participants to acknowledge their status prior to speaking in group meetings. Consequently, in the present studies, we expected affiliation to be positively related to status embracement.

Status Embracement and Psychological Functioning. Embracement of a problematic status should provide certain advantages in terms of psychological functioning. First, it may enhance functioning by allowing persons to use their status to explain, and perhaps to externalize responsibility for, the negative life events they experience (Burk & Sher, 1988). Second, embracing a problematic status may also allow people to perceive others who share this status as an in-group. Such a perception offers individuals sources of social support and sources for social comparisons, two processes that may enhance psychological functioning (Crocker & Major, 1989; Taylor & Lobel, 1989). Third, embracing such a status may free persons from efforts to disguise the status, thereby alleviating the anxiety inherent in such efforts (Goffman, 1963). Given these considerations, we predicted that embracement of a problematic status would be positively related to psychological functioning.

Status-Based Self-Stigmatization

Self-Help Group Involvement and Status-Based Self-Stigmatization. In addition to status embracement, involvement in self-help groups may prompt people to perceive themselves as stigmatized by their status. People who perceive themselves to be stigmatized as a result of their status see themselves as deviant, disadvantaged, and vulnerable. In other words, they have internalized the negative attitudes that others hold toward this status.

Some theorists have suggested that people who attend self-help groups may come to stigmatize themselves as a result of being sensitized to ways that they are deviant (Alexander, 1987; Powell, 1987). However, it has also been argued that self-help groups operate to lessen or at least to normalize deviance (Coates & Winston, 1983). According to this latter view, people may come to feel less deviant as a result of learning that others experience, and cope effectively with, problems similar to their own. Self-help groups may also lessen self-perceptions of deviance by informing participants that they are not responsible for their problems (Barrett, 1978).

In sum, the relation between self-help group affiliation and self-stigmatization was unclear, as some theorists have held that affiliation promotes a sense of deviance whereas others have held that it reduces a sense of deviance. Because both positions seemed to have some validity, no specific hypothesis concerning the direction of this relation was made.

Status-Based Self-Stigmatization and Psychological Functioning. We hypothesized that self-stigmatization would compromise functioning because research has shown that self-perceptions of deviance based on one's negative status were tied to poorer psychological functioning (Jones et al., 1984). Intuitively, perceiving oneself to be deviant as a result of one's status should have a negative impact on psychological functioning in several ways, including increasing deviance through self-fulfilling prophecies. If self-help groups do promote self-perceptions of deviance, then they may actually fuel, rather than prevent, psychological problems.

Attributions for Problems

Self-Help Group Involvement and Attribution. Attribution theory is concerned with the ways people explain their own and others' behaviors and experiences. Although theorists disagree about the number and content of factors that underlie these attributions (e.g., Abramson, Seligman, & Teasdale, 1978; Nicholls, 1975; Weiner, 1985), all concede that the locus of causality dimension is the most basic (see Heider, 1958). In broad terms, this factor captures tendencies to attribute events to either internal or external causes. Internal causes exist inside the individual; they include endowed attributes such as physical appearance and motivational states such as like willpower. By comparison, external causes exist outside the person; they include contextual antecedents such as family and cultural influences. Relative to external attributions, internal attributions for events ascribe responsibility to the persons who experience the event. Thus, in general, people use internal attributions to take personal responsibility for the events they experience.

As with links between self-help group involvement and self-perceptions, several authors have generated hypotheses, but not data, on relations between involvement and attributional patterns. Like embracement and self-stigmatization, these patterns are believed to be shaped by the ideologies or belief systems that are transmitted through self-help group meetings and literature (Maton, Leventhal, Madara, & Julien, 1989), as well as through informal conversations between members.

However, whether affiliation promotes internal or external attributions for one's problems is unclear (Beckman, 1980; Rieff, 1991; Tennen & Affleck, 1990). Consequently, no prediction was made concerning specific relations between affiliation and types of attributions for personal problems.

Attributions and Psychological Functioning. Additionally, there was disagreement concerning which type of attribution is most functional (Baumeister, 1991). To be more specific, scholars have taken different positions with regard to the utility of internal attributions. Whereas the authors who believe that self-help groups foster internal attributions also hold that these attributions bolster personal control and optimism (e.g., Tennen & Affleck, 1990), those who assert that self-help groups encourage external attributions maintain that such explanations protect against the guilt that is associated with internal attributions (Beckman, 1980). Because of this disagreement, we did not make a specific prediction for relations between types of attributions and functioning.

METHODS

Respondents

Studies 1 and 2 included 100 and 128 COAs, respectively, who were recruited from the undergraduate psychology pool at Georgia State University. They volunteered for these particular studies, which were respectively entitled COA Perceptions I and COA Perceptions II, after being presented with various research options for completing course requirements. Having one alcoholic parent was a stipulation for participation in the studies.

Data were continuously collected for Studies 1 and 2 over a period of four academic quarters each. The number of participants in these studies made up roughly 8% of the undergraduate psychology pool at Georgia State, which typically numbers 1,200 students per year. The gender composition (77% female, 23% male in Study 1, 63% female, 37% male in Study 2) and racial composition (66% Caucasian and 29% African-American in Study 1, 66% Caucasian and 27% African-American in Study 2), as well as the average ages (23 in Study 1, 24 in Study 2), were representative of the undergraduate student body at this large urban university.

Study 3 included 188 respondents (123 males, 65 females) who were consecutively admitted to a treatment program for indigent substance abusers. Each respondent was asked to volunteer for this study when admitted to the program, and all but one of the potential respondents agreed to participate. In contrast to Studies 1 and 2, this sample included more African Americans (77%) than Caucasians (22%). The mean age of the participants was 33, and the mean number of years of education was 12. Most (79%) of the sample identified crack as their primary drug of choice. The remainder identified alcohol (18%), marijuana (2%), and heroin (1%) as their drug of choice.

Measures

Self-Help Group Affiliation. In Studies 1 and 2, respondents were asked to indicate their level of COA group affiliation by checking one of five categories (0, 1-5, 6-10, 11-20, more than 20) corresponding to the number of meetings they had attended. Low frequencies in some of these categories subsequently led us to collapse them into two and three categories in Studies 1 and 2, respectively. Whereas the two categories in Study 1 represented either no ($N = 66$) or some ($N = 34$) affiliation, the three categories in Study 2 represented either no ($N = 80$), low ($N = 29$), or high ($N = 19$) levels of affiliation.

In Study 3, on the other hand, an alternative measure of self-help group affiliation was necessary because all of the respondents reported some level of participation in Twelve Step groups. Accordingly, affiliation was assessed indirectly with a nine-item measure of Twelve Step Commitment. Ideas for the items in this subjective measure were garnered from the organizational psychology literature, which has shown that such measures can reliably and validly assess commitment to various types of organizations. For example, workers with high commitment tend to endorse the organization's values, have high job attendance and tenure, and perceive their supervisors and co-workers as supportive (Mowday, Steers, & Porter, 1979). The Twelve

Step commitment measure used in this study showed good internal consistency, $\alpha = .89$, and is presented in Appendix A of this chapter.

Status Embracement. We developed a five-item scale to measure status embracement. Two items tapped the importance of the status to respondents, two items assessed the degree to which respondents viewed similar status persons as an in-group, and one item measured the salience of the status to respondents. This scale can probably be used to measure embracement of any identity; in Study 3, for example, the term *addict* was substituted for COA. The scale, which is presented in Appendix B of this chapter, was internally consistent across all three studies, $\alpha = .74$, .78, and .68, respectively.

Status-Based Self-Stigmatization. A scale was also created to assess status-based self-stigmatization across the three studies. This measure taps the degree to which persons perceive themselves as being different, disadvantaged, vulnerable, and objects of discrimination as a result of their particular status. As with the embracement measure, this one can be used to assess self-stigmatization based on different statuses by substituting one status (e.g., addict) for another (e.g., COA) within constituent items.[1] This scale, which is presented in Appendix C of this chapter, was internally consistent across the three studies, $\alpha = .80$, .78, .80, respectively.

Attribution. Attributional tendencies were assessed by asking respondents to rate the contribution of different causes toward the onset and development of various problems they had experienced. In Study 2—the initial study in which attributions were assessed—COAs rated the degree to which different causes contributed to any substance abuse, emotional, social, and academic problems they had experienced. Different problems were tapped to provide ample opportunity for participants to assign causes for some problem they had experienced. In Study 3, participants made attributions for substance abuse, housing, and emotional problems.

Whereas tendencies to make internal attributions were gauged by including personal causes such as boredom and low willpower, externalizing tendencies were assessed by allowing participants to attribute their problems to insufficient love or inadequate attention from their parents. Parents were used as the potential source for external attributions because COAs and addicts can logically attribute their problems to their parents and because some authors have suggested that self-help groups promote parental blame

(Peele & Brodsky, 1991; Rieff, 1991). By averaging ratings of the personal and parental causes across the different problems, separate measures of personal and parental blame were created. Both the personal blame measure, $\alpha = .91$ and .88, and the parental blame measure, $\alpha = .91$ and .85, were highly reliable across Studies 2 and 3, respectively.

Well-Being. The measures of well-being included a shortened form of the Rosenberg Self-Esteem Scale (Kaniasty, 1991) in Studies 1, 2, and 3 and the Center for Epidemiology Scale for Depression (CES-D; Radloff, 1977) in Studies 2 and 3. Both the esteem, $\alpha = .82$, .88, and .73, respectively, and depression, $\alpha = .88$ and .86, respectively, measures were internally consistent across these studies.

RESULTS

Overview

Because self-help group affiliation was measured with an ordinal scale in Studies 1 and 2, Analysis of Variance (ANOVA) was used to examine relations between it and the other variables in these studies. By comparison, because self-help group affiliation was assessed with a continuous measure of Twelve Step commitment in Study 3, Pearson correlations were used to assess links between it and the other variables in this study.

Self-Help Group Affiliation and Well-Being

Whereas involvement in COA groups was unrelated to the functioning measures in Studies 1 and 2, commitment to Twelve Step groups was related positively to esteem, $r(187) = .27$, $p < .001$, and negatively to depression, $r(187) = -.26$, $p < .001$, in Study 3. Whether these divergent findings were due to variations in the samples (i.e., COA versus addict) or to the affiliation measures used (i.e., involvement versus commitment) could not be determined as both differed in Studies 1 and 2 relative to Study 3.

Self-Help Group Affiliation and Social Cognitions

Results from these studies supported our general hypothesis that self-help group affiliation is positively related to status embracement. In Study 1, respondents who had some involvement in COA groups embraced the COA status more strongly, $M = 2.97$, than those who had no such involvement, $M = 2.64$, $F(1, 98) = 4.27$, $p < .05$. In Study 2, the three groups with varying levels of prior COA group involvement also differed significantly in embracement, $F(1, 126) = 10.42$, $p < .001$. More specifically, posthoc Scheffe' analyses, $p < .05$, indicated that COAs with high involvement, $M = 3.59$, embraced more than those with low involvement, $M = 3.36$, and no involvement, $M = 3.30$. And in Study 3, commitment to Twelve Step groups was positively related to embracement of the addict status, $r(187) = .40$, $p < .001$.

In addition, our hypothesis that self-help group affiliation would be positively related to status-based self-stigmatization was supported across the three studies. In Study 1, respondents with some involvement in COA groups stigmatized themselves, $M = 3.16$, more than did those with no involvement, $M = 2.78$, $F(1, 98) = 8.70$, $p < .01$. Similarly, prior COA group involvement in Study 2 also predicted differences in self-stigmatization, $F(2, 125) = 5.83$, $p < .01$, with posthoc Scheffe' analyses, $p < .05$, indicating that respondents with high prior involvement, $M = 3.40$, engaged in more self-stigmatization than did those with no prior involvement, $M = 2.93$. And in Study 3, Twelve Step commitment was significantly related to self-stigmatization, $r(187) = .18$, $p < .02$.

Regarding the attributions, results from Study 2 indicated that respondents who varied in prior involvement in COA groups differed in personal, $F(2, 125) = 3.81$, $p < .03$, but not parental blame. Posthoc Scheffe' analyses, $p < .05$, revealed that respondents with high prior involvement, $M = 2.73$, and low prior involvement, $M = 2.61$, engaged in more personal blame than did those with no prior involvement, $M = 2.26$. Results from Study 3, on the other hand, indicated that Twelve Step commitment was unrelated to both personal and parental blame. Thus, although COA groups may promote personal blame, these data do not indicate that these groups encourage parental blame. Neither do they indicate that Twelve Step groups promote either personal or parental blame.

Social Cognitions and Well-Being

Bivariate correlations among the social cognition and well-being variables are depicted in Table 15.1. As indicated, the data concerning links between embracement and well-being were inconclusive. Whereas embracement was unrelated to esteem and depression in Studies 1 and 3, it was negatively related to esteem and positively related to depression in Study 2.

TABLE 15.1 Correlations Between the Process and Functioning Measures for the Three Studies

	Status Embracement	Status-Based Self-Esteem	Personal Blame	Parental Blame
Esteem	.06	−.31[c]	—	—
	−.19[a]	−.28[c]	−.32[c]	−.36[c]
	.08	−.31[c]	−.12	−.08
Depression	—	—	—	—
	.26[b]	.34[c]	.40[c]	.40[c]
	.12	.46[c]	.32[c]	.34[c]

NOTE: For both esteem and depression, within each column, the top number is the correlation for the first study, the middle number is the correlation for the second study, and the bottom number is the correlation for the third study.
a. $p < .06$.
b. $p < .01$.
c. $p < .001$.

Thus, although self-help group affiliation was clearly linked with status embracement, it is unclear whether embracement is related to well-being.

Status-based self-stigmatization was negatively linked to esteem and positively related to depression across the different studies. These data are consistent with the position that self-help groups have a negative impact on well-being by leading participants to perceive themselves as stigmatized by their statuses.

In addition, personal and parental blame were negatively related to esteem in Study 2 and positively related to depression in Study 2 and Study 3. Because personal blame was also related to affiliation in Study 2, it is possible that COA groups compromise functioning by promoting personal blame.

Of course, because these data are correlational, firm conclusions cannot be drawn about the causal nature of the links between the different variables. Although it is possible that affiliation leads to embracement, self-stigmatization, and personal blame, it is also possible that these processes lead to affiliation. What is more, it is also possible that some third variable (e.g., severity of status-related problems) leads to both the processes as well as affiliation. Clearly, additional efforts to untangle the nature of these linkages are needed. Nonetheless, the assumption that self-help groups promote these processes seems quite tenable given the consistency of these findings, the theoretical positions on self-help group processes delineated above, and the low likelihood that persons embrace the addict status while engaging in addictive behavior prior to receiving treatment.

DISCUSSION

Summary of Findings

The results from the three studies revealed that status embracement and status-based self-stigmatization were related to self-help group affiliation for both COAs and addicts. Like the COAs with higher involvement in Studies 1 and 2, the addicts with greater commitment in Study 3 engaged in more embracement and self-stigmatization. On the other hand, the relations between self-help group affiliation and attributional tendencies were somewhat ambiguous. More specifically, whereas affiliation with COA group was tied to personal but not parental blame, affiliation with addict groups was not associated with either type of blame.

Moreover, the results revealed that status-based self-stigmatization was negatively related to well-being across the three studies, and that personal blame was negatively related to well-being in Study 2. Taken with the data for affiliation, these findings *suggest* that self-help groups may compromise functioning by encouraging participants to engage in self-stigmatization and personal blame.

The data from these studies also suggest that self-help groups have positive effects that have yet to be clearly documented. For even though affiliation was unrelated to well-being in Studies 1 and 2 and positively related to it in Study 3, the processes that we have linked to self-help groups (i.e., embracement, self-stigmatization, personal blame) had either negative or no effects on esteem and depression. Apparently, some unidentified positive effects of self-help groups effectively canceled out the groups' negative effects that were documented in these studies.

Hypothesized Positive Effects
of Self-Help Group Affiliation

Consequently, three additional social psychological processes are now being investigated in our research on self-help groups. Each of these processes is believed to be affected by self-help group affiliation, and each is believed to bolster well-being.

One of these processes is temporal self-comparison, or the tendency to compare one's present against one's past situation (Albert, 1977). Most people view the present as better than their past, even when their life situations do not show objective improvements (Taylor & Brown, 1988).

Moreover, it seems logical that people are most apt to perceive improvements in their lifestyles when recovering from adverse life events. And although research has confirmed that such self-comparisons enhance coping, little if any effort has been made to identify factors that prompt people to use them.

For two reasons, we expect self-help group affiliation to promote adaptive self-comparisons. First, because these comparisons are more pronounced in times of change, they should be tied to mechanisms (like self-help groups) that promote such change. Second, and more importantly, the format of self-help group meetings actually encourages participants to focus on ways their present life situations have improved over those of their past. Specifically, participants are asked to explain what their past was like, what happened to change it, and what their lives are presently like (Robertson, 1988). Needless to say, testimonies that describe substantial positive change are better received and positively reinforced than are testimonies describing little or no change.

Received and extended social support are the second and third processes that are being investigated. An extensive amount of research has illuminated the psychological and social benefits that people experience by exchanging support. Participants in self-help groups benefit from both receiving and providing empathic understanding, information on coping, and tangible support.

Toward a Theory of Self-Help Group Effects

As indicated above, this research program was designed partly to provide a foundation for a theory of self-help group effects. An initial model of self-help group effects, based on existing data on self-help groups and on social psychological research and theory, is displayed in Figure 15.1. In the model the arrows suggest the causal paths. There are several instances when an arrow indicates that one variable is hypothesized to be caused by another variable and that it, in turn, is causally linked to a third variable. This pattern is referred to as mediation, by which is meant that the middle variable is the causal mechanism through which the first variable affects the third variable.

The model proposes that status embracement either fully or partially mediates links between affiliation and three social psychological processes: (a) status-based self-stigmatization, (b) personal blame, and (c) extended support. The hypothesized mediation involving self-stigmatization and personal blame variables is based on data from the three studies. The hypothe-

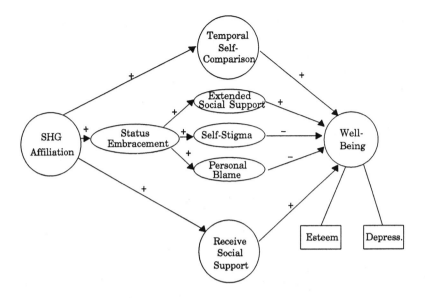

Figure 15.1. Hypothesized Model of Self-Help Group Effects

NOTE: A plus sign (+) indicates a positive causal relationship between the two variables, whereas a minus sign (−) indicates a negative causal relationship.

sized mediation involving the extended support variable, on the other hand, stems from two separate notions: (a) people who embrace a specific status tend to perceive persons who share that status as an in-group (Crocker & Major, 1989) and (b) people are motivated to help members of their in-group (Clark, 1983).

In contrast, temporal self-comparison and received social support are hypothesized to mediate links between affiliation and well-being independent of embracement. More specifically, whether one perceives that he or she has changed significantly, or is receiving significant support from others, should not depend on the extent to which he or she embraces a particular status.[2]

Other Future Directions

Because this research program has indicated that self-help groups generally affect participants in complex ways, efforts should now be directed toward finer and more specific analyses of these effects. In other words, studies that can more tightly link self-help groups to these effects are warranted. Of course, the experimental method would best allow for such analyses, even though some consider it impractical for research on self-help groups (Miller & Mahler, 1991). Although random assignment of naive individuals with no prior involvement in self-help groups to a group for specific-status persons may be unrealistic for both logistic and ethical reasons, experimental and quasi-experimental alternatives could be conducted with relatively few obstacles. For example, participants in residential programs could be randomly assigned to participate in either a self-help group meeting, a recreational activity, or a rest period between two administrations of questionnaires. Such an experiment would be expected to show that the effects of self-help groups on participants are most pronounced immediately following participants' exposure to self-help group processes.

Moreover, this experimental approach ultimately could be expanded to assess linkages between the actions of individual participants during self-help group meetings and the outcomes they experience. For example, the magnitude and content of verbal activity of participants could be assessed by positioning observers in the groups or coding from videotapes. Because reciprocal or mutual sharing is common in these groups, these observers could document the give and take of feedback and its effects on participants.

Eventually, attention should be given to the states and traits of participants and whether they predict how much impact these groups have on individuals. Relevant states would include factors relating to the status targeted by a particular self-help group. In the case of Twelve Step groups, for example, relevant states would include factors relating to addiction, such as time since last drug use, as well as the type(s) and amount(s) of the drug(s) used. Relevant traits, on the other hand, would include characteristics such as authoritarianism and self-monitoring that affect an individual's responsiveness to contextual influences.

Summary

In sum, this research program has successfully documented some correlates effects of self-help groups, some of which had been previously hypothesized but not substantiated. The methodologies and theoretical frameworks that guided each study represent additional contributions of the research. Together, the studies shed some light on the ways in which self-help groups work and provide a foundation for more research on these widely used community resources.

Twelve Step Commitment

These questions assess your attitudes toward Twelve Step groups such as AA, NA, CA, etc. Please respond to these questions by thinking about your preferred Twelve Step group.

1. I am committed to my preferred Twelve Step group.

1	2	3	4	5
Strongly disagree	Disagree	Neither agree nor disagree	Agree	Strongly agree

2. I believe in the slogans of my preferred Twelve Step group.

1	2	3	4	5
Strongly disagree	Disagree	Neither agree nor disagree	Agree	Strongly agree

3. The people who attend the meetings of my preferred Twelve Step group have a lot to offer me.

1	2	3	4	5
Strongly disagree	Disagree	Neither agree nor disagree	Agree	Strongly agree

4. As a recovering person, it is my responsibility to attend the meetings of one of the Twelve Step groups so that I may be of help to other addicts.

1	2	3	4	5
Strongly disagree	Disagree	Neither agree nor disagree	Agree	Strongly agree

5. I believe in what my favorite Twelve Step group stands for.

1	2	3	4	5
Strongly disagree	Disagree	Neither agree nor disagree	Agree	Strongly agree

6. I enjoy the company of persons who attend Twelve Step groups.

1	2	3	4	5
Strongly disagree	Disagree	Neither agree nor disagree	Agree	Strongly agree

7. The only way to recover from addiction is by attending Twelve Step groups.

1	2	3	4	5
Strongly disagree	Disagree	Neither agree nor disagree	Agree	Strongly agree

8. I plan to attend Twelve Step groups for the rest of my life.

1	2	3	4	5
Strongly disagree	Disagree	Neither agree nor disagree	Agree	Strongly agree

9. I feel better after attending Twelve Step group meetings.

1	2	3	4	5
Strongly disagree	Disagree	Neither agree nor disagree	Agree	Strongly agree

APPENDIX B

Status Embracement

The following questions assess the extent to which you identify yourself as a COA (or addict).

1. If asked to describe myself, one of the things I would think about is that I am a COA (addict).

1	2	3	4	5
Strongly disagree	Disagree	Neither agree nor disagree	Agree	Strongly agree

2. On the whole, I feel closer to COAs (addicts) than I do to people who are not COAs (addicts).

1	2	3	4	5
Strongly disagree	Disagree	Neither agree nor disagree	Agree	Strongly agree

3. Being a COA (addict) is an important part of my self-identity.

1	2	3	4	5
Strongly disagree	Disagree	Neither agree nor disagree	Agree	Strongly agree

4. COAs (Addicts) are different from other people.

1	2	3	4	5
Strongly disagree	Disagree	Neither agree nor disagree	Agree	Strongly agree

5. Being a COA (addict) influences the way I think about myself.

1	2	3	4	5
Strongly disagree	Disagree	Neither agree nor disagree	Agree	Strongly agree

APPENDIX C

Status-Based Self-Stigmatization

The following questions assess attitudes toward different aspects of the COA (addict) status. Please respond by circling the number on the scale that best represents your response.

1. I have been handicapped as a result of my (parent's alcoholism) (addiction).

1	2	3	4	5
Strongly disagree	Disagree	Neither agree nor disagree	Agree	Strongly agree

2. As a COA (addict), I am disadvantaged in ways that non-COAs (nonaddicts) are not.

1	2	3	4	5
Strongly disagree	Disagree	Neither agree nor disagree	Agree	Strongly agree

3. People who are not COAs (addicts) do not really understand me.

1	2	3	4	5
Strongly disagree	Disagree	Neither agree nor disagree	Agree	Strongly agree

4. I sometimes feel ashamed of my (parent's alcoholism) (addiction).

1	2	3	4	5
Strongly disagree	Disagree	Neither agree nor disagree	Agree	Strongly agree

5. Revealing to a potential employer that I am a COA (addict) may result in the employer discriminating against me.

1	2	3	4	5
Strongly disagree	Disagree	Neither agree nor disagree	Agree	Strongly agree

NOTES

1. When making these applications, it may be necessary to drop particular items if they are deemed irrelevant or inappropriate for certain status groups. For example, Item 8 was dropped in Study 3 for its lack of relevance to addicts.

2. Although it could be argued that self-help group members extend support only to those who embrace the status, this is doubtful due to the general notion that the participants who need the most help in self-help group meetings are those who are struggling with different aspects of their problems (e.g., Alcoholics Anonymous).

REFERENCES

Abramson, L., Seligman, M., & Teasdale, J. (1978). Learned helplessness in humans: Critique and reformulation. *Journal of Abnormal Psychology, 87,* 49-74.

Albert, S. (1977). Temporal comparison theory. *Psychological Review, 84,* 485-503.

Alexander, B. K. (1987). The disease and adaptive models of addiction: A framework evaluation. *Journal of Drug Issues, 17,* 47-66.

Antze, P. (1979). Role of ideologies in peer psychotherapy groups. In M. A. Lieberman & L. D. Borman (Eds.), *Self-help groups for coping with crisis* (pp. 272-305). San Francisco: Jossey-Bass.

Barrett, C. J. (1978). Effectiveness of widows' groups in facilitating change. *Journal of Consulting and Clinical Psychology, 46,* 20-31.

Baumeister, R. (1991). *Meanings of life.* New York: Guilford.

Beckman, L. (1980). An attributional analysis of Alcoholics Anonymous. *Journal of Studies on Alcohol, 41,* 714-726.

Burk, J. P., & Sher, K. (1988). The "forgotten child" revisted: Neglected areas of COA research. *Clinical Psychology Review, 8,* 285-902.

Clark, M. (1983). Reactions to aid in communal and exchange relationships. In J. Fisher, A. Nadler, & B. DePaulo (Eds.), *New directions in helping: Vol. 1. Recipient reactions to aid.* New York: Academic Press.

Coates, D., & Winston, W. (1983). Counteracting the deviance of depression: Peer support groups for victims. *Journal of Social Issues, 23,* 171-196.

Crocker, J., & Major, B. (1989). Social stigma and self-esteem: The self-protective properties of stigma. *Psychological Review, 96,* 608-630.

Gibbons, F. X. (1986). Stigma and interpersonal relations. In S. C. Ainley, G. Becker, & L. M. Coleman (Eds.), *The dilemma of difference: A multidisciplinary view of stigma* (pp. 123-156). New York: Plenum.

Goffman E. (1963). *Stigma: Notes on the management of spoiled identity.* Englewood Cliffs, NJ: Prentice-Hall.

Heider, F. (1958). *The psychology of interpersonal relations.* New York: John Wiley.

Jacobs, M. K., & Goodman, J. (1989). Psychology and self-help groups: Predictions on a partnership. *American Psychologist, 44,* 536-545.

Jones, E. E., Farina, A., Hastorf, A. H., Markus, H., Miller, D. T., & Scott, R. A. (1984). *Social stigma: The psychology of marked relations.* New York: Freeman.

Kaniasty, K. (1991). *Pretest of candidate measures: Results of two studies.* Louisville, KY: University of Louisville Urban Studies Center.

Kashubeck, S., & Christensen, S. A. (1992). Differences in distress among adult children of alcoholics. *Journal of Counseling Psychology, 39,* 356-362.

Levy, L. (1979). Processes and activities in groups. In M. A. Lieberman & L. D. Borman (Eds.), *Self-help groups for coping with crisis* (pp. 194-233). San Francisco: Jossey-Bass.

Lieberman, M. (1979). Analyzing change mechanisms in groups. In M. A. Lieberman & L. D. Borman (Eds.), *Self-help groups for coping with crisis* (pp. 194-233). San Francisco: Jossey-Bass.

Maton, K., Leventhal, G., Madara, E., & Julien, M. (1989). The birth and death of mutual-help groups: The role of national affiliation, professional involvement, and member focal problem. *American Journal of Community Psychology, 17,* 643-671.

McGuire, W. J., McGuire, C. V., Child, P., & Fujioka, T. (1978). Salience of ethnicity in the spontaneous self-concept as a function of one's ethnic distinctiveness in the social environment. *Journal of Personality and Social Psychology, 36,* 511-520.

Miller, N., & Mahler, J. (1991). Alcoholics Anonymous and the "AA" model for treatment. *Alcoholism Treatment Quarterly, 8,* 39-51.

Mowday, R., Steers, R., & Porter, L. (1979). The measurement of organizational commitment. *Journal of Vocational Behavior, 14,* 224-247.

Nicholls, J. (1975). The development of own attainment and causal attributions for success and failure in reading. *Journal of Personality and Social Psychology, 31,* 379-389.

Peele, S., & Brodsky, A. (1991). *The truth about addiction and recovery.* New York: Simon & Schuster.

Powell, T. J. (1987). *Self-help organizations and professional practice.* Silver Spring, MD: National Association of Social Workers.

Radloff, L. (1977). The CES-D scale: A self-report depression scale for research in the general population. *Applied Psychological Measurement, 1,* 385-401.

Rieff, D. (1991). Victims, all? In S. Sontag & R. Atwan (1992). *The best American essays* (pp. 253-267). New York: Tichnor & Fields.

Riessman F. (1986). Support groups as preventive intervention. In M. Kessler & S. E. Goldston (Eds.), *The primary prevention of psychopathology: Vol 9. A decade of promise in primary prevention* (pp. 275-288). Hanover, NH: University Press of New England.

Robertson, N. (1988). *Getting better inside Alcoholics Anonymous.* New York: William Morrow.

Taylor, S., & Brown, J. (1988). Illusion and well-being: Some social psychological contributions to a theory of mental health. *Psychological Bulletin, 103,* 193-210.

Taylor, S. E., & Lobel, M. (1989). Social comparison activity under threat: Downward evaluation and upward contacts. *Psychological Review, 96,* 569-575.

Tennen, H., & Affleck, G. (1990). Blaming others for threatening events. *Psychological Bulletin, 108,* 209-232.

Weiner, B. (1985). An attributional analysis of achievement motivation and emotion. *Psychological Review, 92,* 548-573.

16. Self-Help Groups for Families With Mental Illness or Alcoholism

LINDA FARRIS KURTZ

People with serious mental illness or alcoholism experience repeated crises and stressful events (Noh & Turner, 1987; Steinglass, 1981). These crises affect not only their own lives but those of their families (Hatfield, 1986-1987; Hatfield, 1987; Jackson, 1954). The family's adjustment to these chronic illnesses is a significant component in treating them. Although mental health agencies assist families, often staff are overburdened and services are limited (Hanson & Rapp, 1992; Steinglass, 1981). Thus, it is important to find other means to alleviate stress and enable families to cope when they endure crises related to mental illness and/or alcoholism among their members. Self-help and support groups are one avenue of assistance to these families.

There are important differences between families with mental illness and families with alcoholism, but there are also many similarities. Differences include the fact that mental illness is not caused by a behavior (such as drinking alcohol) and that mental illness does not respond as predictably to treatment as does alcoholism. Also, family members most affected by serious

AUTHOR'S NOTE: The author thanks the members of the three groups who gave their time and shared their painful memories to further this research project. Indiana University financed the data collection period through a Spring/Summer Research Award to the author in 1989. Ernest Kurtz and Tom Powell were tremendously influential in guiding revisions of the manuscript.

293

mental illness are parents, whereas the family members most affected by alcoholism are more likely to be the spouse and children (Goldman, 1982). Symptoms of mental illness create crises for families when the ill person is acutely psychotic or is suffering from the disabling conditions residual for these patients, such as apathy and inability to live independently; for families of alcoholic members, crises typically are precipitated by behavior when under the influence of intoxicants.

The effects of the two conditions are similar in that those afflicted have difficulty maintaining employment and otherwise taking care of themselves, are stigmatized, blamed for their illness, and denied needed treatment; they face a lifetime of trying to overcome the problem and often must be cared for by others, usually the family (Hatfield, 1987; Paolino, McCrady, Diamond, & Longabaugh, 1976). Another similarity is the fact that most of the caregivers in both situations are female (Ascher-Svanum & Sobel, 1989; Jackson, 1954). Moreover, these women are often viewed as being the cause of the problem (Paolino et al., 1976; Scheyett, 1990; Strecker, 1946). In addition to the symptoms of the illness, stressors for family members with mentally ill or alcoholic relatives include long hours of caregiving, lack of information, and inadequate services (Moos, Finney, & Gamble, 1982; Noh & Turner, 1987; Potasznik & Nelson, 1984; Torrey, 1988). These similarities led the researcher to investigate together groups for families both of alcoholics and of persons with serious mental illness.

Wedenoja (1991) declared that family caretakers of mentally ill individuals need support to care for themselves, advocacy to increase community services for the ailing family member, and empowerment to increase their own coping abilities. Referral to self-help and support groups is one strategy that accomplishes these goals. Potasznik and Nelson (1984) found that families of the mentally ill who participated in self-help groups were less burdened, less isolated, and more informed than nonmembers. Other studies of both National Alliance for the Mentally Ill (NAMI) and Al-Anon groups have found them to be helpful in several ways, such as reframing the nature and cause of the problem, imparting knowledge, and teaching new coping skills (Ablon, 1974; Bailey, 1965; Gidron, Guterman, & Hartman, 1990; Gorman & Rooney, 1979; Medvene & Krauss, 1989; Norton, Wandersman, & Goldman, 1993; Rychtarik, Carstensen, Alford, & Schlundt, 1988).

In this study, the author interviewed members of three groups for families—one chapter of Al-Anon Family Groups, one chapter of NAMI, and one chapter of Together We Learn to Cope (TLC), a statewide support network for families with mentally ill members—to obtain accounts of how their groups had helped in times of crisis.

METHOD

Sample

The investigator used a qualitative research method in which members with at least 1 year of group participation were interviewed about the groups that had been selected for examination. The ideal in qualitative research is to sample to the point of redundancy or until data being collected reveal only information that repeats what has already been found (Patton, 1990, p. 186). A sample of 34 individuals satisfied this requirement, in that later interviews with members from the groups selected produced no new data related to the goals of the study.

The three groups were selected because they represented the oldest, most established of the Al-Anon, NAMI, and TLC groups for families in the area. The Al-Anon group had been in existence over 10 years, met weekly, and had 30-40 regular participants. Ten members of this group were interviewed. The NAMI group had been in existence over 5 years, met biweekly, and had 20-30 regular participants. Fifteen of its members were interviewed. The TLC support group met once a month, had been meeting for 13 years, and had about 15 regular participants. Nine members were interviewed.

Individual members were selected for interviews in ways that conformed to each group's usual way of dealing with researchers. All were asked to volunteer for a study investigating how their group helped them deal with crises related to the ill person in the family. Specific Al-Anon members of the chosen group were invited to be interviewed by the author after a meeting; none of those invited refused. NAMI members were recruited by the author in two meetings through an announcement asking for volunteers who had some experience in the group. About half of the members present in each meeting volunteered. TLC group members were recruited with the assistance of a staff member of the local affiliate of the National Mental Health Association. Nine of approximately 15 members agreed to an interview. Table 16.1 presents characteristics of interviewees and their ill family members.

Despite the similarity of their peer-helping approaches, the groups differed in important ways. The Al-Anon group followed an explicit Twelve

TABLE 16.1 Characteristics of Groups, Interviewees, and Ill Family Members

	Al-Anon	National Alliance for the Mentally Ill	Together We Learn to Cope
Group characteristics			
Primary objective	Personal growth	Advocacy and support	Support
Scope	International	National	State
Situation	Alcoholism	Mental illness	Mental illness
Number of meetings per month	4	2	1
Interviewee characteristics			
Mean age	47	55	62
Race	100% White	87% White	100% White
Gender	100% female	87% female	100% female
Relationship to ill member	90% spouses	80% parents	100% mothers
Meeting attendance per month (Average)	11[a]	1.68	1
Number of years a member	5.4	2.2	9
Ill person characteristics			
Mean age	43	31	33
Gender	100% male	62% male	67% male
Number of times in hospital	1.2	4.3	n/a

NOTE: Al-Anon members often attended Al-Anon groups other than the one in question.

model which focused on the spiritual growth of its members (Al-Anon Family Groups, 1986). The NAMI group offered support to members and an advocacy approach to policy change and community education (Hatfield, 1986-1987). The TLC group, more narrowly defined as a support group, concentrated on providing support and education for its members (Wasserman & Danforth, 1988). The more frequent meetings of the Al-Anon group and the existence of many other Al-Anon groups in the city meant that those members were able to and did attend many more meetings on average than was possible for members of the other two groups.

Procedure

The researcher attended meetings of each group, recruited members for interviews, and performed tape-recorded interviews. Interviews lasted from 30 minutes to 2 hours, with a mean length of 56 minutes. The interviewer began by giving the interviewee a definition of *crisis* as follows: "A crisis is a time in your life when you experience an unsurmountable event that causes shock and a temporary inability to solve problems as you normally would" (Caplan, 1961, as cited by Aguilera, 1990, p. 5). The interview opened with an invitation to describe a crisis event since the illness began and a question asking to whom they turned when the crisis occurred. The crisis event chosen usually was the worst such event the subject had endured. Next, the interviewer asked whether and how the group helped with that or subsequent crises. A review of crisis intervention literature revealed agreement that intervention must assist the person in distress with feelings, cognitions, and behaviors (Aguilera, 1990; Dixon, 1987; Golan, 1978; Parad & Parad, 1990; Roberts, 1990). Aguilera (1990, pp. 23-24) lists the tasks as follows:

1. helping the individual bring into the open his present feelings to which he may not have access
2. helping the individual gain an intellectual understanding of his crisis
3. exploration of coping mechanisms
4. reopening the social world

The interviewer asked four questions, the first three conforming to the first three of the above tasks, which were parallel to tasks listed by others:

1. How did the group help you with feelings about what happened?
2. How has the group helped you understand what happened?
3. What are some ways you handle such events now that you didn't do before?
4. What has changed since you have been in the group?

Questions were asked sequentially, with the answer to one completed before the interviewer revealed the next question. Interviewees did not see the interview format, and the questions were asked in the same order as presented above. The author performed all of the interviews, typing of transcripts, coding of data, and analysis.

Analysis

The investigator used a grounded theory method of analysis (Strauss & Corbin, 1990). In doing grounded theory research, the first interviews should be transcribed and analyzed completely before going on to the next interviews (Strauss & Corbin, 1990, p. 30). These examinations shape the interviews to come. In this study, the investigator departed from the grounded theory methods somewhat by establishing categories from the crisis intervention model; therefore, no changes were made in the interview format, but additional questions were asked about descriptive data when subject's stories suggested interesting aspects for comparison. For example, number of hospitalizations experienced by the ill person was not queried initially, but was added to the second set of interviews.

Grounded theory analysis consists of coding concepts and establishing categories. There are three types of coding: open coding, axial coding, and selective coding (Strauss & Corbin, 1990). Open coding consists of noting on the transcript every idea or event and giving it a name. Once done, these separate notations are grouped and given labels at a very concrete level. For example, basic categories within the discussion of coping skills were grouped into 10 separate ways of coping, such as "increasing meeting attendance at difficult times."

Axial coding is the process of making connections between categories (Strauss & Corbin, 1990). For example, the category above, "increasing meetings at difficult times," was connected with other categories under the label of disengagement, because meeting attendance was one way members had of removing themselves from contact with the ill person.

Selective coding is the process of integrating these categories at a higher level of abstraction into core categories (Strauss & Corbin, 1990). For this analysis, the categories that resulted from axial coding were actually grouped and regrouped repeatedly until a conceptual integration emerged that showed how the findings reflected the process of crisis intervention as it occurred in the groups. Many of the final concepts derived from the interviews illustrated aspects of self-help groups that have been noted before, as the discussion will clarify. Although qualitative data analysis can be accomplished by means of computer (Tesch, 1990), the analysis presented here was performed by hand with ideas and events, concepts, and categories noted on variously colored index cards.

RESULTS

This section will report responses to the questions listed above concerning interviewees' experiences of crisis, who they turned to, and how the groups helped. Table 16.2 gives a numerical breakdown of types of crises, Table 16.3 displays who the interviewees turned to for help, and Table 16.4 shows a cross-tabulation of ways the groups helped.

Did They Experience Crisis?

Most (91%) of those interviewed reported experiencing a crisis as the interviewer defined it. They described episodes of physical violence and other symptoms of psychosis or drunkenness by their family member as precipitating the crisis situation (see Table 16.2). By far, the most frequently mentioned category of stressor involved self-destructive violence or attacks on others in the family. Some interviewees identified their own reaction to the illness as one factor that prompted a crisis. They described themselves as numb and immobilized, having fears of going crazy, being unable to function, to decide, or to problem solve, all indicative of an acute crisis state (Hansell, 1976; Parad & Parad, 1990).

Who Did They Turn To?

When asked what helped them through the crisis period, 38% mentioned friends and family. Three TLC and two NAMI members, but none of the Al-Anon members, turned to a professional for help for themselves. Three of the Al-Anon members had gone directly to the group when in a crisis; all interviewees had eventually done so. Less than half of the Al-Anon members had contact with a professional at any point; in contrast, all the members in NAMI and TLC had contact with a mental health professional after their relative became ill.

How Did the Groups Help?

Under each of the four intervention categories, there were several ways in which the groups helped with accessing feelings, gaining intellectual understanding, and forming new coping mechanisms. A fourth category of helping, the expansion of social worlds, resulted from the analysis, as will be explained further. Discussion of each helping feature follows.

TABLE 16.2 Crisis Categories Discussed by the Participants of Each Group $(N = 32)$[a]

Type of Event	Al-Anon	National Alliance for the Mentally Ill	Together We Learn to Cope	Percent
Violence to self or others	4	7	5	50
Disappearing or packing and leaving	1	2	1	12
Psychotic symptoms	0	1	2	12
Jailings of the ill person	0	2	0	6
Homelessness of the ill person	0	1	1	6
Marital infidelity	2	0	0	6
Physical illness of the ill person	1	0	0	3
Alcoholic symptoms	1	0	0	3
Harassment of family	1	0	0	3
Totals	10	13[a]	9	101[b]

a. In two NAMI families, two members of the same family were interviewed
b. Total percent is more than 100 due to rounding

Opening Up Feelings

Perception of Similarity. Primary help in accessing feelings came through the self-disclosure of similar experiences. Close to half of those interviewed mentioned this factor. A TLC member illustrated the significance of knowing that other members had experienced a similar situation when she said, "It's a closeness. I could talk to my best friend and she wouldn't know what I was talking about." Medvene (1990) emphasized the importance of perception of similarity through self-disclosure in the NAMI group he studied. Self-disclosure produces feelings of safety, belonging, and acceptance in new members and becomes a necessary condition for expressing emotions. Many interviewees echoed this statement by the mother of an alcoholic son who said, "you know you are not the only one living who feels that way. You're not an odd ball."

Redefinition of the Problem. A second way that the groups helped with feelings was through redefining the nature of the problem. The alarming and embarrassing behaviors of mental illness or alcoholism are defined as symptoms of a disease rather than as intentional, immoral, or foolish

TABLE 16.3 Family's First Effort to Obtain Help

	Al-Anon (n = 10)	National Alliance for the Mentally Ill (n = 8)	Together We Learn to Cope (n = 5)
Family	4	3	2
Friends	0	3	1
God, clergy, or church	3	1	0
Professional health care	0	2	3
Self-help group	4	0	0
Neighbor	1	1	0
Co-worker	1	0	0
No one	1	1	0

NOTE: Not all interviewees answered this question; others gave more than one response.

actions. As Ablon (1974) and Medvene and Krauss (1989) have reported, the disease definition relieved members of blame for the illness and helped them be compassionate toward the sick person. A NAMI member illustrated the importance of the disease definition when she stated, "The major feeling is guilt, so the group takes the guilt away. You're supposed to take care of your children and you feel you've done something to cause it, but you learn it's just part of the illness." Another mother said, "I remember I was so frustrated that he smelled and he didn't keep clean and it was causing my house to smell and someone said, 'Ho, ho. Just get a can of deodorant and spray it around.' Then I knew I was taking it too seriously."

Gaining Intellectual Understanding

Acquiring Professional Knowledge. Interviewees described obtaining information and understanding in two ways: (a) from professional speakers and literature and (b) from experiential knowledge given by members to members. NAMI and TLC members most often mentioned the knowledge gained from professional and scientific sources. For example, a TLC member said, "I've attended seminars, workshops, meetings, state conferences, and governor's conferences." These members share their educated opinions on medical matters, insider information on services and service providers, and the "real story" on how to use legal remedies to obtain services. They trade books, journal articles, and newspaper clippings.

TABLE 16.4 Comparison of How Groups Helped

Group Helping Features	Al-Anon	National Alliance for the Mentally Ill	Together We Learn to Cope
Opening up feelings			
Perception of similarity	5 (50%)	6 (40%)	5 (55%)
Reappraisal of problem	3 (30%)	2 (13%)	0
Gaining intellectual understanding			
Professional knowledge	0	12 (80%)	6 (67%)
Experiential knowledge	8 (80%)	3 (20%)	2 (22%)
Exploration of coping mechanisms			
Persuasion to disengage	8 (80%)	2 (13%)	1 (11%)
De-escalation of intensity	1 (10%)	1 (6%)	2 (22%)
Clarification of boundaries	4 (40%)	0	2 (22%)
Expansion of the social world			
Enlarging the social network	5 (50%)	1 (6%)	2 (22%)
Increased self-confidence	3 (30%)	6 (40%)	7 (78%)
Spiritual growth	9 (90%)	3 (20%)	0

Through these efforts, families have learned the symptoms of the illness, remedies for those symptoms, current state of research and knowledge in the field, methods of increasing support for such research, and which sources of expertise were needed for the particular situations in which they found themselves.

Experiential Knowledge. Borkman (1990) identified specialized information and perspectives that people possess when they live through and resolve a problem as different from both the expertise of professionals and the common knowledge of the lay person; she termed this *experiential knowledge.* This understanding that comes from experience was illustrated earlier by the NAMI member who advised her friend to ignore the smell of her unwashed child and "spray deodorant all around." An Al-Anon member illustrated the difference between intellectual and experiential knowledge in the following narrative.

> They told me it (alcoholism) was a disease and I thought I understood that.
> Then one night I heard _____ talk about how her husband died. He had

cirrhosis and he was in her arms hemorrhaging and she was feeding him whiskey by the tablespoon. That's when I *really* understood how alcoholism was a disease.

Experiential knowledge is conveyed through personal stories of learning to cope and using the group's support. The typical story begins with the crisis. The storyteller then tells about joining the group, after which he or she experiences improved coping, relief from shame, and a growing ability to help others. Coping methods learned through the experiential knowledge of group members are discussed below.

Exploration of Coping Mechanisms

Persuasion to Disengage. When asked how they had learned to handle problems that arise, interviewees described one kind of problem solving that the author labeled *disengaging,* although in Al-Anon it is termed *detachment.* When Al-Anon members speak of detachment, they mean letting go of the alcoholic and not trying to control either the person or the course of the illness. The group encourages and supports the member in detaching or disengaging from the situation. For a mother whose child has mental illness, this might mean that the adult child is given more responsibility for self-care. An example of disengagement appears in this account by the mother of an alcoholic son:

> I used to do things for him that he should have done for himself. Like right now he is supposed to attend defensive driving because he got a ticket. If you don't attend, your license is suspended. I put the letter on the refrigerator and that's as much as I have done. In the past I would have just seen to it that he got to the class so he would not have a suspended license.

A NAMI member stated, "You want to do for your child but I've had to accept that that's not the way it's going to be." The effects of both alcoholism and mental illness are intensely destructive to family life, thus provoking a gradual, insidious tendency by the well family members to compensate for, protect, and care for the ill person, even to that person's ultimate detriment (Kellermann, 1993). This learned response must be suppressed, a trying task.

De-escalation of Intensity. One of the similarities between responses by families of alcoholics and families with mentally ill members was their recognition of the need to reduce the intensity of communication. For example, an NAMI member said, "I've learned that I have to soften my voice, watch my body movements, and avoid arguments." Similarly, an Al-Anon member described herself in early recovery:

> My sponsor told me that when I talked to him "just keep to the facts." Before that, I would have been crying and screaming and yelling and everything. So I was talking to him really factual and part of me was looking at this and saying, "is this really me?"

One of the persistent stereotypes of wives of alcoholics is that of the nagging, persecuting woman who drives her husband to drink (Paolino et al., 1976). Although no longer perceived as causal, the image does illustrate the stressful state reached by many spouses of actively drinking alcoholics (Moos et al., 1982). Researchers and clinicians emphasize the importance of reducing tension and intense feelings around persons with major mental illness (Anderson, Hogarty, & Reiss, 1980) and with alcoholics in early recovery (Barnes, 1991). The changes in communication learned in the group are consistent with that advice.

Clarification of Boundaries. One of the complications of living with an alcoholic or mentally ill person is finding it difficult, or even impossible, to set limits. A TLC member, for example, reported that she had to decide not to let her son, who had schizophrenia, live with her: "I had a heart attack right after he went into the hospital. The stress of having a person around like that is pretty awful." Another mother told of being pressured by mental health workers to take her daughter back into her home, despite the fact that she also had serious heart disease and felt she could not do so. In both instances, the group offered a place where these women could obtain support for setting limits and taking care of their own health.

Al-Anon members also learned to set boundaries. For example, a wife stated, "If he started drinking again, I would not stay with him. I've learned to respect myself and I don't have to be bashed around or verbally abused; I will not live that way again." These women learned that they helped themselves and the alcoholic most when they took more responsibility for themselves and less responsibility for the alcoholic. An Al-Anon member illustrated this way, "I used to say, 'that's too bad, let me take care of it,' and now I say, 'if there's anything I can do, let me know.' "

Other Skills Acquired. Other skills mentioned less often than the three just discussed were the ability to reach out to others, to tackle a problem a step at a time, and to convert the frustrated wish to help one's child to social action. A NAMI member said, "It is real important to me to start doing something. I had to be in a group that didn't see everything in completely negative terms." And another, "you realize that you can't do for your child. By working with NAMI, I can help her by changing the public's opinion, by getting legislation, by supporting research on medication to make her life more livable."

Expansion of the Social World

When sorting responses to the final question in the interview, "What has changed since you have been in the group?" the researcher realized that the responses conformed to the fourth crisis intervention technique discussed by Aguilera (1990), that of reopening the social world. Thus, responses to this question were placed under the general heading of social world expansion.

Enlarging the Social Network. Many of those interviewed thought that people in their ordinary support system could not understand the situation and were frightened and embarrassed by requests for help. Joining the group offered contact with people who knew exactly what they were enduring. For example, a TLC member said, "Without the group I wouldn't have any social life at all. I would still be out there wondering what was going on."

When crises occurred, some members increased meeting attendance. This was illustrated in one Al-Anon member's description of her reaction when her alcoholic husband relapsed a day after he finished treatment: "That's when I dropped to my knees and asked God to take all this away from me and I started going to meetings every day." Al-Anon members averaged 11 meetings per month, which they accomplished by attending more than one group. Members of NAMI and TLC were unable to expand attendance in this way due to the smaller number of groups available; many, however, reported more calls to other group members and increased attendance at professionally led groups.

Increased Self-Confidence. Social worlds expanded when interviewees became more assertive and more sure of themselves. A TLC member said,

"I'm out of the closet. I speak out and try to make a difference." A NAMI member said, "I feel I can deal with anything. I look back at how I was floundering about unsure of what my next move was, no direction, no answers to anything. Now, I can say whatever comes up I think I could handle it." And an Al-Anon member confided:

> Before (Al-Anon) I had withdrawn from all people. I couldn't talk to people. I thought whatever I had to say would be dumb and people would be making fun of me. Today, I feel that everything I need to know to be able to live the rest of my life in peace and serenity I can find by going to Al-Anon meetings and sharing my life with others.

Spiritual Growth. Tolerance for others and compassion for the unfortunate also expanded. Members gained self-acceptance, happiness, and gratitude for what they had. One member stated, "I've changed 100%. Today I know myself and why I do what I do." Another stated:

> I can laugh. I'm able to see the beauty in life. I have a spiritual life. God is constantly present in my life and it helps me with things I think I can't handle. I don't have as many crises. Things don't get as serious as they were before.

DISCUSSION

Aguilera's Crisis Intervention Model

Offered a definition of crisis, 91% of the sample identified a point at which they experienced a stressful event that they were unable to deal with using their normal coping skills. Although most of them turned first to family, friends, and professionals, all had found the group most responsive to their crisis situations. Responding to questions about the groups' crisis intervention measures, most described ways that the group helped them open up feelings, gave them intellectual understanding, increased coping skills, and expanded their social network. According to crisis intervention theory, optimal resolution occurs if the person in distress grows in ability to respond to crises in the future (Aguilera, 1990; Dixon, 1987; Golan, 1978; Hansell, 1976). Most of the interviewees were able to report ways that they had benefited from their participation; they described these changes as self-improvements that transcended their normal state before the crises began.

These improvements incorporated skills useful for later difficulties similar to those precipitating the initial crisis.

Aguilera's model of crisis intervention proved to be a particularly useful model for understanding how crises are dealt with in groups of this type. Other models focused on feelings and cognitions but also on more treatment-oriented tasks appropriate for a professional intervention, but less appropriate for an open-ended self-help group (Dixon, 1987; Golan, 1978). For example, Dixon (1987) discusses crisis intervention in a group setting but recommends careful selection of participants and a therapist who will facilitate group interaction to maintain group focus. Of the crisis intervention literature reviewed, few identified groups as a means of intervention, and none mentioned self-help or mutual-aid groups. Golan (1978) described the use of mutual-aid groups for persons in life transition crisis but did not elaborate on the specific processes in these groups.

Aguilera's model also assumes that a professional therapist will intervene either in an individual, family or group setting (Aguilera, 1990). The therapist will perform an assessment, plan an intervention approach, institute intervention measures, and plan for the future (Aguilera, 1990). The intervention itself is well-defined and derives from an article by Morley, Messick, and Aguilera, 1967 (as cited by Aguilera, 1990, p. 23) that includes dealing with feelings, influencing cognitions, teaching skills, and expanding the social world. Despite the assumption of professional intervention, the author found that these four processes were naturally occuring in the self-help groups studied.

One aspect that differentiates hypothesis-generating qualitative research and hypothesis-testing research is that, in the former, researchers may move back and forth between the literature and the data (Patton, 1990, p. 163). In this case, the three tasks of opening up feelings, gaining intellectual understanding, and exploring coping mechanisms formed the initial questions to be asked because these were found in almost every crisis intervention text reviewed. Later in the analytic phase of the study, the author realized that responses to the question, "what has changed since you have been in the group?" conformed to the fourth crisis intervention technique cited by Aguilera, that of reopening the social world. With their broad memberships, self-help groups are especially suited for accomplishing this objective. Indeed, other qualitative and theoretical works on self-help groups have proposed that they, given sufficient size and complexity, can become a social world (Smith, 1991), a subculture (Taylor, 1977), or an alternate community (Denzin, 1987; Mack, 1981). The finding with regard to crisis intervention tasks illustrated how this characteristic of community in self-help groups evolves for people in crisis.

Comparison of Three
Groups and Their Memberships

The members in all three groups were much alike in many ways. They had often experienced domestic violence due to the illness, they were predominantly female, White, and concerned with a male member of the family. They differed in that the relatives of mentally ill persons were predominantly parents and the Al-Anon members were predominantly spouses. In these ways the study sample reflects the typical membership of the three self-help associations. Al-Anon members were more likely to have gone first to the group for help. NAMI and TLC looked for help first from family and professionals and were much more likely to have continued receiving help from professionals. The latter may, in part, be due to the fewer number of groups for families with mental illness. The large number of local Al-Anon groups and the greater frequency of meetings make it more accessible.

Ways groups responded to crises also differed according to type of group. Al-Anon groups emphasize spiritual growth, NAMI groups accent advocacy, and TLC groups stress emotional support. All three groups redefine the problem as an illness, rather than a behavioral problem or moral deficiency, however, the Al-Anon definition is broader than that found in mental illness groups. Alcoholism is generally regarded as a physical, emotional, and spiritual malady, whereas mental illness is seen as a brain disease.

NAMI and TLC members more often seek professional and scientific knowledge; Al-Anon members rely almost solely upon the experiential knowledge of fellow group members and veterans who have written the literature sold by their fellowship. Members from all three groups experienced an increase in self-confidence and self-efficacy; however, this change was framed in different ways. NAMI and TLC members described themselves as more assertive and more willing to enter into efforts toward societal and social policy change. Al-Anon members were more inclined to describe their personal growth in terms of contentment and self-acceptance. These differences were minor, however, compared to the overall finding that all three groups were able to reduce feelings of guilt and blame for the illness, reduce isolation, give cognitive understanding of the illness, teach coping skills, and provide a support system that allowed its members to give and receive mutual aid.

QUALITATIVE RESEARCH
ON SELF-HELP GROUPS

Anselm Strauss's grounded theory approach to qualitative research first originated at the University of Chicago in the 1920s and was influenced by the interactionist and pragmatic writings of such persons as George Herbert Mead and John Dewey (Kurtz, 1984; Strauss & Corbin, 1990). Later, Barney Glaser joined Strauss, and from this partnership came the "systematic set of procedures for coding and testing hypotheses generated during the research process" (Strauss & Corbin, 1990, p. 25). The purpose of grounded theory is "to build theory that is faithful to and illuminates the area under study" (Strauss & Corbin, 1990, p. 24). Grounded theory is an effort to understand how interactions between people lead to constructed meanings by which experience is understood. This method is descriptive and concrete. Observations of tangible events, explicit verbal descriptions, and constant comparisons of these data with each other and with the literature gradually enlarge and enrich existing theory. This method of study is particularly applicable when one's goals are to explore interactive group processes and their impact on members.

Some of the more well-known qualitative studies in which investigators immersed themselves in the field were Znaniecki's study of Polish immigrants attempting to adapt to the New World and Whyte's study of street-corner society in a low-income Italian neighborhood (Kurtz, 1984). More recent studies using the grounded theory approach include such works as Strauss's study of dying and his research on ideologies in psychiatric hospitals (Strauss, 1961; Strauss, 1970).

In the history of research on self-help groups, the grounded theory method of study is most apparent in 50 years of analyzing Alcoholics Anonymous (AA) (Kurtz, 1993). Recently, researchers have investigated, through naturalistic observations and lengthy interviews, aspects of AA such as the process of recovery (Taylor, 1977), the process of affiliation (Rudy, 1986), identity transformation (Denzin, 1987; Nagel, 1988), varieties of AA groups (Johnson, 1987), and how women in AA choose a group (Vourakis, 1989). Using observations and interviews, Smith (1993) described the social construction of group dependency in AA and Bloomfield (1988) described AA as a social movement. In all of these studies, naturalistic inquiry led to the discovery of theory about AA.

Self-help groups for families have not received nearly the sustained research focus that has been lavished upon AA over the past 50 years (Kurtz,

1993). Two recent studies have employed lengthy interviews and observations to investigate family groups (Gidron et al., 1990; Medvene & Krauss, 1989). Gidron et al. compared participants of a self-help group for families in Israel with nonparticipants in the same area. The interviews for this study were conducted using a predetermined, structured interview schedule in order to understand family stress and coping strategies. Medvene and Krauss first interviewed 23 member leaders of a NAMI group in Connecticut to gain basic understanding to develop a more structured mail questionnaire. Although researchers employed interviews and observations in these two studies, the analysis focused on results of predetermined interview items in the first and of mail surveys in the latter. Thus, the analytic methods were more concerned with confirmation of previously formed questions or with quantitative analysis of survey data than with the discovery of theory.

IMPLICATIONS FOR PRACTITIONERS

Families interviewed for this study emphasized the importance of being with others in a similar predicament. They needed to learn about what they were dealing with, to know that they were not alone with the problem, and to find hope for the future from others who shared their problem. The linking process between and among families and family groups is an important service. Especially when the crisis is acute and conditions for successful affiliation are present, it is important to link a family member with the appropriate group.

These findings indicate that increasing attendance in groups helps when stress is most acute. In situations where self-help groups may not meet often, professionally facilitated support groups may provide a welcome addition to the number of groups available to families. Self-help and support groups are useful because of their accessibility and their ability to empower members to be help-givers, not just takers of services. The professional facilitators of support groups should help the groups establish ways in which members can take on the role of help-giving. Moreover, such groups should be easily accessible and open-ended so that dropouts can return when crises occur.

In working individually with family members, social workers can support the processes taking place in the group. For instance, they can recognize and acknowledge the disease theories of mental illness and chemical dependency. They can share professional knowledge about the illness with the individual and with groups when invited. And finally, they can recognize and legitimate experiential knowledge.

CONCLUSION

This was an exploratory case study and, as such, these findings should not be generalized to all families of persons with mental illness and chemical dependency. Nor should differences among the groups be construed as rigorous comparisons. Responses spontaneously generated by open-ended questioning offer a different kind of knowledge than those elicited by the specific inquiries of a large-scale survey. It may be that differences in the selection process account for the dissimilarities noted among groups. It may also be that spouses derive different benefits and involve themselves differently than parents.

Further study with members of these groups should continue to investigate the ways in which self-help groups for families actually do assist them. Group objectives, such as stress management, advocacy, and research could be evaluated more rigorously. One might also explore the ways in which the family's involvement in the group affects the patient. Future qualitative studies should explore demographic differences among members with an eye to discovering what factors facilitate or impede bonding with the group. And finally, because the phenomenon of crisis is experienced in such a personal and idiosyncratic way, more investigation of the kinds of crises families with mentally ill and alcoholic members endure should be pursued. Along with that pursuit, researchers should continue to explore the ways that self-help groups help families to deal and cope with these crisis events.

REFERENCES

Ablon, J. (1974). Al-Anon Family Groups: Impetus for learning and change through the presentation of alternatives. *American Journal of Psychotherapy, 28,* 30-45.

Aguilera, D. A. (1990). Crisis intervention: Theory and methodology (6th. ed.). St. Louis: C. V. Mosby.

Al-Anon Family Groups. (l986). *Al-Anon faces alcoholism* (2nd ed.). New York: Author.

Al-Anon Family Groups. (1990). *Who are the members of Al-Anon and Alateen?* New York: Author.

Anderson, C. M., Hogarty, G. E., & Reiss, D. J.(1980). Family treatment of adult schizophrenic patients: A psycho-educational approach. *Schizophrenia Bulletin, 6,* 490-505.

Ascher-Svanum, H., & Sobel, T. S. (1989). Caregivers of mentally ill adults: A women's agenda. *Hospital and Community Psychiatry, 40,* 843-845.

Bailey, M. B. (1965). Al-Anon Family Groups as an aid to wives of alcoholics. *Social Work, 10,* 68-74.

Barnes, C. (1991). A guide to counseling in early recovery from alcohol dependence. *Alcoholism Treatment Quarterly, 8,* 19-37.

Bloomfield, K. A. (August, 1988). *Beyond sobriety: The cultural significance of Alcoholics Anonymous as a social movement.* Paper presented to the 35th International Congress on Alcohol and Drug Dependence, Oslo, Norway.

Borkman, T. (1990). Experiential, professional and lay frames of reference. In T. J. Powell, *Working with self help* (pp. 3-30). Silver Spring, MD: National Association of Social Workers.

Denzin, N. K. (1987). *The recovering alcoholic.* Newbury Park, CA: Sage.

Dixon, S. (1987). *Working with people in crisis: Theory and practice* (2nd ed). Columbus, OH: Merrill.

Gidron, B., Guterman, N. B., Hartman, H. (1990). Stress and coping patterns of participants and non-participants in self-help groups for parents of the mentally ill. *Community Mental Health Journal, 26,* 483-496.

Golan, N. (1978). *Treatment in crisis situations.* New York: Free Press.

Goldman, H. H. (1982). Mental illness and family burden: A public health perspective. *Hospital and Community Psychiatry, 33,* 557-560.

Gorman, J. M., & Rooney, J. F. (1979). The influence of Al-Anon on the coping behavior of wives of alcoholics. *Journal of Studies on Alcohol, 40,* 1030-1038.

Hansell, N. (1976). *The person in distress: On the biosocial dynamics of adaptation.* New York: Human Sciences Press.

Hanson, J. G., & Rapp, C. A. (1992). Families' perceptions of community mental health programs for their relatives with a severe mental illness. *Community Mental Health Journal, 28,* 181-197.

Hatfield, A. B. (1986-1987). The National Alliance for the Mentally Ill: The meaning of a movement. *International Journal of Mental Health, 15,* 79-93.

Hatfield, A. B. (1987). Families as caregivers: A historical perspective. In A. B. Hatfield & H. P. Lefley (Eds.), *Families of the mentally ill: Coping and Adaptation* (pp. 3-29). New York: Guilford.

Jackson, J. (1954). The adjustment of the family to the crisis of alcoholism. *Quarterly Journal of Studies on Alcohol, 15,* 562-586.

Johnson, H. C. (1987). *Alcoholics Anonymous in the 1980s: Variations on a theme.* Dissertation, University of California, Los Angeles. Ann Arbor: University Microfilms International.

Kellermann, J. L. (1993). *Alcoholism: A merry-go-round named denial* (rev. ed.). Center City, MN: Hazelden.

Kurtz, E. (1993). Research on Alcoholics Anonymous: The historical context. In B. McCrady & W. R. Miller (Eds.), *Research on Alcoholics Anonymous: Opportunities and alternatives,* (pp. 13-26). New Brunswick, NJ: Rutgers Center of Alcohol Studies.

Kurtz, L. R. (1984). *Evaluating Chicago sociology: A guide to the literature.* Chicago: University of Chicago Press.

Mack, J. E. (1981). Alcoholism, A.A., and the governance of the self. In M. H. Bean & N. E. Zinberg (Eds.), *Dynamic approaches to the understanding and treatment of alcoholism* (pp. 128-162). New York: Free Press.

Medvene, L. J. (1990). Family support organizations: The function of similarity. In T. J. Powell, *Working with self-help* (pp. 120-140). Silver Spring, MD: National Association of Social Workers.

Medvene, L. J., & Krauss, D. H. (1989). Causal attributions and parent-child relationships in a self-help group for families of the mentally ill. *Journal of Applied Social Psychology, 19,* 1413-1430.

Moos, R. H., Finney, J. W., & Gamble, W. (1982). The process of recovery from alcoholism: Comparing spouses of alcoholic patients and matched community controls. *Journal of Studies on Alcohol, 43,* 888-909.

Nagel, G. (1988). *Identity reconstruction: Communication and storytelling in Alcoholics Anonymous.* Dissertation, The University of Utah. Ann Arbor, MI: University Microfilms International.

Noh, S., & Turner, R. J. (1987). Living with psychiatric patients: Implications for the mental health of family members. *Social Science and Medicine, 25,* 263-271.

Norton, S., Wandersman, A., & Goldman, C. R. (1993). Perceived costs and benefits of membership in a self-help group: Comparisons of members and nonmembers of the Alliance for the Mentally Ill. *Community Mental Health Journal, 29,* 143-160.

Paolino, T. J., McCrady, B., Diamond, S., & Longabaugh, R. (1976). Psychological disturbances in spouses of alcoholics: An empirical assessment. *Journal of Studies on Alcohol, 37,* 1600-1607.

Parad, H. J., & Parad, L. G. (Eds.). (1990). *Crisis intervention book 2: The practitioner's sourcebook for brief therapy.* Milwaukee, WI: Family Service America.

Patton, M. W. (1990). *Qualitative evaluation and research methods* (2nd ed.). Newbury Park, CA: Sage.

Potasznik, H., & Nelson, G. (1984). Stress and social support: The burden experienced by the family of a mentally ill person. *American Journal of Community Psychology, 12,* 589-607.

Roberts, A. R. (1990). *Crisis intervention handbook: Assessment, treatment and research.* Belmont, CA: Wadsworth.

Rudy, D. R. (1986). *Becoming alcoholic: Alcoholics Anonymous and the reality of alcoholism.* Carbondale, IL: Southern Illinois University Press.

Rychtarik, R. G., Carstensen, L. L., Alford, G. S., & Schlundt, D. G. (1988). Situational assessment of alcohol-related coping skills in wives of alcoholics. *Psychology of Addictive Behaviors, 2,* 66-73.

Scheyett, A. (1990). The oppression of caring: Women caregivers of relatives with mental illness. *Affilia, 5,* 32-48.

Smith, A. R. (1991). *Alcoholics Anonymous: A social world perspective.* Unpublished doctoral dissertation, UC San Diego.

Smith, A. (1993). The social construction of group dependency in Alcoholics Anonymous. *Journal of Drug Issues, 23,* 689-704.

Steinglass, P. (1981). The impact of alcoholism on the family: Relationship between degree of alcoholism and psychiatric symptomatology. *Journal of Studies on Alcohol, 42,* 288-303.

Strauss, A. (1961). *Psychiatric ideologies and institutions.* New York: Macmillan.

Strauss, A. (1970). *Anguish: A case history of a dying trajectory.* Mill Valley, CA: The Sociology Press.

Strauss, A., & Corbin J. (1990). *Basics of qualitative research: Grounded theory procedures and techniques.* Newbury Park, CA: Sage.

Strecker, E. A. (1946). *Their mother's sons: The psychiatrist examines an American problem.* Philadelphia: J. B. Lippincott.

Taylor, M. C. (1977). Alcoholics Anonymous: How it works, recovery processes in a self-help group. *Dissertation Abstracts International, 39,* 7532A. Ann Arbor: University Microfilms.

Tesch, R. (1990). *Qualitative research: Analysis types and software tools.* New York: Falmer.

Torrey, E. F. (1988). *Surviving schizophrenia: A family manual* (rev. ed.) New York: Harper & Row.

Vourakis, C. H. (1989). The process of recovery for women in Alcoholics Anonymous: Seeking groups "like me." Dissertation, University of California, San Francisco. Ann Arbor, MI: University Microfilms International.

Wasserman, H., & Danforth, H. E. (1988). *The human bond: Support groups and mutual aid.* New York: Springer.

Wedenoja, M. (1991). Mothers are not to blame: Confronting cultural bias in the area of serious mental illness. In M. Bricker-Jenkins, N. R. Hooyman, & N. Gottlieb (Eds.), *Feminist social work practice in clinical settings* (pp. 179-196). Newbury Park, CA: Sage.

17. The Role of Self-Help Programs in the Rehabilitation of Persons With Severe Mental Illness and Substance Use Disorders

DOUGLAS L. NOORDSY

BRENDA SCHWAB

LINDY FOX

ROBERT E. DRAKE

The high prevalence of co-occurring substance use disorders among individuals with major mental illness is now widely recognized (Minkoff & Drake, 1991). As dually diagnosed patients have poor short-term outcomes in traditional mental health programs and do not readily fit into traditional substance abuse treatment programs (Ridgely, Goldman, & Willenbring, 1990), models for treatment specifically designed to serve these individuals have been described (Drake, Antosca, Noordsy, Bartels, & Osher, 1991; Drake, Bartels, Teague, Noordsy, & Clark, 1993; Hellerstein & Meehan, 1987; Kofoed, Kania, Walsh, & Atkinson, 1986; Lehman, Herron, & Schwartz, 1993; Minkoff, 1989). Twelve Step models of treatment based on Alcoholics Anonymous (AA) are commonly used in the treatment of addictions in this country and have been included in many of these models. Little information is available on the applicability of either self-help or Twelve Step approaches to the needs of individuals with chronic mental illness.

The New Hampshire-Dartmouth Psychiatric Research Center has been studying systems of providing service to individuals with dual diagnoses since 1987. The systems studied were initially designed with an emphasis on promoting participation in self-help programs. The experience of working with consumers of these services in clinical research settings over time has led to an evolution in our thinking toward a more flexible, multimodal approach. In this chapter we will explore the use of self-help programs for addictions by individuals with severe mental illness and self-help promotion by treatment staff in several of our studies. We will identify several preliminary findings that we hope will stimulate critical debate, attempts at replication, and further research.

This chapter will first review aspects of two recent projects, then abstract ongoing work at our center, and finally present clinical observations generated in the process of conducting these studies. The studies were selected for having generated information about the role of self-help programs in the management of psychoactive substance use disorders among individuals with severe mental illness. The second study also includes information about consumer responses to a vigorous self-help promotion strategy. The studies were conducted in the context of New Hampshire's integrated treatment program for people with major mental illness and substance use disorder, described elsewhere in detail (Drake, Antosca et al., 1991; Drake, Teague, & Warren, 1990; Noordsy & Fox, 1991). The central features are: (a) clinical case management delivered by multidisciplinary teams of clinicians who are trained to address mental health and substance abuse problems individually and in groups, and (b) a four-stage model of substance abuse treatment (engagement, persuasion, active treatment, and relapse prevention) designed for people with major mental illness and aimed at long-term recovery. The program is now being evaluated in a randomized clinical trial across seven sites (Teague, Schwab, & Drake, 1990).

The use of self-help was vigorously promoted in each of these studies, including assistance with motivation to attend meetings, education about the content and format of meetings, transportation, and additional self-help meeting sites within the mental health centers. During the course of these studies, the self-help programs for psychoactive substance abuse available in the communities where study group members lived were limited primarily to AA, Narcotics Anonymous (NA), and Al-Anon. Although the mental health center-based self-help meetings were oriented toward individuals who were dually diagnosed, few such meetings existed elsewhere. Regular community meetings were the major self-help experience for most of the individuals who participated in these studies.

Virtually all study group members were prescribed medications for the management of their mental illness through the course of these studies. Prescribing psychiatrists were integral members of the treatment teams, had training in addictions treatment, and avoided the prescription of potentially addictive medications whenever possible. Medication use was closely monitored. Overuse of medication was viewed as substance abuse and resulted in treatment intervention.

STUDIES REVIEWED

1. Treatment of Alcoholism Among Schizophrenic Outpatients

This is an ongoing study following a pilot sample of alcohol-abusing schizophrenic patients in the community since 1987. We have previously reported the rate and correlates of alcohol use disorders (Drake, Osher et al., 1990; Drake, Wallach et al., 1991; Noordsy et al., 1991; Osher et al., in press) and rate of recovery over a 4-year follow-up period in this study group (Drake, McHugo, & Noordsy, 1993). We will present here previously unreported findings on the use of self-help in this study group.

The study group of 18 people had a mean age of 37.9 (SD = 12.2) years; 11.1% were married, 22.2% were separated, divorced, or widowed, and 66.7% were never married at the time of the original evaluation. Two thirds were male, and all were Caucasian (reflecting the rural New Hampshire population). The distribution of Diagnostic and Statistical Manual of Mental Disorders (DSM-III-R) diagnoses was as follows: schizophrenia, 83.3% (n = 15); schizoaffective disorder, 16.7% (n = 3); alcohol use disorder, 100% (n = 18); marijuana use disorder, 22.2% (n = 4).

The 18 people were treated continuously between 1987 and 1991 and were reevaluated approximately 4 years after their original evaluation. Alcohol and street drug use were assessed through a combination of hospital records, mental health center records, psychiatric interviews, case manager ratings, and intensive case reviews to resolve disagreements. Use of self-help programs was rated by case managers based on frequent behavioral observations in the community and collateral information from families, community contacts, and other caregivers.

The 11 people who had attained full remission from alcohol use disorders as defined in DSM-III-R (Remission group) were compared with the 7 people who did not (Active Abuse group). The two groups did not differ significantly at baseline in age, sex, diagnosis, marital status, or the number of months of prior hospitalization. The Active Abuse group had trends toward a somewhat greater average severity of alcohol use disorder at baseline (average MAST score = 29.3 vs. 20.6 in the Remission group) and a larger proportion of individuals diagnosed with alcohol dependence rather than alcohol abuse (71.4% vs. 45.5% in the Remission group). There were also trends toward greater improvement in certain case manager-rated psychosocial variables and psychiatric symptoms and less institutional time by the Remission group over the 4-year period. Unfortunately, the N was too small to allow for valid statistical comparison. Of particular interest here was a trend toward greater improvement in social relations by the Remission group.

Because none of these clients disappeared from treatment more than temporarily, recovery occurred in the context of active treatment. All clients became actively involved in integrated treatment; 72% attended specialized dual diagnosis treatment groups in the mental health center; 33% attended these groups nearly weekly.

Linkage to self-help meetings was successful for a smaller proportion of clients in this study. Five individuals (28%) in this study attended self-help meetings during the 4-year follow-up interval. One person was actively alcoholic with periods of abstinence lasting several weeks at a time, came to a treatment group weekly, and went to AA on his own 4 to 7 times per week. Another person was in stable remission, came to a treatment group once a month, and went to AA on his own 1 to 2 times per month. The third person was actively abusing alcohol and marijuana, with periods of abstinence lasting 1 to 3 days at a time, attended a treatment group 3 to 4 times per month, and went to AA or NA 3 to 4 times per month with her case manager and 1 to 2 times per month on her own. The fourth used alcohol heavily 5 days a week and abstained for 2-day visits with his family, used other drugs occasionally, attended a treatment group weekly for a year, attended AA 1 to 2 times per week with his case manager for 8 months before refusing to continue, and never attended self-help meetings on his own. The fifth person used alcohol daily with periods of abstinence lasting up to 5 months, came to a treatment group infrequently, and had been to a few AA meetings early in the follow-up interval but had not attended at all for several years.

Use of self-help did not appear to be related to remission in this small sample, so far. Four of the five self-help users, including the regular member, were in the Active Abuse group (Table 17.1). Diagnosis did not appear to be related to self-help use in this study, although the numbers were too small to allow reliable comparison. Four of fifteen individuals (27%) with schizophrenia used self-help, as opposed to one of three (33%) with schizoaffective disorder.

Similar results were found with respect to the use of inpatient addictions treatment programs. All of the inpatient programs available in the communities where these clients lived were based on a Twelve Step model and strongly promoted use of self-help programs during and after inpatient stays. Six individuals (33%) entered inpatient addiction programs at some point during the study interval (Table 17.1). Only one individual completed an inpatient program. Five of the six inpatient treatment attendees, including the one completer, were in the Active Abuse group at follow-up. Three of the five self-help users (60%) had also been in inpatient programs at some point.

One explanation for these results could be that individuals with alcohol abuse have recovered faster with less self-help involvement and are skewing the Remission group. Ongoing attempts at treatment may explain the apparent bias towards self-help and inpatient program use in the Active Abuse group. As many Active Abuse members were showing signs of improvement, a relationship between self-help use and recovery may be more apparent at further follow-up.

2. An Ethnographic Study
of Dual Diagnosis Treatment

This study reports on the ethnographic component of a randomized clinical trial of standard and intensive case management for persons with co-occuring severe mental illness and substance use disorders (Schwab, 1994). The ethnography, carried out at one urban site, examined the process of treatment and the quality of the relationships between case managers and their clients. We will summarize findings of the ethnographic study relevant to clients' response to self-help ideology and jargon when used by clinicians in the process of promoting participation in self-help.

For 2 years, two ethnographers conducted participant observation and ethnographic interviews with clients and case managers in both community

TABLE 17.1 Linkage to Self-Help and Inpatient Treatment Among
Schizophrenic Outpatients: Four-Year Outcomes

| | *Outcome Group* | |
	Remission	*Active Abuse*
Self-help meeting attendance		
None	10	3
Infrequent	1	3
Regular	0	1
Inpatient treatment		
None	10	2
Partial	1	4
Completed	0	1

and treatment settings. Both ethnographers observed interactions between clients and case managers and questioned the participants about expectations of and reactions to the interactions. Both ethnographers also accompanied clients and case managers to self-help meetings and were present when self-help meetings and self-help meeting attendance and philosophy were discussed between clients and case managers. One ethnographer observed and participated in various settings and situations where self-help was discussed among clinicians and interviewed clinicians about self-help (see Schwab, 1994; Schwab, Clark, & Drake, 1991, for a description of the ethnographic procedures). Neither of the ethnographers had any prior experience with self-help programs. Efforts were made throughout the study to minimize researcher bias and faithfully record the study participants' thoughts and reactions to their experience.

Study participants in both treatment conditions (standard and intensive case management) were assigned to experienced, predominantly master's-level clinicians who worked in a large community mental health center that has received national attention for its clinical work. The intensive case management was carried out by interdisciplinary teams of comparable training (some team members had additional substance abuse treatment expertise), which assertively delivered services in the community and integrated substance abuse treatment into the direct delivery of services. The case management teams took responsibility for promoting self-help.

Several clients in this study found self-help programs helpful and were committed to participation (see Clinical Observations below), but many reacted negatively to an approach that they perceived as minimizing the considerable problems they faced living with their disabilities. The ethnographers came to recognize that some clinicians in both case management models relied heavily on the specific jargon and ideology emanating from Twelve Step programs. This approach appeared to create obstacles to communication between clients and their caregivers, leading to a closer analysis of case managers' use of "AA talk," and clients' reactions to it.

AA talk was defined as clinicians' use of phrases and precepts originating from the AA program in discourse with their clients. Clients recognized the domain of AA talk in such comments as, "All he ever talks is AA," and one case manager agreed with a client who commented, "Boy, do you talk a lot of AA" (Schwab, 1991). There was considerable variation among case managers as to how much they talked AA. Recognizing that promoting self-help participation was only one aspect of the complex work of case management and that AA talk is used differently in different treatment settings, we will limit this discussion to ways in which AA talk was experienced as invalidating to clients.

One of the central precepts that seemed to contribute to misunderstandings and impasses in treatment was the concept of denial, defined as a person's inability to link substance abuse to problems in his or her life (Westermeyer, 1992). Case managers who tended to talk more AA responded to explanations clients used for their substance use or resistance to treatment with standard phrases intended to confront denial. For example, clients' explanations were called "stinkin' thinkin'"; clients were told, "It's your disease talking," to signify that an explanation for behavior was not coming from a client him- or herself; or case managers used the phrase, "people, places, and things," referring to a person's blaming problems with other persons or situations for his/her drug use rather than blaming the drug use for causing these problems (Schwab, 1991).

A consequence of using some of the standard responses to statements judged to be demonstrating denial was that sometimes case managers missed opportunities to explore meanings from the clients' perspective, and information that might have been valuable for treatment was left unexplored. In some instances, case managers used the concept of denial to discount clients' complaints about aspects of treatment, explaining to the ethnographer that if a client was complaining about self-help meetings it meant he or she wasn't doing well. In such instances case managers missed opportunities to discuss sources of resistance that might have led to an understanding of more individualized needs.

Clients perceived case managers' use of standard phrases, particularly the concept of denial, as a negation of their reasoning. In frustration, one client exclaimed:

> [Case managers] are like automatons, tell you the same lines over and over again: "Substance abuse is a disease. It's going to kill you. If you drink, you're going to die." If you disagree with them they don't listen to your logic, they just go to their next line, like an automaton: "You're in denial." (Schwab, 1991)

Applying the concept of denial to clients' explanations and statements thus gave many clients the impression that case managers were denying their experience and their suffering (cf. Kleinman, Brodwin, Good, & DelVecchio-Good, 1992).

Clients who perceived that case managers were using a rigid Twelve Step approach developed strategies to deal with AA talk. Some played along, telling case managers what they thought case managers wanted to hear. For example, they said that they were learning that they had a disease or that they had to go to more meetings. By playing along, clients were sometimes able to divert discussion away from matters that were important to treatment. In some cases, clients admitted to alcohol use and declared their intention to attend AA meetings in order to avoid discussion about their cocaine or other drug use and lack of participation in other aspects of treatment. Other clients consented to attend self-help meetings and then reported to the ethnographers that they never listened or they merely left early.

Resistance to self-help was seen by some case managers as noncompliance with treatment or failure to accept therapeutic goals and strategies (cf. Estroff, 1991; Kaljee & Beardsley, 1992). Use of standard phrases or statements about self-help participation became a kind of currency used between clients and case managers to negotiate treatment. In such discussions, self-help meeting attendance was treated as if it was a major goal of treatment, rather than a means to an end. Struggles over self-help meeting attendance between clients and case managers often took on an importance that seemed to overshadow the clinician-client relationship itself or at least took precedence over discussion of issues that clients considered important in their lives, for example, problems with their children or partners.

Significant limitations of this study were that the suitability of the model could not be separated from idiosyncrasies in staff characteristics, and the number of subjects (staff and clients) was small. During the first year of this study, some staff with little previous addictions-treatment training were acquiring experience and expertise on the job. Over time, staff became more sophisticated at integrating AA approaches with other treatment strategies. We speculate that the approach described here may have been reinforcing for staff initially, as it added a sense of sureness to a task filled with ambiguity and frustration. The ethnographic methods had the power to distinguish one fairly clear finding despite the limitations: when attempting to promote self-help among individuals with dual diagnoses, the use of a monolithic, inflexible approach was experienced as alienating for many clients.

It is not clear whether individuals with severe mental illness are less able to tolerate a rigid and confrontive approach than other individuals or how the treatment conditions compare to those in traditional settings. Certainly the use of AA talk was taken out of the context of self-help in this application, as is common practice in addictions treatment programs. The meanings of personal choice and empowerment may have been lost in this setting.

Medical anthropologists working in a variety of clinical settings have written about impasses in treatment that occur when clinicians do not explore or share the explanations or meanings patients attribute to their problems (Good & DelVecchio-Good, 1981; Katon & Kleinman, 1981; Kleinman, 1981, 1988). Research has also shown that consumers of psychiatric services have ideas about their illnesses and medications that affect their behavior (Estroff, 1991, Kaljeee & Beardsley, 1992; Rhodes, 1984). A more meaning-centered approach (Good & DelVecchio-Good 1981, p. 172) to the treatment of substance abuse among mental health clients would emphasize listening to clients' explanatory models of their distress, rather than trying to teach a specific model of addiction to clients. By avoiding a struggle between the correct (clinician's) and incorrect (client's) explanatory models of addiction, clinicians might be better able to identify clients' hidden concerns and come to a fuller understanding of their social system and the social context of their substance use. Clinicians might also become aware of ways in which standard use of AA talk can contribute to impasses in treatment and prevent them from acknowledging the extent to which stigma, poverty, and disenfranchisement are ever present in the experience of individuals with severe mental illness (cf. Estroff, 1981; Hopper, 1988).

3. Preliminary Findings of Ongoing Studies

This section surveys preliminary findings of several forthcoming studies. These studies are taking place in the context of a larger project on the treatment of individuals with severe mental illness and psychoactive substance use disorders described above (Study 2). This section offers an opportunity to preview the use of self-help programs by a subset of individuals in treatment using this model. One is a survey of self-help use among a group of individuals with dual disorders treated by case management teams in the community, and the other is a follow-up of attendees of a residential dual-diagnosis program to evaluate outcomes, including self-help use (Bartels & Thomas, 1991).

Preliminary evaluation of these studies shows some consistent trends in the data. First, both studies show that few individuals become closely linked to self-help program participation, despite the fact that the programs were successful in getting the majority of individuals to attend self-help meetings at some point. Second, diagnosis appears to be associated with intensity of self-help use in these study groups. Close linkage to self-help programs seems to be more common among individuals with an affective-spectrum disorder as their major mental illness. Third, better social ability appeared to be associated with use of self-help programs.

We expect that these studies will demonstrate that self-help programs can be used by dually diagnosed clients, although they do not often participate in them fully. Social impairment may be found to be an intervening variable between diagnosis and difficulty using self-help intensively, and this issue deserves further study. As connection to a social group is a component of self-help programs, social impairment or withdrawal may interfere with using this form of treatment. Social impairment does not appear to be associated with abstinence in these studies, however, suggesting that individuals with social difficulties may benefit from other available forms of addictions treatment.

CLINICAL OBSERVATIONS

As we have carried out these studies we have frequently heard from individuals with severe mental illness about their experiences attempting to link with self-help organizations for addictions treatment. Several recurring themes are described here.

Many individuals reported avoiding initial attendance at self-help meetings because of fear of large crowds and the feeling that everyone would be watching them. Symptoms of mental illness, medication, and the associated side effects made them feel different and may have made them stand out.

Some individuals reported hearing self-help members encouraging them to get off of psychiatric medications because all they needed were meetings. Unless they were attending special dual-diagnosis meetings, the feelings of being and looking different from others were often accurate. This disparity may be conceptualized as poor member-group fit (C. Kaufmann, personal communication).

Individuals who attempted to use self-help programs reported dropping out or finding it hard to make a regular commitment for several reasons. Some individuals stated that once at a meeting, they had difficulty sitting still but felt uncomfortable getting up and leaving. If they were able to listen, many found the stories increased their desire to use substances. They often were unable to relate to the negative side of the stories they heard, as they hadn't experienced the same losses. They usually hadn't had a spouse, job, or car to lose to substance abuse. They did report hearing the alcohol and drug use in the stories and said that this stimulated their desire to use.

Other individuals have had difficulty distinguishing the spiritual recovery of Twelve Step programs from religious themes. Talk of spiritual awakening and advice to "let go and let God" became laden with delusional significance for some. The concept of "working the steps" was also baffling to many and became too abstract to be useful.

Although encouraged to attend self-help in order to develop a sober peer group, many individuals had difficulty finding people there whom they considered peers. They often reported inability to connect to others at meetings and intimidation by the expectations that sponsorship would have placed on them. Their negative symptoms, suspiciousness, and social deficits were frequently poorly understood and responded to with confrontation. Self-help groups offered a value system that people with addictions could use to obtain sobriety and regain some of the losses they had experienced from their use of alcohol and drugs. The person with severe mental illness often lacked similar motivation for abstinence and had difficulty with spirituality as a foundation for recovery.

Those people with dual diagnoses who were successful in linking to community self-help groups for management of their addiction generally described them as extremely helpful. They pointed to the network of support that was readily available to them if they attended meetings. Some individuals obtained several personal sponsors and got a list of phone numbers they could call if they needed help staying away from a drink or a drug.

These people cited availability as another issue of importance. There were self-help meetings available around the clock in the urban sites. For some it seemed easier to get to a meeting than to wait to see their case manager or wait for the next treatment group. They liked the flexibility to just sit and listen, talk about their problem during the meeting, or to talk to someone one on one during a break or after the meeting. In some instances they were able to talk about not only drug and alcohol problems, but also problems in living and coping on a daily basis. The feeling that they were not alone was an experience that consumers who attended self-help groups often talked about as well.

The religious aspects of Twelve Step meetings were very appealing to some clients who had strong religious backgrounds. Some liked the routine and structure the meetings offered to their lives. A self-help meeting in one part of town had many of the same elements as a meeting anywhere. Most regular attendees found this predictability comforting and said that the "one day at a time" philosophy worked for them.

Some of these consumers had accompanied their peers to self-help meetings or helped start special self-help meetings for people with dual disorders. Sharing their experiences, strength, and hope with newcomers is how Twelve Step programs "pass it on." For the individual with dual disorders who was a self-help member, being able to help a fellow addict or alcoholic was a very empowering experience.

DISCUSSION

Psychiatric severity has been associated with poorer outcome from conventional addictions treatment and has been proposed as a marker for matching clients to appropriate treatments (McLellan, 1986; Rounsaville, Dolinsky, Babor, & Meyer, 1987). Study 1 demonstrated that some individuals with schizophrenia and alcohol use disorders can achieve stable remission without using self-help programs. In fact, the majority of individuals who did achieve remission did so through substance abuse treatment that was integrated into their mental health treatment, was flexible and staged in intensity, and which offered addictions treatment options beyond self-help linkage.

Individuals with schizophrenia appeared to have greater difficulty using self-help than did individuals with other major mental illnesses. Study 1 was limited almost entirely to individuals with schizophrenia, and they used self-help programs infrequently. The preliminary findings were similar for individuals with schizophrenia. It is not clear how the intensity of use found here would compare to a sample without mental illness.

These studies may offer some insight into potential reasons that individuals with severe and persistent mental illness have difficulty affiliating with self-help programs for addictions. Connection to an alternative social group and experiencing peer pressure toward abstinence, which are likely essential elements in the effectiveness of self-help for many, may be very difficult for individuals with mental illness to achieve in community meetings. Receiving simultaneous help from separate treatment programs with disparate conceptual frameworks may lead to conflicting advice, confusion, and discouragement (Osher & Kofoed, 1989). Individuals who already feel alienated from society and controlled by the treatment system may have particular difficulty with the intensity and rigidity of conventional Twelve Step approaches. The focus on making amends for past misdeeds may be hard to relate to when mental illness is intertwined with addiction. It may also be that it is problematic to attempt to use Twelve Step material in an assertive fashion outside of the self-help context.

It may also be that less intensive use of self-help is optimal for some individuals. Individuals with serious mental illness may be self-selecting a comfortable level of involvement with self-help programs that does not include establishing a sponsor or frequent attendance.

The preliminary findings also suggested that some individuals with severe mental illness, particularly those with an affective disorder, can participate in self-help programs more intensively under certain conditions. These conditions at minimum included considerable support and assistance in using self-help and the simultaneous availability of extensive community mental health services. Affective disorder is considered a marker for better social function and better outcome in populations with severe, persistent mental illness (Samson, Simpson, & Tsuang, 1988). It would not be surprising if better social function were associated with self-help use, as well. We speculate that social ability may be an important factor in assessing likelihood of successful participation in self-help treatment modalities, and this area deserves further study.

As these studies took place in the context of assertive treatment in residential and community settings with extensive support services available to study group members, the applicability of these findings to other treatment settings is unclear. The context of treatment initiation in these studies was typical of work with individuals with severe mental illness. Clients were often identified by clinicians and research instruments as having substance abuse problems well before they identified such problems themselves. It would seem logical that an approach that emphasized preparation for treatment would be more effective with individuals at this stage. Study 2 suggests that careful attention to clients' explanatory models and tolerance for intensity of intervention may help us to develop individualized treatment plans that clients can comfortably participate in. A firm foundation of understanding and mutual trust would be expected to improve the appropriateness of treatment recommendations, as well as consumer's receptivity to those recommendations and their likelihood of follow-through. The staged model of treatment (Drake, Bartels et al., 1993) may help to guide clinicians in the matching of interventions to individuals' needs.

The trend in Study 1 towards greater improvement in social relations in people with schizophrenia who are recovering from alcoholism may prove relevant to understanding their self-help attendance patterns. As social difficulty likely impairs linkage to self-help, people with severe mental illness, addiction, and poor social function may have nearly insurmountable obstacles to successful linkage to self-help groups at early stages. If social ability improves with reductions in substance abuse or participation in treatment, it may be useful for people to try self-help at more than one stage of treatment. Self-help may be able to play a role in relapse prevention for those who could not use it for active treatment.

We have found that people with severe mental illness can tolerate and make use of a self-help promotion approach as follows:

1. Introduce self-help programs as one treatment option that is helpful for many people, and make other treatment options available.
2. Help clients to sample self-help by offering to accompany them to meetings. Help them overcome the social barriers by introducing them to people at the meeting and translating the meeting during and afterwards.
3. Treat the mental illness, addiction, and underlying social skills deficits aggressively to increase clients ability to function independently in self-help.
4. If the client doesn't like self-help, back-off. Don't pair yourself so tightly with self-help that the client has to reject you to reject self-help. Use other treatment approaches to help the client make progress and gain trust in you. At later treatment stages gently reintroduce self-help options again.

The model we have developed provides an array of addictions treatment services, including self-help promotion, brought to the individual with mental illness in their natural environment and fit to their needs. Basic needs such as housing (Drake, Wallach et al., 1991) and work (Becker & Drake, in press) are attended to in a fashion that supports engagement around substance use issues. Multiple addictions treatment approaches are tried, with their relative effectiveness guiding further application for each individual. We believe that self-help programs have their greatest potential when chosen by individuals in this context.

CONCLUSION

We have compiled several perspectives on the role of self-help interventions from our work on the treatment of addictions among individuals with severe mental illness. Collectively these suggest that a minority achieve linkage to self-help programs, that diagnosis and possibly social function are associated with successful linkage, that most achieve remission without extensive use of self-help, and that pushing a Twelve Step model with those who don't gravitate to it can be counterproductive. Our clinical experience suggests that self-help programs are experienced as most helpful by consumers when consistent with their explanatory models and chosen voluntarily.

REFERENCES

Bartels, S. J., & Thomas, W. (1991). Lessons from a residential program for people with dual diagnoses of severe mental illness and substance use disorder. *Journal of Psychosocial Rehabilitation, 15,* 19-30.

Becker, D. R., & Drake, R. E. (in press). Individual placement and support: A community mental health center approach to vocational rehabilitation. *Journal of Community Mental Health.*

Drake, R. E., Antosca, L., Noordsy, D. L., Bartels, S. J., & Osher, F. C. (1991). New Hampshire's specialized services for the dually diagnosed. In K. Minkoff & R. E. Drake (Eds.), *Dual diagnosis of major mental illness and substance disorder.* San Francisco: Jossey-Bass.

Drake, R. E., Bartels, S. J., Teague, G. B., Noordsy, D. L., & Clark, R. E. (1993). Treatment of substance abuse in severely mentally ill patients. *Journal of Nervous Mental Disorders, 181,* 606-611.

Drake, R. E., McHugo, G. J., & Noordsy, D. L. (1993). Treatment of alcoholism among schizophrenic outpatients: Four-year outcomes. *American Journal of Psychiatry, 150,* 328-329.

Drake, R. E., Osher, F. C., Noordsy, D. L., Hurlbut, S. C., Teague, G. B., & Beaudett, M. S. (1990). Diagnosis of alcohol use disorders in schizophrenia. *Schizophrenia Bulletin, 16,* 57-67.

Drake, R. E., Teague, G. B., & Warren, R. S. (1990). New Hampshire's dual diagnosis program for people with severe mental illness and substance use disorder. *Addiction Recovery, 10,* 35-39.

Drake, R. E., Wallach, M. A., Teague, G. B., Freeman, D. H., Paskus, T. S., & Clark, T. A. (1991). Housing instability and homelessness among rural schizophrenic outpatients. *American Journal of Psychiatry, 148,* 330-336.

Estroff, S. E. (1981). Making it crazy: An ethnography of psychiatric clients in an american community. Berkeley: University of California Press.

Estroff, S. E. (1991). Everybody's got a little mental illness: Accounts of self among people with severe, persistent mental illness. *Medical Anthropology Quarterly, 5,* 331-369.

Good, B. J. & Delvecchio-Good, M. J. (1981). The meaning of symptoms: A cultural hermeneutics model for clinical practice. In L. Eisenberg & A. Kleinman (Eds.), *The relevance of social science for medicine.* Boston: D. Reidel.

Hellerstein, D. J., & Meehan, B. (1987). Outpatient group therapy for schizophrenic substance abusers. *American Journal of Psychiatry, 144,* 1337-1339.

Hopper, K. (1988). More than passing strange: Homelessness and mental illness in New York City. *American Ethnologist, 15,* 155-167.

Kaljee, L. M., & Beardsley, R. (1992). Psychotropic drugs and concepts of compliance in a rural mental health clinic. *Medical Anthropology Quarterly, 6,* 271-287.

Katon, W., & Kleinman, A. (1981). Doctor-patient negotiation and other social science strategies in patient care. In L. Eisenberg & A. Kleinman (Eds.), *The relevance of social science for medicine.* Boston: D. Reidel.

Kleinman, A. (1981). On illness meanings and clinical interpretation. *Culture, Medicine and Psychiatry, 5,* 373-377.

Kleinman, A. (1988). *The illness narratives: Suffering, healing and the human condition.* New York: Basic Books.

Kleinman, A., Brodwin, P. E., Good, B. J., & DelVecchio-Good, M. J. (1992). Pain as human experience: An introduction. In M. J. DelVecchio-Good, P. E. Good, B. J. Good, & A. Kleinman (Eds.) In *Pain as human experience: An anthropological perspective.* Berkeley: University of California Press.

Kofoed, L., Kania, J., Walsh, T., & Atkinson, R. (1986). Outpatient treatment of patients with substance abuse and coexisting psychiatric disorders. *American Journal of Psychiatry, 143,* 867-872.

Lehman, A. F., Herron, J. D., & Schwartz, R. P. (1993). Rehabilitation for young adults with severe mental illness and substance use disorders: A clinical trial. *Journal of Nervous Mental Disorders, 181,* 86-90.

McLellan, A. T. (1986). "Psychiatric severity" as a predictor of outcome from substance abuse treatments. In R. E. Meyer (Ed.), *Psychopathology and addictive disorders.* New York: Guilford.

Minkoff, K. (1989). An integrated treatment model for dual diagnosis of psychosis and addiction. *Hospital and Community Psychiatry, 40,* 1031-1036.

Minkoff, K., & Drake, R. E. (Eds.) (1991). Dual diagnosis of major mental illness and substance disorder. San Francisco: Jossey-Bass.

Noordsy, D. L., Drake, R. E., Teague, G. B., Osher, F. C., Hurlbut, S. C., Beaudett, M. S., & Paskus, T. S. (1991). Subjective experiences related to alcohol use among schizophrenics. *Journal of Nervous Mental Disorders, 179,* 410-414.

Noordsy, D. L., & Fox, L. (1991). Group intervention techniques for people with dual diagnoses. *Journal of Psychosocial Rehabilitation, 15,* 67-78.

Osher, F. C., Drake, R. E., Noordsy, D. L., Teague, G. B., Hurlbut, S. C., Paskus, T. S., & Beaudett, M. S. (in press). Correlates and outcomes of alcohol use disorder among rural schizophrenic outpatients. *Journal of Clinical Psychiatry.*

Osher, F. C., & Kofoed, L. L. (1989). Treatment of patients with psychiatric and psychoactive substance abuse disorders. *Hospital and Community Psychiatry, 40,* 1025-1030.

Rhodes, L. A. (1984). "This will clear your mind": The use of metaphors for medication in psychiatric settings. *Culture, Medicine and Psychiatry, 8,* 49-70.

Ridgely, M. S., Goldman, H. H., & Willenbring, M. (1990). Barriers to the care of persons with dual diagnoses: Organizational and financing issues. *Schizophrenia Bulletin, 16,* 123-132.

Ries, R. K., & Ellingson, T. (1990). A pilot assessment at one month of 17 dual diagnosis patients. *Hospital and Community Psychiatry, 41,* 1230-1233.

Roach, J. (1993). Clinical case management with severely mentally ill adults. In M. Harris & H. C. Bergman (Eds.), *Case management for mentally ill patients: Theory and practice.* Langhorne, PA: Harwood.

Rounsaville, B. J., Dolinsky, Z. S., Babor, T. F., & Meyer, R. E. (1987). Psychopathology as a predictor of treatment outcome in alcoholics. *Archives of General Psychiatry, 44,* 505-513.

Samson, J. A., Simpson, J. C., & Tsuang, M. T. (1988). Outcome studies of schizoaffective disorders. *Schizophrenia Bulletin, 14,* 543-554.

Schwab, B. (1991, November 22). *Explanatory models in conflict: Substance abuse treatment for people with chronic mental illness.* Paper presented at the Annual Meeting of the American Anthropologic Association, Chicago.

Schwab, B. (1994). *Explanatory models in conflict: "AA talk" and substance abuse treatment for persons with chronic mental illness.* Unpublished manuscript.

Schwab, B., Clark, R. E., & Drake, R. E. (1991). An ethnographic note on clients as parents. *Journal of Psychosocial Rehabilitation, 15,* 95-99.

Teague, G. B., Schwab, B., & Drake, R. E. (1990). *Program evaluation for services to young adults with chronic mental illness and substance abuse problems.* Arlington, VA: National Association of State Mental Health Program Directors.

Vaillant, G. E. (1983). *The natural history of alcoholism.* Cambridge, MA: Harvard University Press.

Westermeyer, J. (1992). Schizophrenia and substance aAuse. In A. Tasman & M. B. Riba (Eds.), *Review of psychiatry: Vol. 11.* Washington, DC: American Psychiatric Press.

Index

AA. *See* Alcoholics Anonymous
Abelson, R., 128
Ablon, J., 258, 267
Abuse, 255
Action research, 9, 191
    clearinghouse applications, 199-204
    participatory action research, 227, 229-230, 244
Addiction Severity Index (ASI), 65, 67
Admission, 44-45, 109-110
Adult Children of Alcoholics (ACOA), 249-250. *See also* Children of alcoholics
Affective disorders:
    professional service use and, 6, 38
    sickle cell disease group members, 221-222, 224
    substance abuser programs and, 326
    See also Depression
African Americans, 7-8, 16, 28, 35, 36, 50-60
    common focal problems, 57
    culture and religion, 8, 56, 58, 84
    Epidemiological Catchment Area survey, 52-60
    institutionalized population, 54
    knowledge and access problems, 60
    mental health problems, 55-56, 77-79, 221-222, 224
    mutual help attendance, 77-79
    racial fit, 68-69, 74-76, 80-81, 143
    research problems, 58-59, 81-83
    segregated participation patterns, 62-82
    sickle cell self-help groups, 212-225
Age, self-help participation correlations, 36

Aging network agencies, 21
Aguilera, D., 297, 306-308
Ajzen, I., 202
Al-Anon, 294-306, 308
    detachment and codependency concepts, 258-260, 268
    feminism and, 263, 266
    history and expansion of, 248-251
    lesbian program, 247-248, 251-262
    sexism of, 265-266
    See also Lesbian Al-Anon group
Alcoholics Anonymous (AA), 32
    aggressive recruitment, 15
    attendance, 90
    Beliefs Scale, 65, 68
    cross-meeting variability, 2
    dual recovery groups, 15
    grounded theory research, 309
    growth rate, 33
    jargon and ideology ("AA talk"), 146, 320-322
    lesbian program, 251
    membership data, 34
    mental illness labels and, 195-196
    minority participation, 7, 63
    stories, 130, 184-185
    treatment center growth correlation, 21
    worldview transformation, 183-184
Alcoholism treatment, 21
    disease model, 248-249
    schizophrenia and, 316-318, 325, 327
American Psychiatric Association, 6
Analysis of variance (ANOVA), 280
Anger expression, 249

About the Authors

Thomasina Borkman has been a Professor of Sociology at George Mason University, Fairfax, Virginia, since 1974. She has conducted research on self-help groups since 1970, beginning with groups for people who stutter, then comparative studies of groups for people who stutter, people who have ostomies, and members of Twelve Step groups. She served on the planning committee for the Surgeon General's 1987 Workshop on Self-Help and Public Health. She was a member of the National Council on Self-Help and Public Health and editor of a special issue on self-help groups in the *American Journal of Community Psychology.*

Robert E. Drake, M.D., Ph.D., is Director of the New Hampshire-Dartmouth Psychiatric Research Center and Andrew Thomspon Professor of Psychiatry and Community and Family Medicine at Dartmouth Medical School.

Lindy Fox, M.A., is a Clinical Interviewer and Trainer at the New Hampshire-Dartmouth Psychiatric Research Center.

Keith Humphreys received a Ph.D. in clinical/community psychology from the University of Illinois at Urbana-Champaign in 1993, where his research on mutual-help groups won the Scheiderer Award for Outstanding Research and an American Psychological Association Dissertation Award. He is currently a research scientist at the Center for Health Care Evaluation at the Veterans Affairs and Stanford University Medical Centers in Palo Alto, California. His current research focuses on mutual-help organizations for individuals with alcohol and other drug problems.

340

Caroline A. Kaufmann is Assistant Professor of Psychiatry at the University of Pittsburgh. She is Principal Investigator on research projects dealing with self-help and severe mental illness, funded by the National Institute of Mental Health and the Substance Abuse and Mental Health Services Administration. She holds a Ph.D. in Sociology and has completed postdoctoral studies in Mental Health and Public Policy in Mental Health Services Research. She has published papers on informed consent, social psychological correlates of illness and disabilities, self-help in mental health services, and reasonable accommodation to mental health disabilities.

Mellen Kennedy is Coordinator of The Self-Help Center in Champaign, Illinois, and is a doctoral candidate in Educational Psychology at the University of Illinois. She has been involved in self-help as a researcher, member, and community organizer for the past 10 years.

J. B. (Kip) Kingree, Ph.D, is Director of Programs at Comprehensive Addiction Rehabilitation Programs (CARP) of Georgia, Inc., a community-based residential treatment program for low-income persons. He directs four federally funded addiction treatment programs at CARP: an intensive residential program for homeless persons; an intensive residential program for HIV-infected persons; a long-term program for pregnant women and their children; and an extended transitional housing program for the graduates of the above programs. He holds a doctorate in community psychology from Georgia State University.

Kathryn D. Kramer is a Clinical Assistant Professor in the School of Social Work at the University of North Carolina at Chapel Hill, where she has worked since 1988. Her interests focus on prevention and community interventions, and she has worked on a national study of mutual-help groups in the African American community. She holds a doctoral degree in clinical psychology from Virginia Tech and completed a fellowship at Yale University in 1988. Since 1991 she has been an adjunct faculty member in the UNC School of Public Health since 1991. She has published in psychology, social work, and public health journals.

Linda Farris Kurtz is Professor in the School of Social Work at Eastern Michigan University, Ypsilanti. She has taught courses in self-help and support groups at the University of Chicago, Wayne State University, and Eastern Michigan University. She is the author of numerous articles and book chapters related to her research with mutual-help groups for persons with alcoholism and mental illness. Currently she is working on studies of Alcoholics Anonymous for persons with dual diagnosis and of Recovery, Inc., with the Center for Self-Help Research and Knowledge Dissemination at the University of Michigan in Ann Arbor.

Morton A. Lieberman is Professor of Psychology, University of California, San Francisco, and Director of the Aging & Mental Health Program and The Alzheimer Center. He began his career in the study of small change induction groups at the University of Chicago with studies of sensitivity training. He was a member of the University of Chicago faculty from 1957 to 1983. During the past 40 years, he has studied psychotherapy, encounter, consciousness raising, drug abuse, large-group awareness training, and self-help groups. He has published several books and monographs in the group area, and was co-editor of a special issue on self-help groups of the *Journal of Applied Behavioral Science.*

Douglas A. Luke is an Assistant Professor of community health at St. Louis University School of Public Health. He received his Ph.D. in community and clinical psychology from the University of Illinois at Urbana, and was co-prinicpal investigator of a 5-year study at Michigan State University, evaluating the effectiveness of a specialized treatment program for dual diagnoses. His research and teaching interests include the formal and informal mental health service systems, substance abuse, and innovative analytic methodologies for the social sciences.

Kenneth I. Maton is Associate Professor of Psychology at the University of Maryland, Baltimore County, where he directs the Community-Social Ph.D. Program in Human Services Psychology. He has published widely in community psychology and in the mutual-help group area, with special focus on combining individual and organizational levels of analysis. His research study, *Social Support, Organizational Characteristics, Psychological Well-Being and Group Appraisal in Three Self-Help Populations,* won the 1988 National Research Award of the National Association for Specialists in Group Work. His current research focuses on empowerment in community seetings.

Gregory J. Meissen is Associate Professor of Psychology and Executive Director of the Self-Help Network of Kansas at Wichita State University.

He received his Ph.D. in community psychology from the University of Tennesee and has had visiting appointments at the Harvard and the University of Boston Schools of Medicine. He co-founded and chaired the Interest Group on Self-Help and Mutual Support Research and has served on the National Advisory Council of the Self-Help Mental Health Research Center at the University of Michigan and on the National Council on Self-Help and Public Health. His research interests include access to self-help groups and leadership in self-help groups.

Kermit B. Nash is Professor and Chairman of the Specialization in Health and Medical Care, School of Social Work, University of North Carolina at Chapel Hill. He was previously Professor in the School of Social Work at the University of Washington, Seattle, and Director of the Social Work Department at the university hospital. He has also worked in the Departments of Psychiatry at Yale Medical School, the University of Rochester, and the Albany (NY) Medical College. Recent grants in collaboration with the Comprehensive Sickle Cell Center at Duke University include the establishment of a Psychosocial Research Division and a 5-year national study on the impact of self-help groups on adults with sickle cell anemia.

Douglas L. Noordsy, M.D., is a Staff Psychiatrist at West Central Services, Inc., a Research Associate at the New Hampshire-Dartmouth Psychiatric Research Center, and Assistant Professor of Psychiatry at Darmouth Medical School.

Thomas J. Powell is Professor of Social Work and Director of the Center for Self-Help Research and Knowledge Dissemination at the University of Michigan. His research on volunteer-based and paid consumer-run self-help programs has included studies focusing on the predictors of participation in self-help, professional facilitation of participation in self-help, and the effectiveness of self-help participation. A member of, and an advocate for, numerous self-help groups and organizations, he participated in the Surgeon General's Workshop on Self-Help and Public Health and on the National Council on Self-Help. His previous books include *Self-Help Organizations and Professional Practice* and *Working with Self-Help,* both of which are published by NASW Press.

Julian Rappaport is Professor of Psychology at the University of Illinois at Urbana-Champaign. He is a Past President of the Division of Community Psychology of the American Psychological Association and winner of its award for distinguished career contributions to theory and research. Rappaport is Editor Emeritus of the *American Journal of Community Psychology*. His research has been devoted to understanding and influencing relationships between professional human service programs and individuals dependent on such services. He has written or edited four books and many research articles. Rappaport has served on the National Council for Self-Help and Public Health, an advisory panel to the U.S. Surgeon General.

Linda Roberts is a research Scientist and Principal Investigator for the Research Institute on Addictions, Buffalo, NY, and a Research Assistant Professor at the Department of Psychology, State University of New York at Buffalo. She received her Ph.D. in Clinical and Community Psychology from the University of Illinois at Urbana/Champaign in 1988.

R. Barry Ruback, J.D. Ph.D., is Professor of Psychology and Professor of Criminal Justice at Georgia State University. He is research director of the Georgia Statistical Analsyis Bureau, editor of the *Criminal Justice Review,* and a member of the Bar Associations in Georgia and Texas. He has authored or co-authored over 50 articles and book chapters and co-authored two books. He has held Mellon, Fulbright, and Fulbright-Hays fellowships, and has been a Visiting Fellow at the National Institute of Justice, an Indo-American Fellow, and a South Asia Regional Fullbright Scholar. His research focuses on the interface of law and psychology, primarily decision making by crime victims, and on the effects of environment on behavior.

Christine Flynn Saulnier is a Ph.D. candidate at the School of Social Welfare, University of California at Berkeley. Her areas of interest are women in groups, alcohol problems, and feminist theory. Her publications include articles pertaining to alcohol problem definitions in lesbian communities and group intervention with visually impaired adolescents. Her dissertation involved a study of two alcohol support groups: one for lesbians, the other for African American women. Her book on feminist theories and their applications for social workers will be published by Haworth Press in 1995.

Marsha A. Schubert directs the Content Mastery Program for students with learning disabilities at Boerne Middle School in Texas. Her previous positions as an educator vary from instructing graduate students at Wright State University to working with special education students in public schools at almost every grade level. She co-founded a self-help group for parents of children who are both gifted and learning-disabled. She holds a Doctorate of Arts in Education from George Mason University. Her writing has appeared in several publications, including the *American Journal of Community Psychology*, *Educational Leadership*, and *Exceptional Child*.

Brenda Schwab, Ph.D., is Research Associate at the New Hampshire-Dartmouth Psychiatric Research Center and Research Assistant Professor of Community and Family Medicine at Dartmouth Medical School.

Lonnie R. Snowden is a Professor in the School of Social Welfare at University of California, Berkeley, and Associate Director of the Institute for Mental Health Services Research. He has studied and written extensively on the mental health problems of minority populations and on mental health service delivery.

Mary L. Warren is Director of Operations and Development at the Self-Help Network of Kansas at Wichita State University and has worked with the Network since 1988. She received her M.A. in community psychology from Wichita State University and has been involved in the design and implementation of numerous self-help group research projects. She is Treasurer of the National Network of Mutual-Help Centers. Her research interests include special needs and concerns of rural self-help groups and the role and opportunities for self-help clearinghouses regarding collaborative research with self-help groups.

Michael D. Woods is a Ph.D. candidate in quantitative psychology at the University of Illinois at Urbana-Champaign. His primary interests are applied statistics, psychometric methods, structural equation modelling, and categorical data analysis. His recent research focuses on modelling interactions between latent variables in structural equation models and on the application of this methodology to interactive theories in psychology.